OCA: Oracle®
Certified Associate Java®
SE 8 Programmer I

Study Guide

Exam 1Z0-808

OCA: Oracle®
Certified Associate Java®
SE 8 Programmer I
Study Guide
Exam 1Z0-808

Jeanne Boyarsky

Scott Selikoff

Senior Acquisitions Editor: Kenyon Brown
Development Editor: Alexa Murphy
Technical Editors: Ernest Friedman-Hill, Matt Dalen
Production Editor: Rebecca Anderson
Copy Editor: Liz Welch
Editorial Manager: Pete Gaughan
Vice President and Executive Group Publisher: Richard Swadley
Associate Publisher: Jim Minatel
Production Manager: Kathleen Wisor
Media Supervising Producer: Rich Graves
Book Designers: Judy Fung and Bill Gibson
Proofreader: Scott Klemp, Word One New York
Indexer: Ted Laux
Project Coordinator, Cover: Patrick Redmond
Cover Designer: Wiley
Cover Image: ©Getty Images Inc./Jeremy Woodhouse
Printed and bound by CPI Group (UK) Ltd, Croydon, CR0 4YY

Dear Reader,

Thank you for choosing *OCA: Oracle Certified Associate Java SE 8 Programmer I Study Guide*. This book is part of a family of premium-quality Sybex books, all of which are written by outstanding authors who combine practical experience with a gift for teaching.

Sybex was founded in 1976. More than 30 years later, we're still committed to producing consistently exceptional books. With each of our titles, we're working hard to set a new standard for the industry. From the paper we print on, to the authors we work with, our goal is to bring you the best books available.

I hope you see all that reflected in these pages. I'd be very interested to hear your comments and get your feedback on how we're doing. Feel free to let me know what you think about this or any other Sybex book by sending me an email at contactus@wiley .com. If you think you've found a technical error in this book, please visit http://sybex .custhelp.com. Customer feedback is critical to our efforts at Sybex.

Best regards,

Chris Webb
Associate Publisher
Sybex, an Imprint of Wiley

To the programmers on FIRST robotics team 694.

—Jeanne

To my wife and the two little bundles of joy she is carrying.

—Scott

Acknowledgments

Jeanne and Scott would like to thank numerous individuals for their contribution to this book. Thank you to Developmental Editor Alexa Murphy for teaching us about Wiley's publishing process and making the book better in so many ways. Thank you to Ernest Friedman-Hill for being our Technical Editor as we wrote our first book. Ernest pointed out many subtle errors in addition to the big ones. And thank you to Matt Dalen for being our Technical Proofer and finding the errors we managed to sneak by Ernest. This book also wouldn't be possible without many people at Wiley, including Jeff Kellum, Kenyon Brown, Pete Gaughan, Rebecca Anderson, and so many others.

Jeanne would personally like to thank Chris Kreussling for knowing almost a decade ago that she would someday write a book. Erik Kariyev motivated her to write her first table of contents ever. Countless CodeRanch.com moderators warned Jeanne about how much work writing a book is to get her to the point where she was ready. Michael Ernest gave her extra advice on the Wiley process. Bert Bates let Jeanne dip her toe in by contributing to his Java 7 book and she learned a ton in the process. Scott was a great co-author and was available to bounce ideas off of or remind her to follow her own advice. Finally, Jeanne would like to thank all of the new programmers at CodeRanch.com and FIRST robotics team 694 for the constant reminders of how new programmers think.

Scott could not have reached this point without the help of a small army of people, led by his perpetually understanding wife Patti, without whose love and support this book would never have been possible. Professor Johannes Gehrke of Cornell University always believed in him and knew he would excel in his career. Jeanne's patience and guidance as co-author was invaluable while Scott adjusted to the learning curve of writing a book. Matt Dalen has been a wonderful friend and sounding board over the last year. Joel McNary introduced him to CodeRanch.com and encouraged him to post regularly, a step that changed his life. Finally, Scott would like to thank his mother and retired teacher Barbara Selikoff for teaching him the value of education and his father Mark Selikoff, for instilling in him the benefits of working hard.

About the Authors

Jeanne Boyarsky   has worked as a Java developer for over 12 years at a bank in New York City where she develops, mentors, and conducts training. Besides being a senior moderator at CodeRanch.com in her free time, she works on the forum codebase. Jeanne also mentors the programming division of a FIRST robotics team, where she works with students just getting started with Java.

Jeanne got her Bachelor of Arts in 2002 and her Master's in Computer Information Technology in 2005. She enjoyed getting her Master's degree in an online program while working full time. This was before online education was cool! Jeanne is also a Distinguished Toastmaster and a Scrum Master. You can find out more about Jeanne at www.coderanch.com/how-to/java/BioJeanneBoyarsky.

Scott Selikoff   is a professional software consultant, author, and owner of Selikoff Solutions, LLC, which provides software development solutions to businesses in the tri-state New York City area. Skilled in a plethora of software languages and platforms, Scott specializes in database-driven systems, web-based applications, and service-oriented architectures.

A native of Toms River, NJ, Scott achieved his Bachelor of Arts from Cornell University in Mathematics and Computer Science in 2002, after 3 years of study. In 2003, he received his Master's of Engineering in Computer Science, also from Cornell University.

As someone with a deep love of education, Scott has always enjoyed teaching others new concepts. He's given lectures at Cornell University and Rutgers University, as well as conferences including The Server Side Java Symposium. Scott lives in New Jersey with his loving wife and two very playful dogs, a Siberian husky named Webby and standard poodle named Georgette. You can find out more about Scott at www.linkedin.com/in/selikoff.

Jeanne and Scott are both moderators on the CodeRanch.com forums and can be reached there for questions and comments. They also co-author a technical blog called Down Home Country Coding at www.selikoff.net.

Contents at a Glance

Contents

Introduction

Java, "born" in 1995, is now just about 20 years old. As with anything 20 years old, there is a good amount of history and variation between versions of Java. Over the years, the certification exams have changed to cover different topics. The names of the exams have even changed. This book covers the Java 8 Oracle Certified Associate (OCA) exam.

If you read about "the exam" on the Web, you may see information about the older names for the exam. We've showed the changes in name. Here's what happened. Sun Microsystems used to have two exams. The SCJP (Sun Certified Java Programmer) was meant for programmers and the SCJA (Sun Certified Java Associate) was meant for those who wanted broader knowledge. When Oracle bought Sun Microsystems, they changed all the names from Sun to Oracle, giving us the OCJP and OCJA.

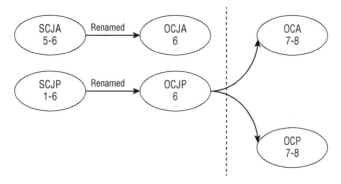

Then Oracle made two strategic decisions with Java 7. They decided to stop updating the OCJA exam. They also decided to cover more on in the programmer space and split it into two exams. Now you first take the OCAJP (Oracle Certified Associate Java Programmer), also known as Java Programmer I, or OCA. That's what this book is about. Then you take the OCPJP (Oracle Certified Professional Java Programmer), also known as Java Programmer II, or OCP. There's also an upgrade exam in case you took an older version of the SCJP or OCPJP and want to upgrade. Most people refer to the current exams as OCA 8, OCP 8, and the Java 8 upgrade exam. We mention when a topic is split between the OCA and OCP so you know which parts are more advanced.

We try to keep the history to a minimum in this book. There are some places on the exam where you need to know both an "old way" and a "new way" of doing things. When that happens, we will be sure to tell you what version of Java introduced it. We will also let you know about topics that are not on the exam anymore in case you see questions in the older free online mock exams.

The OCA Exam

All you need to do to earn the Oracle Certified Associate Java SE 8 Programmer certification is to pass the exam! That's it.

Oracle has a tendency to fiddle with the length of the exam and the passing score once it comes out. Since it's pretty much a guarantee that whatever we tell you here will become obsolete, we will give you a feel for the range of variation. The OCA exam has varied between 60 and 90 questions since it was introduced. The score to pass has varied between 60 percent and 80 percent. The time allowed to take the exam has varied from two hours to two-and-a-half hours.

Oracle has a tendency to "tweak" the exam objectives over time as well. They do make minor additions and removals from what is covered on the exam. Although this tends to affect the OCP exam more than the OCA exam, there are a few topics that were added to the OCA for Java 8. It wouldn't be a surprise for Oracle to make changes.

Although there will likely be minor changes to the scope of the exam, it certainly isn't a secret. We've created a book page on our blog: www.selikoff.net/oca. If there are any changes to the topics on the exam after this book is published, we will note them there.

That book page also contains a link to the official exam page so that you can check the length and passing score that Oracle has chosen for the moment.

Scheduling the Exam

The exam is administered by Pearson VUE and can be taken at any Pearson VUE testing center. To find a testing center or register for the exam, go to www.pearsonvue.com. Choose IT and then Oracle. If you haven't been to the test center before, we recommend visiting in advance. Some testing centers are nice and professionally run. Others stick you in a closet with lots of people talking around you. You don't want to be taking the test with someone complaining about their broken laptop nearby!

At this time, you can reschedule the exam without penalty until up to 24 hours before. This means that you can register for a convenient time slot well in advance, knowing that you can delay if you aren't ready by that time. Rescheduling is easy and can be done on the Pearson VUE website. This may change, so check the rules before paying.

The Day of the Exam

When you go to take the exam, remember to bring two forms of ID, including one that is government issued. See Pearson's list of what is acceptable ID at http://www.pearsonvue.com/policies/1S.pdf. Try not to bring too much extra with you as it will not be allowed into the exam room. While you will be allowed to check your belongings, it is better to leave extra items at home or in the car.

You will not be allowed to bring paper, your phone, and so forth into the exam room with you. Some centers are stricter than others. At one center, tissues were even taken away from us! Most centers allow keeping your ID and money. They watch you taking the exam, though, so don't even think about writing notes on money.

The exam center will give you writing materials to use during the exam. These are used as scratch paper during the exam to figure out answers and keep track of your thought process. The exam center will dispose of them at the end. Notice how we said "writing materials" rather than "pen and paper." Some centers still give pen and paper. Most give a small erasable board and a dry erase marker. If you have a preference to which you receive, call the testing center in advance to inquire.

Finding Out Your Score

In the past, you would find out right after finishing the exam if you passed. Now you have to wait nervously until you can check your score online.

If you go onto the Pearson VUE website, it will just have a status of "Taken" rather than your result. Oracle uses a separate system for scores. You'll need to go to http://certview.oracle.com to find out whether you passed and your score. It doesn't update immediately upon taking the test, but we haven't heard of it taking more than an hour. In addition to your score, you'll also see objectives for which you got a question wrong and instructions on how to get a hardcopy certificate.

At some point, you'll get an electronic certificate and some more time after that you'll receive your printed certificate. Sound vague? It is. The times reported to receive certificates vary widely.

Exam Questions

The OCA exam consists of multiple-choice questions. There are typically five or six possible answers. If a question has more than one answer, the question specifically states exactly how many correct answers there are. This book does not do that. We say "choose all that apply" to make the questions harder. This means the questions in this book are generally harder than those on the exam. The idea is to give you more practice so you can spot the correct answer more easily on the real exam.

Note that exam questions will sometimes have line numbers that begin with numbers higher than 1. This is to indicate that you are looking at a code snippet rather than a complete class. We follow this convention as well to get you used to it.

If you read about older versions of the exam online, you might see references to drag-and-drop questions. These questions had you do a puzzle on how to complete a piece of code. There was also a bug in the exam software that caused your answers to get lost if you reviewed them again. Luckily, these are no longer on the exam.

Getting Started

We recommend reading Appendix B, "Study Tips," before diving into the technical material in this book. Knowing how to approach studying will help you make better use of your study time.

Next, make sure you have downloaded version 8 of the JDK. If you learned Java some time ago, you might have version 7 or even earlier. There have been both big and small changes to the language. You could get a question wrong if you study with the wrong version.

Also, please check our book page to make sure Oracle hasn't changed the objectives. For example, if Oracle decided that lambdas weren't on the exam, you'd want to know that before studying. We will post any updates that you should know about at www.selikoff .net/oca.

Getting Help

Both of the authors are moderators at CodeRanch.com. CodeRanch.com is a very large and active programming forum that is very friendly toward Java beginners. It has a forum just for this exam called OCAJP. It also has a forum called Beginning Java for non-exam-specific questions. As you read the book, feel free to ask your questions in either of those forums. It could be you are having trouble compiling a class or that you are just plain confused about something. You'll get an answer from a knowledgeable Java programmer. It might even be one of us.

Who Should Buy This Book

If you want to become certified as a Java programmer, this book is definitely for you. If you want to acquire a solid foundation in Java and your goal is to prepare for the exam, this book is also for you. You'll find clear explanations of the concepts you need to grasp and plenty of help to achieve the high level of professional competency you need in order to succeed in your chosen field.

This book is intended to be understandable to anyone who has a tiny bit of Java knowledge. If you've never read a Java book before, we recommend starting with a book that teaches programming from the beginning and then returning to this study guide.

This book is for anyone from high school students to those beginning their programming journey to experienced professionals who need a review for the certification.

How This Book Is Organized

This book consists of six chapters, plus supplementary information: a glossary, this introduction, three appendices, and the assessment test after the introduction. You might have noticed that there are more than six exam objectives. We split up what you need to know to make it easy to learn and remember. Each chapter begins with a list of the objectives that are covered in that chapter.

The chapters are organized as follows:

- Chapter 1, "Java Building Blocks," covers the basics of Java such as scoping variables and how to run a program. It also includes calling methods and types of variables.

- Chapter 2, "Operators and Statements," focuses on the core logical constructs such as conditionals and loops. It also talks about the meaning and precedence of operators.

- Chapter 3, "Core Java APIs," introduces you to array, `ArrayList`, `String`, `StringBuilder`, and various date classes.

- Chapter 4, "Methods and Encapsulation," explains how to write methods, including access modifiers. It also shows how to call lambdas.

- Chapter 5, "Class Design," adds interfaces and superclasses. It also includes casting and polymorphism.

- Chapter 6, "Exceptions," shows the different types of exception classes and how to use them.

At the end of each chapter, you'll find a few elements you can use to prepare for the exam:

Summary   This section reviews the most important topics that were covered in the chapter and serves as a good review.

Exam Essentials   This section summarizes highlights that were covered in the chapter. You should be readily familiar with the key points of each chapter and be able to explain them in detail.

Review Questions   Each chapter concludes with at least 20 review questions. You should answer these questions and check your answers against the ones provided in Appendix A.

If you can't answer at least 80 percent of these questions correctly, go back and review the chapter, or at least those sections that seem to be giving you difficulty.

> **WARNING**
>
> The review questions, assessment test, and other testing elements included in this book are *not* derived from the real exam questions, so don't memorize the answers to these questions and assume that doing so will enable you to pass the exam. You should learn the underlying topic, as described in the text of the book. This will let you answer the questions provided with this book *and* pass the exam. Learning the underlying topic is also the approach that will serve you best in the workplace—the ultimate goal of a certification.

To get the most out of this book, you should read each chapter from start to finish before going to the chapter-end elements. They are most useful for checking and reinforcing your understanding. Even if you're already familiar with a topic, you should skim the chapter. There are a number of subtleties to Java that you could easily not encounter even when working with Java, even for years.

Free Online Learning Environment

This book provides a free online interactive learning environment and test bank with several additional elements. The online test bank includes:

Sample Tests All of the questions in this book, including the 20-question assessment test at the end of this introduction and over 130 questions that make up the Review Question sections for each chapter. In addition, there are three 60-question Practice Exams to test your knowledge of the material. The online test bank runs on multiple devices.

Electronic Flashcards Over 200 questions in flashcard format (a question followed by a single correct answer). You can use these to reinforce your learning and provide last-minute test prep before the exam.

Glossary The key terms from this book and their definitions are available as a fully searchable PDF.

> **NOTE**
>
> Go to www.sybex.com/go/ocajavase8 to register and gain access to this comprehensive study tool package.

Conventions Used in This Book

This book uses certain typographic styles in order to help you quickly identify important information and to avoid confusion about the meaning of words, such as onscreen prompts. In particular, look for the following styles:

- *Italicized text* indicates key terms that are described at length for the first time in a chapter. (Italics are also used for emphasis.)

- A monospaced font indicates code or command-line text.

- *Italicized monospaced text* indicates a variable.

In addition to these text conventions, which can apply to individual words or entire paragraphs, a few conventions highlight segments of text:

A note indicates information that's useful or interesting. It is often something to pay special attention to for the exam.

Sidebars

A sidebar is like a note but longer. The information in a sidebar is useful, but it doesn't fit into the main flow of the text.

 Real World Scenario

Real World Scenario

A real world scenario describes a task or an example that's particularly grounded in the real world. Although interesting, the scenario will not show up on the exam.

OCA Exam Objectives

OCA: Oracle Certified Associate Java SE 8 Programmer I Study Guide: Exam 1Z0-808 has been written to cover every OCA exam objective. The following table provides a breakdown of this book's exam coverage, showing you the chapter where each objective or sub-objective is covered:

Exam Objective	Chapter
■ **Java Basics**	
Define the scope of variables	1
Define the structure of a Java class	1
Create executable Java applications with a main method; run a Java program from the command line, including console output	1
Import other Java packages to make them accessible in your code	1
Compare and contrast the features and components of Java such as platform independence, object orientation, encapsulation, etc.	1
■ **Working with Java Data Types**	
Declare and initialize variables (including casting of primitive data types)	1
Differentiate between object reference variables and primitive variables	1
Know how to read or write to object fields	1
Explain an Object's Lifecycle (creation, "dereference by reassignment," and garbage collection)	1
Develop code that uses wrapper classes such as Boolean, Double, and Integer	1
■ **Using Operators and Decision Constructs**	
Use Java operators, including parentheses to override operator precedence	2
Test equality between Strings and other objects using == and equals ()	3
Create if and if/else and ternary constructs	2
Use a switch statement	2
■ **Creating and Using Arrays**	
Declare, instantiate, initialize, and use a one-dimensional array	3
Declare, instantiate, initialize, and use multi-dimensional array	3

Exam Objective	Chapter
■ **Using Loop Constructs**	
Create and use while loops	2
Create and use for loops including the enhanced for loop	2
Create and use do/while loops	2
Compare loop constructs	2
Use break and continue	2
■ **Working with Methods and Encapsulation**	
Create methods with arguments and return values, including overloaded methods	4
Apply the static keyword to methods and fields	4
Create and overload constructors, including impact on default constructors	4
Apply access modifiers	4
Apply encapsulation principles to a class	4
Determine the effect upon object references and primitive values when they are passed into methods that change the values	4
■ **Working with Inheritance**	
Describe inheritance and its benefits	5
Develop code that demonstrates the use of polymorphism, including overriding and object type versus reference type	5
Determine when casting is necessary	5
Use super and this to access objects and constructors	5
Use abstract classes and interfaces	5
■ **Handling Exceptions**	
Differentiate among checked exceptions, unchecked exceptions, and Errors	6
Create a try-catch block and determine how exceptions alter normal program flow	6

(continued)

Exam Objective	Chapter
Describe the advantages of Exception handling	6
Create and invoke a method that throws an exception	6
Recognize common exception classes (such as NullPointerException, ArithmeticException, ArrayIndexOutOfBoundsException, ClassCastException)	6
■ **Working with Selected Classes from the Java API**	
Manipulate data using the StringBuilder class and its methods	3
Creating and manipulating Strings	3
Create and manipulate calendar data using classes from java.time.LocalDateTime, java.time.LocalDate, java.time.LocalTime, java.time.format.DateTimeFormatter, java.time.Period	3
Declare and use an ArrayList of a given type	3
Write a simple Lambda expression that consumes a Lambda Predicate expression	4

Assessment Test

1. What is the result of the following class? (Choose all that apply)

```
1: public class _C {
2:   private static int $;
3:   public static void main(String[] main) {
4:     String a_b;
5:     System.out.print($);
6:     System.out.print(a_b);
7: } }
```

   A. Compiler error on line 1.

   B. Compiler error on line 2.

   C. Compiler error on line 4.

   D. Compiler error on line 5.

   E. Compiler error on line 6.

   F. `0null`

   G. `nullnull`

2. What is the result of the following code?

```
String s1 = "Java";
String s2 = "Java";
StringBuilder sb1 = new StringBuilder();
sb1.append("Ja").append("va");
System.out.println(s1 == s2);
System.out.println(s1.equals(s2));
System.out.println(sb1.toString() == s1);
System.out.println(sb1.toString().equals(s1));
```

   A. true is printed out exactly once.

   B. true is printed out exactly twice.

   C. true is printed out exactly three times.

   D. true is printed out exactly four times.

   E. The code does not compile.

3. What is the output of the following code? (Choose all that apply)

```
1: interface HasTail { int getTailLength(); }
2: abstract class Puma implements HasTail {
3:   protected int getTailLength() {return 4;}
4: }
5: public class Cougar extends Puma {
```

```
6:    public static void main(String[] args) {
7:       Puma puma = new Puma();
8:       System.out.println(puma.getTailLength());
9:    }
10:
11:  public int getTailLength(int length) {return 2;}
12: }
```

A. 2

B. 4

C. The code will not compile because of line 3.

D. The code will not compile because of line 5.

E. The code will not compile because of line 7.

F. The code will not compile because of line 11.

G. The output cannot be determined from the code provided.

4. What is the output of the following program?

```
1: public class FeedingSchedule {
2:  public static void main(String[] args) {
3:     boolean keepGoing = true;
4:     int count = 0;
5:     int x = 3;
6:     while(count++ < 3) {
7:       int y = (1 + 2 * count) % 3;
8:       switch(y) {
9:          default:
10:          case 0: x -= 1; break;
11:          case 1: x += 5;
12:       }
13:    }
14:  System.out.println(x);
15: } }
```

A. 4

B. 5

C. 6

D. 7

E. 13

F. The code will not compile because of line 7.

5. What is the output of the following code snippet?

```
13: System.out.print("a");
14: try {
15:    System.out.print("b");
16:    throw new IllegalArgumentException();
17: } catch (RuntimeException e) {
18:    System.out.print("c");
19: } finally {
20:    System.out.print("d");
21: }
22: System.out.print("e");
```

A. abe

B. abce

C. abde

D. abcde

E. The code does not compile.

F. An uncaught exception is thrown.

6. What is the result of the following program?

```
1: public class MathFunctions {
2:    public static void addToInt(int x, int amountToAdd) {
3:       x = x + amountToAdd;
4:    }
5:    public static void main(String[] args) {
6:       int a = 15;
7:       int b = 10;
8:       MathFunctions.addToInt(a, b);
9:       System.out.println(a);    } }
```

A. 10

B. 15

C. 25

D. Compiler error on line 3.

E. Compiler error on line 8.

F. None of the above.

7. What is the result of the following code?

```
int[] array = {6,9,8};
List<Integer> list = new ArrayList<>();
```

```
list.add(array[0]);
list.add(array[2]);
list.set(1, array[1]);
list.remove(0);
System.out.println(list);
```

A. [8]

B. [9]

C. Something like [Ljava.lang.String;@160bc7c0

D. An exception is thrown.

E. The code does not compile.

8. What is the output of the following code?

```
1: public class Deer {
2:   public Deer() { System.out.print("Deer"); }
3:   public Deer(int age) { System.out.print("DeerAge"); }
4:   private boolean hasHorns() { return false; }
5:   public static void main(String[] args) {
6:     Deer deer = new Reindeer(5);
7:     System.out.println(","+deer.hasHorns());
8:   }
9: }
10: class Reindeer extends Deer {
11:   public Reindeer(int age) { System.out.print("Reindeer"); }
12:   public boolean hasHorns() { return true; }
13: }
```

A. DeerReindeer,false

B. DeerReindeer,true

C. ReindeerDeer,false

D. ReindeerDeer,true

E. DeerAgeReindeer,false

F. DeerAgeReindeer,true

G. The code will not compile because of line 7.

H. The code will not compile because of line 12.

9. Which of the following statements are true? (Choose all that apply)

A. Checked exceptions are intended to be thrown by the JVM (and not the programmer).

B. Checked exceptions are required to be caught or declared.

C. Errors are intended to be thrown by the JVM (and not the programmer).

D. Errors are required to be caught or declared.

E. Runtime exceptions are intended to be thrown by the JVM (and not the programmer).

F. Runtime exceptions are required to be caught or declared.

10. Which are true of the following code? (Choose all that apply)

```
1:   import java.util.*;
2:   public class Grasshopper {
3:   public Grasshopper(String n) {
4:      name = n;
5:   }
6:   public static void main(String[] args) {
7:      Grasshopper one = new Grasshopper("g1");
8:      Grasshopper two = new Grasshopper("g2");
9:      one = two;
10:     two = null;
11:     one = null;
12: }
13:    private String name; }
```

A. Immediately after line 9, no grasshopper objects are eligible for garbage collection.

B. Immediately after line 10, no grasshopper objects are eligible for garbage collection.

C. Immediately after line 9, only one grasshopper object is eligible for garbage collection.

D. Immediately after line 10, only one grasshopper object is eligible for garbage collection.

E. Immediately after line 11, only one grasshopper object is eligible for garbage collection.

F. The code compiles.

G. The code does not compile.

11. What is the output of the following program?

```
1: public class FeedingSchedule {
2: public static void main(String[] args) {
3:    int x = 5, j = 0;
4:    OUTER: for(int i=0; i<3; )
5:      INNER: do {
6:        i++; x++;
7:        if(x > 10) break INNER;
8:        x += 4;
9:        j++;
10:      } while(j <= 2);
11:    System.out.println(x);
12: } }
```

A. 10

B. 12

C. 13

D. 17

E. The code will not compile because of line 4.

F. The code will not compile because of line 6.

12. What is the result of the following program?

```
1: public class Egret {
2:    private String color;
3:    public Egret() {
4:       this("white");
5:    }
6:    public Egret(String color) {
7:       color = color;
8:    }
9:    public static void main(String[] args) {
10:      Egret e = new Egret();
11:      System.out.println("Color:" + e.color);
12:   }
13: }
```

  A. Color:

  B. Color:null

  C. Color:White

  D. Compiler error on line 4.

  E. Compiler error on line 10.

  F. Compiler error on line 11.

13. What is the output of the following program?

```
1: public class BearOrShark {
2:    public static void main(String[] args) {
3:       int luck = 10;
4:       if((luck>10 ? luck++: --luck)<10) {
5:          System.out.print("Bear");
6:       } if(luck<10) System.out.print("Shark");
7: } }
```

  A. Bear

  B. Shark

  C. BearShark

  D. The code will not compile because of line 4.

  E. The code will not compile because of line 6.

  F. The code compiles without issue but does not produce any output.

14. Assuming we have a valid, non-null HenHouse object whose value is initialized by the blank line shown here, which of the following are possible outputs of this application? (Choose all that apply)

```
1: class Chicken {}
2: interface HenHouse { public java.util.List<Chicken> getChickens(); }
3: public class ChickenSong {
```

Introduction **xxxvii**

```
4:    public static void main(String[] args) {
5:       HenHouse house = _____
6:       Chicken chicken = house.getChickens().get(0);
7:       for(int i=0; i<house.getChickens().size();
8:         chicken = house.getChickens().get(i++)) {
9:         System.out.println("Cluck");
10: } } }
```

A. The code will not compile because of line 6.

B. The code will not compile because of lines 7–8.

C. The application will compile but not produce any output.

D. The application will output Cluck exactly once.

E. The application will output Cluck more than once.

F. The application will compile but produce an exception at runtime.

15. Which of the following statements can be inserted in the blank line so that the code will compile successfully? (Choose all that apply)

```
public interface CanSwim {}
public class Amphibian implements CanSwim {}
class Tadpole extends Amphibian {}
public class FindAllTadPole {
  public static void main(String[] args) {
    List<Tadpole> tadpoles = new ArrayList<Tadpole>();
    for(Amphibian amphibian : tadpoles) {
      _____ tadpole = amphibian;
} } }
```

A. CanSwim

B. Long

C. Amphibian

D. Tadpole

E. Object

16. What individual changes, if any, would allow the following code to compile? (Choose all that apply)

```
1: public interface Animal { public default String getName() { return null; } }
2: interface Mammal { public default String getName() { return null; } }
3: abstract class Otter implements Mammal, Animal {}
```

A. The code compiles without issue.

B. Remove the default method modifier and method implementation on line 1.

C. Remove the default method modifier and method implementation on line 2.

D. Remove the default method modifier and method implementation on lines 1 and 2.

E. Change the return value on line 1 from null to "Animal".

   F. Override the `getName()` method with an `abstract` method in the `Otter` class.

   G. Override the `getName()` method with a concrete method in the `Otter` class.

17. Which of the following lines can be inserted at line 11 to print `true`? (Choose all that apply)

```
10: public static void main(String[] args) {
11:    // INSERT CODE HERE
12: }
13: private static boolean test(Predicate<Integer> p) {
14:    return p.test(5);
15: }
```

   A. `System.out.println(test(i -> i == 5));`

   B. `System.out.println(test(i -> {i == 5;}));`

   C. `System.out.println(test((i) -> i == 5));`

   D. `System.out.println(test((int i) -> i == 5);`

   E. `System.out.println(test((int i) -> {return i == 5;}));`

   F. `System.out.println(test((i) -> {return i == 5;}));`

18. Which of the following print out a date representing April 1, 2015? (Choose all that apply)

   A. `System.out.println(LocalDate.of(2015, Calendar.APRIL, 1));`

   B. `System.out.println(LocalDate.of(2015, Month.APRIL, 1));`

   C. `System.out.println(LocalDate.of(2015, 3, 1));`

   D. `System.out.println(LocalDate.of(2015, 4, 1));`

   E. `System.out.println(new LocalDate(2015, 3, 1));`

   F. `System.out.println(new LocalDate(2015, 4, 1));`

19. Bytecode is in a file with which extension?

   A. `.bytecode`

   B. `.bytes`

   C. `.class`

   D. `.exe`

   E. `.javac`

   F. `.java`

20. Which of the following are checked exceptions? (Choose all that apply)

   A. `Exception`

   B. `IllegalArgumentException`

   C. `IOException`

   D. `NullPointerException`

   E. `NumberFormatException`

   F. `StackOverflowError`

Answers to Assessment Test

1. E. Option E is correct because local variables require assignment before referencing them. Option D is incorrect because class and instance variables have default values and allow referencing. `$` defaults to `0`. Options A, B, and C are incorrect because identifiers may begin with a letter, underscore, or dollar sign. Options F and G are incorrect because the code does not compile. If `a_b` was an instance variable, the code would compile and output `0null`. For more information, see Chapter 1.

2. C. String literals are used from the string pool. This means that `s1` and `s2` refer to the same object and are equal. Therefore, the first two print statements print `true`. The third print statement prints `false` because `toString()` uses a method to compute the value and it is not from the string pool. The final print statement again prints `true` because `equals()` looks at the values of `String` objects. For more information, see Chapter 3.

3. C, D, E. First, the method `getTailLength()` in the interface `HasTail` is assumed to be `public`, since it is part of an interface. The implementation of the method on line 3 is therefore an invalid override, as `protected` is a more restrictive access modifier than `public`, so option C is correct. Next, the class `Cougar` implements an overloaded version of `getTailLength()`, but since the declaration in the parent class `Cougar` is invalid, it needs to implement a public version of the method. Since it does not, the declaration of `Cougar` is invalid, so option D is correct. Option E is correct, since `Puma` is marked `abstract` and cannot be instantiated. The overloaded method on line 11 is declared correctly, so option F is not correct. Finally, as the code has multiple compiler errors, options A, B, and G can be eliminated. For more information, see Chapter 5.

4. C. The code compiles and runs without issue; therefore, option F is incorrect. This type of problem is best examined one loop iteration at a time:

   - The loop starts as count loop expression evaluates to `0 < 3`, which is `true`, With count taking a new value of 1. The value of y is set to:

     ```
     y = (1 + 2 * 1) % 3
       = (1 + 2) % 3
       = 3 % 3
       = 0
     ```

   - The first case block is called and the value of x is then set to:

     ```
     x = 3 - 1 = 2
     ```

   - The loop continues as count loop expression evaluates to `1 < 3`, which is `true`, with y taking a new value of 2. The value of y is set to:

     ```
     y = (1 + 2 * 2) % 3
       = (1 + 5) % 3
       = 4 % 3
       = 2
     ```

- The default block is called and the value of x is set to:

  x = 2 - 1 = 1

- The loop continues as the count loop expression evaluates to 2 < 3, which is true, with y taking a new value of 3. The value of y is set to:

  y = (1 + 2 * 3) % 3

    = (1 + 6) % 3

    = 7 % 3

    = 1

- The second case block is called and the value of x is then set to:

  x = 1 + 5 = 6

- The loop ends as the count loop expression evaluates to 3 < 3, with y also taking a new value of 4. The most recent value of x, 6, is output, so the answer is option C. For more information, see Chapter 2.

5. D. The code starts running and prints a and b on lines 13 and 15. Line 16 throws an exception, which is caught on line 17. After line 18 prints c, the finally block is run and d is printed. Then the try statement ends and e is printed on line 22. For more information, see Chapter 6.

6. B. The code compiles successfully, so options D and E are incorrect. The value of *a* cannot be changed by the addToInt method, no matter what the method does, because only a copy of the variable is passed into the parameter *x*. Therefore, *a* does not change and the output on line 9 is 15. For more information, see Chapter 4.

7. B. The array is allowed to use an anonymous initializer because it is in the same line as the declaration. The ArrayList uses the diamond operator allowed since Java 7. This specifies the type matches the one on the left without having to re-type it. After adding the two elements, *list* contains [6, 8]. We then replace the element at index 1 with 9, resulting in [6, 9]. Finally, we remove the element at index 0, leaving [9]. Option C is incorrect because arrays output something like that rather than an ArrayList. For more information, see Chapter 3.

8. A. The code compiles and runs without issue, so options G and H are incorrect. First, the Reindeer object is instantiated using the constructor that takes an int value. Since there is no explicit call to the parent constructor, the default no-argument super() is inserted as the first line of the constructor. The output is then Deer, followed by Reindeer in the child constructor, so only options A and B can be correct. Next, the method hasHorns() looks like an overridden method, but it is actually a hidden method since it is declared private in the parent class. Because the hidden method is referenced in the parent class, the parent version is used, so the code outputs false, and option A is the correct answer.

9. B, C. Only checked exceptions are required to be handled (caught) or declared. Run-time exceptions are commonly thrown by both the JVM and programmer code. Checked exceptions are usually thrown by programmer code. Errors are intended to be

thrown by the JVM. While a programmer could throw one, this would be a horrible practice. For more information, see Chapter 6.

10. C, D, F. Immediately after line 9, only Grasshopper g1 is eligible for garbage collection since both one and two point to Grasshopper g2. Immediately after line 10, we still only have Grasshopper g1 eligible for garbage collection. Reference two points to g2 and reference two is null. Immediately after line 11, both Grasshopper objects are eligible for garbage collection since both one and two point to null. The code does compile. Although it is traditional to declare instance variables early in the class, you don't have to. For more information, see Chapter 1.

11. B. The code compiles and runs without issue; therefore, options E and F are incorrect. This type of problem is best examined one loop iteration at a time:

- On the first iteration of the outer loop i is 0, so the loop continues.

- On the first iteration of the inner loop, i is updated to 1 and x to 6. The if-then statement branch is not executed, and x is increased to 10 and j to 1.

- On the second iteration of the inner loop (since j = 1 and 1 <= 2), i is updated to 2 and x to 11. At this point, the if-then branch will evaluate to true for the remainder of the program run, which causes the flow to break out of the inner loop each time it is reached.

- On the second iteration of the outer loop (since i = 2), i is updated to 3 and x to 12. As before, the inner loop is broken since x is still greater than 10.

- On the third iteration of the outer loop, the outer loop is broken, as i is already not less than 3. The most recent value of x, 12, is output, so the answer is option B. For more information, see Chapter 2.

12. B. Line 10 calls the constructor on lines 3–5. That constructor calls the other constructor. However, the constructor on lines 6–8 assigns the method parameter to itself, which leaves the *color* instance variable on line 2 set to its default value of *null*. For more information, see Chapter 4.

13. C. The code compiles and runs without issue, so options D and E are incorrect. Remember that only one of the right-hand ternary expressions will be evaluated at runtime. Since luck is not less than 10, the second expression, --luck, will be evaluated, and since the pre-increment operator was used, the value returned will be 9, which is less than 10. So the first if-then statement will be visited and Bear will be output. Notice there is no else statement on line 6. Since luck is still less than 10, the second if-then statement will also be reached and Shark will be output; therefore, the correct answer is option C. For more information, see Chapter 2.

14. D, E, F. The code compiles without issue, so options A and B are incorrect. If house .getChickens() returns an array of one element, the code will output Cluck once, so option D is correct. If house.getChickens() returns an array of multiple elements, the code will output Cluck once for each element in the array, so option E is correct. Alternatively, if house.getChickens() returns an array of zero elements, then the code will throw an IndexOutOfBoundsException on the call to house.getChickens().get(0); therefore, option C is not possible and option F is correct. The code will also throw an exception if the array returned by house.getChickens() is null, so option F is possible under multiple circumstances. For more information, see Chapter 2.

15. A, C, E. The for-each loop automatically casts each Tadpole object to an Amphibian reference, which does not require an explicit cast because Tadpole is a subclass of Amphibian. From there, any parent class or interface that Amphibian inherits from is permitted without an explicit cast. This includes CanSwim, the interface Amphibian implements, and Object, which all classes extend from, so options A and E are correct. Option C is also correct since the reference is being cast to the same type, so no explicit cast is required. Option B is incorrect, since Long is not a parent of Amphibian. Option D is incorrect as well, although an explicit cast to Tadpole on the right-hand side of the expression would be required to allow the code to compile. For more information, see Chapter 5.

16. D, F, G. The code does not compile, since a class cannot inherit two interfaces that both define default methods with the same signature, unless the class implementing the interfaces overrides it with an abstract or concrete method. Therefore, option A is incorrect and options F and G are correct. The alternate approach is to make the getName() method abstract in the interfaces, because a class may inherit two abstract methods with the same signature. The change must be made to both interfaces, though, so options B and C are incorrect if taken individually, and option D is correct since the changes are taken together. For more information, see Chapter 5.

17. A, C, F. The only functional programming interface you need to memorize for the exam is Predicate. It takes a single parameter and returns a boolean. Lambda expressions with one parameter are allowed to omit the parentheses around the parameter list, making options A and C correct. The return statement is optional when a single statement is in the body, making option F correct. Option B is incorrect because a return statement must be used if braces are included around the body. Options D and E are incorrect because the type is Integer in the predicate and int in the lambda. Autoboxing works for collections not inferring predicates. If these two were changed to Integer, they would be correct. For more information, see Chapter 4.

18. B, D. The new date APIs added in Java 8 use static methods rather than a constructor to create a new date, making options E and F incorrect. The months are indexed starting with 1 in these APIs, making options A and C incorrect. Option A uses the old Calendar constants which are indexed from 0. Therefore, options B and D are correct. For more information, see Chapter 3.

19. C. Files with the .java extension contain the Java source code and are compiled to files with the .class extension that contain the bytecode. For more information, see Chapter 1.

20. A, C. Option A is the exception base class, which is a checked exception. Options B, D, and E extend RuntimeException directly or indirectly and therefore are unchecked exceptions. Option F is a throwable and not an exception, and so should not be caught or declared. For more information, see Chapter 6.

OCA: Oracle®
Certified Associate Java®
SE 8 Programmer I
Study Guide
Exam 1Z0-808

Chapter 1

Java Building Blocks

OCA EXAM OBJECTIVES COVERED IN THIS CHAPTER:

✓ **Java Basics**

- Define the scope of variables

- Define the structure of a Java class

- Create executable Java applications with a main method; run a Java program from the command line; including console output

- Import other Java packages to make them accessible in your code

- Compare and contrast the features and components of Java such as platform independence, object orientation, encapsulation, etc.

✓ **Working with Java Data Types**

- Declare and initialize variables (including casting or primitive types)

- Differentiate between object reference variables and primitive variables

- Know how to read or write to object fields

- Explain an Object's Lifecycle (creation, "dereference by reassignment" and garbage collection

Welcome to the beginning of your journey to become certified on Java. We assume this isn't the first Java programming book you've read. Although we do talk about the basics, we do so only because we want to make sure you have all the terminology and detail you'll need for the OCA exam. If you've never written a Java program before, we recommend you pick up an introductory book on any version of Java—something like *Head First Java, 2nd Edition* (O'Reilly Media, 2005); *Java for Dummies* (For Dummies, 2014), or *Thinking in Java, 4th Edition* (Prentice Hall, 2006). (It's okay if the book covers an older version of Java—even Java 1.3 is fine.) Then come back to this certification study guide.

This chapter covers the fundamentals of Java. You'll see how to define and run a Java class, and learn about packages, variables, and the object life cycle.

Understanding the Java Class Structure

In Java programs, classes are the basic building blocks. When defining a *class*, you describe all the parts and characteristics of one of those building blocks. To use most classes, you have to create objects. An *object* is a runtime instance of a class in memory. All the various objects of all the different classes represent the state of your program.

In the following sections, we'll look at fields, methods, and comments. We'll also explore the relationship between classes and files.

Fields and Methods

Java classes have two primary elements: *methods*, often called functions or procedures in other languages, and *fields*, more generally known as variables. Together these are called the *members* of the class. Variables hold the state of the program, and methods operate on that state. If the change is important to remember, a variable stores that change. That's all classes really do. It's the programmer who creates and arranges these elements in such a way that the resulting code is useful and, ideally, easy for other programmers to understand.

Other building blocks include interfaces, which you'll learn about in Chapter 5, "Class Design," and enums, which you'll learn about when you start studying for the OCP exam.

The simplest Java class you can write looks like this:

```
1: public class Animal {
2: }
```

Java calls a word with special meaning a *keyword*. The `public` keyword on line 1 means the class can be used by other classes. The `class` keyword indicates you're defining a class. `Animal` gives the name of the class. Granted, this isn't a very interesting class, so add your first field:

```
1: public class Animal {
2:   String name;
3: }
```

 NOTE   The line numbers aren't part of the program; they're just there to make the code easier to talk about.

On line 2, we define a variable named name. We also define the type of that variable to be a `String`. A `String` is a value that we can put text into, such as `"this is a string"`. `String` is also a class supplied with Java. Next you can add methods:

```
1: public class Animal {
2:   String name;
3:   public String getName() {
4:     return name;
5:   }
6:   public void setName(String newName) {
7:     name = newName;
8:   }
9: }
```

On lines 3–5, you've defined your first method. A method is an operation that can be called. Again, `public` is used to signify that this method may be called from other classes. Next comes the return type—in this case, the method returns a `String`. On lines 6–8 is another method. This one has a special return type called *void*. `void` means that no value at all is returned. This method requires information be supplied to it from the calling method; this information is called a *parameter*. setName has one parameter named *newName*, and it is of type `String`. This means the caller should pass in one `String` parameter and expect nothing to be returned.

The full declaration of a method is called a *method signature*. In this example, can you identify the return type and parameters?

```
public int numberVisitors(int month)
```

The return type is int, which is a numeric type. There's one parameter named *month*, which is of type int as well.

Comments

Another common part of the code is called a *comment*. Because comments aren't executable code, you can place them anywhere. Comments make your code easier to read. You won't see many comments on the exam—the exam creators are trying to make the code difficult to read—but you'll see them in this book as we explain the code. And we hope you use them in your own code. There are three types of comments in Java. The first is called a single-line comment:

```
// comment until end of line
```

A single-line comment begins with two slashes. Anything you type after that on the same line is ignored by the compiler. Next comes the multiple-line comment:

```
/* Multiple
 * line comment
 */
```

A multiple-line comment (also known as a multiline comment) includes anything starting from the symbol /* until the symbol */. People often type an asterisk (*) at the beginning of each line of a multiline comment to make it easier to read, but you don't have to. Finally, we have a Javadoc comment:

```
/**
 * Javadoc multiple-line comment
 * @author Jeanne and Scott
 */
```

This comment is similar to a multiline comment except it starts with /**. This special syntax tells the Javadoc tool to pay attention to the comment. Javadoc comments have a specific structure that the Javadoc tool knows how to read. You won't see a Javadoc comment on the exam—just remember it exists so you can read up on it online when you start writing programs for others to use.

As a bit of practice, can you identify which type of comment each of these six words is in? Is it a single-line or a multiline comment?

```
/*
 * // anteater
 */
// bear
// // cat
```

```
// /* dog */
/* elephant */
/*
 * /* ferret */
 */
```

Did you look closely? Some of these are tricky. Even though comments technically aren't on the exam, it is good to practice to look at code carefully.

Okay, on to the answers. anteater is in a multiline comment. Everything between /* and */ is part of a multiline comment—even if it includes a single-line comment within it! bear is your basic single-line comment. cat and dog are also single-line comments. Everything from // to the end of the line is part of the comment, even if it is another type of comment. elephant is your basic multiline comment.

The line with ferret is interesting in that it doesn't compile. Everything from the first /* to the first */ is part of the comment, which means the compiler sees something like this:

```
/* */ */
```

We have a problem. There is an extra */. That's not valid syntax—a fact the compiler is happy to inform you about.

Classes vs. Files

Most of the time, each Java class is defined in its own *.java file. It is usually public, which means any code can call it. Interestingly, Java does not require that the class be public. For example, this class is just fine:

```
1: class Animal {
2:   String name;
3: }
```

You can even put two classes in the same file. When you do so, at most one of the classes in the file is allowed to be public. That means a file containing the following is also fine:

```
1: public class Animal {
2:     private String name;
3: }
4: class Animal2 {
5: }
```

If you do have a public class, it needs to match the filename. public class Animal2 would not compile in a file named Animal.java. In Chapter 5, we will discuss what non-public access means.

Writing a *main()* Method

A Java program begins execution with its main() *method*. A main() method is the gateway between the startup of a Java process, which is managed by the *Java Virtual Machine* (JVM), and the beginning of the programmer's code. The JVM calls on the underlying system to allocate memory and CPU time, access files, and so on.

The main() method lets us hook our code into this process, keeping it alive long enough to do the work we've coded. The simplest possible class with a main() method looks like this:

```
1: public class Zoo {
2:   public static void main(String[] args) {
3:
4:   }
5:}
```

This code doesn't do anything useful (or harmful). It has no instructions other than to declare the entry point. It does illustrate, in a sense, that what you can put in a main() method is arbitrary. Any legal Java code will do. In fact, the only reason we even need a class structure to start a Java program is because the language requires it. To compile and execute this code, type it into a file called Zoo.java and execute the following:

```
$ javac Zoo.java
$ java Zoo
```

If you don't get any error messages, you were successful. If you do get error messages, check that you've installed a Java Development Kit (JDK) and not a Java Runtime Environment (JRE), that you have added it to the PATH, and that you didn't make any typos in the example. If you have any of these problems and don't know what to do, post a question with the error message you received in the Beginning Java forum at CodeRanch (www.coderanch.com/forums/f-33/java).

To compile Java code, the file must have the extension .java. The name of the file must match the name of the class. The result is a file of *bytecode* by the same name, but with a .class filename extension. Bytecode consists of instructions that the JVM knows how to execute. Notice that we must omit the .class extension to run Zoo.java because the period has a reserved meaning in the JVM.

The rules for what a Java code file contains, and in what order, are more detailed than what we have explained so far (there is more on this topic later in the chapter). To keep things simple for now, we'll follow a subset of the rules:

- Each file can contain only one class.
- The filename must match the class name, including case, and have a .java extension.

Suppose we replace line 3 in Zoo.java with System.out.println("Welcome!");. When we compile and run the code again, we'll get the line of output that matches what's between the quotes. In other words, the program will output Welcome!.

Let's first review the words in the main() method's signature, one at a time. The keyword public is what's called an *access modifier*. It declares this method's level of exposure to potential callers in the program. Naturally, public means anyplace in the program. You'll learn about access modifiers in Chapter 4, "Methods and Encapsulation."

The keyword *static* binds a method to its class so it can be called by just the class name, as in, for example, Zoo.main(). Java doesn't need to create an object to call the main() method—which is good since you haven't learned about creating objects yet! In fact, the JVM does this, more or less, when loading the class name given to it. If a main() method isn't present in the class we name with the .java executable, the process will throw an error and terminate. Even if a main() method is present, Java will throw an exception if it isn't static. A nonstatic main() method might as well be invisible from the point of view of the JVM. We'll see static again in Chapter 4.

The keyword *void* represents the *return type*. A method that returns no data returns control to the caller silently. In general, it's good practice to use void for methods that change an object's state. In that sense, the main() method changes the program state from started to finished. We will explore return types in Chapter 4 as well. Excited for Chapter 4 yet?

Finally we arrive at the main() method's parameter list, represented as an array of java.lang.String objects. In practice, you can write String[] args, String args[] or String... args; the compiler accepts any of these. The variable name *args* hints that this list contains values that were read in (arguments) when the JVM started. You can use any name you like, though. The characters [] are brackets and represent an array. An array is a fixed-size list of items that are all of the same type. The characters ... are called varargs (variable argument lists). You will learn about String in Chapter 2, "Operators and Statements." Arrays and varargs will follow in Chapter 3, "Core Java APIs."

Let's see how to use the *args* parameter. First we modify the Zoo program to print out the first two arguments passed in:

```
public class Zoo {
  public static void main(String[] args) {
    System.out.println(args[0]);
    System.out.println(args[1]);
} }
```

args[0] accesses the first element of the array. That's right: array indexes begin with 0 in Java. To run it, type this:

```
$ javac Zoo.java
$ java Zoo Bronx Zoo
```

The output is what you might expect:

```
Bronx
Zoo
```

The program correctly identifies the first two "words" as the arguments. Spaces are used to separate the arguments. If you want spaces inside an argument, you need to use quotes as in this example:

```
$ javac Zoo.java
$ java Zoo "San Diego" Zoo
```

Now we have a space in the output:

```
San Diego
Zoo
```

All command-line arguments are treated as String objects, even if they represent another data type:

```
$ javac Zoo.java
$ java Zoo Zoo 2
```

No matter. You still get the values output as Strings. In Chapter 2, you'll learn how to convert Strings to numbers.

```
Zoo
2
```

Finally, what happens if you don't pass in enough arguments?

```
$ javac Zoo.java
$ java Zoo Zoo
```

Reading args[0] goes fine and Zoo is printed out. Then Java panics. There's no second argument! What to do? Java prints out an exception telling you it has no idea what to do with this argument at position 1. (You'll learn about exceptions in Chapter 6, "Exceptions.")

```
ZooException in thread "main"
java.lang.ArrayIndexOutOfBoundsException: 1
        at Zoo.main(Zoo.java:4)
```

To review, you need to have a JDK to compile because it includes a compiler. You do not need to have a JDK to run the code—a JRE is enough. Java class files run on the JVM and therefore run on any machine with Java rather than just the machine or operating system they happened to have been compiled on.

Understanding Package Declarations and Imports

Java comes with thousands of built-in classes, and there are countless more from developers like you. With all those classes, Java needs a way to organize them. It handles this in a way similar to a file cabinet. You put all your pieces of paper in folders. Java puts classes in *packages*. These are logical groupings for classes.

We wouldn't put you in front of a file cabinet and tell you to find a specific paper. Instead, we'd tell you which folder to look in. Java works the same way. It needs you to tell it which packages to look in to find code.

Suppose you try to compile this code:

```
public class ImportExample {
  public static void main(String[] args) {
    Random r = new Random();   // DOES NOT COMPILE
    System.out.println(r.nextInt(10));
  }
}
```

The Java compiler helpfully gives you an error that looks like this:

```
Random cannot be resolved to a type
```

This error could mean you made a typo in the name of the class. You double-check and discover that you didn't. The other cause of this error is omitting a needed *import* statement. Import statements tell Java which packages to look in for classes. Since you didn't tell Java where to look for Random, it has no clue.

Trying this again with the import allows you to compile:

```
import java.util.Random;  // import tells us where to find Random
public class ImportExample {
  public static void main(String[] args) {
    Random r = new Random();
    System.out.println(r.nextInt(10));  // print a number between 0 and 9
  }
}
```

Now the code runs; it prints out a random number between 0 and 9. Just like arrays, Java likes to begin counting with 0.

Java classes are grouped into packages. The import statement tells the compiler which package to look in to find a class. This is similar to how mailing a letter works.

Imagine you are mailing a letter to 123 Main St., Apartment 9. The mail carrier first brings the letter to 123 Main St. Then she looks for the mailbox for apartment number 9. The address is like the package name in Java. The apartment number is like the class name in Java. Just as the mail carrier only looks at apartment numbers in the building, Java only looks for class names in the package.

Package names are hierarchical like the mail as well. The postal service starts with the top level, looking at your country first. You start reading a package name at the beginning too. If it begins with java or javax, this means it came with the JDK. If it starts with something else, it likely shows where it came from using the website name in reverse. For example, com.amazon.java8book tells us the code came from amazon.com. After the website name, you can add whatever you want. For example, com.amazon.java8.my.name also came from amazon.com. Java calls more detailed packages *child packages*. com.amazon .java8book is a child package of com.amazon. You can tell because it's longer and thus more specific.

You'll see package names on the exam that don't follow this convention. Don't be surprised to see package names like a.b.c. The rule for package names is that they are mostly letters or numbers separated by dots. Technically, you're allowed a couple of other characters between the dots. The rules are the same as for variable names, which you'll see later in the chapter. The exam may try to trick you with invalid variable names. Luckily, it doesn't try to trick you by giving invalid package names.

In the following sections, we'll look at imports with wildcards, naming conflicts with imports, how to create a package of your own, and how the exam formats code.

Wildcards

Classes in the same package are often imported together. You can use a shortcut to import all the classes in a package:

```
import java.util.*;    // imports java.util.Random among other things
public class ImportExample {
  public static void main(String[] args) {
    Random r = new Random();
    System.out.println(r.nextInt(10));
  }
}
```

In this example, we imported java.util.Random and a pile of other classes. The * is a wildcard that matches all classes in the package. Every class in the java.util package is available to this program when Java compiles it. It doesn't import child packages, fields, or methods; it imports only classes. (Okay, it's only classes for now, but there's a special type of import called the "static import" that imports other types. You'll learn more about that in Chapter 4.)

You might think that including so many classes slows down your program, but it doesn't. The compiler figures out what's actually needed. Which approach you choose is personal preference.

Listing the classes used makes the code easier to read, especially for new programmers. Using the wildcard can shorten the import list. You'll see both approaches on the exam.

Redundant Imports

Wait a minute! We've been referring to System without an import and Java found it just fine. There's one special package in the Java world called java.lang. This package is special in that it is automatically imported. You can still type this package in an import statement, but you don't have to. In the following code, how many of the imports do you think are redundant?

```
1: import java.lang.System;
2: import java.lang.*;
3: import java.util.Random;
4: import java.util.*;
5: public class ImportExample {
6:   public static void main(String[] args) {
7:     Random r = new Random();
8:     System.out.println(r.nextInt(10));
9:   }
10: }
```

The answer is that three of the imports are redundant. Lines 1 and 2 are redundant because everything in java.lang is automatically considered to be imported. Line 4 is also redundant in this example because Random is already imported from java.util.Random. If line 3 wasn't present, java.util.* wouldn't be redundant, though, since it would cover importing Random.

Another case of redundancy involves importing a class that is in the same package as the class importing it. Java automatically looks in the current package for other classes.

Let's take a look at one more example to make sure you understand the edge cases for imports. For this example, Files and Paths are both in the package java.nio.file. You don't need to memorize this package for the OCA exam (but you should know it for the OCP exam). When testing your understanding of packages and imports, the OCA exam will use packages you may never have seen before. The question will let you know which package the class is in if you need to know that in order to answer the question.

What imports do you think would work to get this code to compile?

```
public class InputImports {
  public void read(Files files) {
    Paths.get("name");
  }
}
```

There are two possible answers. The shorter one is to use a wildcard to import both at the same time:

```
import java.nio.file.*;
```

The other answer is to import both classes explicitly:

```
import java.nio.file.Files;
import java.nio.file.Paths;
```

Now let's consider some imports that don't work:

```
import java.nio.*; // NO GOOD - a wildcard only matches
                   //class names, not "file.*Files"
import java.nio.*.*; // NO GOOD - you can only have one wildcard
                     //and it must be at the end
import java.nio.file.Paths.*; // NO GOOD - you cannot import methods
                              //only class names
```

Naming Conflicts

One of the reasons for using packages is so that class names don't have to be unique across all of Java. This means you'll sometimes want to import a class that can be found in multiple places. A common example of this is the Date class. Java provides implementations of java.util.Date and java.sql.Date. This is another example where you don't need to know the package names for the OCA exam—they will be provided to you. What import could we use if we want the java.util.Date version?

```
public class Conflicts {
  Date date;
  // some more code
}
```

The answer should be easy by now. You can write either **import java.util.*;** or **import java.util.Date;**. The tricky cases come about when other imports are present:

```
import java.util.*;
import java.sql.*; // DOES NOT COMPILE
```

When the class is found in multiple packages, Java gives you the compiler error:

```
The type Date is ambiguous
```

In our example, the solution is easy—remove the java.sql.Date import that we don't need. But what do we do if we need a whole pile of other classes in the java.sql package?

```
import java.util.Date;
import java.sql.*;
```

Ah, now it works. If you explicitly import a class name, it takes precedence over any wildcards present. Java thinks, "Okay! The programmer really wants me to assume use of the java.util.Date class."

One more example. What does Java do with "ties" for precedence?

```
import java.util.Date;
import java.sql.Date;
```

Java is smart enough to detect that this code is no good. As a programmer, you've claimed to explicitly want the default to be both the java.util.Date and java.sql.Date implementations. Because there can't be two defaults, the compiler tells you:

```
The import java.sql.Date collides with another import statement
```

If You Really Need to Use Two Classes with the Same Name...

Sometimes you really do want to use Date from two different packages. When this happens, you can pick one to use in the import and use the other's fully qualified class name (the package name, a dot, and the class name) to specify that it's special. For example:

```
import java.util.Date;

public class Conflicts {
        Date date;
        java.sql.Date sqlDate;

}
```

Or you could have neither with an import and always use the fully qualified class name:

```
public class Conflicts {
        java.util.Date date;
        java.sql.Date sqlDate;

}
```

Creating a New Package

Up to now, all the code we've written in this chapter has been in the *default package*. This is a special unnamed package that you should use only for throwaway code. You can tell the code is in the default package, because there's no package name. On the exam, you'll see the default package used a lot to save space in code listings. In real life, always name your packages to avoid naming conflicts and to allow others to reuse your code.

Now it's time to create a new package. The directory structure on your computer is related to the package name. Suppose we have these two classes:

```
C:\temp\packagea\ClassA.java

package packagea;
public class ClassA {
}

C:\temp\packageb\ClassB.java

package packageb;
import packagea.ClassA;
public class ClassB {
  public static void main(String[] args) {
    ClassA a;
    System.out.println("Got it");
  }
}
```

When you run a Java program, Java knows where to look for those package names. In this case, running from C:\temp works because both packagea and packageb are underneath it.

Compiling Code with Packages

You'll learn Java much more easily by using the command line to compile and test your examples. Once you know the Java syntax well, you can switch to an integrated development environment (IDE) like Eclipse. An IDE will save you time in coding. But for the exam, your goal is to know details about the language and not have the IDE hide them for you.

Follow this example to make sure you know how to use the command line. If you have any problems following this procedure, post a question in the Beginning Java forum at CodeRanch (www.coderanch.com/forums/f-33/java). Describe what you tried and what the error said.

Windows Setup
Create the two files:

- C:\temp\packagea\ClassA.java

- C:\temp\packageb\ClassB.java

Then type this command:

```
cd C:\temp
```

Mac/Linux Setup

Create the two files:

- /tmp/packagea/ClassA.java

- /tmp/packageb/ClassB.java

Then type this command:

```
cd /tmp
```

To Compile

Type this command:

```
javac packagea/ClassA.java packageb/ClassB.java
```

If this command doesn't work, you'll get an error message. Check your files carefully for typos against the provided files. If the command does work, two new files will be created:

packagea/ClassA.class and packageb/ClassB.class.

To Run

Type this command:

```
java packageb.ClassB
```

If it works, you'll see Got it printed. You might have noticed we typed ClassB rather than ClassB.class. In Java you don't pass the extension when running a program.

Class Paths and JARs

You can also specify the location of the other files explicitly using a class path. This technique is useful when the class files are located elsewhere or in special JAR files. A JAR file is like a zip file of mainly Java class files. This goes beyond what you'll need to do on version 8 of the exam, although it appears on older versions.

On Windows, you type the following:

```
java -cp ".;C:\temp\someOtherLocation;c:\temp\myJar.jar" myPackage.MyClass
```

And on Mac OS/Linux, you type this:

```
java -cp ".:/tmp/someOtherLocation:/tmp/myJar.jar" myPackage.MyClass
```

The dot indicates you want to include the current directory in the class path. The rest of the command says to look for loose class files (or packages) in someOtherLocation and within myJar.jar. Windows uses semicolons to separate parts of the class path; other operating systems use colons.

Finally, you can use a wildcard (*) to match all the JARs in a directory. Here's an example:

```
java -cp "C:\temp\directoryWithJars\*" myPackage.MyClass
```

This command will add all the JARs to the class path that are in directoryWithJars. It won't include any JARs in the class path that are in a subdirectory of directoryWithJars.

Code Formatting on the Exam

Not all questions will include the imports. If the exam isn't asking about imports in the question, it will often omit the imports to save space. You'll see examples with line numbers that don't begin with 1 in this case. The question is telling you, "Don't worry—imagine the code we omitted is correct; just focus on what I'm giving you." This means when you do see the line number 1 or no line numbers at all, you have to make sure imports aren't missing. Another thing the exam does to save space is to merge code on the same line. You should expect to see code like the following and to be asked whether it compiles. (You'll learn about ArrayList in Chapter 3—assume that part is good for now.)

```
6: public void method(ArrayList list) {
7:  if (list.isEmpty()) { System.out.println("e");
8:  } else { System.out.println("n");
9: }  }
```

The answer here is that it does compile because the code starts below the imports. Now, what about this one? Does it compile?

```
1: public class LineNumbers {
2: public void method(ArrayList list) {
3:  if (list.isEmpty()) { System.out.println("e");
4:  } else { System.out.println("n");
5: }  } }
```

For this one, you would answer "Does not compile." Since the code begins with line 1, you don't get to assume that valid imports were provided earlier. The exam will let you know what package classes are in unless they're covered in the objectives. You'll be expected to know that ArrayList is in java.util—at least you will once you get to Chapter 3 of this book!

You'll also see code that doesn't have a main() method. When this happens, assume the main() method, class definition, and all necessary imports are present. You're just being asked if the part of the code you're shown compiles when dropped into valid surrounding code.

Creating Objects

Our programs wouldn't be able to do anything useful if we didn't have the ability to create new objects. Remember that an object is an instance of a class. In the following sections, we'll look at constructors, object fields, instance initializers, and the order in which values are initialized.

Constructors

To create an instance of a class, all you have to do is write new before it. For example:

```
Random r = new Random();
```

First you declare the type that you'll be creating (Random) and give the variable a name (r). This gives Java a place to store a reference to the object. Then you write new Random() to actually create the object.

Random() looks like a method since it is followed by parentheses. It's called a *constructor*, which is a special type of method that creates a new object. Now it's time to define a constructor of your own:

```
public class Chick {
  public Chick() {
    System.out.println("in constructor");
  }
}
```

There are two key points to note about the constructor: the name of the constructor matches the name of the class, and there's no return type. You'll likely see a method like this on the exam:

```
public void Chick() { } // NOT A CONSTRUCTOR
```

When you see a method name beginning with a capital letter and having a return type, pay special attention to it. It is *not* a constructor since there's a return type. It's a regular method that won't be called when you write new Chick().

The purpose of a constructor is to initialize fields, although you can put any code in there. Another way to initialize fields is to do so directly on the line on which they're declared. This example shows both approaches:

```
public class Chicken {
  int numEggs = 0;// initialize on line
  String name;
  public Chicken() {
    name = "Duke";// initialize in constructor
  } }
```

For most classes, you don't have to code a constructor—the compiler will supply a "do nothing" default constructor for you. There's one scenario that requires you to declare a constructor that you'll learn about in Chapter 5.

Reading and Writing Object Fields

It's possible to read and write instance variables directly from the caller. In this example, a mother swan lays eggs:

```java
public class Swan {
  int numberEggs;// instance variable
  public static void main(String[] args) {
    Swan mother = new Swan();
    mother.numberEggs = 1;    // set variable
    System.out.println(mother.numberEggs);  // read variable
  }
}
```

Reading a variable is known as *getting* it. The class gets *numberEggs* directly to print it out. Writing to a variable is known as *setting* it. This class sets *numberEggs* to 1.

In Chapter 4, you'll learn how to protect the Swan class from having someone set a negative number of eggs.

You can even read and write fields directly on the line declaring them:

```java
1: public class Name {
2:    String first = "Theodore";
3:    String last = "Moose";
4:    String full = first + last;
5: }
```

Lines 2 and 3 both write to fields. Line 4 does both. It reads the fields *first* and *last*. It then writes the field *full*.

Instance Initializer Blocks

When you learned about methods, you saw braces ({}). The code between the braces is called a *code block*. Sometimes this code is called being inside the braces. Anywhere you see braces is a code block.

Sometimes code blocks are inside a method. These are run when the method is called. Other times, code blocks appear outside a method. These are called *instance initializers*. In Chapter 5, you'll learn how to use a static initializer.

How many blocks do you see in this example? How many instance initializers do you see?

```java
3: public static void main(String[] args) {
4:    { System.out.println("Feathers"); }
5: }
6: { System.out.println("Snowy"); }
```

There are three code blocks and one instance initializer. Counting code blocks is easy: you just count the number of pairs of braces. If there aren't the same number of open ({) and close (}) braces, the code doesn't compile. It doesn't matter that one set of braces is inside the main() method—it still counts.

When counting instance initializers, keep in mind that it does matter whether the braces are inside a method. There's only one pair of braces outside a method. Line 6 is an instance initializer.

Order of Initialization

When writing code that initializes fields in multiple places, you have to keep track of the order of initialization. We'll add some more rules to the order of initialization in Chapters 4 and 5. In the meantime, you need to remember:

- Fields and instance initializer blocks are run in the order in which they appear in the file.
- The constructor runs after all fields and instance initializer blocks have run.

Let's look at an example:

```
1: public class Chick {
2:   private String name = "Fluffy";
3:   { System.out.println("setting field"); }
4:   public Chick() {
5:     name = "Tiny";
6:     System.out.println("setting constructor");
7:   }
8:   public static void main(String[] args) {
9:     Chick chick = new Chick();
10:    System.out.println(chick.name); } }
```

Running this example prints this:

```
setting field
setting constructor
Tiny
```

Let's look at what's happening here. We start with the main() method because that's where Java starts execution. On line 9, we call the constructor of Chick. Java creates a new object. First it initializes name to "Fluffy" on line 2. Next it executes the print statement in the instance initializer on line 3. Once all the fields and instance initializers have run, Java returns to the constructor. Line 5 changes the value of name to "Tiny" and line 6 prints another statement. At this point, the constructor is done executing and goes back to the print statement on line 10.

   Order matters for the fields and blocks of code. You can't refer to a variable before it has been initialized:

```
{ System.out.println(name); }   // DOES NOT COMPILE
private String name = "Fluffy";
```

   You should expect to see a question about initialization on the exam. Let's try one more. What do you think this code prints out?

```
public class Egg {
  public Egg() {
    number = 5;
  }
  public static void main(String[] args) {
    Egg egg = new Egg();
    System.out.println(egg.number);
  }
  private int number = 3;
  { number = 4; } }
```

   If you answered 5, you got it right. Fields and blocks are run first in order, setting *number* to 3 and then 4. Then the constructor runs, setting *number* to 5.

Distinguishing Between Object References and Primitives

Java applications contain two types of data: primitive types and reference types. In this section, we'll discuss the differences between a primitive type and a reference type.

Primitive Types

Java has eight built-in data types, referred to as the Java *primitive types*. These eight data types represent the building blocks for Java objects, because all Java objects are just a complex collection of these primitive data types. The exam assumes you are well versed in the eight primitive data types, their relative sizes, and what can be stored in them.

Table 1.1 shows the Java primitive types together with their size in bytes and the range of values that each holds.

TABLE 1.1   Java primitive types

Keyword	Type	Example
boolean	true or false	true
byte	8-bit integral value	123
short	16-bit integral value	123
int	32-bit integral value	123
long	64-bit integral value	123
float	32-bit floating-point value	123.45f
double	64-bit floating-point value	123.456
char	16-bit Unicode value	'a'

There's a lot of information in Table 1.1. Let's look at some key points:

- float and double are used for floating-point (decimal) values.
- A float requires the letter f following the number so Java knows it is a float.
- byte, short, int, and long are used for numbers without decimal points.
- Each numeric type uses twice as many bits as the smaller similar type. For example, short uses twice as many bits as byte does.

You won't be asked about the exact sizes of most of these types. You should know that a byte can hold a value from –128 to 127. So you aren't stuck memorizing this, let's look at how Java gets that. A byte is 8 bits. A bit has two possible values. (These are basic computer science definitions that you should memorize.) 2^8 is $2 \times 2 = 4 \times 2 = 8 \times 2 = 16 \times 2 = 32 \times 2 = 64 \times 2 = 128 \times 2 = 256$. Since 0 needs to be included in the range, Java takes it away from the positive side. Or if you don't like math, you can just memorize it.

The number of bits is used by Java when it figures out how much memory to reserve for your variable. For example, Java allocates 32 bits if you write this:

```
int num;
```

⊕ Real World Scenario

What Is the Largest int?

You do not have to know this for the exam, but the maximum number an int can hold is 2,147,483,647. How do we know this? One way is to have Java tell us:

```
System.out.println(Integer.MAX_VALUE);
```

The other way is with math. An int is 32 bits. 2^{32} is 4,294,967,296. Divide that by 2 and you get 2,147,483,648. Then subtract 1 as we did with bytes and you get 2,147,483,647. It's easier to just ask Java to print the value, isn't it?

There are a few more things you should know about numeric primitives. When a number is present in the code, it is called a *literal*. By default, Java assumes you are defining an int value with a literal. In this example, the number listed is bigger than what fits in an int. Remember, you aren't expected to memorize the maximum value for an int. The exam will include it in the question if it comes up.

```
long max = 3123456789;  // DOES NOT COMPILE
```

Java complains the number is out of range. And it is—for an int. However, we don't have an int. The solution is to add the character L to the number:

```
long max = 3123456789L;  // now Java knows it is a long
```

Alternatively, you could add a lowercase l to the number. But please use the uppercase L. The lowercase l looks like the number 1.

Another way to specify numbers is to change the "base." When you learned how to count, you studied the digits 0–9. This numbering system is called base 10 since there are 10 numbers. It is also known as the decimal number system. Java allows you to specify digits in several other formats:

- octal (digits 0–7), which uses the number 0 as a prefix—for example, 017
- hexadecimal (digits 0–9 and letters A–F), which uses the number 0 followed by x or X as a prefix—for example, 0xFF
- binary (digits 0–1), which uses the number 0 followed by b or B as a prefix—for example, 0b10

You won't need to convert between number systems on the exam. You'll have to recognize valid literal values that can be assigned to numbers.

Converting Back to Binary

Although you don't need to convert between number systems on the exam, we'll look at one example in case you're curious:

```
System.out.println(56);      // 56
System.out.println(0b11);    // 3
System.out.println(017);     // 15
System.out.println(0x1F);    // 31
```

First we have our normal base 10 value. We know you already know how to read that, but bear with us. The rightmost digit is 6, so it's "worth" 6. The second-to-rightmost digit is 5, so it's "worth" 50 (5 times 10.) Adding these together, we get 56.

Next we have binary, or base 2. The rightmost digit is 1 and is "worth" 1. The second-to-rightmost digit is also 1. In this case, it's "worth" 2 (1 times 2) because the base is 2. Adding these gets us 3.

Then comes octal, or base 8. The rightmost digit is 7 and is "worth" 7. The second-to-rightmost digit is 1. In this case, it's "worth" 8 (1 times 8) because the base is 8. Adding these gets us 15.

Finally, we have hexadecimal, or base 16, which is also known as hex. The rightmost "digit" is F and it's "worth" 15 (9 is "worth" 9, A is "worth" 10, B is "worth" 11, and so forth). The second-to-rightmost digit is 1. In this case, it's "worth" 16 (1 times 16) because the base is 16. Adding these gets us 31.

The last thing you need to know about numeric literals is a feature added in Java 7. You can have underscores in numbers to make them easier to read:

```
int million1 = 1000000;
int million2 = 1_000_000;
```

We'd rather be reading the latter one because the zeroes don't run together. You can add underscores anywhere except at the beginning of a literal, the end of a literal, right before a decimal point, or right after a decimal point. Let's look at a few examples:

```
double notAtStart = _1000.00;        // DOES NOT COMPILE
double notAtEnd = 1000.00_;          // DOES NOT COMPILE
double notByDecimal = 1000_.00;      // DOES NOT COMPILE
double annoyingButLegal = 1_00_0.0_0;  // this one compiles
```

Reference Types

A *reference type* refers to an object (an instance of a class). Unlike primitive types that hold their values in the memory where the variable is allocated, references do not hold the value of the object they refer to. Instead, a reference "points" to an object by storing the memory address where the object is located, a concept referred to as a *pointer*. Unlike other languages, Java does not allow you to learn what the physical memory address is. You can only use the reference to refer to the object.

Let's take a look at some examples that declare and initialize reference types. Suppose we declare a reference of type java.util.Date and a reference of type String:

```
java.util.Date today;
String greeting;
```

The *today* variable is a reference of type Date and can only point to a Date object. The *greeting* variable is a reference that can only point to a String object. A value is assigned to a reference in one of two ways:

- A reference can be assigned to another object of the same type.
- A reference can be assigned to a new object using the new keyword.

For example, the following statements assign these references to new objects:

```
today = new java.util.Date();
greeting = "How are you?";
```

The *today* reference now points to a new Date object in memory, and *today* can be used to access the various fields and methods of this Date object. Similarly, the *greeting* reference points to a new String object, "How are you?". The String and Date objects do not have names and can be accessed only via their corresponding reference. Figure 1.1 shows how the reference types appear in memory.

FIGURE 1.1   An object in memory can be accessed only via a reference.

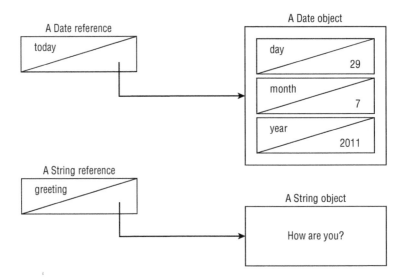

Key Differences

There are a few important differences you should know between primitives and reference types. First, reference types can be assigned `null`, which means they do not currently refer to an object. Primitive types will give you a compiler error if you attempt to assign them `null`. In this example, *value* cannot point to `null` because it is of type `int`:

```
int value = null;    // DOES NOT COMPILE
String s = null;
```

Next, reference types can be used to call methods when they do not point to `null`. Primitives do not have methods declared on them. In this example, we can call a method on *reference* since it is of a reference type. You can tell `length` is a method because it has () after it. The following line is gibberish. No methods exist on *len* because it is an `int` primitive. Primitives do not have methods.

```
String reference = "hello";
int len = reference.length();
int bad = len.length(); // DOES NOT COMPILE
```

Finally, notice that all the primitive types have lowercase type names. All classes that come with Java begin with uppercase. You should follow this convention for classes you create as well.

Declaring and Initializing Variables

We've seen some variables already. A *variable* is a name for a piece of memory that stores data. When you declare a variable, you need to state the variable type along with giving it a name. For example, the following code declares two variables. One is named *zooName* and is of type `String`. The other is named *numberAnimals* and is of type `int`.

```
String zooName;
int numberAnimals;
```

Now that we've declared a variable, we can give it a value. This is called initializing a variable. To initialize a variable, you just type the variable name followed by an equal sign, followed by the desired value:

```
zooName = "The Best Zoo";
numberAnimals = 100;
```

Since you often want to initialize a variable right away, you can do so in the same statement as the declaration. For example, here we merge the previous declarations and initializations into more concise code:

```
String zooName = "The Best Zoo";
int numberAnimals = 100;
```

In the following sections, we'll look at how to declare multiple variables in one-line and legal identifiers.

Declaring Multiple Variables

You can also declare and initialize multiple variables in the same statement. How many variables do you think are declared and initialized in the following two lines?

```
String s1, s2;
String s3 = "yes", s4 = "no";
```

Four String variables were declared: *s1*, *s2*, *s3*, and *s4*. You can declare many variables in the same declaration as long as they are all of the same type. You can also initialize any or all of those values inline. In the previous example, we have two initialized variables: *s3* and *s4*. The other two variables remain declared but not yet initialized.

This is where it gets tricky. Pay attention to tricky things! The exam will attempt to trick you. Again, how many variables do you think are declared and initialized in this code?

```
int i1, i2, i3 = 0;
```

As you should expect, three variables were declared: *i1*, *i2*, and *i3*. However, only one of those values was initialized: *i3*. The other two remain declared but not yet initialized. That's the trick. Each snippet separated by a comma is a little declaration of its own. The initialization of *i3* only applies to *i3*. It doesn't have anything to do with *i1* or *i2* despite being in the same statement.

Another way the exam could try to trick you is to show you code like this line:

```
int num, String value; // DOES NOT COMPILE
```

This code doesn't compile because it tries to declare multiple variables of *different* types in the same statement. The shortcut to declare multiple variables in the same statement only works when they share a type.

To make sure you understand this, see if you can figure out which of the following are legal declarations. "Legal," "valid," and "compiles" are all synonyms in the Java exam world. We try to use all the terminology you could encounter on the exam.

```
boolean b1, b2;
String s1 = "1", s2;
double d1, double d2;
int i1; int i2;
int i3; i4;
```

The first statement is legal. It declares two variables without initializing them. The second statement is also legal. It declares two variables and initializes only one of them.

The third statement is *not* legal. Java does not allow you to declare two different types in the same statement. Wait a minute! Variables *d1* and *d2* are the same type. They are both of type double. Although that's true, it still isn't allowed. If you want to declare multiple variables in the same statement, they must share the same type declaration and not repeat it. double d1, d2; would have been legal.

The fourth statement is legal. Although int does appear twice, each one is in a separate statement. A semicolon (;) separates statements in Java. It just so happens there are two completely different statements on the same line. The fifth statement is *not* legal. Again, we have two completely different statements on the same line. The second one is not a valid declaration because it omits the type. When you see an oddly placed semicolon on the exam, pretend the code is on separate lines and think about whether the code compiles that way. In this case, we have the following:

```
int i1;
int i2;
int i3;
i4;// DOES NOT COMPILE
```

Looking at the last line on its own, you can easily see that the declaration is invalid. And yes, the exam really does cram multiple statements onto the same line—partly to try to trick you and partly to fit more code on the screen. In the real world, please limit yourself to one declaration per statement and line. Your teammates will thank you for the readable code.

Identifiers

It probably comes as no surprise that Java has precise rules about *identifier* names. Luckily, the same rules for identifiers apply to anything you are free to name, including variables, methods, classes, and fields.

There are only three rules to remember for legal identifiers:

- The name must begin with a letter or the symbol $ or _.
- Subsequent characters may also be numbers.
- You cannot use the same name as a Java *reserved word*. As you might imagine, a reserved word is a keyword that Java has reserved so that you are not allowed to use it. Remember that Java is case sensitive, so you can use versions of the keywords that only differ in case. Please don't, though.

Don't worry—you won't need to memorize the full list of reserved words. The exam will only ask you about ones you've already learned, such as class. The following is a list of all the reserved words in Java. const and goto aren't actually used in Java. They are reserved so that people coming from other languages don't use them by accident—and in theory, in case Java wants to use them one day.

abstract	assert	boolean	break	byte
case	catch	char	class	const*
continue	default	do	double	else
enum	extends	false	final	finally
float	for	goto*	if	implements
import	instanceof	int	interface	long
native	new	null	package	private
protected	public	return	short	static
strictfp	super	switch	synchronized	this
throw	throws	transient	true	try
void	volatile	while		

Prepare to be tested on these rules. The following examples are legal:

```
okidentifier
$OK2Identifier
_alsoOK1d3ntifi3r
__SStillOkbutKnotsonice$
```

These examples are not legal:

```
3DPointClass  // identifiers cannot begin with a number
hollywood@vine // @ is not a letter, digit, $ or _
*$coffee // * is not a letter, digit, $ or _
public   // public is a reserved word
```

Although you can do crazy things with identifier names, you shouldn't. Java has conventions so that code is readable and consistent. This consistency includes CamelCase. In CamelCase, each word begins with an uppercase letter. This makes multiple-word variable names easier to read. Which would you rather read: *Thisismyclass name* or *ThisIsMyClass name*? The exam will mostly use common conventions for identifiers, but not always. When you see a nonstandard identifier, be sure to check if it is legal. If not, you get to mark the answer "does not compile" and skip analyzing everything else in the question.

Real World Scenario

Identifiers in the Real World

Most Java developers follow these conventions for identifier names:

- Method and variables names begin with a lowercase letter followed by CamelCase.

- Class names begin with an uppercase letter followed by CamelCase. Don't start any identifiers with $. The compiler uses this symbol for some files.

Also, know that valid letters in Java are not just characters in the English alphabet. Java supports the Unicode character set, so there are more than 45,000 characters that can start a legal Java identifier. A few hundred more are non-Arabic numerals that may appear after the first character in a legal identifier. Luckily, you don't have to worry about memorizing those for the exam. If you are in a country that doesn't use the English alphabet, this is useful to know for a job.

Understanding Default Initialization of Variables

Before you can use a variable, it needs a value. Some types of variables get this value set automatically, and others require the programmer to specify it. In the following sections, we'll look at the differences between the defaults for local, instance, and class variables.

Local Variables

A *local variable* is a variable defined within a method. Local variables must be initialized before use. They do not have a default value and contain garbage data until initialized. The compiler will not let you read an uninitialized value. For example, the following code generates a compiler error:

```
4: public int notValid() {
5:   int y = 10;
6:   int x;
7:   int reply = x + y; // DOES NOT COMPILE
8:   return reply;
9: }
```

y is initialized to 10. However, because *x* is not initialized before it is used in the expression on line 7, the compiler generates the following error:

```
Test.java:7: variable x might not have been initialized
        int reply = x + y;
              ^
```

Until *x* is assigned a value, it cannot appear within an expression, and the compiler will gladly remind you of this rule. The compiler knows your code has control of what happens inside the method and can be expected to initialize values.

The compiler is smart enough to recognize variables that have been initialized after their declaration but before they are used. Here's an example:

```
public int valid() {
  int y = 10;
  int x; // x is declared here
  x = 3; // and initialized here
  int reply = x + y;
  return reply;
}
```

The compiler is also smart enough to recognize initializations that are more complex. In this example, there are two branches of code. *answer* is initialized in both of them so the compiler is perfectly happy. *onlyOneBranch* is only initialized if *check* happens to be true. The compiler knows there is the possibility for *check* to be false, resulting in uninitialized code, and gives a compiler error. You'll learn more about the if statement in the next chapter.

```
public void findAnswer(boolean check) {
  int answer;
  int onlyOneBranch;
  if (check) {
    onlyOneBranch = 1;
    answer = 1;
  } else {
    answer = 2;
  }
  System.out.println(answer);
  System.out.println(onlyOneBranch); // DOES NOT COMPILE
}
```

Instance and Class Variables

Variables that are not local variables are known as *instance variables* or *class variables*. Instance variables are also called fields. Class variables are shared across multiple objects.

You can tell a variable is a class variable because it has the keyword `static` before it. You'll learn about this in Chapter 4. For now, just know that a variable is a class variable if it has the `static` keyword in its declaration.

Instance and class variables do not require you to initialize them. As soon as you declare these variables, they are given a default value. You'll need to memorize everything in table 1.2 except the default value of `char`. To make this easier, remember that the compiler doesn't know what value to use and so wants the simplest value it can give the type: `null` for an object and `0`/`false` for a primitive.

TABLE 1.2   Default initialization values by type

Variable type	Default initialization value
boolean	false
byte, short, int, long	0 (in the type's bit-length)
float, double	0.0 (in the type's bit-length)
char	'\u0000' (NUL)
All object references (everything else)	null

Understanding Variable Scope

You've learned that local variables are declared within a method. How many local variables do you see in this example?

```
public void eat(int piecesOfCheese) {
   int bitesOfCheese = 1;
}
```

There are two local variables in this method. *bitesOfCheese* is declared inside the method. *piecesOfCheese* is called a method parameter. It is also local to the method. Both of these variables are said to have a *scope* local to the method. This means they cannot be used outside the method.

Local variables can never have a scope larger than the method they are defined in. However, they can have a smaller scope. Consider this example:

```
3: public void eatIfHungry(boolean hungry) {
4:   if (hungry) {
5:     int bitesOfCheese = 1;
```

```
6:  }  // bitesOfCheese goes out of scope here
7:  System.out.println(bitesOfCheese);// DOES NOT COMPILE
8: }
```

hungry has a scope of the entire method. *bitesOfCheese* has a smaller scope. It is only available for use in the if statement because it is declared inside of it. When you see a set of braces ({ }) in the code, it means you have entered a new block of code. Each block of code has its own scope. When there are multiple blocks, you match them from the inside out. In our case, the if statement block begins at line 4 and ends at line 6. The method's block begins at line 3 and ends at line 8.

Since *bitesOfCheese* is declared in such a block, the scope is limited to that block. When the compiler gets to line 7, it complains that it doesn't know anything about this *bitesOf-Cheese* thing and gives an error:

```
bitesOfCheese cannot be resolved to a variable
```

Remember that blocks can contain other blocks. These smaller contained blocks can reference variables defined in the larger scoped blocks, but not vice versa. For example:

```
16: public void eatIfHungry(boolean hungry) {
17:   if (hungry) {
18:     int bitesOfCheese = 1;
19:     {
20:       boolean teenyBit = true;
21:       System.out.println(bitesOfCheese);
22:     }
23:   }
24:   System.out.println(teenyBit);  // DOES NOT COMPILE
25: }
```

The variable defined on line 18 is in scope until the block ends on line 23. Using it in the smaller block from lines 19 to 22 is fine. The variable defined on line 20 goes out of scope on line 22. Using it on line 24 is not allowed.

The exam may attempt to trick you with questions on scope. You'll probably see a question that appears to be about something complex and fails to compile because one of the variables is out of scope. Let's try one. Don't worry if you aren't familiar with if statements or while loops yet. It doesn't matter what the code does since we are talking about scope. See if you can figure out on which line each of the five local variables goes into and out of scope:

```
11: public void eatMore(boolean hungry, int amountOfFood) {
12:   int roomInBelly = 5;
13:   if (hungry) {
14:     boolean timeToEat = true;
15:     while (amountOfFood > 0) {
16:       int amountEaten = 2;
```

```
17:        roomInBelly = roomInBelly - amountEaten;
18:        amountOfFood = amountOfFood - amountEaten;
19:      }
20:   }
21:   System.out.println(amountOfFood);
22: }
```

The first step in figuring out the scope is to identify the blocks of code. In this case, there are three blocks. You can tell this because there are three sets of braces. Starting from the innermost set, we can see where the while loop's block starts and ends. Repeat this as we go out for the if statement block and method block. Table 1.3 shows the line numbers that each block starts and ends on.

TABLE 1.3   Blocks for scope

Line	First line in block	Last line in block
while	15	19
if	13	20
Method	11	22

You'll want to practice this skill a lot. Identifying blocks needs to be second nature for the exam. The good news is that there are lots of code examples to practice on. You can look at any code example in this book on any topic and match up braces.

Now that we know where the blocks are, we can look at the scope of each variable. *hungry* and *amountOfFood* are method parameters, so they are available for the entire method. This means their scope is lines 11 to 22. *roomInBelly* goes into scope on line 12 because that is where it is declared. It stays in scope for the rest of the method and so goes out of scope on line 22. *timeToEat* goes into scope on line 14 where it is declared. It goes out of scope on line 20 where the if block ends. *amountEaten* goes into scope on line 16 where it is declared. It goes out of scope on line 19 where the while block ends.

All that was for local variables. Luckily the rule for instance variables is easier: they are available as soon as they are defined and last for the entire lifetime of the object itself. The rule for class (static) variables is even easier: they go into scope when declared like the other variables types. However, they stay in scope for the entire life of the program.

Let's do one more example to make sure you have a handle on this. Again, try to figure out the type of the four variables and when they go into and out of scope.

```
1:  public class Mouse {
2:     static int MAX_LENGTH = 5;
3:     int length;
```

```
4:    public void grow(int inches) {
5:      if (length < MAX_LENGTH) {
6:        int newSize = length + inches;
7:        length = newSize;
8:      }
9:    }
10: }
```

In this class, we have one class variable (*MAX_LENGTH*), one instance variable (*length*), and two local variables (*inches* and *newSize*.) *MAX_LENGTH* is a class variable because it has the static keyword in its declaration. *MAX_LENGTH* goes into scope on line 2 where it is declared. It stays in scope until the program ends. *length* goes into scope on line 3 where it is declared. It stays in scope as long as this Mouse object exists. *inches* goes into scope where it is declared on line 4. It goes out of scope at the end of the method on line 9. *newSize* goes into scope where it is declared on line 6. Since it is defined inside the if statement block, it goes out of scope when that block ends on line 8.

Got all that? Let's review the rules on scope:

- Local variables—in scope from declaration to end of block
- Instance variables—in scope from declaration until object garbage collected
- Class variables—in scope from declaration until program ends

Ordering Elements in a Class

Now that you've seen the most common parts of a class, let's take a look at the correct order to type them into a file. Comments can go anywhere in the code. Beyond that, you need to memorize the rules in Table 1.4.

TABLE 1.4   Elements of a class

Element	Example	Required?	Where does it go?
Package declaration	package abc;	No	First line in the file
Import statements	import java.util.*;	No	Immediately after the package
Class declaration	public class C	Yes	Immediately after the import
Field declarations	int value;	No	Anywhere inside a class
Method declarations	void method()	No	Anywhere inside a class

Let's look at a few examples to help you remember this. The first example contains one of each element:

```
package structure;   // package must be first non-comment
import java.util.*; // import must come after package
public class Meerkat { // then comes the class
  double weight;        // fields and methods can go in either order
  public double getWeight() {
    return weight; }
  double height;    //  another field - they don't need to be together
 }
```

So far so good. This is a common pattern that you should be familiar with. How about this one?

```
/* header */
package structure;
// class Meerkat
public class Meerkat { }
```

Still good. We can put comments anywhere, and imports are optional. In the next example, we have a problem:

```
import java.util.*;
package structure;   // DOES NOT COMPILE
String name;  // DOES NOT COMPILE
public class Meerkat { }
```

There are two problems here. One is that the `package` and `import` statements are reversed. Though both are optional, `package` must come before `import` if present. The other issue is that a field attempts declaration outside a class. This is not allowed. Fields and methods must be within a class.

Got all that? Think of the acronym PIC (picture): package, import, and class. Fields and methods are easier to remember because they merely have to be inside of a class.

You need to know one more thing about class structure for the OCA exam: multiple classes can be defined in the same file, but only one of them is allowed to be public. The public class matches the name of the file. For example, these two classes must be in a file named `Meerkat.java`:

```
1: public class Meerkat { }
2: class Paw { }
```

A file is also allowed to have neither class be public. As long as there isn't more than one public class in a file, it is okay. On the OCP exam, you'll also need to understand inner classes, which are classes within a class.

Destroying Objects

Now that we've played with our objects, it is time to put them away. Luckily, Java automatically takes care of that for you. Java provides a garbage collector to automatically look for objects that aren't needed anymore.

All Java objects are stored in your program memory's *heap*. The heap, which is also referred to as the free store, represents a large pool of unused memory allocated to your Java application. The heap may be quite large, depending on your environment, but there is always a limit to its size. If your program keeps instantiating objects and leaving them on the heap, eventually it will run out of memory.

In the following sections, we'll look at garbage collection and the `finalize()` method.

Garbage Collection

Garbage collection refers to the process of automatically freeing memory on the heap by deleting objects that are no longer reachable in your program. There are many different algorithms for garbage collection, but you don't need to know any of them for the exam. You *do* need to know that `System.gc()` is not guaranteed to run, and you should be able to recognize when objects become eligible for garbage collection.

Let's start with the first one. Java provides a method called `System.gc()`. Now you might think from the name that this tells Java to run garbage collection. Nope! It meekly *suggests* that now might be a good time for Java to kick off a garbage collection run. Java is free to ignore the request.

The more interesting part of garbage collection is when the memory belonging to an object can be reclaimed. Java waits patiently until the code no longer needs that memory. An object will remain on the heap until it is no longer reachable. An object is no longer reachable when one of two situations occurs:

- The object no longer has any references pointing to it.
- All references to the object have gone out of scope.

Objects vs. References

Do not confuse a reference with the object that it refers to; they are two different entities. The reference is a variable that has a name and can be used to access the contents of an object. A reference can be assigned to another reference, passed to a method, or returned from a method. All references are the same size, no matter what their type is.

An object sits on the heap and does not have a name. Therefore, you have no way to access an object except through a reference. Objects come in all different shapes and sizes and consume varying amounts of memory. An object cannot be assigned to another object, nor can an object be passed to a method or returned from a method. It is the object that gets garbage collected, not its reference.

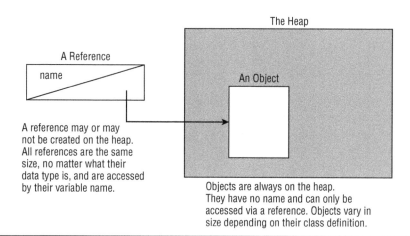

The Heap

A Reference

name

An Object

A reference may or may not be created on the heap. All references are the same size, no matter what their data type is, and are accessed by their variable name.

Objects are always on the heap. They have no name and can only be accessed via a reference. Objects vary in size depending on their class definition.

Realizing the difference between a reference and an object goes a long way toward understanding garbage collection, the new operator, and many other facets of the Java language. Look at this code and see if you can figure out when each object first becomes eligible for garbage collection:

```
1: public class Scope {
2:   public static void main(String[] args) {
3:     String one, two;
4:     one = new String("a");
5:     two = new String("b");
6:     one = two;
7:     String three = one;
8:     one = null;
9:   } }
```

When you get asked a question about garbage collection on the exam, we recommend you draw what's going on. There's a lot to keep track of in your head and it's easy to make a silly mistake trying to keep it all in your memory. Let's try it together now. Really. Get a pencil and paper. We'll wait.

Got that paper? Okay, let's get started. On line 3, we write *one* and *two*. Just the words. No need for boxes or arrows yet since no objects have gone on the heap yet. On line 4, we have our first object. Draw a box with the string "a" in it and draw an arrow from the word *one* to that box. Line 5 is similar. Draw another box with the string "b" in it this time and an arrow from the word *two*. At this point, your work should look like Figure 1.2.

FIGURE 1.2   Your drawing after line 5

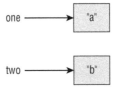

On line 6, the variable *one* changes to point to "b". Either erase or cross out the arrow from *one* and draw a new arrow from *one* to "b". On line 7, we have a new variable, so write the word *three* and draw an arrow from *three* to "b". Notice that *three* points to what *one* is pointing to right now and not what it was pointing to at the beginning. This is why we are drawing pictures. It's easy to forget something like that. At this point, your work should look like Figure 1.3.

FIGURE 1.3   Your drawing after line 7

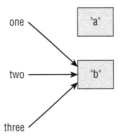

Finally, cross out the line between *one* and "b" since line 8 sets this variable to null. Now, we were trying to find out when the objects were first eligible for garbage collection. On line 6, we got rid of the only arrow pointing to "a", making that object eligible for garbage collection. "b" has arrows pointing to it until it goes out of scope. This means "b" doesn't go out of scope until the end of the method on line 9.

finalize()

Java allows objects to implement a method called `finalize()` that might get called. This method gets called if the garbage collector tries to collect the object. If the garbage collector doesn't run, the method doesn't get called. If the garbage collector fails to collect the object and tries to run it again later, the method doesn't get called a second time.

In practice, this means you are highly unlikely to use it in real projects. Luckily, there isn't much to remember about `finalize()` for the exam. Just keep in mind that it might not get called and that it definitely won't be called twice.

With that said, this call produces no output when we run it:

```
public class Finalizer {
  protected void finalize() {
```

```
    System.out.println("Calling finalize");
  }
  public static void main(String[] args) {
    Finalizer f = new Finalizer();
} }
```

The reason is that the program exits before there is any need to run the garbage collector. While *f* is eligible for garbage collection, Java has better things to do than take out the trash constantly. For the exam, you need to know that this finalize() call could run zero or one time. Now for a more interesting example:

```
public class Finalizer {
  private static List objects = new ArrayList();
  protected void finalize()  {
    objects.add(this);  // Don't do this
} }
```

Remember, finalize() is only run when the object is eligible for garbage collection. The problem here is that by the end of the method, the object is no longer eligible for garbage collection because a static variable is referring to it and static variables stay in scope until the program ends. Java is smart enough to realize this and aborts the attempt to throw out the object. Now suppose later in the program *objects* is set to null. Oh, good, we can finally remove the object from memory. Java remembers already running finalize() on this object and will not do so again. The lesson is that the finalize() call could run zero or one time. This is the exact same lesson as the simple example—that's why it's so easy to remember.

Benefits of Java

Java has some key benefits that you'll need to know for the exam:

Object Oriented   Java is an object-oriented language, which means all code is defined in classes and most of those classes can be instantiated into objects. We'll discuss this more throughout the book. Many languages before Java were procedural, which meant there were routines or methods but no classes. Another common approach is functional programming. Java allows for functional programming within a class, but object oriented is still the main organization of code.

Encapsulation   Java supports access modifiers to protect data from unintended access and modification. Most people consider encapsulation to be an aspect of object-oriented languages. Since the exam objectives call attention to it specifically, so do we.

Platform Independent   Java is an interpreted language because it gets compiled to bytecode. A key benefit is that Java code gets compiled once rather than needing to be recompiled for different operating systems. This is known as "write once, run everywhere." On the OCP exam, you'll learn that it is possible to write code that does not run everywhere. For example, you might refer to a file in a specific directory. If you get asked on the OCA exam, the answer is that the same class files run everywhere.

Robust   One of the major advantages of Java over C++ is that it prevents memory leaks. Java manages memory on its own and does garbage collection automatically. Bad memory management in C++ is a big source of errors in programs.

Simple   Java was intended to be simpler than C++. In addition to eliminating pointers, it got rid of operator overloading. In C++, you could write a + b and have it mean almost anything.

Secure   Java code runs inside the JVM. This creates a sandbox that makes it hard for Java code to do evil things to the computer it is running on.

Summary

In this chapter, you saw that Java classes consist of members called fields and methods. An object is an instance of a Java class. There are three styles of comment: a single-line comment (//), a multiline comment (/* */), and a Javadoc comment (/** */).

Java begins program execution with a main() method. The most common signature for this method run from the command line is public static void main(String[] args). Arguments are passed in after the class name, as in java NameOfClass firstArgument. Arguments are indexed starting with 0.

Java code is organized into folders called packages. To reference classes in other packages, you use an import statement. A wildcard ending an import statement means you want to import all classes in that package. It does not include packages that are inside that one. java.lang is a special package that does not need to be imported.

Constructors create Java objects. A constructor is a method matching the class name and omitting the return type. When an object is instantiated, fields and blocks of code are initialized first. Then the constructor is run.

Primitive types are the basic building blocks of Java types. They are assembled into reference types. Reference types can have methods and be assigned to null. In addition to "normal" numbers, numeric literals are allowed to begin with 0 (octal), 0x (hex), 0X (hex), 0b (binary), or 0B (binary). Numeric literals are also allowed to contain underscores as long as they are directly between two other numbers.

Declaring a variable involves stating the data type and giving the variable a name. Variables that represent fields in a class are automatically initialized to their corresponding "zero" or null value during object instantiation. Local variables must be specifically initialized. Identifiers may contain letters, numbers, $, or _. Identifiers may not begin with numbers.

Scope refers to that portion of code where a variable can be accessed. There are three kinds of variables in Java, depending on their scope: instance variables, class variables, and local variables. Instance variables are the nonstatic fields of your class. Class variables are the static fields within a class. Local variables are declared within a method.

For some class elements, order matters within the file. The package statement comes first if present. Then comes the import statements if present. Then comes the class declaration. Fields and methods are allowed to be in any order within the class.

Garbage collection is responsible for removing objects from memory when they can never be used again. An object becomes eligible for garbage collection when there are no more references to it or its references have all gone out of scope. The finalize() method will run once for each object if/when it is first garbage collected.

Java code is object oriented, meaning all code is defined in classes. Access modifiers allow classes to encapsulate data. Java is platform independent, compiling to bytecode. It is robust and simple by not providing pointers or operator overloading. Finally, Java is secure because it runs inside a virtual machine.

Exam Essentials

Be able to write code using a main() method. A main() method is usually written as public static void main(String[] args). Arguments are referenced starting with args[0]. Accessing an argument that wasn't passed in will cause the code to throw an exception.

Understand the effect of using packages and imports. Packages contain Java classes. Classes can be imported by class name or wildcard. Wildcards do not look at subdirectories. In the event of a conflict, class name imports take precedence.

Be able to recognize a constructor. A constructor has the same name as the class. It looks like a method without a return type.

Be able to identify legal and illegal declarations and initialization. Multiple variables can be declared and initialized in the same statement when they share a type. Local variables require an explicit initialization; others use the default value for that type. Identifiers may contain letters, numbers, $, or _. Identifiers may not begin with numbers. Numeric literals may contain underscores between two digits and begin with 1–9, 0, 0x, 0X, 0b, and 0B.

Be able to determine where variables go into and out of scope. All variables go into scope when they are declared. Local variables go out of scope when the block they are declared in ends. Instance variables go out of scope when the object is garbage collected. Class variables remain in scope as long as the program is running.

Be able to recognize misplaced statements in a class. Package and import statements are optional. If present, both go before the class declaration in that order. Fields and methods are also optional and are allowed in any order within the class declaration.

Know how to identify when an object is eligible for garbage collection. Draw a diagram to keep track of references and objects as you trace the code. When no arrows point to a box (object), it is eligible for garbage collection.

Review Questions

1. Which of the following are valid Java identifiers? (Choose all that apply)

   A. A$B

   B. _helloWorld

   C. true

   D. java.lang

   E. Public

   F. 1980_s

2. What is the output of the following program?

```
1: public class WaterBottle {
2: private String brand;
3: private boolean empty;
4: public static void main(String[] args) {
5:   WaterBottle wb = new WaterBottle();
6:   System.out.print("Empty = " + wb.empty);
7:   System.out.print(", Brand = " + wb.brand);
8: } }
```

   A. Line 6 generates a compiler error.

   B. Line 7 generates a compiler error.

   C. There is no output.

   D. Empty = false, Brand = null

   E. Empty = false, Brand =

   F. Empty = null, Brand = null

3. Which of the following are true? (Choose all that apply)

```
4: short numPets = 5;
5: int numGrains = 5.6;
6: String name = "Scruffy";
7: numPets.length();
8: numGrains.length();
9: name.length();
```

   A. Line 4 generates a compiler error.

   B. Line 5 generates a compiler error.

   C. Line 6 generates a compiler error.

   D. Line 7 generates a compiler error.

   E. Line 8 generates a compiler error.

 F. Line 9 generates a compiler error.

 G. The code compiles as is.

4. Given the following class, which of the following is true? (Choose all that apply)

```
1: public class Snake {
2:
3:  public void shed(boolean time) {
4:
5:    if (time) {
6:
7:    }
8:    System.out.println(result);
9:
10: }
11: }
```

 A. If `String result = "done";` is inserted on line 2, the code will compile.

 B. If `String result = "done";` is inserted on line 4, the code will compile.

 C. If `String result = "done";` is inserted on line 6, the code will compile.

 D. If `String result = "done";` is inserted on line 9, the code will compile.

 E. None of the above changes will make the code compile.

5. Given the following classes, which of the following can independently replace `INSERT IMPORTS HERE` to make the code compile? (Choose all that apply)

```
package aquarium;
public class Tank { }
```

```
package aquarium.jellies;
public class Jelly { }
```

```
package visitor;
INSERT IMPORTS HERE
public class AquariumVisitor {
  public void admire(Jelly jelly) { } }
```

 A. `import aquarium.*;`

 B. `import aquarium.*.Jelly;`

 C. `import aquarium.jellies.Jelly;`

 D. `import aquarium.jellies.*;`

 E. `import aquarium.jellies.Jelly.*;`

 F. None of these can make the code compile.

6. Given the following classes, what is the maximum number of imports that can be removed and have the code still compile?

```
package aquarium; public class Water { }
```

```
package aquarium;
import java.lang.*;
import java.lang.System;
import aquarium.Water;
import aquarium.*;
public class Tank {
  public void print(Water water) {
   System.out.println(water); } }
```

  A. 0

  B. 1

  C. 2

  D. 3

  E. 4

  F. Does not compile.

7. Given the following classes, which of the following snippets can be inserted in place of INSERT IMPORTS HERE and have the code compile? (Choose all that apply)

```
package aquarium;
public class Water {
  boolean salty = false;
}
package aquarium.jellies;
public class Water {
  boolean salty = true;
}
package employee;
 INSERT IMPORTS HERE
public class WaterFiller {
  Water water;
}
```

  A. import aquarium.*;

  B. import aquarium.Water;
     import aquarium.jellies.*;

  C. import aquarium.*;
     import aquarium.jellies.Water;

    D. `import aquarium.*;`
       `import aquarium.jellies.*;`

    E. `import aquarium.Water;`
       `import aquarium.jellies.Water;`

    F. None of these imports can make the code compile.

8. Given the following class, which of the following calls print out Blue Jay? (Choose all that apply)

```
public class BirdDisplay {
   public static void main(String[] name) {
      System.out.println(name[1]);
} }
```

    A. `java BirdDisplay Sparrow Blue Jay`

    B. `java BirdDisplay Sparrow "Blue Jay"`

    C. `java BirdDisplay Blue Jay Sparrow`

    D. `java BirdDisplay "Blue Jay" Sparrow`

    E. `java BirdDisplay.class Sparrow "Blue Jay"`

    F. `java BirdDisplay.class "Blue Jay" Sparrow`

    G. Does not compile.

9. Which of the following legally fill in the blank so you can run the main() method from the command line? (Choose all that apply)

```
public static void main(_____)
```

    A. `String[] _names`

    B. `String[] 123`

    C. `String abc[]`

    D. `String _Names[]`

    E. `String... $n`

    F. `String names`

    G. None of the above.

10. Which of the following are legal entry point methods that can be run from the command line? (Choose all that apply)

    A. `private static void main(String[] args)`

    B. `public static final main(String[] args)`

    C. `public void main(String[] args)`

    D. `public static void test(String[] args)`

    E. `public static void main(String[] args)`

    F. `public static main(String[] args)`

    G. None of the above.

11. Which of the following are true? (Choose all that apply)

   A. An instance variable of type double defaults to null.

   B. An instance variable of type int defaults to null.

   C. An instance variable of type String defaults to null.

   D. An instance variable of type double defaults to 0.0.

   E. An instance variable of type int defaults to 0.0.

   F. An instance variable of type String defaults to 0.0.

   G. None of the above.

12. Which of the following are true? (Choose all that apply)

   A. A local variable of type boolean defaults to null.

   B. A local variable of type float defaults to 0.

   C. A local variable of type Object defaults to null.

   D. A local variable of type boolean defaults to false.

   E. A local variable of type boolean defaults to true.

   F. A local variable of type float defaults to 0.0.

   G. None of the above.

13. Which of the following are true? (Choose all that apply)

   A. An instance variable of type boolean defaults to false.

   B. An instance variable of type boolean defaults to true.

   C. An instance variable of type boolean defaults to null.

   D. An instance variable of type int defaults to 0.

   E. An instance variable of type int defaults to 0.0.

   F. An instance variable of type int defaults to null.

   G. None of the above.

14. Given the following class in the file /my/directory/named/A/Bird.java:

```
INSERT CODE HERE
public class Bird { }
```

Which of the following replaces INSERT CODE HERE if we compile from /my/directory?
(Choose all that apply)

   A. package my.directory.named.a;

   B. package my.directory.named.A;

   C. package named.a;

   D. package named.A;

   E. package a;

   F. package A;

   G. Does not compile.

15. Which of the following lines of code compile? (Choose all that apply)

A. `int i1 = 1_234;`

B. `double d1 = 1_234_.0;`

C. `double d2 = 1_234._0;`

D. `double d3 = 1_234.0_;`

E. `double d4 = 1_234.0;`

F. None of the above.

16. Given the following class, which of the following lines of code can replace INSERT CODE
HERE to make the code compile? (Choose all that apply)

```
public class Price {
    public void admission() {
            INSERT CODE HERE
        System.out.println(amount);
    } }
```

A. `int amount = 9L;`

B. `int amount = 0b101;`

C. `int amount = 0xE;`

D. `double amount = 0xE;`

E. `double amount = 1_2_.0_0;`

F. `int amount = 1_2_;`

G. None of the above.

17. Which of the following are true? (Choose all that apply)

```
public class Bunny {
        public static void main(String[] args) {
            Bunny bun = new Bunny();
} }
```

A. Bunny is a class.

B. bun is a class.

C. main is a class.

D. Bunny is a reference to an object.

E. bun is a reference to an object.

F. main is a reference to an object.

G. None of the above.

18. Which represent the order in which the following statements can be assembled into a program that will compile successfully? (Choose all that apply)

```
A: class Rabbit {}
B: import java.util.*;
C: package animals;
```

A. A, B, C

B. B, C, A

C. C, B, A

D. B, A

E. C, A

F. A, C

G. A, B

19. Suppose we have a class named `Rabbit`. Which of the following statements are true? (Choose all that apply)

```
1:  public class Rabbit {
2:   public static void main(String[] args) {
3:    Rabbit one = new Rabbit();
4:    Rabbit two = new Rabbit();
5:    Rabbit three = one;
6:    one = null;
7:    Rabbit four = one;
8:    three = null;
9:    two = null;
10:    two = new Rabbit();
11:    System.gc();
12: } }
```

A. The Rabbit object from line 3 is first eligible for garbage collection immediately following line 6.

B. The Rabbit object from line 3 is first eligible for garbage collection immediately following line 8.

C. The Rabbit object from line 3 is first eligible for garbage collection immediately following line 12.

D. The Rabbit object from line 4 is first eligible for garbage collection immediately following line 9.

E. The Rabbit object from line 4 is first eligible for garbage collection immediately following line 11.

F. The Rabbit object from line 4 is first eligible for garbage collection immediately following line 12.

20. What is true about the following code? (Choose all that apply)

```
public class Bear {
  protected void finalize() {
    System.out.println("Roar!");
  }
}
```

```
public static void main(String[] args) {
  Bear bear = new Bear();
  bear = null;
  System.gc();
} }
```

A. `finalize()` is guaranteed to be called.

B. `finalize()` might or might not be called

C. `finalize()` is guaranteed not to be called.

D. Garbage collection is guaranteed to run.

E. Garbage collection might or might not run.

F. Garbage collection is guaranteed not to run.

G. The code does not compile.

21. What does the following code output?

```
1: public class Salmon {
2:   int count;
3:   public void Salmon() {
4:     count = 4;
5:   }
6: public static void main(String[] args) {
7:   Salmon s = new Salmon();
8:   System.out.println(s.count);
9: } }
```

A. 0

B. 4

C. Compilation fails on line 3.

D. Compilation fails on line 4.

E. Compilation fails on line 7.

F. Compilation fails on line 8.

22. Which of the following are true statements? (Choose all that apply)

A. Java allows operator overloading.

B. Java code compiled on Windows can run on Linux.

C. Java has pointers to specific locations in memory.

D. Java is a procedural language.

E. Java is an object-oriented language.

F. Java is a functional programming language.

23. Which of the following are true? (Choose all that apply)

    A. javac compiles a `.class` file into a `.java` file.

    B. javac compiles a `.java` file into a `.bytecode` file.

    C. javac compiles a `.java` file into a `.class` file.

    D. Java takes the name of the class as a parameter.

    E. Java takes the name of the `.bytecode` file as a parameter.

    F. Java takes the name of the `.class` file as a parameter.

Chapter

2

Operators and Statements

Like many programming languages, Java is composed primarily of variables, operators, and statements put together in some logical order. In the previous chapter, we discussed variables and gave some examples; in this chapter we'll discuss the various operators and statements available to you within the language. This knowledge will allow you to build complex functions and class structures that you'll see in later chapters.

Understanding Java Operators

A Java *operator* is a special symbol that can be applied to a set of variables, values, or literals—referred to as operands—and that returns a result. Three flavors of operators are available in Java: unary, binary, and ternary. These types of operators can be applied to one, two, or three operands, respectively. For the OCA exam, you'll need know a specific subset of Java operators, how to apply them, and the order in which they should be applied.

Java operators are not necessarily evaluated from left-to-right order. For example, the following Java expression is actually evaluated from right-to-left given the specific operators involved:

```
int y = 4;
double x = 3 + 2 * --y;
```

In this example, you would first decrement y to 3, and then multiply the resulting value by 2, and finally add 3. The value would then be automatically upcast from 9 to 9.0 and assigned to x. The final values of x and y would be 9.0 and 3, respectively. If you didn't follow that evaluation, don't worry. By the end of this chapter, solving problems like this should be second nature.

Unless overridden with parentheses, Java operators follow *order of operation*, listed in Table 2.1, by decreasing order of *operator precedence*. If two operators have the same level of precedence, then Java guarantees left-to-right evaluation. You need to know only those operators in bold for the OCA exam.

TABLE 2.1 Order of operator precedence

Operator	Symbols and examples
Post-unary operators	*expression*++, *expression*--
Pre-unary operators	++*expression*, --*expression*

Operator	Symbols and examples
Other unary operators	~, +, -, !
Multiplication/Division/Modulus	*, /, %
Addition/Subtraction	+, -
Shift operators	<<, >>, >>>
Relational operators	<, >, <=, >=, `instanceof`
Equal to/not equal to	==, !=
Logical operators	&, ^, |
Short-circuit logical operators	&&, ||
Ternary operators	`boolean expression ? expression1 : expression2`
Assignment operators	=, +=, -=, *=, /=, %=, &=, ^=, |=, <<=, >>=, >>>=

We'll spend the first half of this chapter discussing many of the operators in this list as well as how operator precedence determines which operators should be applied first. Note that you won't be tested on some operators, although we recommend that you be aware of their existence.

Working with Binary Arithmetic Operators

We'll begin our discussion with *binary operators*, by far the most common operators in the Java language. They can be used to perform mathematical operations on variables, create logical expressions, as well as perform basic variable assignments. Binary operators are commonly combined in complex expressions with more than two variables; therefore, operator precedence is very important in evaluating expressions.

Arithmetic Operators

Arithmetic operators are often encountered in early mathematics and include addition (+), subtraction (-), multiplication (*), division (/), and modulus (%). They also include the unary operators, ++ and --, although we cover them later in this chapter. As you may have noticed in Table 2.1, the *multiplicative* operators (*, /, %) have a higher order of precedence than the *additive* operators (+, -). That means when you see an expression such as this:

```
int x = 2 * 5 + 3 * 4 - 8;
```

you first evaluate the 2 * 5 and 3 * 4, which reduces the expression to the following:

```
int x = 10 + 12 - 8;
```

Then, you evaluate the remaining terms in left-to-right order, resulting in a value of x of *14*. Make sure you understand why the result is *14* as you'll likely see this kind of operator precedence question on the exam.

Notice that we said "Unless overridden with parentheses…" prior to Table 2.1. That's because you can change the order of operation explicitly by wrapping parentheses around the sections you want evaluated first. Compare the previous example with the following one containing the same values and operators, in the same order, but with two sets of parentheses:

```
int x = 2 * ((5 + 3) * 4 - 8);
```

This time you would evaluate the addition operator 5 + 3, which reduces the expression to the following:

```
int x = 2 * (8 * 4 - 8);
```

You can further reduce this expression by multiplying the first two values within the parentheses:

```
int x = 2 * (32 - 8);
```

Next, you subtract the values within the parentheses before applying terms outside the parentheses:

```
int x = 2 * 24;
```

Finally, you would multiply the result by 2, resulting in a value of 48 for x.

All of the arithmetic operators may be applied to any Java primitives, except `boolean` and `String`. Furthermore, only the addition operators + and += may be applied to `String` values, which results in `String` concatenation.

Although we are sure you have seen most of the arithmetic operators before, the modulus operator, %, may be new to you. The modulus, or remainder operator, is simply the remainder when two numbers are divided. For example, 9 divided by 3 divides evenly and has no remainder; therefore, the remainder, or 9 % 3, is 0. On the other hand, 11 divided by 3 does not divide evenly; therefore, the remainder, or 11 % 3, is 2.

Be sure to understand the difference between arithmetic division and modulus. For integer values, division results in the floor value of the nearest integer that fulfills the operation, whereas modulus is the remainder value. The following examples illustrate this distinction:

```
System.out.print(9 / 3);  // Outputs 3
System.out.print(9 % 3);  // Outputs 0
```

```
System.out.print(10 / 3);   // Outputs 3
System.out.print(10 % 3);   // Outputs 1

System.out.print(11 / 3);   // Outputs 3
System.out.print(11 % 3);   // Outputs 2

System.out.print(12 / 3);   // Outputs 4
System.out.print(12 % 3);   // Outputs 0
```

Note that the division results only increase when the value on the left-hand side goes from 9 to 12, whereas the modulus remainder value increases by 1 each time the left-hand side is increased until it wraps around to zero. For a given divisor y, which is 3 in these examples, the modulus operation results in a value between 0 and (y - 1) for positive dividends. This means that the result of a modulus operation is always 0, 1, or 2.

The modulus operation is not limited to positive integer values in Java and may also be applied to negative integers and floating-point integers. For a given divisor y and negative dividend, the resulting modulus value is between and (-y + 1) and 0. For the OCA exam, though, you are not required to be able to take the modulus of a negative integer or a floating-point number.

Numeric Promotion

Now that you understand the basics of arithmetic operators, it is vital we talk about primitive *numeric promotion*, as Java may do things that seem unusual to you at first. If you recall in Chapter 1, "Java Building Blocks," where we listed the primitive numeric types, each primitive has a bit-length. You don't need to know the exact size of these types for the exam, but you should know which are bigger than others. For example, you should know that a long takes up more space than an int, which in turn takes up more space than a short, and so on.

You should memorize certain rules Java will follow when applying operators to data types:

Numeric Promotion Rules

1. If two values have different data types, Java will automatically promote one of the values to the larger of the two data types.
2. If one of the values is integral and the other is floating-point, Java will automatically promote the integral value to the floating-point value's data type.

3. Smaller data types, namely byte, short, and char, are first promoted to int any time they're used with a Java binary arithmetic operator, even if neither of the operands is int.

4. After all promotion has occurred and the operands have the same data type, the result-ing value will have the same data type as its promoted operands.

The last two rules are the ones most people have trouble with, and the ones likely to trip you up on the exam. For the third rule, note that unary operators are excluded from this rule. For example, applying ++ to a short value results in a short value. We'll discuss unary operators in the next section.

Let's tackle some examples for illustrative purposes:

- What is the data type of x * y?

  ```
  int x = 1;
  long y = 33;
  ```

  If we follow the first rule, since one of the values is long and the other is int, and long is larger than int, then the int value is promoted to a long, and the resulting value is long.

- What is the data type of x + y?

  ```
  double x = 39.21;
  float y = 2.1;
  ```

  This is actually a trick question, as this code will not compile! As you may remember from Chapter 1, floating-point literals are assumed to be double, unless postfixed with an f, as in 2.1f. If the value was set properly to 2.1f, then the promotion would be similar to the last example, with both operands being promoted to a double, and the result would be a double value.

- What is the data type of x / y?

  ```
  short x = 10;
  short y = 3;
  ```

  In this case, we must apply the third rule, namely that x and y will both be promoted to int before the operation, resulting in an output of type int. Pay close attention to the fact that the resulting output is not a short, as we'll come back to this example in the upcoming section on assignment operators.

- What is the data type of x * y / z?

  ```
  short x = 14;
  float y = 13;
  double z = 30;
  ```

  In this case, we must apply all of the rules. First, x will automatically be promoted to int solely because it is a short and it is being used in an arithmetic binary operation.

The promoted x value will then be automatically promoted to a float so that it can be multiplied with y. The result of x * y will then be automatically promoted to a double, so that it can be divided with z, resulting in a double value.

Working with Unary Operators

By definition, a *unary* operator is one that requires exactly one operand, or variable, to function. As shown in Table 2.2, they often perform simple tasks, such as increasing a numeric variable by one, or negating a boolean value.

TABLE 2.2   Java unary operators

Unary operator	Description
+	Indicates a number is positive, although numbers are assumed to be positive in Java unless accompanied by a negative unary operator
-	Indicates a literal number is negative or negates an expression
++	Increments a value by 1
--	Decrements a value by 1
!	Inverts a Boolean's logical value

Logical Complement and Negation Operators

The *logical complement operator,* !, flips the value of a boolean expression. For example, if the value is true, it will be converted to false, and vice versa. To illustrate this, compare the outputs of the following statements:

```
boolean x = false;
System.out.println(x);  // false
x = !x;
System.out.println(x);  // true
```

Likewise, the *negation operator,* -, reverses the sign of a numeric expression, as shown in these statements:

```
double x = 1.21;
```

```
System.out.println(x);  // 1.21
x = -x;
System.out.println(x);  // -1.21
x = -x;
System.out.println(x);  // 1.21
```

Based on the description, it might be obvious that some operators require the variable or expression they're acting upon to be of a specific type. For example, you cannot apply a negation operator, -, to a boolean expression, nor can you apply a logical complement operator, !, to a numeric expression. Be wary of questions on the exam that try to do this, as they'll cause the code to fail to compile. For example, none of the following lines of code will compile:

```
int x = !5;  // DOES NOT COMPILE
boolean y = -true;  // DOES NOT COMPILE
boolean z = !0;  // DOES NOT COMPILE
```

The first statement will not compile due the fact that in Java you cannot perform a logical inversion of a numeric value. The second statement does not compile because you cannot numerically negate a boolean value; you need to use the logical inverse operator. Finally, the last statement does not compile because you cannot take the logical complement of a numeric value, nor can you assign an integer to a boolean variable.

Keep an eye out for questions on the exam that use the logical complement operator or numeric values with boolean expressions or variables. Unlike some other programming languages, in Java 1 and true are not related in any way, just as 0 and false are not related.

Increment and Decrement Operators

Increment and decrement operators, ++ and --, respectively, can be applied to numeric operands and have the higher order or precedence, as compared to binary operators. In other words, they often get applied first to an expression.

Increment and decrement operators require special care because the order they are applied to their associated operand can make a difference in how an expression is processed. If the operator is placed before the operand, referred to as the *pre-increment operator* and the *pre-decrement operator*, then the operator is applied first and the value return is the *new value* of the expression. Alternatively, if the operator is placed after the operand, referred to as the *post-increment operator* and the *post-decrement operator*, then the *original value* of the expression is returned, with operator applied after the value is returned.

The following code snippet illustrates this distinction:

```
int counter = 0;
System.out.println(counter);  // Outputs 0
System.out.println(++counter);  // Outputs 1
System.out.println(counter); // Outputs 1
System.out.println(counter--);  // Outputs 1
System.out.println(counter);  // Outputs 0
```

The first pre-increment operator updates the value for counter and outputs the new value of 1. The next post-decrement operator also updates the value of counter but outputs the value before the decrement occurs.

One common practice in a certification exam, albeit less common in the real world, is to apply multiple increment or decrement operators to a single variable on the same line:

```
int x = 3;
int y = ++x * 5 / x-- + --x;
System.out.println("x is " + x);
System.out.println("y is " + y);
```

This one is more complicated than the previous example because x is modified three times on the same line. Each time it is modified, as the expression moves from left to right, the value of x changes, with different values being assigned to the variable. As you'll recall from our discussion on operator precedence, order of operation plays an important part in evaluating this example.

So how do you read this code? First, the x is incremented and returned to the expression, which is multiplied by 5. We can simplify this:

```
int y = 4 * 5 / x-- + --x;  // x assigned value of 4
```

Next, x is decremented, but the original value of 4 is used in the expression, leading to this:

```
int y = 4 * 5 / 4 + --x;  // x assigned value of 3
```

The final assignment of x reduces the value to 2, and since this is a pre-increment operator, that value is returned to the expression:

```
int y = 4 * 5 / 4 + 2;  // x assigned value of 2
```

Finally, we evaluate the multiple and division from left-to-right, and finish with the addition. The result is then printed:

```
x is 2
y is 7
```

Using Additional Binary Operators

We'll now expand our discussion of binary operators to include all other binary operators that you'll need to know for the exam. This includes operators that perform assignments, those that compare arithmetic values and return `boolean` results, and those that compare `boolean` and object values and return `boolean` results.

Assignment Operators

An *assignment operator* is a binary operator that modifies, or assigns, the variable on the left-hand side of the operator, with the result of the value on the right-hand side of the equation. The simplest assignment operator is the = assignment, which you have seen already:

```
int x = 1;
```

This statement assigns x the value of 1.

Java will automatically promote from smaller to larger data types, as we saw in the previous section on arithmetic operators, but it will throw a compiler exception if it detects you are trying to convert from larger to smaller data types.

Let's return to some examples similar to what you saw in Chapter 1 in order to show how casting can resolve these issues:

```
int x = 1.0;  // DOES NOT COMPILE
short y = 1921222;  // DOES NOT COMPILE
int z = 9f;  // DOES NOT COMPILE
long t = 192301398193810323;  // DOES NOT COMPILE
```

The first statement does not compile because you are trying to assign a double 1.0 to an integer value. Even though the value is a mathematic integer, by adding .0, you're instructing the compiler to treat it as a double. The second statement does not compile because the literal value 1921222 is outside the range of short and the compiler detects this. The third statement does not compile because of the f added to the end of the number that instructs the compiler to treat the number as floating-point value. Finally, the last statement does not compile because Java interprets the literal as an int and notices that the value is larger than int allows. The literal would need a postfix L to be considered a long.

Casting Primitive Values

We can fix the examples in the previous section by casting the results to a smaller data type. Casting primitives is required any time you are going from a larger numerical data type to a smaller numerical data type, or converting from a floating-point number to an integral value.

```
int x = (int)1.0;
short y = (short)1921222;  // Stored as 20678
```

```
int z = (int)9f;
long t = 192301398193810323L;
```

Overflow and Underflow

The expressions in the previous example now compile, although there's a cost. The second value, 1,921,222, is too large to be stored as a short, so numeric overflow occurs and it becomes 20,678. *Overflow* is when a number is so large that it will no longer fit within the data type, so the system "wraps around" to the next lowest value and counts up from there. There's also an analogous *underflow*, when the number is too low to fit in the data type.

This is beyond the scope of the exam, but something to be careful of in your own code. For example, the following statement outputs a negative number:

```
System.out.print(2147483647+1);   // -2147483648
```

Since 2147483647 is the maximum int value, adding any strictly positive value to it will cause it to wrap to the next negative number.

Let's return to one of our earlier examples for a moment:

```
short x = 10;
short y = 3;
short z = x * y;  // DOES NOT COMPILE
```

Based on everything you have learned up until now, can you understand why the last line of this statement will not compile? If you remember, short values are automatically promoted to int when applying any arithmetic operator, with the resulting value being of type int. Trying to set a short variable to an int results in a compiler error, as Java thinks you are trying to implicitly convert from a larger data type to a smaller one.

There are times that you may want to override the default behavior of the compiler. For example, in the preceding example, we know the result of 10 * 3 is 30, which can easily fit into a short variable. If you need the result to be a short, though, you can override this behavior by casting the result of the multiplication:

```
short x = 10;
short y = 3;
short z = (short)(x * y);
```

By performing this explicit cast of a larger value into a smaller data type, you are instructing the compiler to ignore its default behavior. In other words, you are telling the compiler that you have taken additional steps to prevent overflow or underflow. It is also possible that in your particular application and scenario, overflow or underflow would result in acceptable values.

Compound Assignment Operators

Besides the simple assignment operator, =, there are also numerous *compound assignment operators*. Only two of the compound operators listed in Table 2.1 are required for the exam, += and -=. Complex operators are really just glorified forms of the simple assignment operator, with a built-in arithmetic or logical operation that applies the left- and right-hand sides of the statement and stores the resulting value in a variable in the left-hand side of the statement. For example, the following two statements after the declaration of x and z are equivalent:

```
int x = 2, z = 3;
x = x * z;  // Simple assignment operator
x *= z;  // Compound assignment operator
```

The left-hand side of the compound operator can only be applied to a variable that is already defined and cannot be used to declare a new variable. In the previous example, if x was not already defined, then the expression x *= z would not compile.

Compound operators are useful for more than just shorthand—they can also save us from having to explicitly cast a value. For example, consider the following example, in which the last line will not compile due to the result being promoted to a long and assigned to an int variable:

```
long x = 10;
int y = 5;
y = y * x;  // DOES NOT COMPILE
```

Based on the last two sections, you should be able to spot the problem in the last line. This last line could be fixed with an explicit cast to (int), but there's a better way using the compound assignment operator:

```
long x = 10;
int y = 5;
y *= x;
```

The compound operator will first cast y to a long, apply the multiplication of two long values, and then cast the result to an int. Unlike the previous example, in which the compiler threw an exception, in this example we see that the compiler will automatically cast the resulting value to the data type of the value on the left-hand side of the compound operator.

One final thing to know about the assignment operator is that the result of the assignment is an expression in and of itself, equal to the value of the assignment. For example, the following snippet of code is perfectly valid, if not a little odd looking:

```
long x = 5;
long y = (x=3);
System.out.println(x); // Outputs 3
System.out.println(y); // Also, outputs 3
```

The key here is that (x=3) does two things. First, it sets the value of the variable x to be 3. Second, it returns a value of the assignment, which is also 3. The exam creators are fond of inserting the assignment operator = in the middle of an expression and using the value of the assignment as part of a more complex expression.

Relational Operators

We now move on to *relational operators*, which compare two expressions and return a boolean value. The first four relational operators (see Table 2.3) are applied to numeric primitive data types only. If the two numeric operands are not of the same data type, the smaller one is promoted in the manner as previously discussed.

TABLE 2.3   Relational operators

<	Strictly less than
<=	Less than or equal to
>	Strictly greater than
>=	Greater than or equal to

Let's look at examples of these operators in action:

```
int x = 10, y = 20, z = 10;
System.out.println(x < y);   // Outputs true
System.out.println(x <= y);  // Outputs true
System.out.println(x >= z);  // Outputs true
System.out.println(x > z);   // Outputs false
```

Notice that the last example outputs false, because although x and z are the same value, x is not strictly greater than z.

The fifth relational operator (Table 2.4) is applied to object references and classes or interfaces.

TABLE 2.4   Relational instanceof operator

a instanceof b	True if the reference that a points to is an instance of a class, subclass, or class that implements a particular interface, as named in b

The instanceof operator, while useful for determining whether an arbitrary object is a member of a particular class or interface, is out of scope for the OCA exam.

Logical Operators

If you have studied computer science, you may have already come across logical operators before. If not, no need to panic—we'll be covering them in detail in this section.

The *logical operators*, (&), (|), and (^), may be applied to both numeric and boolean data types. When they're applied to boolean data types, they're referred to as *logical operators*. Alternatively, when they're applied to numeric data types, they're referred to as *bitwise operators*, as they perform bitwise comparisons of the bits that compose the number. For the exam, though, you don't need to know anything about numeric bitwise comparisons, so we'll leave that educational aspect to other books.

You should familiarize with the truth tables in Figure 2.1, where x and y are assumed to be boolean data types.

FIGURE 2.1   The logical truth tables for &, |, and ^

x & y (AND)	y = true	y = false
x = true	true	false
x = false	false	false

x | y (INCLUSIVE OR)	y = true	y = false
x = true	true	true
x = false	true	false

x ^ y (EXCLUSIVE OR)	y = true	y = false
x = true	false	true
x = false	true	false

Here are some tips to help remember this table:

- AND is only true if both operands are true.
- Inclusive OR is only false if both operands are false.
- Exclusive OR is only true if the operands are different.

Finally, we present the conditional operators, && and ||, which are often referred to as short-circuit operators. The *short-circuit operators* are nearly identical to the logical operators, & and |, respectively, except that the right-hand side of the expression may never be evaluated if the final result can be determined by the left-hand side of the expression. For example, consider the following statement:

```
boolean x = true || (y < 4);
```

Referring to the truth tables, the value x can only be false if both sides of the expression are false. Since we know the left-hand side is true, there's no need to evaluate the right-hand side, since no value of y will ever make the value of x anything other than true. It may help you to illustrate this concept by executing the previous line of code for various values of y.

A more common example of where short-circuit operators are used is checking for `null` objects before performing an operation, such as this:

```
if(x != null && x.getValue() < 5) {
  // Do something
}
```

In this example, if x was *null*, then the short-circuit prevents a `NullPointerException` from ever being thrown, since the evaluation of `x.getValue() < 5` is never reached. Alternatively, if we used a logical &, then both sides would always be evaluated and when x was `null` this would throw an exception:

```
if(x != null & x.getValue() < 5) { // Throws an exception if x is null
  // Do something
}
```

Be wary of short-circuit behavior on the exam, as questions are known to alter a variable on the right-hand side of the expression that may never be reached. For example, what is the output of the following code?

```
int x = 6;
boolean y = (x >= 6) || (++x <= 7);
System.out.println(x);
```

Because `x >= 6` is true, the increment operator on the right-hand side of the expression is never evaluated, so the output is 6.

Equality Operators

Determining equality in Java can be a nontrivial endeavor as there's a semantic difference between "two objects are the same" and "two objects are equivalent." It is further complicated by the fact that for numeric and `boolean` primitives, there is no such distinction.

Let's start with the basics, the *equals* operator == and *not equals* operator !=. Like the relational operators, they compare two operands and return a `boolean` value about whether the expressions or values are equal, or not equal, respectively.

The equality operators are used in one of three scenarios:

1. Comparing two numeric primitive types. If the numeric values are of different data types, the values are automatically promoted as previously described. For example, `5 == 5.00` returns true since the left side is promoted to a double.

2. Comparing two boolean values.

3. Comparing two objects, including `null` and `String` values.

The comparisons for equality are limited to these three cases, so you cannot mix and match types. For example, each of the following would result in a compiler error:

```
boolean x = true == 3;   // DOES NOT COMPILE
boolean y = false != "Giraffe";   // DOES NOT COMPILE
boolean z = 3 == "Kangaroo";   // DOES NOT COMPILE
```

Pay close attention to the data types when you see an equality operator on the exam. The exam creators also have a habit of mixing assignment operators and equality operators, as in the following snippet:

```
boolean y = false;
boolean x = (y = true);
System.out.println(x);   // Outputs true
```

At first glance, you might think the output should be false, and if the expression was (y == true), then you would be correct. In this example, though, the expression is assigning the value of true to y, and as you saw in the section on assignment operators, the assignment itself has the value of the assignment. Therefore, the output would be true.

For object comparison, the equality operator is applied to the references to the objects, not the objects they point to. Two references are equal if and only if they point to the same object, or both point to null. Let's take a look at some examples:

```
File x = new File("myFile.txt");
File y = new File("myFile.txt");
File z = x;
System.out.println(x == y);   // Outputs false
System.out.println(x == z);   // Outputs true
```

Even though all of the variables point to the same file information, only two, x and z, are equal in terms of ==. In this example, as well as during the OCA exam, you may be presented with classnames that are unfamiliar, such as File. Many times you can answer questions about these classes without knowing the specific details of these classes. In particular, you should be able to answer questions that indicate x and y are two separate and distinct objects, even if you do not know the data types of these objects.

In Chapter 3, "Core Java APIs," we'll continue the discussion of object equality by introducing what it means for two different objects to be equivalent. We'll also cover String equality and show how this can be a nontrivial topic.

Understanding Java Statements

Java operators allow you to create a lot of complex expressions, but they're limited in the manner in which they can control program flow. For example, imagine you want a section of code to only be executed under certain conditions that cannot be evaluated until runtime. Or suppose you want a particular segment of code to repeat once for every item in some list.

As you may recall from Chapter 1, a Java *statement* is a complete unit of execution in Java, terminated with a semicolon (;). For the remainder of the chapter, we'll be introducing you to various Java control flow statements. *Control flow statements* break up the flow of execution by using decision making, looping, and branching, allowing the application to selectively execute particular segments of code.

These statements can be applied to single expressions as well as a block of Java code. As described in the previous chapter, a *block* of code in Java is a group of zero or more statements between balanced braces, ({}), and can be used anywhere a single statement is allowed.

The *if-then* Statement

Often, we only want to execute a block of code under certain circumstances. The *if-then* statement, as shown in Figure 2.2, accomplishes this by allowing our application to execute a particular block of code if and only if a boolean expression evaluates to true at runtime.

FIGURE 2.2   The structure of an if-then statement

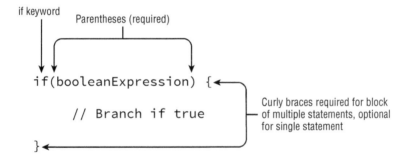

For example, imagine we had a function that used the hour of day, an integer value from 0 to 23, to display a message to the user:

```
if(hourOfDay < 11)
    System.out.println("Good Morning");
```

If the hour of the day is less than 11, then the message will be displayed. Now let's say we also wanted to increment some value, morningGreetingCount, every time the greeting is printed. We could write the if-then statement twice, but luckily Java offers us a more natural approach using a block:

```
if(hourOfDay < 11) {
    System.out.println("Good Morning");
    morningGreetingCount++;
}
```

The block allows multiple statements to be executed based on the if-then evaluation. Notice that the first statement didn't contain a block around the print section, but it easily could have. For readability, it is considered good coding practice to put blocks around the execution component of if-then statements, as well as many other control flow statements, although it is not required.

Watch Indentation and Braces

One area that the exam writers will try to trip you up is on if-then statements without braces ({}). For example, take a look at this slightly modified form of our example:

```
if(hourOfDay < 11)
   System.out.println("Good Morning");
   morningGreetingCount++;
```

Based on the indentation, you might be inclined to think the variable morningGreeting-Count is only going to be incremented if the hourOfDay is less than 11, but that's not what this code does. It will execute the print statement only if the condition is met, but it will always execute the increment operation.

Remember that in Java, unlike some other programming languages, tabs are just whitespace and are not evaluated as part of the execution. When you see a control flow statement in a question, be sure to trace the open and close braces of the block and ignore any indentation you may come across.

The *if-then-else* Statement

Let's expand our example a little. What if we want to display a different message if it is 11 a.m. or later? Could we do it using only the tools we have? Of course we can!

```
if(hourOfDay < 11) {
   System.out.println("Good Morning");
}
if(hourOfDay >= 11) {
   System.out.println("Good Afternoon");
}
```

This seems a bit redundant, though, since we're performing an evaluation on hourOfDay twice. It's also wasteful because in some circumstances the cost of the boolean expression we're evaluating could be computationally expensive. Luckily, Java offers us a more useful approach in the form of an *if-then-else* statement, as shown in Figure 2.3.

FIGURE 2.3   The structure of an if-then-else statement

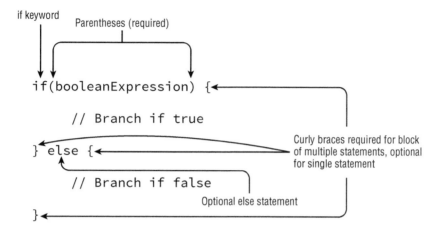

Let's return to this example:

```java
if(hourOfDay < 11) {
    System.out.println("Good Morning");
} else {
    System.out.println("Good Afternoon");
}
```

Now our code is truly branching between one of the two possible options, with the boolean evaluation happening only once. The else operator takes a statement or block of statements, in the same manner as the if statement does. In this manner, we can append additional if-then statements to an else block to arrive at a more refined example:

```java
if(hourOfDay < 11) {
    System.out.println("Good Morning");
} else if(hourOfDay < 15) {
    System.out.println("Good Afternoon");
} else {
    System.out.println("Good Evening");
}
```

In this example, the Java process will continue execution until it encounters an if-then statement that evaluates to true. If neither of the first two expressions are true, it will execute the final code of the else block. One thing to keep in mind in creating complex `if-then-else` statements is that order is important. For example, see what happens if we reorder the previous snippet of code as follows:

```
if(hourOfDay < 15) {
  System.out.println("Good Afternoon");
} else if(hourOfDay < 11) {
  System.out.println("Good Morning");  // UNREACHABLE CODE
} else {
  System.out.println("Good Evening");
}
```

For hours of the day less than 11, this code behaves very differently than the previous set of code. See if you can determine why the second block can never be executed regardless of the value of hourOfDay.

If a value is less than 11, then it must be also less than 15 by definition. Therefore, if the second branch in the example can be reached, the first branch can also be reached. Since execution of each branch is mutually exclusive in this example—that is, only one branch can be executed—if the first branch is executed, then the second cannot be executed. Therefore, there is no way the second branch will ever be executed, and the code is deemed unreachable.

Verifying the *if* Statement Evaluates to a Boolean Expression

Another common place the exam may try to lead you astray is by providing code where the boolean expression inside the `if-then` statement is not actually a boolean expression. For example, take a look at the following lines of code:

```
int x = 1;
if(x) {  // DOES NOT COMPILE
  ...
}
```

This statement may be valid in some other programming and scripting languages, but not in Java, where 0 and 1 are not considered boolean values. Also, be wary of assignment operators being used as if they were equals `==` operators in `if-then` statements:

```
int x = 1;
if(x = 5) {  // DOES NOT COMPILE
  ...
}
```

Ternary Operator

Now that we have discussed if-then-else statements, we can briefly return to our discussion of operators and present the final operator that you need to learn for the exam. The conditional operator, ? :, otherwise known as the *ternary operator*, is the only operator that takes three operands and is of the form:

```
booleanExpression ? expression₁ : expression₂
```

The first operand must be a boolean expression, and the second and third can be any expression that returns a value. The ternary operation is really a condensed form of an if-then-else statement that returns a value. For example, the following two snippets of code are equivalent:

```java
int y = 10;
int x;
if(y > 5) {
  x = 2 * y;
} else {
  x = 3 * y;
}
```

Compare the previous code snippet with the following equivalent ternary operator code snippet:

```java
int y = 10;
int x = (y > 5) ? (2 * y) : (3 * y);
```

Note that it is often helpful for readability to add parentheses around the expressions in ternary operations, although it is certainly not required.

There is no requirement that second and third expressions in ternary operations have the same data types, although it may come into play when combined with the assignment operator. Compare the following two statements:

```java
System.out.println((y > 5) ? 21 : "Zebra");
int animal = (y < 91) ? 9 : "Horse";   // DOES NOT COMPILE
```

Both expressions evaluate similar boolean values and return an int and a String, although only the first line will compile. The System.out.println() does not care that the statements are completely different types, because it can convert both to String. On the other hand, the compiler does know that "Horse" is of the wrong data type and cannot be assigned to an int; therefore, it will not allow the code to be compiled.

Ternary Expression Evaluation

Only one of the right-hand expressions of the ternary operator will be evaluated at runtime. In a manner similar to the short-circuit operators, if one of the two right-hand expressions in a ternary operator performs a side effect, then it may not be applied at runtime. Let's illustrate this principle with the following example:

```
int y = 1;
int z = 1;
final int x = y<10 ? y++ : z++;
System.out.println(y+","+z); // Outputs 2,1
```

Notice that since the left-hand boolean expression was true, only y was incremented. Contrast the preceding example with the following modification:

```
int y = 1;
int z = 1;
final int x = y>=10 ? y++ : z++;
System.out.println(y+","+z); // Outputs 1,2
```

Now that the left-hand boolean expression evaluates to false, only z was incremented. In this manner, we see how the expressions in a ternary operator may not be applied if the particular expression is not used.

For the exam, be wary of any question that includes a ternary expression in which a variable is modified in one of the right-hand side expressions.

The *switch* Statement

We now expand on our discussion of if-then-else statements by discussing a switch statement. A *switch* statement, as shown in Figure 2.4, is a complex decision-making structure in which a single value is evaluated and flow is redirected to the first matching branch, known as a *case* statement. If no such case statement is found that matches the value, an optional *default* statement will be called. If no such default option is available, the entire switch statement will be skipped.

Supported Data Types

As shown in Figure 2.4, a switch statement has a target variable that is not evaluated until runtime. Prior to Java 5.0, this variable could only be int values or those values that could be promoted to int, specifically byte, short, char, or int. When enum was added in Java 5.0, support was added to switch statements to support enum values. In Java 7, switch statements were further updated to allow matching on String values. Finally, the switch statement also supports any of the primitive numeric wrapper classes, such as Byte, Short, Character, or Integer.

FIGURE 2.4   The structure of a switch statement

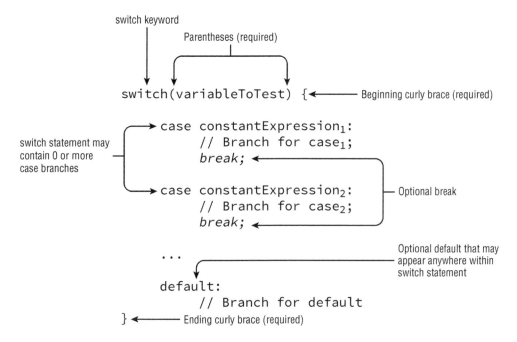

Data types supported by switch statements include the following:

- byte and Byte
- short and Short
- char and Character
- int and Integer
- String
- enum values

For the exam, we recommend you memorize this list. Note that boolean and long, and their associated wrapper classes, are not supported by switch statements.

Compile-time Constant Values

The values in each case statement must be compile-time constant values of the same data type as the switch value. This means you can use only literals, enum constants, or final constant variables of the same data type. By final constant, we mean that the variable must be marked with the final modifier and initialized with a literal value in the same expression in which it is declared.

Let's look at a simple example using the day of the week, with 0 for Sunday, 1 for Monday, and so on:

```
int dayOfWeek = 5;
switch(dayOfWeek) {
  default:
    System.out.println("Weekday");
    break;
  case 0:
    System.out.println("Sunday");
    break;
  case 6:
    System.out.println("Saturday");
    break;
}
```

With a value of dayOfWeek of 5, this code will output:

```
Weekday
```

The first thing you may notice is that there is a break statement at the end of each case and default section. We'll discuss break statements in detail when we discuss loops, but for now all you need to know is that they terminate the switch statement and return flow control to the enclosing statement. As we'll soon see, if you leave out the break statement, flow will continue to the next proceeding case or default block automatically.

Another thing you might notice is that the default block is not at the end of the switch statement. There is no requirement that the case or default statements be in a particular order, unless you are going to have pathways that reach multiple sections of the switch block in a single execution.

To illustrate both of the preceding points, consider the following variation:

```
int dayOfWeek = 5;
switch(dayOfWeek) {
  case 0:
    System.out.println("Sunday");
  default:
    System.out.println("Weekday");
  case 6:
    System.out.println("Saturday");
    break;
}
```

This code looks a lot like the previous example except two of the break statements have been removed and the order has been changed. This means that for the given value of day-OfWeek, 5, the code will jump to the default block and then execute all of the proceeding case statements in order until it finds a break statement or finishes the structure:

```
Weekday
Saturday
```

The order of the case and default statements is now important since placing the default statement at the end of the switch statement would cause only one word to be output.

What if the value of dayOfWeek was 6 in this example? Would the default block still be executed? The output of this example with dayOfWeek set to 6 would be:

```
Saturday
```

Even though the default block was before the case block, only the case block was executed. If you recall the definition of the default block, it is only branched to if there is no matching case value for the switch statement, regardless of its position within the switch statement.

Finally, if the value of dayOfWeek was 0, all three statements would be output:

```
Sunday
```

```
Weekday
Saturday
```

Notice that in this last example, the default is executed since there was no break statement at the end of the preceding case block. While the code will not branch to the default statement if there is a matching case value within the switch statement, it will execute the default statement if it encounters it after a case statement for which there is no terminating break statement.

The exam creators are fond of switch *examples that are missing* break *statements!* When evaluating switch statements on the exam, always consider that multiple branches may be visited in a single execution.

We conclude our discussion on switch statements by acknowledging that the data type for case statements must all match the data type of the switch variable. As already discussed, the case statement value must also be a literal, enum constant, or final constant variable. For example, given the following switch statement, notice which case statements will compile and which will not:

```java
private int getSortOrder(String firstName, final String lastName) {
  String middleName = "Patricia";
  final String suffix = "JR";
  int id = 0;
  switch(firstName) {
    case "Test":
      return 52;
```

```
      case middleName:  // DOES NOT COMPILE
        id = 5;
        break;
      case suffix:
        id = 0;
        break;
      case lastName:  // DOES NOT COMPILE
        id = 8;
        break;
      case 5:  // DOES NOT COMPILE
        id = 7;
        break;
      case 'J':  // DOES NOT COMPILE
        id = 10;
        break;
      case java.time.DayOfWeek.SUNDAY:  // DOES NOT COMPILE
        id=15;
        break;
    }
    return id;
}
```

The first case statement compiles without issue using a String literal and is a good example of how a return statement, like a break statement, can be used to exit the switch statement early. The second case statement does not compile because middleName is not a final variable, despite having a known value at this particular line of execution. The third case statement compiles without issue because suffix is a final constant variable.

In the fourth case statement, despite lastName being final, it is not constant as it is passed to the function; therefore, this line does not compile as well. Finally, the last three case statements don't compile because none of them have a matching type of String; the last one is an enum value.

The *while* Statement

A repetition control structure, which we refer to as a *loop*, executes a statement of code multiple times in succession. By using nonconstant variables, each repetition of the statement may be different. For example, a statement that iterates over a list of unique names and outputs them would encounter a new name on every execution of the loop.

The simplest such repetition control structure in Java is the *while* statement, described in Figure 2.5. Like all repetition control structures, it has a termination condition, implemented as a boolean expression, that will continue as long as the expression evaluates to true.

FIGURE 2.5 The structure of a while statement

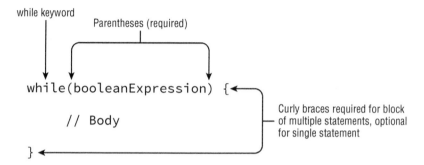

As shown in Figure 2.5, a while loop is similar to an if-then statement in that it is composed of a boolean expression and a statement, or block of statements. During execution, the boolean expression is evaluated before each iteration of the loop and exits if the evaluation returns false. It is important to note that a while loop may terminate after its first evaluation of the boolean expression. In this manner, the statement block may never be executed.

Let's return to our mouse example from Chapter 1 and show a loop can be used to model a mouse eating a meal:

```java
int roomInBelly = 5;

public void eatCheese(int bitesOfCheese) {
  while (bitesOfCheese > 0 && roomInBelly > 0) {
    bitesOfCheese--;
    roomInBelly--;
  }
  System.out.println(bitesOfCheese+" pieces of cheese left");
}
```

This method takes an amount of food, in this case cheese, and continues until the mouse has no room in its belly or there is no food left to eat. With each iteration of the loop, the mouse "eats" one bite of food and loses one spot in its belly. By using a compound boolean statement, you ensure that the while loop can end for either of the conditions.

 **Real World Scenario**

Infinite Loops

Consider the following segment of code:

```
int x = 2;
int y = 5;
while(x < 10)
   y++;
```

You may notice one glaring problem with this statement: it will never end! The boolean expression that is evaluated prior to each loop iteration is never modified, so the expression (x < 10) will always evaluate to true. The result is that the loop will never end, creating what is commonly referred to as an *infinite loop*.

Infinite loops are something you should be aware of any time you create a loop in your application. You should be absolutely certain that the loop will eventually terminate under some condition. First, make sure the loop variable is modified. Then, ensure that the termination condition will be eventually reached in all circumstances. As you'll see in the upcoming section "Understanding Advanced Flow Control," a loop may also exit under other conditions such as a break statement.

The *do-while* Statement

Java also allows for the creation of a *do-while* loop, which like a while loop, is a repetition control structure with a termination condition and statement, or block of statements, as shown in Figure 2.6. Unlike a while loop, though, a do-while loop guarantees that the statement or block will be executed at least once.

FIGURE 2.6   The structure of a do-while statement

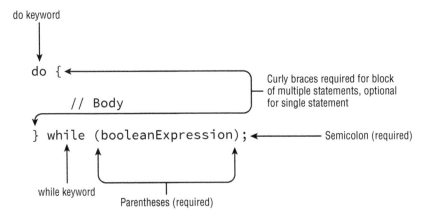

The primary difference between the syntactic structure of a do-while loop and a while loop is that a do-while loop purposely orders the statement or block of statements before the conditional expression, in order to reinforce that the statement will be executed before the expression is ever evaluated. For example, take a look at the output of the following statements:

```
int x = 0;
do {
  x++;
} while(false);
System.out.println(x);   // Outputs 1
```

Java will execute the statement block first, and then check the loop condition. Even though the loop exits right away, the statement block was still executed once and the program outputs a 1.

When to Use *while* vs. *do-while* Loops

In practice, it might be difficult to determine when you should use a while loop and when you should use a do-while loop. The short answer is that it does not actually matter. Any while loop can be converted to a do-while loop, and vice versa. For example, compare this while loop:

```
while(x > 10) {
  x--;
}
```

and this do-while loop:

```
if(x > 10) {
  do {
    x--;
  } while(x > 10);
}
```

Though one of the loops is certainly easier to read, they are functionally equivalent. Java recommends you use a while loop when a loop might not be executed at all and a do-while loop when the loop is executed at least once. But determining whether you should use a while loop or a do-while loop in practice is sometimes about personal preference and code readability.

For example, although the first statement is shorter, the second has the advantage that you could leverage the existing if-then statement and perform some other operation in a new else branch, as shown in the following example:

continues

continued

```
if(x > 10) {
  do {
    x--;
  } while(x > 10);
} else {
  x++;
}
```

The *for* Statement

Now that you can build applications with simple while and do-while statements, we expand our discussion of loops to a more complex repetition control structure called a for loop.

Starting in Java 5.0, there are now two types of for statements. The first is referred to as the basic for loop, and the second is often called the enhanced for loop. For clarity, we'll refer to the enhanced for loop as the for-each statement throughout the book.

The Basic *for* Statement

A basic *for loop* has the same conditional boolean expression and statement, or block of statements, as the other loops you have seen, as well as two new sections: an *initialization block* and an *update* statement. Figure 2.7 shows how these components are laid out.

FIGURE 2.7   The structure of a basic for statement

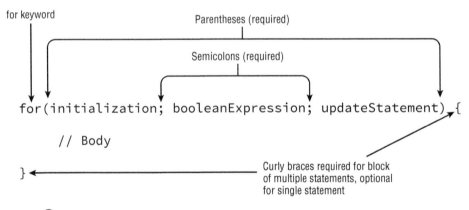

for keyword

Parentheses (required)

Semicolons (required)

```
for(initialization; booleanExpression; updateStatement) {

      // Body

}
```

Curly braces required for block of multiple statements, optional for single statement

① Initialization statement executes
② If booleanExpression is true continue, else exit loop
③ Body executes
④ Execute updateStatements
⑤ Return to Step 2

Although Figure 2.7 might seem a little confusing and almost arbitrary at first, the organization of the components and flow allow us to create extremely powerful statements in a very small amount of space that otherwise would take multiple lines with a standard while loop. Note that each section is separated by a semicolon. The initialization and update sections may contain multiple statements, separated by commas.

Variables declared in the initialization block of a for loop have limited scope and are only accessible within the for loop. Be wary of any exam questions in which a variable declared within the initialization block of a for loop is available outside the loop. Alternatively, variables declared before the for loop and assigned a value in the initialization block may be used outside the for loop because their scope precedes the for loop creation.

Let's take a look at an example that prints the numbers 0 to 9:

```java
for(int i = 0; i < 10; i++) {
   System.out.print(i + " ");
}
```

The local variable i is initialized first to 0. The variable i is only in scope for the duration of the loop and is not available outside the loop once the loop has completed. Like a while loop, the boolean condition is evaluated on every iteration of the loop *before* the loop executes. Since it returns true, the loop executes and outputs the 0 followed by a space. Next, the loop executes the update section, which in this case increases the value of i to 1. The loop then evaluates the boolean expression a second time, and the process repeats multiple times, printing:

```
0 1 2 3 4 5 6 7 8 9
```

On the 10th iteration of the loop, the value of i reaches 9 and is incremented by 1 to reach 10. On the 11th iteration of the loop, the boolean expression is evaluated and since (10 < 10) returns false, the loop terminates without executing the statement loop body.

Although most for loops you are likely to encounter in practice will be well defined and similar to the previous example, there are a number of variations and edge cases you could see on the exam. You should familiarize yourself with the following five examples: variations of these are likely to be seen on the exam.

Let's tackle some examples for illustrative purposes:

1. Creating an Infinite Loop

```java
for( ; ; ) {
   System.out.println("Hello World");
}
```

Although this for loop may look like it will throw a compiler error, it will in fact compile and run without issue. It is actually an infinite loop that will print the same statement repeatedly. This example reinforces the fact that the components of the for loop are each optional. Note that the semicolons separating the three sections are required, as for(;) and for( ) will not compile.

2. Adding Multiple Terms to the **for** Statement

```
int x = 0;
for(long y = 0, z = 4; x < 5 && y < 10; x++, y++) {
  System.out.print(y + " ");
}
```

This code demonstrates three variations of the for loop you may not have seen. First, you can declare a variable, such as x in this example, before the loop begins and use it after it completes. Second, your initialization block, boolean expression, and update statements can include extra variables that may not reference each other. For example, z is defined in the initialization block and is never used. Finally, the update statement can modify multiple variables. This code will print the following when executed:

```
0 1 2 3 4
```

Keep this example in mind when we look at the next three examples, none of which compile.

3. Redeclaring a Variable in the Initialization Block

```
int x = 0;
for(long y = 0, x = 4; x < 5 && y < 10; x++, y++) {    // DOES NOT COMPILE
  System.out.print(x + " ");
}
```

This example looks similar to the previous one, but it does not compile because of the initialization block. The difference is that x is repeated in the initialization block after already being declared before the loop, resulting in the compiler stopping because of a duplicate variable declaration. We can fix this loop by changing the declaration of x and y as follows:

```
int x = 0;
long y = 10;
for(y = 0, x = 4; x < 5 && y < 10; x++, y++) {
  System.out.print(x + " ");
}
```

Note that this variation will now compile because the initialization block simply assigns a value to x and does not declare it.

4. Using Incompatible Data Types in the Initialization Block

```
for(long y = 0, int x = 4; x < 5 && y<10; x++, y++) {    // DOES NOT COMPILE
  System.out.print(x + " ");
}
```

This example also looks a lot like our second example, but like the third example will not compile, although this time for a different reason. The variables in the initialization block must all be of the same type. In the multiple terms example, y and z were both long, so the code compiled without issue, but in this example they have differing types, so the code will not compile.

5. Using Loop Variables Outside the Loop

```
for(long y = 0, x = 4; x < 5 && y < 10; x++, y++) {
  System.out.print(y + " ");
}
System.out.print(x);   // DOES NOT COMPILE
```

The final variation on the second example will not compile for a different reason than the previous examples. If you notice, x is defined in the initialization block of the loop, and then used after the loop terminates. Since x was only scoped for the loop, using it outside the loop will throw a compiler error.

The *for-each* Statement

Starting with Java 5.0, Java developers have had a new type of enhanced for loop at their disposal, one specifically designed for iterating over arrays and Collection objects. This enhanced for loop, which for clarity we'll refer to as a *for-each* loop, is shown in Figure 2.8.

FIGURE 2.8   The structure of an enhanced for-each statement

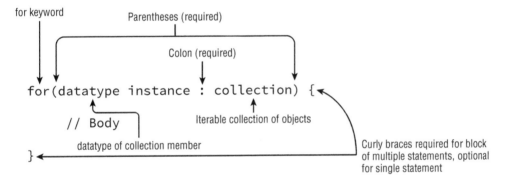

The for-each loop declaration is composed of an initialization section and an object to be iterated over. The right-hand side of the for-each loop statement must be a built-in Java array or an object whose class implements java.lang.Iterable, which includes most of the Java Collections framework. The left-hand side of the for-each loop must include a declaration for an instance of a variable, whose type matches the type of a member of the array or collection in the right-hand side of the statement. On each iteration of the loop, the named variable on the left-hand side of the statement is assigned a new value from the array or collection on the right-hand side of the statement.

For the OCA exam, the only members of the Collections framework that you need to be aware of are List and ArrayList. In this chapter, we'll show how to iterate over List objects, and in Chapter 3 we'll go into detail about how to create List objects and how they differ from traditional Java arrays.

Let's review some examples:

- What will this code output?

```java
final String[] names = new String[3];
names[0] = "Lisa";
names[1] = "Kevin";
names[2] = "Roger";
for(String name : names) {
  System.out.print(name + ", ");
}
```

This code will compile and print:

```java
Lisa, Kevin, Roger,
```

- What will this code output?

```java
java.util.List<String> values = new java.util.ArrayList<String>();
values.add("Lisa");
values.add("Kevin");
values.add("Roger");
for(String value : values) {
  System.out.print(value + ", ");
}
```

This code will compile and print the same values:

```java
Lisa, Kevin, Roger,
```

When you see a for-each loop on the exam, make sure the right-hand side is an array or Iterable object and the left-hand side has a matching type. For example, the two examples that follow will not compile.

- Why will the following fail to compile?

```java
String names = "Lisa";
for(String name : names) {    // DOES NOT COMPILE
  System.out.print(name + " ");
}
```

In this example, the String names is not an array, nor does it implement java.lang.Iterable, so the compiler will throw an exception since it does not know how to iterate over the String.

- Why will the following fail to compile?

```java
String[] names = new String[3];
for(int name : names) {  // DOES NOT COMPILE
  System.out.print(name + " ");
}
```

This code will fail to compile because the left-hand side of the for-each statement does not define an instance of String. Notice that in this last example, the array is initialized with three null pointer values. In and of itself, that will not cause the code to not compile, as a corrected loop would just output null three times.

 Real World Scenario

Comparing *for* and *for-each* Loops

Since for and for-each both use the same keyword, you might be wondering how they are related. While this discussion is out of scope for the exam, let's take a moment to explore how for-each loops are converted to for loops by the compiler.

When for-each was introduced in Java 5, it was added as a compile-time enhancement. This means that Java actually converts the for-each loop into a standard for loop during compilation. For example, assuming names is an array of String[] as we saw in the first example, the following two loops are equivalent:

```
for(String name : names) {
   System.out.print(name + ", ");
}
for(int i=0; i < names.length; i++) {
   String name = names[i];
   System.out.print(name + ", ");
}
```

For objects that inherit java.lang.Iterable, there is a different, but similar, conversion. For example, assuming values is an instance of List<Integer>, as we saw in the second example, the following two loops are equivalent:

```
for(int value : values) {
   System.out.print(value + ", ");
}
for(java.util.Iterator<Integer> i = values.iterator(); i.hasNext(); ) {
   int value = i.next();
   System.out.print(value + ", ");
}
```

Notice that in the second version, there is no update statement as it is not required when using the java.util.Iterator class.

You may have noticed that in the previous for-each examples, there was an extra comma printed at the end of the list:

```
Lisa, Kevin, Roger,
```

While the `for-each` statement is convenient for working with lists in many cases, it does hide access to the loop iterator variable. If we wanted to print only the comma between names, we could convert the example into a standard `for` loop, as in the following example:

```java
java.util.List<String> names = new java.util.ArrayList<String>();
names.add("Lisa");
names.add("Kevin");
names.add("Roger");
for(int i=0; i<names.size(); i++) {
  String name = names.get(i);
  if(i>0) {
    System.out.print(", ");
  }
  System.out.print(name);
}
```

This sample code would output the following:

```
Lisa, Kevin, Roger
```

It is also common to use a standard `for` loop over a `for-each` loop if comparing multiple elements in a loop within a single iteration, as in the following example. Notice that we skip the first loop's execution, since `value[-1]` is not defined and would throw an `IndexOutOfBoundsException` error.

```java
int[] values = new int[3];
values[0] = 10;
values[1] = new Integer(5);
values[2] = 15;
for(int i=1; i<values.length; i++) {
  System.out.print((values[i]-values[i-1]) + ",");
}
```

This sample code would output the following:

```
-5, 10,
```

Despite these examples, enhanced `for-each` loops are quite useful in Java in a variety of circumstances. As a developer, though, you can always revert to a standard `for` loop if you need fine-grain control.

Understanding Advanced Flow Control

Up to now, we have been dealing with single loops that only ended when their `boolean` expression evaluated to `false`. We'll now show you other ways loops could end, or branch, and you'll see that the path taken during runtime may not be as straightforward as in previous examples.

Nested Loops

First off, loops can contain other loops. For example, consider the following code that iterates over a two-dimensional array, an array that contains other arrays as its members. We'll cover multidimensional arrays in detail in Chapter 3, but for now assume the following is how you would declare a two-dimensional array.

```
int[][] myComplexArray = {{5,2,1,3},{3,9,8,9},{5,7,12,7}};
for(int[] mySimpleArray : myComplexArray) {
  for(int i=0; i<mySimpleArray.length; i++) {
    System.out.print(mySimpleArray[i]+"\t");
  }
  System.out.println();
}
```

Notice that we intentionally mix a `for` and `for-each` loop in this example. The outer loops will execute a total of three times. Each time the outer loop executes, the inner loop is executed four times. When we execute this code, we see the following output:

```
5       2       1       3
3       9       8       9
5       7       12      7
```

Nested loops can include `while` and `do-while`, as shown in this example. See if you can determine what this code will output.

```
int x = 20;
while(x>0) {
  do {
    x -= 2
  } while (x>5);
  x--;
  System.out.print(x+"\t");
}
```

The first time this loop executes, the inner loop repeats until the value of x is 4. The value will then be decremented to 3 and that will be the output at the end of the first iteration of the outer loop. On the second iteration of the outer loop, the inner `do-while` will be executed once, even though x is already not greater than 5. As you may recall, `do-while` statements always execute the body at least once. This will reduce the value to 1, which will be further lowered by the decrement operator in the outer loop to 0. Once the value reaches 0, the outer loop will terminate. The result is that the code will output the following:

```
3       0
```

Adding Optional Labels

One thing we skipped when we presented `if-then` statements, `switch` statements, and loops is that they can all have optional labels. A *label* is an optional pointer to the head of a statement that allows the application flow to jump to it or break from it. It is a single word that is proceeded by a colon (:). For example, we can add optional labels to one of the previous examples:

```
int[][] myComplexArray = {{5,2,1,3},{3,9,8,9},{5,7,12,7}};
OUTER_LOOP:  for(int[] mySimpleArray : myComplexArray) {
  INNER_LOOP:  for(int i=0; i<mySimpleArray.length; i++) {
    System.out.print(mySimpleArray[i]+"\t");
  }
  System.out.println();
}
```

When dealing with only one loop, they add no value, but as we'll see in the next section, they are extremely useful in nested environments. Optional labels are often only used in loop structures. While this topic is not on the OCA exam, it is possible to add optional labels to control and block structures. That said, it is rarely considered good coding practice to do so.

For formatting, labels follow the same rules for identifiers. For readability, they are commonly expressed in uppercase, with underscores between words, to distinguish them from regular variables.

The *break* Statement

As you saw when working with switch statements, a *break* statement transfers the flow of control out to the enclosing statement. The same holds true for break statements that appear inside of while, do-while, and for loops, as it will end the loop early, as shown in Figure 2.9

FIGURE 2.9   The structure of a break statement

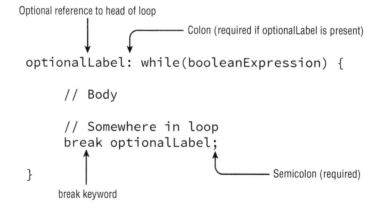

Notice in Figure 2.9 that the break statement can take an optional label parameter. Without a label parameter, the break statement will terminate the nearest inner loop it is currently in the process of executing. The optional label parameter allows us to break out of a higher level outer loop. In the following example, we search for the first (x,y) array index position of a number within an unsorted two-dimensional array:

```java
public class SearchSample {
  public static void main(String[] args) {
    int[][] list = {{1,13,5},{1,2,5},{2,7,2}};
    int searchValue = 2;
    int positionX = -1;
    int positionY = -1;
    PARENT_LOOP: for(int i=0; i<list.length; i++) {
      for(int j=0; j<list[i].length; j++) {
        if(list[i][j]==searchValue) {
          positionX = i;
          positionY = j;
          break PARENT_LOOP;
        }
      }
    }
    if(positionX==-1 || positionY==-1) {
      System.out.println("Value "+searchValue+" not found");
    } else {
      System.out.println("Value "+searchValue+" found at: " +
        "("+positionX+","+positionY+")");
    }
  }
}
```

When executed, this code will output:

```
Value 2 found at: (1,1)
```

In particular, take a look at the statement break PARENT_LOOP. This statement will break out of the entire loop structure as soon as the first matching value is found. Now, imagine what would happen if we replaced the body of the inner loop with the following:

```java
if(list[i][j]==searchValue) {
  positionX = i;
  positionY = j;
  break;
}
```

How would this change our flow and would the output change? Instead of exiting when the first matching value is found, the program will now only exit the inner loop when the condition is met. In other words, the structure will now find the first matching value of the last inner loop to contain the value, resulting in the following output:

```
Value 2 found at: (2,0)
```

Finally, what if we removed the break altogether?

```
if(list[i][j]==searchValue) {
  positionX = i;
  positionY = j;
}
```

In this case, the code will search for the last value in the entire structure that has the matching value. The output will look like this:

```
Value 2 found at: (2,2)
```

You can see from this example that using a label on a break statement in a nested loop, or not using the break statement at all, can cause the loop structure to behave quite differently.

The *continue* Statement

Let's now complete our discussion of advanced loop control with the *continue* statement, a statement that causes flow to finish the execution of the current loop, as shown in Figure 2.10.

FIGURE 2.10   The structure of a continue statement

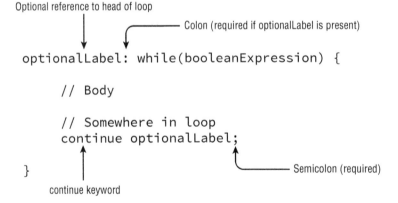

You may notice the syntax of the continue statement mirrors that of the break statement. In fact, the statements are similar in how they are used, but with different results. While the break statement transfers control to the enclosing statement, the continue statement transfers control to the boolean expression that determines if the loop should continue. In other words, it ends the current iteration of the loop. Also like the break statement, the continue statement is applied to the nearest inner loop under execution using optional label statements to override this behavior. Let's take a look at the following example:

```
public class SwitchSample {
  public static void main(String[] args) {
    FIRST_CHAR_LOOP: for (int a = 1; a <= 4; a++) {
      for (char x = 'a'; x <= 'c'; x++) {
        if (a == 2 || x == 'b')
          continue FIRST_CHAR_LOOP;
        System.out.print(" " + a + x);
      }
    }
  }
}
```

With the structure as defined, the loop will return control to the parent loop any time the first value is 2 or the second value is b. This results in one execution of the inner loop for each of three outer loop calls. The output looks like this:

```
1a 3a 4a
```

Now, imagine we removed the FIRST_CHAR_LOOP label in the continue statement so that control is returned to the inner loop instead of the outer. See if you can understand how the output will be changed to:

```
1a 1c 3a 3c 4a 4c
```

Finally, if we remove the continue statement and associated if-then statement altogether, we arrive at a structure that outputs all the values, such as:

```
1a 1b 1c 2a 2b 2c 3a 3b 3c 4a 4b 4c
```

Table 2.5 will help remind you when labels, break, and continue statements are permitted in Java. Although for illustrative purposes our examples have included using these statements in nested loops, they can be used inside single loops as well.

TABLE 2.5   Advanced flow control usage

	Allows optional labels	Allows unlabeled break	Allows *continue* statement
if	Yes *	No	No
while	Yes	Yes	Yes
do while	Yes	Yes	Yes
for	Yes	Yes	Yes
switch	Yes	Yes	No

* Labels are allowed for any block statement, including those that are preceded with an if-then statement.

Summary

This chapter covered a wide variety of topics, including dozens of Java operators, along with numerous control flow statements. Many of these operators and statements may have been new to you.

It is important that you understand how to use all of the required Java operators covered in this chapter and know how operator precedence influences the way a particular expression is interpreted. There will likely be numerous questions on the exam that appear to test one thing, such as StringBuilder or exception handling, when in fact the answer is related to the misuse of a particular operator that causes the application to fail to compile. When you see an operator on the exam, always check that the appropriate data types are used and that they match each other where applicable.

For statements, this chapter covered two types of control structures: decision-making controls structures, including if-then, if-then-else, and switch statements, as well as repetition control structures including for, for-each, while, and do-while. Remember that most of these structures require the evaluation of a particular boolean expression either for branching decisions or once per repetition. The switch statement is the only one that supports a variety of data types, including String variables as of Java 7.

With a for-each statement you don't need to explicitly write a boolean expression, since the compiler builds them implicitly. For clarity, we referred to an enhanced for loop as a for-each loop, but syntactically they are written as a for statement.

We concluded this chapter by discussing advanced control options and how flow can be enhanced through nested loops, break statements, and continue statements. Be wary of questions on the exam that use nested statements, especially ones with labels, and verify they are being used correctly.

This chapter is especially important because at least one component of this chapter will likely appear in every exam question with sample code. Many of the questions on the exam focus on proper syntactic use of the structures, as they will be a large source of questions that end in "Does not compile." You should be able to answer all of the review questions correctly or fully understand those that you answered incorrectly before moving on to later chapters.

Exam Essentials

Be able to write code that uses Java operators.   This chapter covered a wide variety of operator symbols. Go back and review them several times so that you are familiar with them throughout the rest of the book.

Be able to recognize which operators are associated with which data types.   Some operators may be applied only to numeric primitives, some only to boolean values, and some only to objects. It is important that you notice when an operator and operand(s) are mismatched, as this issue is likely to come up in a couple of exam questions.

Understand Java operator precedence.   Most Java operators you'll work with are binary, but the number of expressions is often greater than two. Therefore, you must understand the order in which Java will evaluate each operator symbol.

Be able to write code that uses parentheses to override operator precedence.   You can use parentheses in your code to manually change the order of precedence.

Understand `if` and `switch` decision control statements.   The `if-then` and `switch` statements come up frequently throughout the exam in questions unrelated to decision control, so make sure you fully understand these basic building blocks of Java.

Understand loop statements.   Know the syntactical structure of all loops, including `while`, `do-while`, and `for`. Each loop has its own special properties and structures. Also, be familiar with the enhanced `for-each` loops that iterate over lists.

Understand how `break` and `continue` can change flow control.   Know how to change the flow control within a statement by applying a `break` or `continue` command. Also know which control statements can accept `break` statements and which can accept `continue` statements. Finally, understand how these statements work inside embedded loops or `switch` statements.

Review Questions

1. Which of the following Java operators can be used with `boolean` variables? (Choose all that apply)

   A. `==`

   B. `+`

   C. `--`

   D. `!`

   E. `%`

   F. `<=`

2. What data type (or types) will allow the following code snippet to compile? (Choose all that apply)

   ```
   byte x = 5;
   byte y = 10;
   _____ z = x + y;
   ```

   A. `int`

   B. `long`

   C. `boolean`

   D. `double`

   E. `short`

   F. `byte`

3. What is the output of the following application?

   ```
   1: public class CompareValues {
   2:   public static void main(String[] args) {
   3:     int x = 0;
   4:     while(x++ < 10) {}
   5:     String message = x > 10 ? "Greater than" : false;
   6:     System.out.println(message+","+x);
   7:   }
   8: }
   ```

   A. `Greater than,10`

   B. `false,10`

   C. `Greater than,11`

   D. `false,11`

   E. The code will not compile because of line 4.

   F. The code will not compile because of line 5.

4. What change would allow the following code snippet to compile? (Choose all that apply)

```
3: long x = 10;
4: int y = 2 * x;
```

A. No change; it compiles as is.

B. Cast x on line 4 to int.

C. Change the data type of x on line 3 to short.

D. Cast 2 * x on line 4 to int.

E. Change the data type of y on line 4 to short.

F. Change the data type of y on line 4 to long.

5. What is the output of the following code snippet?

```
3: java.util.List<Integer> list = new java.util.ArrayList<Integer>();
4: list.add(10);
5: list.add(14);
6: for(int x : list) {
7:   System.out.print(x + ", ");
8:   break;
9: }
```

A. 10, 14,

B. 10, 14

C. 10,

D. The code will not compile because of line 7.

E. The code will not compile because of line 8.

F. The code contains an infinite loop and does not terminate.

6. What is the output of the following code snippet?

```
3: int x = 4;
4: long y = x * 4 - x++;
5: if(y<10) System.out.println("Too Low");
6: else System.out.println("Just right");
7: else System.out.println("Too High");
```

A. Too Low

B. Just Right

C. Too High

D. Compiles but throws a NullPointerException.

E. The code will not compile because of line 6.

F. The code will not compile because of line 7.

7. What is the output of the following code?

```
1: public class TernaryTester {
2:    public static void main(String[] args) {
3:       int x = 5;
4:       System.out.println(x > 2 ? x < 4 ? 10 : 8 : 7);
5: }}
```

A. 5

B. 4

C. 10

D. 8

E. 7

F. The code will not compile because of line 4.

8. What is the output of the following code snippet?

```
3: boolean x = true, z = true;
4: int y = 20;
5: x = (y != 10) ^ (z=false);
6: System.out.println(x+", "+y+", "+z);
```

A. true, 10, true

B. true, 20, false

C. false, 20, true

D. false, 20, false

E. None of the above

F. The code will not compile because of line 5.

9. How many times will the following code print "Hello World"?

```
3: for(int i=0; i<10 ; ) {
4:    i = i++;
5:    System.out.println("Hello World");
6: }
```

A. 9

B. 10

C. 11

D. The code will not compile because of line 3.

E. The code will not compile because of line 5.

F. The code contains an infinite loop and does not terminate.

10. What is the output of the following code?

```
3: byte a = 40, b = 50;
4: byte sum = (byte) a + b;
5: System.out.println(sum);
```

A. 40

B. 50

C. 90

D. The code will not compile because of line 4.

E. An undefined value.

11. What is the output of the following code?

```
1: public class ArithmeticSample {
2:   public static void main(String[] args) {
3:     int x = 5 * 4 % 3;
4:     System.out.println(x);
5: }}
```

A. 2

B. 3

C. 5

D. 6

E. The code will not compile because of line 3.

12. What is the output of the following code snippet?

```
3: int x = 0;
4: String s = null;
5: if(x == s) System.out.println("Success");
6: else System.out.println("Failure");
```

A. Success

B. Failure

C. The code will not compile because of line 4.

D. The code will not compile because of line 5.

13. What is the output of the following code snippet?

```
3: int x1 = 50, x2 = 75;
4: boolean b = x1 >= x2;
5: if(b = true) System.out.println("Success");
6: else System.out.println("Failure");
```

A. Success

B. Failure

C. The code will not compile because of line 4.

D. The code will not compile because of line 5.

14. What is the output of the following code snippet?

```
3: int c = 7;
4: int result = 4;
```

```
5: result += ++c;
6: System.out.println(result);
```

A. 8

B. 11

C. 12

D. 15

E. 16

F. The code will not compile because of line 5.

15. What is the output of the following code snippet?

```
3: int x = 1, y = 15;
4: while x < 10
5:    y--;
6:    x++;
7: System.out.println(x+", "+y);
```

A. 10, 5

B. 10, 6

C. 11, 5

D. The code will not compile because of line 3.

E. The code will not compile because of line 4.

F. The code contains an infinite loop and does not terminate.

16. What is the output of the following code snippet?

```
3: do {
4:    int y = 1;
5:    System.out.print(y++ + " ");
6: } while(y <= 10);
```

A. 1 2 3 4 5 6 7 8 9

B. 1 2 3 4 5 6 7 8 9 10

C. 1 2 3 4 5 6 7 8 9 10 11

D. The code will not compile because of line 6.

E. The code contains an infinite loop and does not terminate.

17. What is the output of the following code snippet?

```
3: boolean keepGoing = true;
4: int result = 15, i = 10;
5: do {
6:    i--;
7:    if(i==8) keepGoing = false;
8:    result -= 2;
9: } while(keepGoing);
```

```
10: System.out.println(result);
```
A. 7

B. 9

C. 10

D. 11

E. 15

F. The code will not compile because of line 8.

18. What is the output of the following code snippet?
```
3: int count = 0;
4: ROW_LOOP: for(int row = 1; row <=3; row++)
5:   for(int col = 1; col <=2 ; col++) {
6:     if(row * col % 2 == 0) continue ROW_LOOP;
7:     count++;
8:   }
9: System.out.println(count);
```
A. 1

B. 2

C. 3

D. 4

E. 6

F. The code will not compile because of line 6.

19. What is the result of the following code snippet?
```
3: int m = 9, n = 1, x = 0;
4: while(m > n) {
5:   m--;
6:   n += 2;
7:   x += m + n;
8: }
9: System.out.println(x);
```
A. 11

B. 13

C. 23

D. 36

E. 50

F. The code will not compile because of line 7.

20. What is the result of the following code snippet?
```
3: final char a = 'A', d = 'D';
4: char grade = 'B';
```

```
5: switch(grade) {
6:   case a:
7:   case 'B': System.out.print("great");
8:   case 'C': System.out.print("good"); break;
9:   case d:
10:  case 'F': System.out.print("not good");
11: }
```

A. great

B. greatgood

C. The code will not compile because of line 3.

D. The code will not compile because of line 6.

E. The code will not compile because of lines 6 and 9.

Chapter

3

Core Java APIs

OCA EXAM OBJECTIVES COVERED IN THIS CHAPTER:

✓ **Using Operators and Decision Constructs**

- Test equality between Strings and other objects using == and equals()

✓ **Creating and Using Arrays**

- Declare, instantiate, initialize and use a one-dimensional array

- Declare, instantiate, initialize and use a multi-dimensional array

✓ **Working with Selected classes from the Java API**

- Creating and manipulating Strings

- Manipulate data using the StringBuilder class and its methods

- Declare and use an ArrayList of a given type

- Create and manipulate calendar data using classes from java.time.LocalDateTime, java.time.LocalDate, java.time.Local-Time, java.time.format.DateTimeFormatter, java.time.Period

✓ **Working with Java Data Types**

- Develop code that uses wrapper classes such as Boolean, Double, and Integer.

The OCA exam expects you to know the core data structures and classes used in Java, and in this chapter readers will learn about the most common methods available. For example, `String` and `StringBuilder` are used for text data. An array and an `ArrayList` are used when you have multiple values. A variety of classes are used for working with dates. In this chapter, you'll also learn how to determine whether two objects are equal.

API stands for application programming interface. In Java, an interface is something special. In the context of an API, it can be a group of class or interface definitions that gives you access to a service or functionality. You will learn about the most common APIs for each of the classes covered in this chapter.

Creating and Manipulating Strings

The `String` class is such a fundamental class that you'd be hard-pressed to write code without it. After all, you can't even write a `main()` method without using the `String` class. A *string* is basically a sequence of characters; here's an example:

```
String name = "Fluffy";
```

As you learned in Chapter 1, "Java Building Blocks," this is an example of a reference type. You also learned that reference types are created using the `new` keyword. Wait a minute. Something is missing from the previous example: it doesn't have new in it! In Java, these two snippets both create a `String`:

```
String name = "Fluffy";
String name = new String("Fluffy");
```

Both give you a reference variable of type *name* pointing to the `String` object `"Fluffy"`. They are subtly different, as you'll see in the section "String Pool," later in this chapter. For now, just remember that the `String` class is special and doesn't need to be instantiated with new.

In this section, we'll look at concatenation, immutability, the string pool, common methods, and method chaining.

Concatenation

In Chapter 2, "Operators and Statements," you learned how to add numbers. 1 + 2 is clearly 3. But what is `"1"` + `"2"`? It's actually `"12"` because Java combines the two `String` objects.

Placing one String before the other String and combining them together is called string *concatenation*. The OCA exam creators like string concatenation because the + operator can be used in two ways within the same line of code. There aren't a lot of rules to know for this, but you have to know them well:

1. If both operands are numeric, + means numeric addition.

2. If either operand is a String, + means concatenation.

3. The expression is evaluated left to right.

Now let's look at some examples:

```
System.out.println(1 + 2);          // 3
System.out.println("a" + "b");      // ab
System.out.println("a" + "b" + 3);  // ab3
System.out.println(1 + 2 + "c");    // 3c
```

The first example uses the first rule. Both operands are numbers, so we use normal addition. The second example is simple string concatenation, described in the second rule. The quotes for the String are only used in code—they don't get output.

The third example combines both the second and third rules. Since we start on the left, Java figures out what "a" + "b" evaluates to. You already know that one: it's "ab". Then Java looks at the remaining expression of "ab" + 3. The second rule tells us to concatenate since one of the operands is a String.

In the fourth example, we start with the third rule, which tells us to consider 1 + 2. Both operands are numeric, so the first rule tells us the answer is 3. Then we have 3 + "c", which uses the second rule to give us "3c". Notice all three rules get used in one line? The exam takes this a step further and will try to trick you with something like this:

```
int three = 3;
String four = "4";
System.out.println(1 + 2 + three + four);
```

When you see this, just take it slow and remember the three rules—and be sure to check the variable types. In this example, we start with the third rule, which tells us to consider 1 + 2. The first rule gives us 3. Next we have 3 + three. Since three is of type int, we still use the first rule, giving us 6. Next we have 6 + four. Since four is of type String, we switch to the second rule and get a final answer of "64". When you see questions like this, just take your time and check the types. Being methodical pays off.

There is only one more thing to know about concatenation, but it is an easy one. In this example, you just have to remember what += does. s += "2" means the same thing as s = s + "2".

```
4: String s = "1";         // s currently holds "1"
5: s += "2";               // s currently holds "12"
6: s += 3;                 // s currently holds "123"
7: System.out.println(s);  // 123
```

On line 5, we are "adding" two strings, which means we concatenate them. Line 6 tries to trick you by adding a number, but it's just like we wrote s = s + 3. We know that a string "plus" anything else means to use concatenation.

To review the rules one more time: use numeric addition if two numbers are involved, use concatenation otherwise, and evaluate from left to right. Have you memorized these three rules yet? Be sure to do so before the exam!

Immutability

Once a `String` object is created, it is not allowed to change. It cannot be made larger or smaller, and you cannot change one of the characters inside it.

You can think of a string as a storage box you have perfectly full and whose sides can't bulge. There's no way to add objects, nor can you replace objects without disturbing the entire arrangement. The trade-off for the optimal packing is zero flexibility.

Mutable is another word for changeable. *Immutable* is the opposite—an object that can't be changed once it's created. On the OCA exam, you need to know that `String` is immutable.

More on Immutability

You won't be asked to identify whether custom classes are immutable on the exam, but it's helpful to see an example. Consider the following code:

```
class Mutable {
  private String s;
  public void setS(String newS){ s = newS; }  // Setter makes it mutable
  public String getS() { return s; }
}
final class Immutable {
  private String s = "name";
  public String getS() { return s; }
}
```

Immutable only has a getter. There's no way to change the value of s once it's set. Mutable has a setter as well. This allows the reference s to change to point to a different String later. Note that even though the String class is immutable, it can still be used in a mutable class. You can even make the instance variable final so the compiler reminds you if you accidentally change s.

Also, immutable classes in Java are final, and subclasses can't add mutable behavior.

You learned that + is used to do String concatenation in Java. There's another way, which isn't used much on real projects but is great for tricking people on the exam. What does this print out?

```
String s1 = "1";
String s2 = s1.concat("2");
s2.concat("3");
System.out.println(s2);
```

Did you say "12"? Good. The trick is to see if you forget that the String class is immutable by throwing a method at you.

The String Pool

Since strings are everywhere in Java, they use up a lot of memory. In some production applications, they can use up 25–40 percent of the memory in the entire program. Java realizes that many strings repeat in the program and solves this issue by reusing common ones. The *string pool*, also known as the intern pool, is a location in the Java virtual machine (JVM) that collects all these strings.

The string pool contains literal values that appear in your program. For example, "name" is a literal and therefore goes into the string pool. myObject.toString() is a string but not a literal, so it does not go into the string pool. Strings not in the string pool are garbage collected just like any other object.

Remember back when we said these two lines are subtly different?

```
String name = "Fluffy";
String name = new String("Fluffy");
```

The former says to use the string pool normally. The second says "No, JVM. I really don't want you to use the string pool. Please create a new object for me even though it is less efficient." When you write programs, you wouldn't want to do this. For the exam, you need to know that it is allowed.

Important String Methods

The String class has dozens of methods. Luckily, you need to know only a handful for the exam. The exam creators pick most of the methods developers use in the real world.

For all these methods, you need to remember that a string is a sequence of characters and Java counts from 0 when indexed. Figure 3.1 shows how each character in the string "animals" is indexed.

FIGURE 3.1   Indexing for a string

a	n	i	m	a	l	s
0	1	2	3	4	5	6

Let's look at thirteen methods from the String class. Many of them are straightforward so we won't discuss them at length. You need to know how to use these methods.

length()

The method length() returns the number of characters in the String. The method signature is as follows:

```
int length()
```

The following code shows how to use length():

```
String string = "animals";
System.out.println(string.length());  // 7
```

Wait. It outputs 7? Didn't we just tell you that Java counts from 0? The difference is that zero counting happens only when you're using indexes or positions within a list. When determining the total size or length, Java uses normal counting again.

charAt()

The method charAt() lets you query the string to find out what character is at a specific index. The method signature is as follows:

```
char charAt(int index)
```

The following code shows how to use charAt():

```
String string = "animals";
System.out.println(string.charAt(0));  // a
System.out.println(string.charAt(6));  // s
System.out.println(string.charAt(7));  // throws exception
```

Since indexes start counting with 0, charAt(0) returns the "first" character in the sequence. Similarly, charAt(6) returns the "seventh" character in the sequence. charAt(7) is a problem. It asks for the "eighth" character in the sequence, but there are only seven characters present. When something goes wrong that Java doesn't know how to deal with, it throws an exception, as shown here. You'll learn more about exceptions in Chapter 6, "Exceptions."

```
java.lang.StringIndexOutOfBoundsException: String index out of range: 7
```

indexOf()

The method indexOf() looks at the characters in the string and finds the first index that matches the desired value. indexOf can work with an individual character or a whole String as input. It can also start from a requested position. The method signatures are as follows:

```
int indexOf(int ch)
int indexOf(int ch, int fromIndex)
int indexOf(String str)
int indexOf(String str, int fromIndex)
```

The following code shows how to use indexOf():

```
String string = "animals";
System.out.println(string.indexOf('a'));        // 0
System.out.println(string.indexOf("al"));       // 4
System.out.println(string.indexOf('a', 4));     // 4
System.out.println(string.indexOf("al", 5));    // -1
```

Since indexes begin with 0, the first 'a' matches at that position. The second statement looks for a more specific string and so matches later on. The third statement says Java shouldn't even look at the characters until it gets to index 4. The final statement doesn't find anything because it starts looking after the match occurred. Unlike charAt(), the indexOf() method doesn't throw an exception if it can't find a match. indexOf() returns –1 when no match is found. Because indexes start with 0, the caller knows that –1 couldn't be a valid index. This makes it a common value for a method to signify to the caller that no match is found.

substring()

The method substring() also looks for characters in a string. It returns parts of the string. The first parameter is the index to start with for the returned string. As usual, this is a zero-based index. There is an optional second parameter, which is the end index you want to stop at.

Notice we said "stop at" rather than "include." This means the endIndex parameter is allowed to be 1 past the end of the sequence if you want to stop at the end of the sequence. That would be redundant, though, since you could omit the second parameter entirely in that case. In your own code, you want to avoid this redundancy. Don't be surprised if the exam uses it though. The method signatures are as follows:

```
String substring(int beginIndex)
String substring(int beginIndex, int endIndex)
```

The following code shows how to use substring():

```
String string = "animals";
System.out.println(string.substring(3));  // mals
System.out.println(string.substring(string.indexOf('m'))); // mals
System.out.println(string.substring(3, 4)); // m
System.out.println(string.substring(3, 7)); // mals
```

The substring() method is the trickiest String method on the exam. The first example says to take the characters starting with index 3 through the end, which gives us "mals". The second example does the same thing: it calls indexOf() to get the index rather than hard-coding it. This is a common practice when coding because you may not know the index in advance.

The third example says to take the characters starting with index 3 until, but not including, the character at index 4—which is a complicated way of saying we want a String with one character: the one at index 3. This results in "m". The final example says to take the characters starting with index 3 until we get to index 7. Since index 7 is the same as the end of the string, it is equivalent to the first example.

We hope that wasn't too confusing. The next examples are less obvious:

```
System.out.println(string.substring(3, 3)); // empty string
System.out.println(string.substring(3, 2));  // throws exception
System.out.println(string.substring(3, 8)); // throws exception
```

The first example in this set prints an empty string. The request is for the characters starting with index 3 until you get to index 3. Since we start and end with the same index, there are *no* characters in between. The second example in this set throws an exception because the indexes can't be backward. Java knows perfectly well that it will never get to index 2 if it starts with index 3. The third example says to continue until the eighth character. There is no eighth position, so Java throws an exception. Granted, there is no seventh character either, but at least there is the "end of string" invisible position.

Let's review this one more time since substring() is so tricky. The method returns the string starting from the requested index. If an end index is requested, it stops right before that index. Otherwise, it goes to the end of the string.

toLowerCase() and *toUpperCase()*

Whew. After that mental exercise, it is nice to have methods that do exactly what they sound like! These methods make it easy to convert your data. The method signatures are as follows:

```
String toLowerCase()
String toUpperCase()
```

The following code shows how to use these methods:

```
String string = "animals";
System.out.println(string.toUpperCase()); // ANIMALS
System.out.println("Abc123".toLowerCase()); // abc123
```

These methods do what they say. toUpperCase() converts any lowercase characters to uppercase in the returned string. toLowerCase() converts any uppercase characters to lowercase in the returned string. These methods leave alone any characters other than letters. Also, remember that strings are immutable, so the original string stays the same.

equals() and *equalsIgnoreCase()*

The equals() method checks whether two String objects contain exactly the same characters in the same order. The equalsIgnoreCase() method checks whether two String objects contain the same characters with the exception that it will convert the characters' case if needed. The method signatures are as follows:

```
boolean equals(Object obj)
boolean equalsIgnoreCase(String str)
```

The following code shows how to use these methods:

```
System.out.println("abc".equals("ABC"));  // false
System.out.println("ABC".equals("ABC"));  // true
System.out.println("abc".equalsIgnoreCase("ABC"));  // true
```

This example should be fairly intuitive. In the first example, the values aren't exactly the same. In the second, they are exactly the same. In the third, they differ only by case, but it is okay because we called the method that ignores differences in case.

startsWith() and *endsWith()*

The startsWith() and endsWith() methods look at whether the provided value matches part of the String. The method signatures are as follows:

```
boolean startsWith(String prefix)
boolean endsWith(String suffix)
```

The following code shows how to use these methods:

```
System.out.println("abc".startsWith("a")); // true
System.out.println("abc".startsWith("A")); // false
System.out.println("abc".endsWith("c")); // true
System.out.println("abc".endsWith("a")); // false
```

Again, nothing surprising here. Java is doing a case-sensitive check on the values provided.

contains()

The contains() method also looks for matches in the String. It isn't as particular as startsWith() and endsWith()—the match can be anywhere in the String. The method signature is as follows:

```
boolean contains(String str)
```

The following code shows how to use these methods:

```
System.out.println("abc".contains("b")); // true
System.out.println("abc".contains("B")); // false
```

Again, we have a case-sensitive search in the String. The contains() method is a convenience method so you don't have to write **str·indexOf(otherString) != -1**.

replace()

The replace() method does a simple search and replace on the string. There's a version that takes char parameters as well as a version that takes CharSequence parameters. A CharSequence is a general way of representing several classes, including String and StringBuilder. It's called an interface, which we'll cover in Chapter 5, "Class Design." The method signatures are as follows:

```
String replace(char oldChar, char newChar)
String replace(CharSequence oldChar, CharSequence newChar)
```

The following code shows how to use these methods:

```
System.out.println("abcabc".replace('a', 'A')); // AbcAbc
System.out.println("abcabc".replace("a", "A")); // AbcAbc
```

The first example uses the first method signature, passing in char parameters. The second example uses the second method signature, passing in String parameters.

trim()

You've made it through the all the String methods you need to know except one. We left the easy one for last. The trim() method removes whitespace from the beginning and end of a String. In terms of the exam, whitespace consists of spaces along with the \t (tab) and \n (newline) characters. Other characters, such as \r (carriage return), are also included in what gets trimmed. The method signature is as follows:

```
public String trim()
```

The following code shows how to use this method:

```
System.out.println("abc".trim());            // abc
System.out.println("\t   a b c\n".trim()); // a b c
```

The first example prints the original string because there are no whitespace characters at the beginning or end. The second example gets rid of the leading tab, subsequent spaces, and the trailing newline. It leaves the spaces that are in the middle of the string.

Method Chaining

It is common to call multiple methods on the same String, as shown here:

```
String start = "AniMaL    ";
String trimmed = start.trim();                    // "AniMaL"
```

```
String lowercase = trimmed.toLowerCase();      // "animal"
String result = lowercase.replace('a', 'A');   // "AnimAl"
System.out.println(result);
```

This is just a series of `String` methods. Each time one is called, the returned value is put in a new variable. There are four `String` values along the way, and `AnimAl` is output.

However, on the exam there is a tendency to cram as much code as possible into a small space. You'll see code using a technique called method chaining. Here's an example:

```
String result = "AniMaL   ".trim().toLowerCase().replace('a', 'A');
System.out.println(result);
```

This code is equivalent to the previous example. It also creates four `String` objects and outputs `Animal`. To read code that uses method chaining, start at the left and evaluate the first method. Then call the next method on the returned value of the first method. Keep going until you get to the semicolon.

Remember that `String` is immutable. What do you think the result of this code is?

```
5: String a = "abc";
6: String b = a.toUpperCase();
7: b = b.replace("B", "2").replace('C', '3');
8: System.out.println("a=" + a);
9: System.out.println("b=" + b);
```

On line 5, we set *a* to point to `"abc"` and never pointed *a* to anything else. Since we are dealing with an immutable object, none of the code on lines 6 or 7 changes *a*.

b is a little trickier. Line 6 has *b* pointing to `"ABC"`, which is straightforward. On line 7, we have method chaining. First, `"ABC".replace("B", "2")` is called. This returns `"A2C"`. Next, `"A2C".replace('C', '3')` is called. This returns `"A23"`. Finally, *b* changes to point to this returned `String`. When line 9 executes, *b* is `"A23"`.

Using the *StringBuilder* Class

A small program can create a lot of `String` objects very quickly. For example, how many do you think this piece of code creates?

```
10: String alpha = "";
11: for(char current = 'a'; current <= 'z'; current++)
12:   alpha += current;
13: System.out.println(alpha);
```

The empty `String` on line 10 is instantiated, and then line 12 appends an `"a"`. However, because the `String` object is immutable, a new `String` object is assigned to *alpha* and the

"" object becomes eligible for garbage collection. The next time through the loop, *alpha* is assigned a new String object, "ab", and the "a" object becomes eligible for garbage collection. The next iteration assigns *alpha* to "abc" and the "ab" object becomes eligible for garbage collection, and so on.

This sequence of events continues, and after 26 iterations through the loop, a total of 27 objects are instantiated, most of which are immediately eligible for garbage collection.

This is very inefficient. Luckily, Java has a solution. The StringBuilder class creates a String without storing all those interim String values. Unlike the String class, StringBuilder is not immutable.

```
15: StringBuilder alpha = new StringBuilder();
16: for(char current = 'a'; current <= 'z'; current++)
17:   alpha.append(current);
18: System.out.println(alpha);
```

On line 15, a new StringBuilder object is instantiated. The call to append() on line 17 adds a character to the StringBuilder object each time through the for loop and appends the value of current to the end of *alpha*. This code reuses the same StringBuilder without creating an interim String each time.

In this section, we'll look at creating a StringBuilder, common methods, and a comparison to StringBuffer.

Mutability and Chaining

We're sure you noticed this from the previous example, but StringBuilder is not immutable. In fact, we gave it 27 different values in the example (blank plus adding each letter in the alphabet). The exam will likely try to trick you with respect to String and StringBuilder being mutable.

Chaining makes this even more interesting. When we chained String method calls, the result was a new String with the answer. Chaining StringBuilder objects doesn't work this way. Instead, the StringBuilder changes its own state and returns a reference to itself! Let's look at an example to make this clearer:

```
4: StringBuilder sb = new StringBuilder("start");
5: sb.append("+middle");                  // sb = "start+middle"
6: StringBuilder same = sb.append("+end");  // "start+middle+end"
```

Line 5 adds text to the end of *sb*. It also returns a reference to *sb*, which is ignored. Line 6 also adds text to the end of *sb* and returns a reference to *sb*. This time the reference is stored in *same*—which means *sb* and *same* point to the exact same object and would print out the same value.

The exam won't always make the code easy to read by only having one method per line. What do you think this example prints?

```
4: StringBuilder a = new StringBuilder("abc");
5: StringBuilder b = a.append("de");
```

```
6: b = b.append("f").append("g");
7: System.out.println("a=" + a);
8: System.out.println("b=" + b);
```

Did you say both print "abcdefg"? Good. There's only one StringBuilder object here. We know that because new StringBuilder() was called only once. On line 5, there are two variables referring to that object, which has a value of "abcde". On line 6, those two variables are still referring to that same object, which now has a value of "abcdefg". Incidentally, the assignment back to *b* does absolutely nothing. *b* is already pointing to that StringBuilder.

Creating a *StringBuilder*

There are three ways to construct a StringBuilder:

```
StringBuilder sb1 = new StringBuilder();
StringBuilder sb2 = new StringBuilder("animal");
StringBuilder sb3 = new StringBuilder(10);
```

The first says to create a StringBuilder containing an empty sequence of characters and assign *sb1* to point to it. The second says to create a StringBuilder containing a specific value and assign *sb2* to point to it. For the first two, it tells Java to manage the implementation details. The final example tells Java that we have some idea of how big the eventual value will be and would like the StringBuilder to reserve a certain number of slots for characters.

Size vs. Capacity

The behind-the-scenes process of how objects are stored isn't on the exam, but some knowledge of this process may help you better understand and remember String-Builder.

Size is the number of characters currently in the sequence, and capacity is the number of characters the sequence can currently hold. Since a String is immutable, the size and capacity are the same. The number of characters appearing in the String is both the size and capacity.

For StringBuilder, Java knows the size is likely to change as the object is used. When StringBuilder is constructed, it may start at the default capacity (which happens to be 16) or one of the programmer's choosing. In the example, we request a capacity of 5. At this point, the size is 0 since no characters have been added yet, but we have space for 5.

---

continues

(continued)

Next we add four characters. At this point, the size is 4 since four slots are taken. The capacity is still 5. Then we add three more characters. The size is now 7 since we have used up seven slots. Because the capacity wasn't large enough to store seven characters, Java automatically increased it for us.

```
StringBuilder sb = new StringBuilder(5);
```

0	1	2	3	4

```
sb.append("anim");
```

a	n	i	m	
0	1	2	3	4

```
sb.append("als");
```

a	n	i	m	a	l	s		
0	1	2	3	4	5	6	7	...

Important *StringBuilder* Methods

As with `String`, we aren't going to cover every single method in the `StringBuilder` class. These are the ones you might see on the exam.

charAt(), indexOf(), length(), and substring()

These four methods work exactly the same as in the `String` class. Be sure you can identify the output of this example:

```
StringBuilder sb = new StringBuilder("animals");
String sub = sb.substring(sb.indexOf("a"), sb.indexOf("al"));
int len = sb.length();
char ch = sb.charAt(6);
System.out.println(sub + " " + len + " " + ch);
```

The correct answer is anim 7 s. The `indexOf()` method calls return 0 and 4, respectively. `substring()` returns the `String` starting with index 0 and ending right before index 4.

`length()` returns 7 because it is the number of characters in the `StringBuilder` rather than an index. Finally, `charAt()` returns the character at index 6. Here we do start with 0 because we are referring to indexes. If any of this doesn't sound familiar, go back and read the section on `String` again.

Notice that substring() returns a String rather than a StringBuilder. That is why *sb* is not changed. substring() is really just a method that inquires about where the substring happens to be.

append()

The append() method is by far the most frequently used method in StringBuilder. In fact, it is so frequently used that we just started using it without comment. Luckily, this method does just what it sounds like: it adds the parameter to the StringBuilder and returns a reference to the current StringBuilder. One of the method signatures is as follows:

```
StringBuilder append(String str)
```

Notice that we said *one* of the method signatures. There are more than 10 method signatures that look similar but that take different data types as parameters. All those methods are provided so you can write code like this:

```
StringBuilder sb = new StringBuilder().append(1).append('c');
sb.append("-").append(true);
System.out.println(sb);        // 1c-true
```

Nice method chaining, isn't it? append() is called directly after the constructor. By having all these method signatures, you can just call append() without having to convert your parameter to a String first.

insert()

The insert() method adds characters to the StringBuilder at the requested index and returns a reference to the current StringBuilder. Just like append(), there are lots of method signatures for different types. Here's one:

```
StringBuilder insert(int offset, String str)
```

Pay attention to the offset in these examples. It is the index where we want to insert the requested parameter.

```
3: StringBuilder sb = new StringBuilder("animals");
4: sb.insert(7, "-");              // sb = animals-
5: sb.insert(0, "-");              // sb = -animals-
6: sb.insert(4, "-");              // sb = -ani-mals-
7: System.out.println(sb);
```

Line 4 says to insert a dash at index 7, which happens to be the end of sequence of characters. Line 5 says to insert a dash at index 0, which happens to be the very beginning. Finally, line 6 says to insert a dash right before index 4. The exam creators will try to trip you up on this. As we add and remove characters, their indexes change. When you see a question dealing with such operations, draw what is going on so you won't be confused.

delete() and deleteCharAt()

The delete() method is the opposite of the insert() method. It removes characters from the sequence and returns a reference to the current StringBuilder. The deleteCharAt() method is convenient when you want to delete only one character. The method signatures are as follows:

```
StringBuilder delete(int start, int end)
StringBuilder deleteCharAt(int index)
```

The following code shows how to use these methods:

```
StringBuilder sb = new StringBuilder("abcdef");
sb.delete(1, 3);                    // sb = adef
sb.deleteCharAt(5);                       // throws an exception
```

First, we delete the characters starting with index 1 and ending right before index 3. This gives us adef. Next, we ask Java to delete the character at position 5. However, the remaining value is only four characters long, so it throws a StringIndexOutOfBoundsException.

reverse()

After all that, it's time for a nice, easy method. The reverse() method does just what it sounds like: it reverses the characters in the sequences and returns a reference to the current StringBuilder. The method signature is as follows:

```
StringBuilder reverse()
```

The following code shows how to use this method:

```
StringBuilder sb = new StringBuilder("ABC");
sb.reverse();
System.out.println(sb);
```

As expected, this prints CBA. This method isn't that interesting. Maybe the exam creators like to include it to encourage you to write down the value rather than relying on memory for indexes.

toString()

The last method converts a StringBuilder into a String. The method signature is as follows:

```
String toString()
```

The following code shows how to use this method:

```
String s = sb.toString();
```

Often `StringBuilder` is used internally for performance purposes but the end result needs to be a `String`. For example, maybe it needs to be passed to another method that is expecting a `String`.

StringBuilder vs. *StringBuffer*

When writing new code that concatenates a lot of `String` objects together, you should use `StringBuilder`. `StringBuilder` was added to Java in Java 5. If you come across older code, you will see `StringBuffer` used for this purpose. `StringBuffer` does the same thing but more slowly because it is thread safe. You'll learn about threads for the OCP exam. In theory, you don't need to know about `StringBuffer` on the exam at all. However, we bring this up anyway, since an older question might still be left on the exam.

Understanding Equality

In Chapter 2, you learned how to use == to compare numbers and that object references refer to the same object.

```
StringBuilder one = new StringBuilder();
StringBuilder two = new StringBuilder();
StringBuilder three = one.append("a");
System.out.println(one == two); // false
System.out.println(one == three); // true
```

Since this example isn't dealing with primitives, we know to look for whether the references are referring to the same object. *one* and *two* are both completely separate `StringBuilder`s, giving us two objects. Therefore, the first print statement gives us `false`. *three* is more interesting. Remember how `StringBuilder` methods like to return the current reference for chaining? This means *one* and *three* both point to the same object and the second print statement gives us `true`.

Let's now visit the more complex and confusing scenario, `String` equality, made so in part because of the way the JVM reuses `String` literals:

```
String x = "Hello World";
String y = "Hello World";
System.out.println(x == y);     // true
```

Remember that `String`s are immutable and literals are pooled. The JVM created only one literal in memory. *x* and *y* both point to the same location in memory; therefore, the statement outputs true. It gets even trickier. Consider this code:

```
String x = "Hello World";
String z = " Hello World".trim();
System.out.println(x == z); // false
```

In this example, we don't have two of the same String literal. Although *x* and *z* happen to evaluate to the same string, one is computed at runtime. Since it isn't the same at compile-time, a new String object is created.

You can even force the issue by creating a new String:

```
String x = new String("Hello World");
String y = "Hello World";
System.out.println(x == y); // false
```

Since you have specifically requested a different String object, the pooled value isn't shared.

The lesson is to never use == to compare String objects. The only time you should have to deal with == for Strings is on the exam.

You saw earlier that you can say you want logical equality rather than object equality for String objects:

```
String x = "Hello World";
String z = " Hello World".trim();
System.out.println(x.equals(z)); // true
```

This works because the authors of the String class implemented a standard method called equals to check the values inside the String rather than the String itself. If a class doesn't have an equals method, Java determines whether the references point to the same object—which is exactly what == does. In case you are wondering, the authors of StringBuilder did not implement equals(). If you call equals() on two StringBuilder instances, it will check reference equality.

The exam will test you on your understanding of equality with objects they define too. For example:

```
1: public class Tiger {
2:    String name;
3:    public static void main(String[] args) {
4:      Tiger t1 = new Tiger();
5:      Tiger t2 = new Tiger();
6:      Tiger t3 = t1;
7:      System.out.println(t1 == t3); // true
8:      System.out.println(t1 == t2); // false
9:      System.out.println(t1.equals(t2)); // false
10:  } }
```

The first two statements check object reference equality. Line 7 prints true because we are comparing references to the same object. Line 8 prints false because the two object references are different. Line 9 prints `false` since `Tiger` does not implement `equals()`. Don't worry—you aren't expected to know how to implement `equals()` for the OCA exam.

Understanding Java Arrays

Up to now, we've been referring to the `String` and `StringBuilder` classes as a "sequence of characters." This is true. They are implemented using an *array* of characters. An array is an area of memory on the heap with space for a designated number of elements. A `String` is implemented as an array with some methods that you might want to use when dealing with characters specifically. A `StringBuilder` is implemented as an array where the array object is replaced with a new bigger array object when it runs out of space to store all the characters. A big difference is that an array can be of any other Java type. If we didn't want to use a `String` for some reason, we could use an array of `char` primitives directly:

```
char[] letters;
```

This wouldn't be very convenient because we'd lose all the special properties `String` gives us, such as writing "Java". Keep in mind that *letters* is a reference variable and not a primitive. `char` is a primitive. But `char` is what goes into the array and not the type of the array itself. The array itself is of type `char[]`. You can mentally read the brackets (`[]`) as "array."

In other words, an array is an ordered list. It can contain duplicates. You will learn about data structures that cannot contain duplicates for the OCP exam. In this section, we'll look at creating an array of primitives and objects, sorting, searching, varargs, and multidimensional arrays.

Creating an Array of Primitives

The most common way to create an array looks like this:

```
int[] numbers1 = new int[3];
```

The basic parts are shown in Figure 3.2. It specifies the type of the array (`int`) and the size (3). The brackets tell you this is an array.

FIGURE 3.2 The basic structure of an array

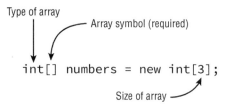

When using this form to instantiate an array, all elements are set to the default value for that type. As you learned in Chapter 1, the default value of an int is 0. Since *numbers1* is a reference variable, it points to the array object, as shown in Figure 3.3. As you can see, the default value for all the elements is 0. Also, the indexes start with 0 and count up, just as they did for a String.

FIGURE 3.3   An empty array

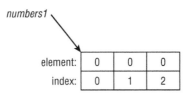

Another way to create an array is to specify all the elements it should start out with:

```
int[] numbers2 = new int[] {42, 55, 99};
```

In this example, we also create an int array of size 3. This time, we specify the initial values of those three elements instead of using the defaults. Figure 3.4 shows what this array looks like.

FIGURE 3.4   An initialized array

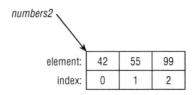

Java recognizes that this expression is redundant. Since you are specifying the type of the array on the left side of the equal sign, Java already knows the type. And since you are specifying the initial values, it already knows the size. As a shortcut, Java lets you write this:

```
int[] numbers2 = {42, 55, 99};
```

This approach is called an anonymous array. It is anonymous because you don't specify the type and size.

Finally, you can type the [] before or after the name, and adding a space is optional. This means that all four of these statements do the exact same thing:

```
int[] numAnimals;
int [] numAnimals2;
int numAnimals3[];
int numAnimals4 [];
```

Most people use the first one. You could see any of these on the exam, though, so get used to seeing the brackets in odd places.

Multiple "Arrays" in Declarations

What types of reference variables do you think the following code creates?

```
int[] ids, types;
```

The correct answer is two variables of type `int[]`. This seems logical enough. After all, `int a, b;` created two `int` variables. What about this example?

```
int ids[], types;
```

All we did was move the brackets, but it changed the behavior. This time we get one variable of type `int[]` and one variable of type `int`. Java sees this line of code and thinks something like this: "They want two variables of type `int`. The first one is called `ids[]`. This one is a `int[]` called *ids*. The second one is just called *types*. No brackets, so it is a regular integer."

Needless to say, you shouldn't write code that looks like this. But you do still need to understand it for the exam.

Creating an Array with Reference Variables

You can choose any Java type to be the type of the array. This includes classes you create yourself. Let's take a look at a built-in type with `String`:

```
public class ArrayType {
  public static void main(String args[]) {
    String [] bugs = { "cricket", "beetle", "ladybug" };
    String [] alias = bugs;
    System.out.println(bugs.equals(alias));    // true
    System.out.println(bugs.toString()); // [Ljava.lang.String;@160bc7c0
} }
```

We can call `equals()` because an array is an object. It returns `true` because of reference equality. The `equals()` method on arrays does not look at the elements of the array. Remember, this would work even on an `int[]` too. `int` is a primitive; `int[]` is an object.

The second print statement is even more interesting. What on earth is `[Ljava.lang.String;@160bc7c0`? You don't have to know this for the exam, but `[L` means it is an array, `java.lang.String` is the reference type, and `160bc7c0` is the hash code.

NOTE   Since Java 5, Java has provided a method that prints an array nicely: `java .util.Arrays.toString(bugs)` would print `[cricket, beetle, lady-bug]`. The exam tends not to use it because most of the questions on arrays were written a long time ago. Regardless, this is a useful method when testing your own code.

Make sure you understand Figure 3.5. The array does not allocate space for the `String` objects. Instead, it allocates space for a reference to where the objects are really stored.

FIGURE 3.5   An array pointing to strings

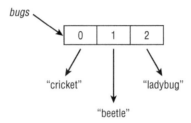

As a quick review, what do you think this array points to?

```
class Names {
  String names[];
}
```

You got us. It was a review of Chapter 1 and not our discussion on arrays. The answer is `null`. The code never instantiated the array so it is just a reference variable to `null`. Let's try that again—what do you think this array points to?

```
class Names {
  String names[] = new String[2];
}
```

It is an array because it has brackets. It is an array of type `String` since that is the type mentioned in the declaration. It has two elements because the length is 2. Each of those two slots currently is `null`, but has the potential to point to a `String` object.

Remember casting from the previous chapter when you wanted to force a bigger type into a smaller type? You can do that with arrays too:

```
3: String[] strings = { "stringValue" };
4: Object[] objects = strings;
5: String[] againStrings = (String[]) objects;
6: againStrings[0] = new StringBuilder();   // DOES NOT COMPILE
7: objects[0] = new StringBuilder();        // careful!
```

Line 3 creates an array of type `String`. Line 4 doesn't require a cast because `Object` is a broader type than `String`. On line 5, a cast is needed because we are moving to a more specific type. Line 6 doesn't compile because a `String[]` only allows `String` objects and `StringBuilder` is not a `String`.

Line 7 is where this gets interesting. From the point of view of the compiler, this is just fine. A `StringBuilder` object can clearly go in an `Object[]`. The problem is that we don't actually have an `Object[]`. We have a `String[]` referred to from an `Object[]` variable. At runtime, the code throws an `ArrayStoreException`. You don't need to memorize the name of this exception, but you do need to know that the code will throw an exception.

Using an Array

Now that we know how to create an array, let's try accessing one:

```
4: String[] mammals = {"monkey", "chimp", "donkey"};
5: System.out.println(mammals.length);          // 3
6: System.out.println(mammals[0]);              // monkey
7: System.out.println(mammals[1]);              // chimp
8: System.out.println(mammals[2]);              // donkey
```

Line 4 declares and initializes the array. Line 5 tells us how many elements the array can hold. The rest of the code prints the array. Notice elements are indexed starting with 0. This should be familiar from `String` and `StringBuilder`, which also start counting with 0. Those classes also counted `length` as the number of elements.

To make sure you understand how `length` works, what do you think this prints?

```
String[] birds = new String[6];
System.out.println(birds.length);
```

The answer is 6. Even though all 6 elements of the array are `null`, there are still 6 of them. `length` does not consider what is in the array; it only considers how many slots have been allocated.

It is very common to use a loop when reading from or writing to an array. This loop sets each element of number to 5 higher than the current index:

```
5: int[] numbers = new int[10];
6: for (int i = 0; i < numbers.length; i++)
7:   numbers[i] = i + 5;
```

Line 5 simply instantiates an array with 10 slots. Line 6 is a for loop using an extremely common pattern. It starts at index 0, which is where an array begins as well. It keeps going, one at a time, until it hits the end of the array. Line 7 sets the current element of *numbers*.

The exam will test whether you are being observant by trying to access elements that are not in the array. Can you tell why each of these throws an `ArrayIndexOutOfBoundsException` for our array of size 10?

```
numbers[10] = 3;
numbers[numbers.length] = 5;
for (int i = 0; i <= numbers.length; i++) numbers[i] = i + 5;
```

The first one is trying to see if you know that indexes start with 0. Since we have 10 elements in our array, this means only numbers[0] through numbers[9] are valid. The second example assumes you are clever enough to know 10 is invalid and disguises it by using the length field. However, the length is always one more than the maximum valid index. Finally, the for loop incorrectly uses <= instead of <, which is also a way of referring to that 10th element.

Sorting

Java makes it easy to sort an array by providing a sort method—or rather, a bunch of sort methods. Just like StringBuilder allowed you to pass almost anything to append(), you can pass almost any array to Arrays.sort().

Arrays is the first class provided by Java we have used that requires an import. To use it, you must have either of the following two statements in your class:

```
import java.util.*;         // import whole package including Arrays
import java.util.Arrays;    // import just Arrays
```

There is one exception, although it doesn't come up often on the exam. You can write java.util.Arrays every time it is used in the class instead of specifying it as an import.

Remember that if you are shown a code snippet with a line number that doesn't begin with 1, you can assume the necessary imports are there. Similarly, you can assume the imports are present if you are shown a snippet of a method.

This simple example sorts three numbers:

```
int[] numbers = { 6, 9, 1 };
Arrays.sort(numbers);
for (int i = 0; i < numbers.length; i++)
  System.out.print (numbers[i] +  " ");
```

The result is 1 6 9, as you should expect it to be. Notice that we had to loop through the output to print the values in the array. Just printing the array variable directly would give the annoying hash of [I@2bd9c3e7.

Try this again with String types:

```
String[] strings = { "10", "9", "100" };
Arrays.sort(strings);
for (String string : strings)
  System.out.print(string + " ");
```

This time the result might not be what you expect. This code outputs 10 100 9. The problem is that String sorts in alphabetic order, and 1 sorts before 9. (Numbers sort before letters and uppercase sorts before lowercase, in case you were wondering.) For the OCP exam, you'll learn how to create custom sort orders using something called a comparator.

Did you notice we snuck in the enhanced for loop in this example? Since we aren't using the index, we don't need the traditional for loop. That won't stop the exam creators from using it, though, so we'll be sure to use both to keep you sharp!

Searching

Java also provides a convenient way to search—but only if the array is already sorted. Table 3.1 covers the rules for binary search.

TABLE 3.1 Binary search rules

Scenario	Result
Target element found in sorted array	Index of match
Target element not found in sorted array	Negative value showing one smaller than the negative of index, where a match needs to be inserted to preserve sorted order
Unsorted array	A surprise—this result isn't predictable

Let's try out these rules with an example:

```
3: int[] numbers = {2,4,6,8};
4: System.out.println(Arrays.binarySearch(numbers, 2)); // 0
5: System.out.println(Arrays.binarySearch(numbers, 4)); // 1
6: System.out.println(Arrays.binarySearch(numbers, 1)); // -1
7: System.out.println(Arrays.binarySearch(numbers, 3)); // -2
8: System.out.println(Arrays.binarySearch(numbers, 9)); // -5
```

Take note of the fact that line 3 is a sorted array. If it weren't, we couldn't apply either of the other rules. Line 4 searches for the index of 2. The answer is index 0. Line 5 searches for the index of 4, which is 1.

Line 6 searches for the index of 1. Although 1 isn't in the list, the search can determine that it should be inserted at element 0 to preserve the sorted order. Since 0 already means something for array indexes, Java needs to subtract 1 to give us the answer of –1. Line 7 is similar. Although 3 isn't in the list, it would need to be inserted at element 1 to preserve the sorted order. We negate and subtract 1 for consistency, getting –1 –1, also known as –2. Finally, line 8 wants to tell us that 9 should be inserted at index 4. We again negate and subtract 1, getting –4 –1, also known as –5.

What do you think happens in this example?

```
5: int[] numbers = new int[] {3,2,1};
6: System.out.println(Arrays.binarySearch(numbers, 2));
7: System.out.println(Arrays.binarySearch(numbers, 3));
```

Note that on line 5, the array isn't sorted. This means the output will not be predictable. When testing this example, line 6 correctly gave 1 as the output. However, line 7 gave the wrong answer. The exam creators will not expect you to know what incorrect values come out. As soon as you see the array isn't sorted, look for an answer choice about unpredictable output.

On the exam, you need to know what a binary search returns in various scenarios. Oddly, you don't need to know why "binary" is in the name. In case you are curious, a binary search splits the array into two equal pieces (remember 2 is binary) and determines which half the target it is. It repeats this process until only one element is left.

Varargs

When creating an array yourself, it looks like what we've seen thus far. When one is passed to your method, there is another way it can look. Here are three examples with a main() method:

```
public static void main(String[] args)
public static void main(String args[])
public static void main(String... args) // varargs
```

The third example uses a syntax called varargs (variable arguments), which you saw in Chapter 1. You'll learn how to call a method using varargs in Chapter 4, "Methods and Encapsulation." For now, all you need to know is that you can use a variable defined using varargs as if it were a normal array. For example args.length and args[0] are legal.

Multidimensional Arrays

Arrays are objects, and of course array components can be objects. It doesn't take much time, rubbing those two facts together, to wonder if arrays can hold other arrays, and of course they can.

Creating a Multidimensional Array

Multiple array separators are all it takes to declare arrays with multiple dimensions. You can locate them with the type or variable name in the declaration, just as before:

```
int[][] vars1;          // 2D array
int vars2 [][];         // 2D array
int[] vars3[];          // 2D array
int[] vars4 [], space [][];  // a 2D AND a 3D array
```

The first two examples are nothing surprising and declare a two-dimensional (2D) array. The third example also declares a 2D array. There's no good reason to use this style other than to confuse readers of your code. The final example declares two arrays on the same line. Adding up the brackets, we see that the vars4 is a 2D array and space is a 3D array. Again, there' no reason to use this style other than to confuse readers of your code. The exam creators like to try to confuse you, though. Luckily you are on to them and won't let this happen to you!

You can specify the size of your multidimensional array in the declaration if you like:

```
String [][] rectangle = new String[3][2];
```

The result of this statement is an array rectangle with three elements, each of which refers to an array of two elements. You can think of the addressable range as [0][0] through [2][1], but don't think of it as a structure of addresses like [0,0] or [2,1].

Now suppose we set one of these values:

```
rectangle[0][1] = "set";
```

You can visualize the result as shown in Figure 3.6. This array is sparsely populated because it has a lot of null values. You can see that rectangle still points to an array of three elements and that we have three arrays of two elements. You can also follow the trail from reference to the one value pointing to a String. First you start at index 0 in the top array. Then you go to index 1 in the next array.

FIGURE 3.6   A sparsely populated multidimensional array

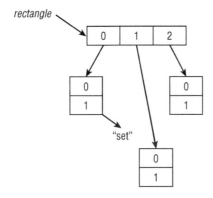

While that array happens to be rectangular in shape, an array doesn't need to be. Consider this one:

```
int[][] differentSize = {{1, 4}, {3}, {9,8,7}};
```

We still start with an array of three elements. However, this time the elements in the next level are all different sizes. One is of length 2, the next length 1, and the last length 3 (see Figure 3.7). This time the array is of primitives, so they are shown as if they are in the array themselves.

FIGURE 3.7   An asymmetric multidimensional array

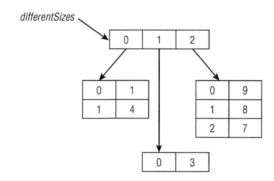

Another way to create an asymmetric array is to initialize just an array's first dimension, and define the size of each array component in a separate statement:

```
int [][] args = new int[4][];
args[0] = new int[5];
args[1] = new int[3];
```

This technique reveals what you really get with Java: arrays of arrays that, properly managed, offer a multidimensional effect.

Using a Multidimensional Array

The most common operation on a multidimensional array is to loop through it. This example prints out a 2D array:

```
int[][] twoD = new int[3][2];
for (int i = 0; i < twoD.length; i++) {
  for (int j = 0; j < twoD[i].length; j++)
    System.out.print(twoD[i][j] + " "); // print element
  System.out.println();                 // time for a new row
}
```

We have two loops here. The first uses index i and goes through the first subarray for twoD. The second uses a different loop variable j. It is very important these be different variable names so the loops don't get mixed up. The inner loop looks at how many elements are in the second-level array. The inner loop prints the element and leaves a space for readability. When the inner loop completes, the outer loop goes to a new line and repeats the process for the next element.

This entire exercise would be easier to read with the enhanced for loop.

```
for (int[] inner : twoD) {
  for (int num : inner)
```

```
    System.out.print(num + " ");
  System.out.println();
}
```

We'll grant you that it isn't fewer lines, but each line is less complex and there aren't any loop variables or terminating conditions to mix up.

Understanding an *ArrayList*

An array has one glaring shortcoming: you have to know how many elements will be in the array when you create it and then you are stuck with that choice. Just like a StringBuilder, ArrayList can change size at runtime as needed. Like an array, an ArrayList is an ordered sequence that allows duplicates.

As when we used Arrays.sort, ArrayList requires an import. To use it, you must have either of the following two statements in your class:

```
import java.util.*;         // import whole package including ArrayList
import java.util.ArrayList; // import just ArrayList
```

Remember that if you are shown a code snippet with a line number that doesn't begin with 1, you can assume the necessary imports are there. Similarly, you can assume the imports are present if you are shown a snippet of a method.

In this section, we'll look at creating an ArrayList, common methods, autoboxing, conversion, and sorting.

Experienced programmers, take note: This section is simplified and doesn't cover a number of topics that are out of scope for the OCA exam.

Creating an *ArrayList*

As with StringBuilder, there are three ways to create an ArrayList:

```
ArrayList list1 = new ArrayList();
ArrayList list2 = new ArrayList(10);
ArrayList list3 = new ArrayList(list2);
```

The first says to create an ArrayList containing space for the default number of elements but not to fill any slots yet. The second says to create an ArrayList containing a specific number of slots, but again not to assign any. The final example tells Java that we want to make a copy of another ArrayList. We copy both the size and contents of that ArrayList. Granted, *list2* is empty in this example so it isn't particularly interesting.

Although these are the only three constructors you need to know, you do need to learn some variants of it. The previous examples were the old pre–Java 5 way of creating an ArrayList. They still work and you still need to know they work. You also need to know the new and improved way. Java 5 introduced *generics*, which allow you to specify the type of class that the `ArrayList` will contain.

```
ArrayList<String> list4 = new ArrayList<String>();
ArrayList<String> list5 = new ArrayList<>();
```

Java 5 allows you to tell the compiler what the type would be by specifying it between < and >. Starting in Java 7, you can even omit that type from the right side. The < and > are still required, though. This is called the diamond operator because <> looks like a diamond.

Just when you thought you knew everything about creating an `ArrayList`, there is one more thing you need to know. `ArrayList` implements an interface called `List`. In other words, an `ArrayList` is a `List`. You will learn about interfaces in Chapter 5. In the meantime, just know that you can store an `ArrayList` in a `List` reference variable but not vice versa. The reason is that `List` is an interface and interfaces can't be instantiated.

```
List<String> list6 = new ArrayList<>();
ArrayList<String> list7 = new List<>(); // DOES NOT COMPILE
```

Using an *ArrayList*

`ArrayList` has many methods, but you only need to know a handful of them—even fewer than you did for `String` and `StringBuilder`.

Before reading any further, you are going to see something new in the method signatures: a "class" named E. Don't worry—it isn't really a class. E is used by convention in generics to mean "any class that this array can hold." If you didn't specify a type when creating the `ArrayList`, E means `Object`. Otherwise, it means the class you put between < and >.

You should also know that `ArrayList` implements `toString()` so you can easily see the contents just by printing it. Arrays do not do produce such pretty output.

add()

The `add()` methods insert a new value in the `ArrayList`. The method signatures are as follows:

```
boolean add(E element)
void add(int index, E element)
```

Don't worry about the `boolean` return value. It always returns `true`. It is there because other classes in the collections family need a return value in the signature when adding an element.

Since `add()` is the most critical `ArrayList` method you need to know for the exam, we are going to show a few sets of examples for it. Let's start with the most straightforward case:

```
ArrayList list = new ArrayList();
list.add("hawk");          // [hawk]
```

```
list.add(Boolean.TRUE);    // [hawk, true]
System.out.println(list);  // [hawk, true]
```

add() does exactly what we expect: it stores the String in the no longer empty ArrayList. It then does the same thing for the boolean. This is okay because we didn't specify a type for ArrayList; therefore, the type is Object, which includes everything except primitives. It may not have been what we intended, but the compiler doesn't know that. Now, let's use generics to tell the compiler we only want to allow String objects in our ArrayList:

```
ArrayList<String> safer = new ArrayList<>();
safer.add("sparrow");
safer.add(Boolean.TRUE);    // DOES NOT COMPILE
```

This time the compiler knows that only String objects are allowed in and prevents the attempt to add a boolean. Now let's try adding multiple values to different positions.

```
4: List<String> birds = new ArrayList<>();
5: birds.add("hawk");              // [hawk]
6: birds.add(1, "robin");          // [hawk, robin]
7: birds.add(0, "blue jay");       // [blue jay, hawk, robin]
8: birds.add(1, "cardinal");       // [blue jay, cardinal, hawk, robin]
9: System.out.println(birds);      // [blue jay, cardinal, hawk, robin]
```

When a question has code that adds objects at indexed positions, draw it so that you won't lose track of which value is at which index. In this example, line 5 adds "hawk" to the end of birds. Then line 6 adds "robin" to index 1 of birds, which happens to be the end. Line 7 adds "blue jay" to index 0, which happens to be the beginning of birds. Finally, line 8 adds "cardinal" to index 1, which is now near the middle of birds.

remove()

The remove() methods remove the first matching value in the ArrayList or remove the element at a specified index. The method signatures are as follows:

```
boolean remove(Object object)
E remove(int index)
```

This time the boolean return value tells us whether a match was removed. The E return type is the element that actually got removed. The following shows how to use these methods:

```
3: List<String> birds = new ArrayList<>();
4: birds.add("hawk");       // [hawk]
5: birds.add("hawk");       // [hawk, hawk]
6: System.out.println(birds.remove("cardinal")); // prints false
7: System.out.println(birds.remove("hawk")); // prints true
```

```
8: System.out.println(birds.remove(0)); // prints hawk
9: System.out.println(birds);        // []
```

Line 6 tries to remove an element that is not in birds. It returns false because no such element is found. Line 7 tries to remove an element that is in birds and so returns true. Notice that it removes only one match. Line 8 removes the element at index 0, which is the last remaining element in the ArrayList.

Since calling remove() with an int uses the index, an index that doesn't exist will throw an exception. For example, birds.remove(100) throws an IndexOutOfBoundsException.

There is also a removeIf() method. We'll cover it in the next chapter because it uses lambda expressions (a topic in that chapter).

set()

The set() method changes one of the elements of the ArrayList without changing the size. The method signature is as follows:

```
E set(int index, E newElement)
```

The E return type is the element that got replaced. The following shows how to use this method:

```
15: List<String> birds = new ArrayList<>();
16: birds.add("hawk");                  // [hawk]
17: System.out.println(birds.size());   // 1
18: birds.set(0, "robin");              // [robin]
19: System.out.println(birds.size());   // 1
20: birds.set(1, "robin");              // IndexOutOfBoundsException
```

Line 16 adds one element to the array, making the size 1. Line 18 replaces that one element and the size stays at 1. Line 20 tries to replace an element that isn't in the ArrayList. Since the size is 1, the only valid index is 0. Java throws an exception because this isn't allowed.

isEmpty() and size()

The isEmpty() and size() methods look at how many of the slots are in use. The method signatures are as follows:

```
boolean isEmpty()
int size()
```

The following shows how to use these methods:

```
System.out.println(birds.isEmpty());    // true
System.out.println(birds.size());    // 0
birds.add("hawk");                   // [hawk]
birds.add("hawk");                   // [hawk, hawk]
```

```
System.out.println(birds.isEmpty());      // false
System.out.println(birds.size());      // 2
```

At the beginning, birds has a size of 0 and is empty. It has a capacity that is greater than 0. However, as with StringBuilder, we don't use the capacity in determining size or length. After adding elements, the size becomes positive and it is no longer empty.

clear()

The clear() method provides an easy way to discard all elements of the ArrayList. The method signature is as follows:

```
void clear()
```

The following shows how to use this method:

```
List<String> birds = new ArrayList<>();
birds.add("hawk");                      // [hawk]
birds.add("hawk");                      // [hawk, hawk]
System.out.println(birds.isEmpty());      // false
System.out.println(birds.size());      // 2
birds.clear();                           // []
System.out.println(birds.isEmpty());      // true
System.out.println(birds.size());      // 0
```

After we call clear(), birds is back to being an empty ArrayList of size 0.

contains()

The contains() method checks whether a certain value is in the ArrayList. The method signature is as follows:

```
boolean contains(Object object)
```

The following shows how to use this method:

```
List<String> birds = new ArrayList<>();
birds.add("hawk");                          // [hawk]
System.out.println(birds.contains("hawk")); // true
System.out.println(birds.contains("robin")); // false
```

This method calls equals() on each element of the ArrayList to see whether there are any matches. Since String implements equals(), this works out well.

equals()

Finally, ArrayList has a custom implementation of equals() so you can compare two lists to see if they contain the same elements in the same order.

```
boolean equals(Object object)
```

The following shows an example:

```
31: List<String> one = new ArrayList<>();
32: List<String> two = new ArrayList<>();
33: System.out.println(one.equals(two));      // true
34: one.add("a");                        // [a]
35: System.out.println(one.equals(two));    // false
36: two.add("a");                        // [a]
37: System.out.println(one.equals(two));    // true
38: one.add("b");                      // [a,b]
39: two.add(0, "b");                  // [b,a]
40: System.out.println(one.equals(two));    // false
```

On line 33, the two ArrayList objects are equal. An empty list is certainly the same elements in the same order. On line 35, the ArrayList objects are not equal because the size is different. On line 37, they are equal again because the same one element is in each. On line 40, they are not equal. The size is the same and the values are the same, but they are not in the same order.

Wrapper Classes

Up to now, we've only put String objects in the ArrayList. What happens if we want to put primitives in? Each primitive type has a wrapper class, which is an object type that corresponds to the primitive. Table 3.2 lists all the wrapper classes along with the constructor for each.

TABLE 3.2 Wrapper classes

Primitive type	Wrapper class	Example of constructing
boolean	Boolean	new Boolean(true)
byte	Byte	new Byte((byte) 1)
short	Short	new Short((short) 1)
int	Integer	new Integer(1)
long	Long	new Long(1)
float	Float	new Float(1.0)
double	Double	new Double(1.0)
char	Character	new Character('c')

The wrapper classes also have a method that converts back to a primitive. You don't need to know much about the constructors or intValue() type methods for the exam because autoboxing has removed the need for them (see the next section). You might encounter this syntax on questions that have been on the exam for many years. However, you just need to be able to read the code and not look for tricks in it.

There are also methods for converting a String to a primitive or wrapper class. You do need to know these methods. The parse methods, such as parseInt(), return a primitive, and the valueOf() method returns a wrapper class. This is easy to remember because the name of the returned primitive is in the method name. For example:

```
int primitive = Integer.parseInt("123");
Integer wrapper = Integer.valueOf("123");
```

The first line converts a String to an int primitive. The second converts a String to an Integer wrapper class. If the String passed in is not valid for the given type, Java throws an exception. In these examples, letters and dots are not valid for an integer value:

```
int bad1 = Integer.parseInt("a");           // throws NumberFormatException
Integer bad2 = Integer.valueOf("123.45");   // throws NumberFormatException
```

Before you worry, the exam won't make you recognize that the method parseInt() is used rather than parseInteger(). You simply need to be able to recognize the methods when put in front of you. Also, the Character class doesn't participate in the parse/valueOf methods. Since a String is made up of characters, you can just call charAt() normally.

Table 3.3 lists the methods you need to recognize for creating a primitive or wrapper class object from a String. In real coding, you won't be so concerned which is returned from each method due to autoboxing.

TABLE 3.3   Converting from a String

Wrapper class	Converting String to primitive	Converting String to wrapper class
Boolean	Boolean.parseBoolean("true");	Boolean.valueOf("TRUE");
Byte	Byte.parseByte("1");	Byte.valueOf("2");
Short	Short.parseShort("1");	Short.valueOf("2");
Integer	Integer.parseInt("1");	Integer.valueOf("2");
Long	Long.parseLong("1");	Long.valueOf("2");
Float	Float.parseFloat("1");	Float.valueOf("2.2");
Double	Double.parseDouble("1");	Double.valueOf("2.2");
Character	None	None

Autoboxing

Why won't you need to be concerned with whether a primitive or wrapper class is returned, you ask? Since Java 5, you can just type the primitive value and Java will convert it to the relevant wrapper class for you. This is called *autoboxing*. Let's look at an example:

```
4: List<Double> weights = new ArrayList<>();
5: weights.add(50.5);              // [50.5]
6: weights.add(new Double(60));    // [50.5, 60.0]
7: weights.remove(50.5);            // [60.0]
8: double first = weights.get(0);   // 60.0
```

Line 5 autoboxes the double primitive into a Double object and adds that to the List. Line 6 shows that you can still write code the long way and pass in a wrapper object. Line 7 again autoboxes into the wrapper object and passes it to remove(). Line 8 retrieves the Double and unboxes it into a double primitive.

What do you think happens if you try to unbox a null?

```
3: List<Integer> heights = new ArrayList<>();
4: heights.add(null);
5: int h = heights.get(0);         // NullPointerException
```

On line 4, we add a null to the list. This is legal because a null reference can be assigned to any reference variable. On line 5, we try to unbox that null to an int primitive. This is a problem. Java tries to get the int value of null. Since calling any method on null gives a NullPointerException, that is just what we get. Be careful when you see null in relation to autoboxing.

Be careful when autoboxing into Integer. What do you think this code outputs?

```
List<Integer> numbers = new ArrayList<>();
numbers.add(1);
numbers.add(2);
numbers.remove(1);
System.out.println(numbers);
```

It actually outputs [1]. After adding the two values, the List contains [1, 2]. We then request the element with index 1 be removed. That's right: index 1. Because there's already a remove() method that takes an int parameter, Java calls that method rather than autoboxing. If you want to remove the 2, you can write numbers.remove(new Integer(2)) to force wrapper class use.

Converting Between *array* and *List*

You should know how to convert between an array and an ArrayList. Let's start with turning an ArrayList into an array:

```
3: List<String> list = new ArrayList<>();
4: list.add("hawk");
```

```
5: list.add("robin");
6: Object[] objectArray = list.toArray();
7: System.out.println(objectArray.length);     // 2
8: String[] stringArray = list.toArray(new String[0]);
9: System.out.println(stringArray.length);     // 2
```

Line 6 shows that an ArrayList knows how to convert itself to an array. The only problem is that it defaults to an array of class Object. This isn't usually what you want. Line 8 specifies the type of the array and does what we actually want. The advantage of specifying a size of 0 for the parameter is that Java will create a new array of the proper size for the return value. If you like, you can suggest a larger array to be used instead. If the ArrayList fits in that array, it will be returned. Otherwise, a new one will be created.

Converting from an array to a List is more interesting. The original array and created array backed List are linked. When a change is made to one, it is available in the other. It is a fixed-size list and is also known a *backed* List because the array changes with it. Pay careful attention to the values here:

```
20: String[] array = { "hawk", "robin" };     // [hawk, robin]
21: List<String> list = Arrays.asList(array); // returns fixed size list
22: System.out.println(list.size());     // 2
23: list.set(1, "test");          // [hawk, test]
24: array[0] = "new";             // [new, test]
25: for (String b : array) System.out.print(b + " "); // new test
26: list.remove(1);     // throws UnsupportedOperation Exception
```

Line 21 converts the array to a List. Note that it isn't the java.util.ArrayList we've grown used to. It is a fixed-size, backed version of a List. Line 23 is okay because set() merely replaces an existing value. It updates both *array* and *list* because they point to the same data store. Line 24 also changes both *array* and *list*. Line 25 shows the array has changed to new test. Line 26 throws an exception because we are not allowed to change the size of the list.

A Cool Trick with Varargs

This topic isn't on the exam, but merging varargs with ArrayList conversion allows you to create an ArrayList in a cool way:

```
List<String> list = Arrays.asList("one", "two");
```

asList() takes varargs, which let you pass in an array or just type out the String values. This is handy when testing because you can easily create and populate a List on one line.

Sorting

Sorting an ArrayList is very similar to sorting an array. You just use a different helper class:

```
List<Integer> numbers = new ArrayList<>();
numbers.add(99);
numbers.add(5);
numbers.add(81);
Collections.sort(numbers);
System.out.println(numbers); [5, 81, 99]
```

As you can see, the numbers got sorted, just like you'd expect. Isn't it nice to have something that works just like you think it will?

Working with Dates and Times

In Java 8, Oracle completely revamped how we work with dates and times. You can still write code the "old way," but those classes aren't on the exam. We'll mention the "old way" in real-world scenarios so that you can learn the "new way" more easily if you first learned Java before version 8. Even if you are learning Java starting with version 8, this will help you when you need to read older code. Just know that the "old way" is not on the exam.

As with an ArrayList, you need an import statement to work with the date and time classes. Most of them are in the java.time package. To use it, add this import to your program:

```
import java.time.*;          // import time classes
```

In the following sections, we'll look at creating, manipulating, and formatting dates and times.

Creating Dates and Times

In the real world, we usually talk about dates and time zones as if the other person is located near us. For example, if you say "I'll call you at 11:00 on Tuesday morning," we assume that 11:00 means the same thing to both of us. But if you live in New York and we live in California, you need to be more specific. California is three hours earlier than New York because the states are in different time zones. You would instead say, "I'll call you at 11:00 EST on Tuesday morning." Luckily, the exam doesn't cover time zones, so discussing dates and times is easier.

When working with dates and times, the first thing to do is decide how much information you need. The exam gives you three choices:

LocalDate Contains just a date—no time and no time zone. A good example of LocalDate is your birthday this year. It is your birthday for a full day regardless of what time it is.

LocalTime   Contains just a time—no date and no time zone. A good example of LocalTime is midnight. It is midnight at the same time every day.

LocalDateTime   Contains both a date and time but no time zone. A good example of LocalDateTime is "the stroke of midnight on New Year's." Midnight on January 2 isn't nearly as special, and clearly an hour after midnight isn't as special either.

Oracle recommends avoiding time zones unless you really need them. Try to act as if everyone is in the same time zone when you can. If you do need to communicate across time zones, ZonedDateTime handles them.

Ready to create your first date and time objects?

```
System.out.println(LocalDate.now());
System.out.println(LocalTime.now());
System.out.println(LocalDateTime.now());
```

Each of the three classes has a static method called now() that gives the current date and time. Your output is going to depend on what date/time you run it and where you live. The authors live in the United States, making the output look like the following when run on January 20 at 12:45 p.m.:

```
2015-01-20
12:45:18.401
2015-01-20T12:45:18.401
```

The key is to notice the type of information in the output. The first one contains only a date and no time. The second contains only a time and no date. This time displays hours, minutes, seconds, and nanoseconds. The third contains both date and time. Java uses T to separate the date and time when converting LocalDateTime to a String.

Wait—I Don't Live in the United States

The exam recognizes that exam takers live all over the world and will not ask you about the details of United States date and time formats.

In the United States, the month is written before the date. The exam won't ask you about the difference between 02/03/2015 and 03/02/2015. That would be mean and not internationally friendly, and it would be testing your knowledge of United States dates rather than your knowledge of Java. That said, our examples do use United States date and time formats as will the questions on the exam. Just remember that the month comes before the date. Also, Java tends to use a 24-hour clock even though the United States uses a 12-hour clock with a.m./p.m.

Now that you know how to create the current date and time, let's look at other specific dates and times. To begin, let's create just a date with no time. Both of these examples create the same date:

```
LocalDate date1 = LocalDate.of(2015, Month.JANUARY, 20);
LocalDate date2 = LocalDate.of(2015, 1, 20);
```

Both pass in the year, month, and date. Although it is good to use the Month constants (to make the code easier to read), you can pass the int number of the month directly. Just use the number of the month the same way you would if you were writing the date in real life.

The method signatures are as follows:

```
public static LocalDate of(int year, int month, int dayOfMonth)
public static LocalDate of(int year, Month month, int dayOfMonth)
```

Month is a special type of class called an enum. You don't need to know about enums on the OCA exam and can just treat them as constants.

Up to now, we've been like a broken record telling you that Java counts starting with 0. Well, months are an exception. For months in the new date and time methods, Java counts starting from 1 like we human beings do.

When creating a time, you can choose how detailed you want to be. You can specify just the hour and minute, or you can add the number of seconds. You can even add nanoseconds if you want to be very precise. (A nanosecond is a billionth of a second—you probably won't need to be that specific.)

```
LocalTime time1 = LocalTime.of(6, 15);              // hour and minute
LocalTime time2 = LocalTime.of(6, 15, 30);          // + seconds
LocalTime time3 = LocalTime.of(6, 15, 30, 200);     // + nanoseconds
```

These three times are all different but within a minute of each other. The method signatures are as follows:

```
public static LocalTime of(int hour, int minute)
public static LocalTime of(int hour, int minute, int second)
public static LocalTime of(int hour, int minute, int second, int nanos)
```

Finally, we can combine dates and times:

```
LocalDateTime dateTime1 = LocalDateTime.of(2015, Month.JANUARY, 20, 6, 15, 30);
LocalDateTime dateTime2 = LocalDateTime.of(date1, time1);
```

The first line of code shows how you can specify all the information about the LocalDateTime right in the same line. There are many method signatures allowing you to specify different things. Having that many numbers in a row gets to be hard to read, though. The second line of code shows how you can create LocalDate and LocalTime objects separately first and then combine them to create a LocalDateTime object.

This time there are a lot of method signatures since there are more combinations. The method signatures are as follows:

```
public static LocalDateTime of(int year, int month,
  int dayOfMonth, int hour, int minute)
public static LocalDateTime of(int year, int month,
  int dayOfMonth, int hour, int minute, int second)
public static LocalDateTime of(int year, int month,
  int dayOfMonth, int hour, int minute, int second, int nanos)
public static LocalDateTime of(int year, Month month,
  int dayOfMonth, int hour, int minute)
public static LocalDateTime of(int year, Month month,
  int dayOfMonth, int hour, int minute, int second)
public static LocalDateTime of(int year, Month month,
  int dayOfMonth, int hour, int minute, int second, int nanos)
public static LocalDateTime of(LocalDate date, LocalTime time)
```

Did you notice that we did not use a constructor in any of the examples? The date and time classes have private constructors to force you to use the static methods. The exam creators may try to throw something like this at you:

```
LocalDate d = new LocalDate(); // DOES NOT COMPILE
```

Don't fall for this. You are not allowed to construct a date or time object directly. Another trick is to see what happens when you pass invalid numbers to of(). For example:

```
LocalDate.of(2015, Month.January, 32);     // throws DateTimeException
```

You don't need to know the exact exception that's thrown, but it's a clear one:

```
java.time.DateTimeException: Invalid value for DayOfMonth
  (valid values 1 - 28/31): 32
```

 Real World Scenario

Creating Dates in Java 7 and Earlier

You can see some of the problems with the "old way" in the following table. There wasn't a way to specify just a date without the time. The Date class represented both the date and time whether you wanted it to or not. Trying to create a specific date required more code than it should have. Month indexes were 0 based instead of 1 based, which was confusing.

continues

continued

There's an old way to create a date. In Java 1.1, you created a specific Date with this: Date jan = new Date(2015, Calendar.JANUARY, 1);. You could use the Calendar class beginning with Java 1.2. Date exists mainly for backward compatibility and so that Calendar can work with code—making the "new way" the third way. The "new way" is much better so it looks like this is a case of the third time is the charm!

	Old way	New way (Java 8 and later)
Importing	`import java.util.*;`	`import java .time.*;`
Creating an object with the current date	`Date d = new Date();`	`LocalDate d = LocalDate .now();`
Creating an object with the current date and time	`Date d = new Date();`	`LocalDateTime dt = LocalDateTime. now();`

Creating an object representing January 1, 2015	`Calendar c = Calendar.getInstance();`
	`c.set(2015, Calendar.JANUARY, 1);`
	`Date jan = c.getTime();`
	
	or
	
	`Calendar c = new GregorianCalendar(2015,`
	`Calendar.JANUARY, 1);`
	`Date jan = c.getTime();`
		`LocalDate jan = LocalDate.of(2015, Month.JANUARY, 1);`

Creating January 1, 2015 without the constant	`Calendar c = Calendar.getInstance();`
	`c.set(2015, 0, 1);`
	`Date jan = c.getTime();`
		`LocalDate jan = LocalDate.of(2015, 1, 1)`

Manipulating Dates and Times

Adding to a date is easy. The date and time classes are immutable, just like String was. This means that we need to remember to assign the results of these methods to a reference variable so they are not lost.

```
12: LocalDate date = LocalDate.of(2014, Month.JANUARY, 20);
13: System.out.println(date);          // 2014-01-20
14: date = date.plusDays(2);
15: System.out.println(date);          // 2014-01-22
16: date = date.plusWeeks(1);
```

```
17: System.out.println(date);         // 2014-01-29
18: date = date.plusMonths(1);
19: System.out.println(date);         // 2014-02-28
20: date = date.plusYears(5);
21: System.out.println(date);         // 2019-02-28
```

This code is nice because it does just what it sounds like. We start out with January 20, 2014. On line 14, we add two days to it and reassign it to our reference variable. On line 16, we add a week. This method allows us to write clearer code than plusDays(7). Now date is January 29, 2014. On line 18, we add a month. This would bring us to February 29, 2014. However, 2014 is not a leap year. (2012 and 2016 are leap years.) Java is smart enough to realize February 29, 2014 does not exist and gives us February 28, 2014 instead. Finally, line 20 adds five years.

There are also nice easy methods to go backward in time. This time, let's work with LocalDateTime.

```
22: LocalDate date = LocalDate.of(2020, Month.JANUARY, 20);
23: LocalTime time = LocalTime.of(5, 15);
24: LocalDateTime dateTime = LocalDateTime.of(date, time);
25: System.out.println(dateTime);     // 2020-01-20T05:15
26: dateTime = dateTime.minusDays(1);
27: System.out.println(dateTime);     // 2020-01-19T05:15
28: dateTime = dateTime.minusHours(10);
29: System.out.println(dateTime);     // 2020-01-18T19:15
30: dateTime = dateTime.minusSeconds(30);
31: System.out.println(dateTime);     // 2020-01-18T19:14:30
```

Line 25 prints the original date of January 20, 2020 at 5:15 a.m. Line 26 subtracts a full day, bringing us to January 19, 2020 at 5:15 a.m. Line 28 subtracts 10 hours, showing that the date will change if the hours cause it to and brings us to January 18, 2020 at 19:15 (7:15 p.m.). Finally, line 30 subtracts 30 seconds. We see that all of a sudden the display value starts displaying seconds. Java is smart enough to hide the seconds and nanoseconds when we aren't using them.

It is common for date and time methods to be chained. For example, without the print statements, the previous example could be rewritten as follows:

```
LocalDate date = LocalDate.of(2020, Month.JANUARY, 20);
LocalTime time = LocalTime.of(5, 15);
LocalDateTime dateTime = LocalDateTime.of(date, time)
   .minusDays(1).minusHours(10).minusSeconds(30);
```

When you have a lot of manipulations to make, this chaining comes in handy. There are two ways the exam creators can try to trick you. What do you think this prints?

```
LocalDate date = LocalDate.of(2020, Month.JANUARY, 20);
date.plusDays(10);
System.out.println(date);
```

It prints January 20, 2020. Adding 10 days was useless because we ignored the result. Whenever you see immutable types, pay attention to make sure the return value of a method call isn't ignored.

The exam also may test to see if you remember what each of the date and time objects includes. Do you see what is wrong here?

```
LocalDate date = LocalDate.of(2020, Month.JANUARY, 20);
date = date.plusMinutes(1);    // DOES NOT COMPILE
```

LocalDate does not contain time. This means you cannot add minutes to it. This can be tricky in a chained sequence of additions/subtraction operations, so make sure you know which methods in Table 3.4 can be called on which of the three objects.

TABLE 3.4   Methods in LocalDate, LocalTime, and LocalDateTime

	Can call on LocalDate?	Can call on LocalTime?	Can call on LocalDateTime?
plusYears/minusYears	Yes	No	Yes
plusMonths/minusMonths	Yes	No	Yes
plusWeeks/minusWeeks	Yes	No	Yes
plusDays/minusDays	Yes	No	Yes
plusHours/minusHours	No	Yes	Yes
plusMinutes/minusMinutes	No	Yes	Yes
plusSeconds/minusSeconds	No	Yes	Yes
plusNanos/minusNanos	No	Yes	Yes

Manipulating Dates in Java 7 and Earlier

As you look at all the code in the following table to do time calculations in the "old way," you can see why Java needed to revamp the date and time APIs! The "old way" took a lot of code to do something simple.

	Old way	New way (Java 8 and later)
Adding a day	```public Date addDay(Date date) { Calendar cal = Calendar .getInstance(); cal.setTime(date); cal.add(Calendar.DATE, 1); return cal.getTime(); }```	```public LocalDate addDay(LocalDate date) { return date. plusDays(1); }```
Subtracting a day	```public Date subtractDay(Date date) { Calendar cal = Calendar .getInstance(); cal.setTime(date); cal.add(Calendar.DATE, -1); return cal.getTime(); }```	```public LocalDate subtractDay(LocalDate date) { return date. minusDays(1); }```

Working with Periods

Now we know enough to do something fun with dates! Our zoo performs animal enrichment activities to give the animals something fun to do. The head zookeeper has decided to switch the toys every month. This system will continue for three months to see how it works out.

```
public static void main(String[] args) {
  LocalDate start = LocalDate.of(2015, Month.JANUARY, 1);
  LocalDate end = LocalDate.of(2015, Month.MARCH, 30);
  performAnimalEnrichment(start, end);
}
private static void performAnimalEnrichment(LocalDate start, LocalDate end) {
  LocalDate upTo = start;
  while (upTo.isBefore(end)) {          // check if still before end
   System.out.println("give new toy: " + upTo);
   upTo  = upTo.plusMonths(1);              // add a month
  }}
```

This code works fine. It adds a month to the date until it hits the end date. The problem is that this method can't be reused. Our zookeeper wants to try different schedules to see which works best.

Converting to a long

LocalDate and LocalDateTime have a method to convert them into long equivalents in relation to 1970. What's special about 1970? That's what UNIX started using for date standards, so Java reused it. And don't worry—you don't have to memorize the names for the exam.

- LocalDate has toEpochDay(), which is the number of days since January 1, 1970.

- LocalDateTime has toEpochSecond(), which is the number of seconds since January 1, 1970.

- LocalTime does not have an epoch method. Since it represents a time that occurs on any date, it doesn't make sense to compare it in 1970. Although the exam pretends time zones don't exist, you may be wondering if this special January 1, 1970 is in a specific time zone. The answer is yes. This special time refers to when it was January 1, 1970 in GMT (Greenwich Mean Time). Greenwich is in England and GMT does not participate in daylight savings time. This makes it a good reference point. (Again, you don't have to know about GMT for the exam.)

Luckily, Java has a Period class that we can pass in. This code does the same thing as the previous example:

```java
public static void main(String[] args) {
  LocalDate start = LocalDate.of(2015, Month.JANUARY, 1);
  LocalDate end = LocalDate.of(2015, Month.MARCH, 30);
  Period period = Period.ofMonths(1);              // create a period
  performAnimalEnrichment(start, end, period);
}
private static void performAnimalEnrichment(LocalDate start, LocalDate end,
  Period period) {                  // uses the generic period
  LocalDate upTo = start;
  while (upTo.isBefore(end)) {
    System.out.println("give new toy: " + upTo);
    upTo = upTo.plus(period);       // adds the period
}}
```

The method can add an arbitrary period of time that gets passed in. This allows us to reuse the same method for different periods of time as our zookeeper changes her mind.

There are five ways to create a Period class:

```java
Period annually = Period.ofYears(1);              // every 1 year
Period quarterly = Period.ofMonths(3);             // every 3 months
```

```
Period everyThreeWeeks = Period.ofWeeks(3);        // every 3 weeks
Period everyOtherDay = Period.ofDays(2);           // every 2 days
Period everyYearAndAWeek = Period.of(1, 0, 7);      // every year and 7 days
```

There's one catch. You cannot chain methods when creating a Period. The following code looks like it is equivalent to the everyYearAndAWeek example, but it's not. Only the last method is used because the Period.ofXXX methods are static methods.

```
Period wrong = Period.ofYears(1).ofWeeks(1);        // every week
```

This tricky code is really like writing the following:

```
Period wrong = Period.ofYears(1);
wrong = Period.ofWeeks(1);
```

This is clearly not what you intended! That's why the of() method allows us to pass in the number of years, months, and days. They are all included in the same period. You will get a compiler warning about this. Compiler warnings tell you something is wrong or suspicious without failing compilation.

You've probably noticed by now that a Period is a day or more of time. There is also Duration, which is intended for smaller units of time. For Duration, you can specify the number of days, hours, minutes, seconds, or nanoseconds. And yes, you could pass 365 days to make a year, but you really shouldn't—that's what Period is for. Duration isn't on the exam since it roughly works the same way as Period. It's good to know it exists, though.

The last thing to know about Period is what objects it can be used with. Let's look at some code:

```
3: LocalDate date = LocalDate.of(2015, 1, 20);
4: LocalTime time = LocalTime.of(6, 15);
5: LocalDateTime dateTime = LocalDateTime.of(date, time);
6: Period period = Period.ofMonths(1);
7: System.out.println(date.plus(period));         // 2015-02-20
8: System.out.println(dateTime.plus(period));       // 2015-02-20T06:15
9: System.out.println(time.plus(period));   // UnsupportedTemporalTypeException
```

Lines 7 and 8 work as expected. They add a month to January 20, 2015, giving us February 20, 2015. The first has only the date, and the second has both the date and time.

Line 9 attempts to add a month to an object that only has a time. This won't work. Java throws an exception and complains that we attempt to use an Unsupported unit: Months.

As you can see, you'll have to pay attention to the type of date and time objects every place you see them.

Formatting Dates and Times

The date and time classes support many methods to get data out of them:

```
LocalDate date = LocalDate.of(2020, Month.JANUARY, 20);
System.out.println(date.getDayOfWeek());      // MONDAY
System.out.println(date.getMonth());           // JANUARY
System.out.println(date.getYear());           // 2020
System.out.println(date.getDayOfYear());      // 20
```

We could use this information to display information about the date. However, it would be more work than necessary. Java provides a class called DateTimeFormatter to help us out. Unlike the LocalDateTime class, DateTimeFormatter can be used to format any type of date and/or time object. What changes is the format. DateTimeFormatter is in the package java.time.format.

```
LocalDate date = LocalDate.of(2020, Month.JANUARY, 20);
LocalTime time = LocalTime.of(11, 12, 34);
LocalDateTime dateTime = LocalDateTime.of(date, time);
System.out.println(date.format(DateTimeFormatter.ISO_LOCAL_DATE));
System.out.println(time.format(DateTimeFormatter.ISO_LOCAL_TIME));
System.out.println(dateTime.format(DateTimeFormatter.ISO_LOCAL_DATE_TIME));
```

ISO is a standard for dates. The output of the previous code looks like this:

```
2020-01-20
11:12:34
2020-01-20T11:12:34
```

This is a reasonable way for computers to communicate, but probably not how you want to output the date and time in your program. Luckily there are some predefined formats that are more useful:

```
DateTimeFormatter shortDateTime =
  DateTimeFormatter.ofLocalizedDate(FormatStyle.SHORT);
System.out.println(shortDateTime.format(dateTime));    // 1/20/20
System.out.println(shortDateTime.format(date));        // 1/20/20
System.out.println(
  shortDateTime.format(time)); // UnsupportedTemporalTypeException
```

Here we say we want a localized formatter in the predefined short format. The last line throws an exception because a time cannot be formatted as a date. The format() method is declared on both the formatter objects and the date/time objects, allowing you to reference the objects in either order. The following statements print exactly the same thing as the previous code:

```
DateTimeFormatter shortDateTime =
  DateTimeFormatter.ofLocalizedDate(FormatStyle.SHORT);
System.out.println(dateTime.format(shortDateTime));
System.out.println(date.format(shortDateTime));
System.out.println(time.format(shortDateTime));
```

In this book, we'll change around the orders to get you used to seeing it both ways. Table 3.5 shows the legal and illegal localized formatting methods.

TABLE 3.5 ofLocalized methods

DateTimeFormatter f = DateTimeFormatter._____ (FormatStyle.SHORT);	Calling f.format (localDate)	Calling f.format (localDateTime)	Calling f.format (localTime)
ofLocalizedDate	Legal – shows whole object	Legal – shows just date part	Throws runtime exception
ofLocalizedDateTime	Throws runtime exception	Legal – shows whole object	Throws runtime exception
ofLocalizedTime	Throws runtime exception	Legal – shows just time part	Legal – shows whole object

There are two predefined formats that can show up on the exam: SHORT and MEDIUM. The other predefined formats involve time zones, which are not on the exam.

```
LocalDate date = LocalDate.of(2020, Month.JANUARY, 20);
LocalTime time = LocalTime.of(11, 12, 34);
LocalDateTime dateTime = LocalDateTime.of(date, time);

DateTimeFormatter shortF = DateTimeFormatter
   .ofLocalizedDateTime(FormatStyle.SHORT);
DateTimeFormatter mediumF = DateTimeFormatter
   .ofLocalizedDateTime(FormatStyle.MEDIUM);
System.out.println(shortF.format(dateTime));    // 1/20/20 11:12 AM
System.out.println(mediumF.format(dateTime));    // Jan 20, 2020 11:12:34 AM
```

If you don't want to use one of the predefined formats, you can create your own. For example, this code spells out the month:

```
DateTimeFormatter f = DateTimeFormatter.ofPattern("MMMM dd, yyyy, hh:mm");
System.out.println(dateTime.format(f));    // January 20, 2020, 11:12
```

Before we look at the syntax, know you are not expected to memorize what different numbers of each symbol mean. The most you will need to do is recognize the date and time pieces.

MMMM M represents the month. The more Ms you have, the more verbose the Java output. For example, M outputs 1, MM outputs 01, MMM outputs Jan, and MMMM outputs January.

dd d represents the date in the month. As with month, the more ds you have, the more verbose the Java output. dd means to include the leading zero for a single-digit day.

, Use , if you want to output a comma (this also appears after the year).

yyyy y represents the year. yy outputs a two-digit year and yyyy outputs a four-digit year.

hh h represents the hour. Use hh to include the leading zero if you're outputting a single-digit hour.

: Use : if you want to output a colon.

mm m represents the minute.

 Real World Scenario

Formatting Dates in Java 7 and Earlier

Formatting is roughly equivalent to the "old way"; it just uses a different class.

	Old way	**New way (Java 8 and later)**
Formatting the times	`SimpleDateFormat sf = new SimpleDateFormat("hh:mm");` `sf.format(jan3);`	`DateTimeFormatter f = DateTimeFormatter.ofPattern("hh:mm");` `dt.format(f);`

Let's do a quick review. Can you figure out which of these lines will throw an exception?

```
4: DateTimeFormatter f = DateTimeFormatter.ofPattern("hh:mm");
5: f.format(dateTime);
6: f.format(date);
7: f.format(time);
```

If you get this question on the exam, think about what the symbols represent. We have h for hour and m for minute. Remember M (uppercase) is month and m (lowercase) is minute. We can only use this formatter with objects containing times. Therefore, line 6 will throw an exception.

Parsing Dates and Times

Now that you know how to convert a date or time to a formatted String, you'll find it easy to convert a String to a date or time. Just like the format() method, the parse() method takes a formatter as well. If you don't specify one, it uses the default for that type.

```
DateTimeFormatter f = DateTimeFormatter.ofPattern("MM dd yyyy");
LocalDate date = LocalDate.parse("01 02 2015", f);
LocalTime time = LocalTime.parse("11:22");
System.out.println(date);        // 2015-01-02
System.out.println(time);        // 11:22
```

Here we show using both a custom formatter and a default value. This isn't common, but you might have to read code that looks like this on the exam. Parsing is consistent in that if anything goes wrong, Java throws a runtime exception. That could be a format that doesn't match the String to be parsed or an invalid date.

Summary

In this chapter, you learned that Strings are immutable sequences of characters. The new operator is optional. The concatenation operator (+) creates a new String with the content of the first String followed by the content of the second String. If either operand involved in the + expression is a String, concatenation is used; otherwise, addition is used. String literals are stored in the string pool. The String class has many methods. You need to know charAt(), concat(), endsWith(), equals(), equalsIgnoreCase(), indexOf(), length(), replace(), startsWith(), substring(), toLowerCase(), toUpperCase(), and trim().

StringBuilders are mutable sequences of characters. Most of the methods return a reference to the current object to allow method chaining. The StringBuilder class has many methods. You need to know append(), charAt(), delete(), deleteCharAt(), indexOf(), insert(), length(), reverse(), substring(), and toString(). StringBuffer is the same as StringBuilder except that it is thread safe.

Calling == on String objects will check whether they point to the same object in the pool. Calling == on StringBuilder references will check whether they are pointing to the same StringBuilder object. Calling equals() on String objects will check whether the sequence of characters is the same. Calling equals() on StringBuilder objects will check whether they are pointing to the same object rather than looking at the values inside.

An array is a fixed-size area of memory on the heap that has space for primitives or pointers to objects. You specify the size when creating it—for example, int[] a = new int[6];. Indexes begin with 0 and elements are referred to using a[0]. The Arrays.sort() method sorts an array. Arrays.binarySearch() searches a sorted array and returns the index of a match. If no match is found, it negates the position where the element would need to be inserted and subtracts 1. Methods that are passed varargs (…) can be used as if a normal array was passed in. In a multidimensional array, the second-level arrays and beyond can be different sizes.

An `ArrayList` can change size over its life. It can be stored in an `ArrayList` or `List` reference. Generics can specify the type that goes in the `ArrayList`. You need to know the methods `add()`, `clear()`, `contains()`, `equals()`, `isEmpty()`, `remove()`, `set()`, and `size()`. Although an `ArrayList` is not allowed to contain primitives, Java will autobox parameters passed in to the proper wrapper type. `Collections.sort()` sorts an `ArrayList`.

A `LocalDate` contains just a date, a `LocalTime` contains just a time, and a `LocalDateTime` contains both a date and time. All three have private constructors and are created using `LocalDate.now()` or `LocalDate.of()` (or the equivalents for that class). Dates and times can be manipulated using plus*XXX* or minus*XXX* methods. The `Period` class represents a number of days, months, or years to add or subtract from a `LocalDate` or `LocalDateTime`. `DateTimeFormatter` is used to output dates and times in the desired format. The date and time classes are all immutable, which means the return value must be used.

Exam Essentials

Be able to determine the output of code using String.   Know the rules for concatenating `String`s and how to use common `String` methods. Know that `String`s are immutable. Pay special attention to the fact that indexes are zero based and that `substring()` gets the string up until right before the index of the second parameter.

Be able to determine the output of code using StringBuilder.   Know that `StringBuilder` is mutable and how to use common `StringBuilder` methods. Know that `substring()` does not change the value of a `StringBuilder` whereas `append()`, `delete()`, and `insert()` do change it. Also note that most `StringBuilder` methods return a reference to the current instance of `StringBuilder`.

Understand the difference between == and equals.   == checks object equality. `equals()` depends on the implementation of the object it is being called on. For `String`s, `equals()` checks the characters inside of it.

Be able to determine the output of code using arrays.   Know how to declare and instantiate one-dimensional and multidimensional arrays. Be able to access each element and know when an index is out of bounds. Recognize correct and incorrect output when searching and sorting.

Be able to determine the output of code using ArrayList.   Know that `ArrayList` can increase in size. Be able to identify the different ways of declaring and instantiating an `ArrayList`. Identify correct output from `ArrayList` methods, including the impact of autoboxing.

Recognize invalid uses of dates and times.   `LocalDate` does not contain time fields and `LocalTime` does not contain date fields. Watch for operations being performed on the wrong time. Also watch for adding or subtracting time and ignoring the result.

Review Questions

1. What is output by the following code? (Choose all that apply)

```
1: public class Fish {
2:  public static void main(String[] args) {
3:     int numFish = 4;
4:     String fishType = "tuna";
5:     String anotherFish = numFish + 1;
6:     System.out.println(anotherFish + " " + fishType);
7:     System.out.println(numFish + " " + 1);
8: } }
```

   A. 4 1
   B. 41
   C. 5
   D. 5 tuna
   E. 5tuna
   F. 51tuna
   G. The code does not compile.

2. Which of the following are output by this code? (Choose all that apply)

```
3: String s = "Hello";
4: String t = new String(s);
5: if ("Hello".equals(s)) System.out.println("one");
6: if (t == s) System.out.println("two");
7: if (t.equals(s)) System.out.println("three");
8: if ("Hello" == s) System.out.println("four");
9: if ("Hello" == t) System.out.println("five");
```

   A. one
   B. two
   C. three
   D. four
   E. five
   F. The code does not compile.

3. Which are true statements? (Choose all that apply)

   A. An immutable object can be modified.
   B. An immutable object cannot be modified.
   C. An immutable object can be garbage collected.

D. An immutable object cannot be garbage collected.

E. `String` is immutable.

F. `StringBuffer` is immutable.

G. `StringBuilder` is immutable.

4. What is the result of the following code?

```
7: StringBuilder sb = new StringBuilder();
8: sb.append("aaa").insert(1, "bb").insert(4, "ccc");
9: System.out.println(sb);
```

A. abbaaccc

B. abbaccca

C. bbaaaccc

D. bbaaccca

E. An exception is thrown.

F. The code does not compile.

5. What is the result of the following code?

```
2: String s1 = "java";
3: StringBuilder s2 = new StringBuilder("java");
4: if (s1 == s2)
5:   System.out.print("1");
6: if (s1.equals(s2))
7:   System.out.print("2");
```

A. 1

B. 2

C. 12

D. No output is printed.

E. An exception is thrown.

F. The code does not compile.

6. What is the result of the following code?

```
public class Lion {
  public void roar(String roar1, StringBuilder roar2) {
    roar1.concat("!!!");
    roar2.append("!!!");
  }
  public static void main(String[] args) {
    String roar1 = "roar";
    StringBuilder roar2 = new StringBuilder("roar");
    new Lion().roar(roar1, roar2);
```

```
System.out.println(roar1 + " " + roar2);
} }
```

A. roar roar

B. roar roar!!!

C. roar!!! roar

D. roar!!! roar!!!

E. An exception is thrown.

F. The code does not compile.

7. Which are the results of the following code? (Choose all that apply)

```
String letters = "abcdef";
System.out.println(letters.length());
System.out.println(letters.charAt(3));
System.out.println(letters.charAt(6));
```

A. 5

B. 6

C. c

D. d

E. An exception is thrown.

F. The code does not compile.

8. Which are the results of the following code? (Choose all that apply)

```
String numbers = "012345678";
System.out.println(numbers.substring(1, 3));
System.out.println(numbers.substring(7, 7));
System.out.println(numbers.substring(7));
```

A. 12

B. 123

C. 7

D. 78

E. A blank line.

F. An exception is thrown.

G. The code does not compile.

9. What is the result of the following code?

```
3: String s = "purr";
4: s.toUpperCase();
5: s.trim();
6: s.substring(1, 3);
```

```
7: s += " two";
8: System.out.println(s.length());
```

A. 2

B. 4

C. 8

D. 10

E. An exception is thrown.

F. The code does not compile.

10. What is the result of the following code? (Choose all that apply)

```
13: String a = "";
14: a += 2;
15: a += 'c';
16: a += false;
17: if ( a == "2cfalse") System.out.println("==");
18: if ( a.equals("2cfalse")) System.out.println("equals");
```

A. Compile error on line 14.

B. Compile error on line 15.

C. Compile error on line 16.

D. Compile error on another line.

E. ==

F. equals

G. An exception is thrown.

11. What is the result of the following code?

```
4: int total = 0;
5: StringBuilder letters = new StringBuilder("abcdefg");
6: total += letters.substring(1, 2).length();
7: total += letters.substring(6, 6).length();
8: total += letters.substring(6, 5).length();
9: System.out.println(total);
```

A. 1

B. 2

C. 3

D. 7

E. An exception is thrown.

F. The code does not compile.

12. What is the result of the following code? (Choose all that apply)
```
StringBuilder numbers = new StringBuilder("0123456789");
numbers.delete(2,  8);
numbers.append("-").insert(2, "+");
System.out.println(numbers);
```
  A. 01+89-

  B. 012+9-

  C. 012+-9

  D. 0123456789

  E. An exception is thrown.

  F. The code does not compile.

13. What is the result of the following code?
```
StringBuilder b = "rumble";
b.append(4).deleteCharAt(3).delete(3, b.length() - 1);
System.out.println(b);
```
  A. rum

  B. rum4

  C. rumb4

  D. rumble4

  E. An exception is thrown.

  F. The code does not compile.

14. Which of the following can replace line 4 to print "avaJ"? (Choose all that apply)
```
3: StringBuilder puzzle = new StringBuilder("Java");
4: // INSERT CODE HERE
5: System.out.println(puzzle);
```
  A. puzzle.reverse();

  B. puzzle.append("vaJ$").substring(0, 4);

  C. puzzle.append("vaJ$").delete(0, 3).deleteCharAt(puzzle.length() - 1);

  D. puzzle.append("vaJ$").delete(0, 3).deleteCharAt(puzzle.length());

  E. None of the above.

15. Which of these array declarations is not legal? (Choose all that apply)
  A. int[][] scores = new int[5][];

  B. Object[][][] cubbies = new Object[3][0][5];

  C. String beans[] = new beans[6];

  D. java.util.Date[] dates[] = new java.util.Date[2][];

  E. int[][] types = new int[];

  F. int[][] java = new int[][];

16. Which of these compile when replacing line 8? (Choose all that apply)

```
7: char[]c = new char[2];
8: // INSERT CODE HERE
```

A. `int length = c.capacity;`

B. `int length = c.capacity();`

C. `int length = c.length;`

D. `int length = c.length();`

E. `int length = c.size;`

F. `int length = c.size();`

G. None of the above.

17. Which of these compile when replacing line 8? (Choose all that apply)

```
7: ArrayList l = new ArrayList();
8: // INSERT CODE HERE
```

A. `int length = l.capacity;`

B. `int length = l.capacity();`

C. `int length = l.length;`

D. `int length = l.length();`

E. `int length = l.size;`

F. `int length = l.size();`

G. None of the above.

18. Which of the following are true? (Choose all that apply)

A. An array has a fixed size.

B. An `ArrayList` has a fixed size.

C. An array allows multiple dimensions.

D. An array is ordered.

E. An `ArrayList` is ordered.

F. An array is immutable.

G. An `ArrayList` is immutable.

19. Which of the following are true? (Choose all that apply)

A. Two arrays with the same content are equal.

B. Two `ArrayList`s with the same content are equal.

C. If you call `remove(0)` using an empty `ArrayList` object, it will compile successfully.

D. If you call `remove(0)` using an empty `ArrayList` object, it will run successfully.

E. None of the above.

20. What is the result of the following statements?

```
6:  List<String> list = new ArrayList<String>();
7:  list.add("one");
8:  list.add("two");
9:  list.add(7);
10: for(String s : list)  System.out.print(s);
```

- **A.** onetwo
- **B.** onetwo7
- **C.** onetwo followed by an exception
- **D.** Compiler error on line 9.
- **E.** Compiler error on line 10.

21. What is the result of the following statements?

```
3: ArrayList<Integer> values = new ArrayList<>();
4: values.add(4);
5: values.add(5);
6: values.set(1, 6);
7: values.remove(0);
8: for (Integer v : values) System.out.print(v);
```

- **A.** 4
- **B.** 5
- **C.** 6
- **D.** 46
- **E.** 45
- **F.** An exception is thrown.
- **G.** The code does not compile.

22. What is the result of the following?

```
int[] random = { 6, -4, 12, 0, -10 };
int x = 12;
int y = Arrays.binarySearch(random, x);
System.out.println(y);
```

- **A.** 2
- **B.** 4
- **C.** 6
- **D.** The result is undefined.
- **E.** An exception is thrown.
- **F.** The code does not compile.

23. What is the result of the following?

```
4: List<Integer> list = Arrays.asList(10, 4, -1, 5);
5: Collections.sort(list);
6: Integer array[] = list.toArray(new Integer[4]);
7: System.out.println(array[0]);
```

A. -1

B. 10

C. Compiler error on line 4.

D. Compiler error on line 5.

E. Compiler error on line 6.

F. An exception is thrown.

24. What is the result of the following?

```
6: String [] names = {"Tom", "Dick", "Harry"};
7: List<String> list = names.asList();
8: list.set(0, "Sue");
9: System.out.println(names[0]);
```

A. Sue

B. Tom

C. Compiler error on line 7.

D. Compiler error on line 8.

E. An exception is thrown.

25. What is the result of the following?

```
List<String> hex = Arrays.asList("30", "8", "3A", "FF");
Collections.sort(hex);
int x = Collections.binarySearch(hex, "8");
int y = Collections.binarySearch(hex, "3A");
int z = Collections.binarySearch(hex, "4F");
System.out.println(x + " " + y + " " + z);
```

A 0 1 –2

B. 0 1 –3

C. 2 1 –2

D. 2 1 –3

E. None of the above.

F. The code doesn't compile.

26. Which of the following are true statements about the following code? (Choose all that apply)

```
4: List<Integer> ages = new ArrayList<>();
5: ages.add(Integer.parseInt("5"));
```

```
6: ages.add(Integer.valueOf("6"));
7: ages.add(7);
8: ages.add(null);
9: for (int age : ages) System.out.print(age);
```

A. The code compiles.

B. The code throws a runtime exception.

C. Exactly one of the add statements uses autoboxing.

D. Exactly two of the add statements use autoboxing.

E. Exactly three of the add statements use autoboxing.

27. What is the result of the following?

```
List<String> one = new ArrayList<String>();
one.add("abc");
List<String> two = new ArrayList<>();
two.add("abc");
if (one == two)
  System.out.println("A");
else if (one.equals(two))
  System.out.println("B");
else
  System.out.println("C");
```

A. A

B. B

C. C

D. An exception is thrown.

E. The code does not compile.

28. Which of the following can be inserted into the blank to create a date of June 21, 2014? (Choose all that apply)

```
import java.time.*;

public class StartOfSummer {

  public static void main(String[] args) {
    LocalDate date = _____
  }

}
```

A. new LocalDate(2014, 5, 21);

B. new LocalDate(2014, 6, 21);

C. LocalDate.of(2014, 5, 21);

D. `LocalDate.of(2014, 6, 21);`

E. `LocalDate.of(2014, Calendar.JUNE, 21);`

F. `LocalDate.of(2014, Month.JUNE, 21);`

29. What is the output of the following code?

```
LocalDate date = LocalDate.parse("2018-04-30", DateTimeFormatter.ISO_LOCAL_
DATE);
date.plusDays(2);
date.plusHours(3);
System.out.println(date.getYear() + " " + date.getMonth() + " "
+ date.getDayOfMonth());
```

A. `2018 APRIL 2`

B. `2018 APRIL 30`

C. `2018 MAY 2`

D. The code does not compile.

E. A runtime exception is thrown.

30. What is the output of the following code?

```
LocalDate date = LocalDate.of(2018, Month.APRIL, 40);
System.out.println(date.getYear() + " " + date.getMonth() + " "
+ date.getDayOfMonth());
```

A. `2018 APRIL 4`

B. `2018 APRIL 30`

C. `2018 MAY 10`

D. Another date.

E. The code does not compile.

F. A runtime exception is thrown.

31. What is the output of the following code?

```
LocalDate date = LocalDate.of(2018, Month.APRIL, 30);
date.plusDays(2);
date.plusYears(3);
System.out.println(date.getYear() + " " + date.getMonth() + " "
+ date.getDayOfMonth());
```

A. `2018 APRIL 2`

B. `2018 APRIL 30`

C. `2018 MAY 2`

D. `2021 APRIL 2`

E. 2021 APRIL 30

F. 2021 MAY 2

G. A runtime exception is thrown.

32. What is the output of the following code?

```
LocalDateTime d = LocalDateTime.of(2015, 5, 10, 11, 22, 33);
Period p = Period.of(1, 2, 3);
d = d.minus(p);
DateTimeFormatter f = DateTimeFormatter.ofLocalizedTime(FormatStyle.SHORT);
System.out.println(d.format(f));
```

A. 3/7/14 11:22 AM

B. 5/10/15 11:22 AM

C. 3/7/14

D. 5/10/15

E. 11:22 AM

F. The code does not compile.

G. A runtime exception is thrown.

33. What is the output of the following code?

```
LocalDateTime d = LocalDateTime.of(2015, 5, 10, 11, 22, 33);
Period p = Period.ofDays(1).ofYears(2);
d = d.minus(p);
DateTimeFormatter f = DateTimeFormatter.ofLocalizedDateTime(FormatStyle
.SHORT);
System.out.println(f.format(d));
```

A. 5/9/13 11:22 AM

B. 5/10/13 11:22 AM

C. 5/9/14

D. 5/10/14

E. The code does not compile.

F. A runtime exception is thrown.

Chapter

4

Methods and Encapsulation

OCA EXAM OBJECTIVES COVERED IN THIS CHAPTER:

✓ **Working with Methods and Encapsulation**

- ▪ Create methods with arguments and return values; including overloaded methods

- ▪ Apply the static keyword to methods and fields

- ▪ Create and overload constructors; include impact on default constructors

- ▪ Apply access modifiers

- ▪ Apply encapsulation principles to a class

- ▪ Determine the effect upon object references and primitive values when they are passed into methods that change the values

✓ **Working with Selected classes from the Java API**

- ▪ Write a simple Lambda expression that consumes a Lambda Predicate expression

In previous chapters, we've used methods and constructors without examining them in detail. In this chapter, we'll explore methods and constructors in depth and cover everything you need to know about them for the OCA exam. (Well, almost—Chapter 5, "Class Design," will explain the effects of inheritance on both methods and constructors.) This chapter discusses instance variables, the `final` keyword, access modifiers, and initialization. You'll also learn how to write a simple lambda expression.

Designing Methods

Every interesting Java program we've seen has had a `main()` method. We can write other methods, too. For example, we can write a basic method to take a nap, as shown in Figure 4.1.

FIGURE 4.1 Method signature

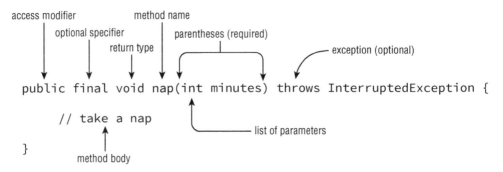

This is called a *method declaration*, which specifies all the information needed to call the method. There are a lot of parts, and we'll cover each one in more detail. Table 4.1 is a brief reference to the elements of a method declaration. Don't worry if it seems like a lot of information—by the time you finish this chapter, it will all fit together.

TABLE 4.1 Parts of a method declaration

Element	Value in nap() example	Required?
Access modifier	`public`	No
Optional specifier	`final`	No

Element	Value in nap() example	Required?
Return type	`void`	Yes
Method name	`nap`	Yes
Parameter list	`(int minutes)`	Yes, but can be empty parentheses
Optional exception list	`throws InterruptedException`	No

Method body	`{`
	`  // take a nap`
	`}`
		Yes, but can be empty braces

To call this method, just type its name, followed by a single `int` value in parentheses:

`nap(10);`

Let's start by taking a look at each of these parts of a basic method.

Access Modifiers

Java offers four choices of access modifier:

public   The method can be called from any class.

private   The method can only be called from within the same class.

protected   The method can only be called from classes in the same package or subclasses. You'll learn about subclasses in Chapter 5.

Default (Package Private) Access   The method can only be called from classes in the same package. This one is tricky because there is no keyword for default access. You simply omit the access modifier.

> There's a `default` keyword in Java. You saw it in the `switch` statement in Chapter 2, "Operators and Statements," and you'll see it again in the next chapter when we discuss interfaces. It's not used for access control.

We'll explore the impact of the various access modifiers later in this chapter. For now, just master identifying valid syntax of methods. The exam creators like to trick you by putting method elements in the wrong order or using incorrect values.

We'll have practice examples as we go through each of the method elements in this section. Make sure you understand why each of these is a valid or invalid method declaration. Pay attention to the access modifiers as you figure out what is wrong with the ones that don't compile:

```
public void walk1() {}
default void walk2() {} // DOES NOT COMPILE
```

```
void public walk3() {} // DOES NOT COMPILE
void walk4() {}
```

walk1() is a valid method declaration with public access. walk4() is a valid method declaration with default access. walk2() doesn't compile because default is not a valid access modifier. walk3() doesn't compile because the access modifier is specified after the return type.

Optional Specifiers

There are a number of optional specifiers, but most of them aren't on the exam. Optional specifiers come from the following list. Unlike with access modifiers, you can have multiple specifiers in the same method (although not all combinations are legal). When this happens, you can specify them in any order. And since it is optional, you are allowed to not have any of them at all. This means you can have zero or more specifiers in a method declaration.

static   Covered later in this chapter. Used for class methods.

abstract   Covered in Chapter 5. Used when not providing a method body.

final   Covered in Chapter 5. Used when a method is not allowed to be overridden by a subclass.

synchronized   On the OCP but not the OCA exam.

native   Not on the OCA or OCP exam. Used when interacting with code written in another language such as C++.

strictfp   Not on the OCA or OCP exam. Used for making floating-point calculations portable.

Again, just focus on syntax for now. Do you see why these compile or don't compile?

```
public void walk1() {}
public final void walk2() {}
public static final void walk3() {}
public final static void walk4() {}
public modifier void walk5() {} // DOES NOT COMPILE
public void final walk6() {} // DOES NOT COMPILE
final public void walk7() {}
```

walk1() is a valid method declaration with no optional specifier. This is okay; it is optional, after all. walk2() is a valid method declaration, with final as the optional specifier. walk3() and walk4() are valid method declarations with both final and static as optional specifiers. The order of these two keywords doesn't matter. walk5() doesn't compile because *modifier* is not a valid optional specifier. walk6() doesn't compile because the optional specifier is after the return type.

walk7() does compile. Java allows the optional specifiers to appear before the access modifier. This is a weird case and not one you need to know for the exam. We are mentioning it so you don't get confused when practicing.

Return Type

The next item in a method declaration is the return type. The return type might be an actual Java type such as String or int. If there is no return type, the void keyword is used. This special return type comes from the English language: *void* means without contents. In Java, we have no type there.

Remember that a method must have a return type. If no value is returned, the return type is void. You cannot omit the return type.

When checking return types, you also have to look inside the method body. Methods with a return type other than void are required to have a return statement inside the method body. This return statement must include the primitive or object to be returned. Methods that have a return type of void are permitted to have a return statement with no value returned or omit the return statement entirely.

Ready for some examples? Can you explain why these methods compile or don't?

```
public void walk1() { }
public void walk2() { return; }
public String walk3() { return ""; }
public String walk4() { }  // DOES NOT COMPILE
public walk5() { }  // DOES NOT COMPILE
String walk6(int a) { if (a == 4) return ""; }  // DOES NOT COMPILE
```

Since the return type of walk1() is void, the return statement is optional. walk2() shows the optional return statement that correctly doesn't return anything. walk3() is a valid method with a String return type and a return statement that returns a String. walk4() doesn't compile because the return statement is missing. walk5() doesn't compile because the return type is missing.

walk6() is a little tricky. There is a return statement, but it doesn't always get run. If a is 6, the return statement doesn't get executed. Since the String always needs to be returned, the compiler complains.

When returning a value, it needs to be assignable to the return type. Imagine there is a local variable of that type to which it is assigned before being returned. Can you think of how to add a line of code with a local variable in these two methods?

```
int integer() {
  return 9;
}
int longMethod(){
  return 9L; // DOES NOT COMPILE
}
```

It is a fairly mechanical exercise. You just add a line with a local variable. The type of the local variable matches the return type of the method. Then you return that local variable instead of the value directly:

```
int integerExpanded() {
  int temp = 9;
  return temp;
}
int longExpanded() {
  int temp = 9L; // DOES NOT COMPILE
  return temp;
}
```

This shows more clearly why you can't return a long primitive in a method that returns an int. You can't stuff that long into an int variable, so you can't return it directly either.

Method Name

Method names follow the same rules as we practiced with variable names in Chapter 1, "Java Building Blocks." To review, an identifier may only contain letters, numbers, $, or _. Also, the first character is not allowed to be a number, and reserved words are not allowed. By convention, methods begin with a lowercase letter but are not required to. Since this is a review of Chapter 1, we can jump right into practicing with some examples:

```
public void walk1() { }
public void 2walk() { } // DOES NOT COMPILE
public walk3 void() { } // DOES NOT COMPILE
public void Walk_$() { }
public void() { } // DOES NOT COMPILE
```

walk1() is a valid method declaration with a traditional name. 2walk() doesn't compile because identifiers are not allowed to begin with numbers. walk3() doesn't compile because the method name is before the return type. Walk_$() is a valid method declaration. While it certainly isn't good practice to start a method name with a capital letter and end with punctuation, it is legal. The final line of code doesn't compile because the method name is missing.

Parameter List

Although the parameter list is required, it doesn't have to contain any parameters. This means you can just have an empty pair of parentheses after the method name, such as void nap(){}. If you do have multiple parameters, you separate them with a comma. There are a couple more rules for the parameter list that you'll see when we cover varargs shortly. For now, let's practice looking at method signatures with "regular" parameters:

```java
public void walk1() { }
public void walk2 { } // DOES NOT COMPILE
public void walk3(int a) { }
public void walk4(int a; int b) { }  // DOES NOT COMPILE
public void walk5(int a, int b) { }
```

walk1() is a valid method declaration without any parameters. walk2() doesn't compile because it is missing the parentheses around the parameter list. walk3() is a valid method declaration with one parameter. walk4() doesn't compile because the parameters are separated by a semicolon rather than a comma. Semicolons are for separating statements, not parameter lists. walk5() is a valid method declaration with two parameters.

Optional Exception List

In Java, code can indicate that something went wrong by throwing an exception. We'll cover this in Chapter 6, "Exceptions." For now, you just need to know that it is optional and where in the method signature it goes if present. In the example, InterruptedException is a type of Exception. You can list as many types of exceptions as you want in this clause separated by commas. For example:

```java
public void zeroExceptions() { }
public void oneException() throws IllegalArgumentException { }
public void twoExceptions() throws
  IllegalArgumentException, InterruptedException { }
```

You might be wondering what methods do with these exceptions. The calling method can throw the same exceptions or handle them. You'll learn more about this in Chapter 6.

Method Body

The final part of a method declaration is the method body (except for abstract methods and interfaces, but you don't need to know about either of those until next chapter). A method body is simply a code block. It has braces that contain zero or more Java statements. We've spent several chapters looking at Java statements by now, so you should find it easy to figure out why these compile or don't:

```
public void walk1() { }
public void walk2(); // DOES NOT COMPILE
public void walk3(int a) { int name = 5; }
```

Walk1() is a valid method declaration with an empty method body. walk2() doesn't compile because it is missing the braces around the empty method body. walk3() is a valid method declaration with one statement in the method body.

You've made it through the basics of identifying correct and incorrect method declarations. Now we can delve into more detail.

Working with Varargs

As you saw in the previous chapter, a method may use a vararg parameter (variable argument) as if it is an array. It is a little different than an array, though. A vararg parameter must be the last element in a method's parameter list. This implies you are only allowed to have one vararg parameter per method.

Can you identify why each of these does or doesn't compile? (Yes, there is a lot of practice in this chapter. You have to be really good at identifying valid and invalid methods for the exam.)

```
public void walk1(int... nums) { }
public void walk2(int start, int... nums) { }
public void walk3(int... nums, int start) { } // DOES NOT COMPILE
public void walk4(int... start, int... nums) { } // DOES NOT COMPILE
```

walk1() is a valid method declaration with one vararg parameter. walk2() is a valid method declaration with one int parameter and one vararg parameter. walk3() and walk4() do not compile because they have a vararg parameter in a position that is not the last one.

When calling a method with a vararg parameter, you have a choice. You can pass in an array, or you can list the elements of the array and let Java create it for you. You can even omit the vararg values in the method call and Java will create an array of length zero for you.

Finally! We get to do something other than identify whether method declarations are valid. Instead we get to look at method calls. Can you figure out why each method call outputs what it does?

```
15: public static void walk(int start, int... nums) {
16:   System.out.println(nums.length);
17: }
18: public static void main(String[] args) {
19:   walk(1);                    // 0
20:   walk(1, 2);                 // 1
```

```
21:  walk(1, 2, 3);              // 2
22:  walk(1, new int[] {4, 5});   // 2
23: }
```

Line 19 passes 1 as start but nothing else. This means Java creates an array of length 0 for nums. Line 20 passes 1 as start and one more value. Java converts this one value to an array of length 1. Line 21 passes 1 as start and two more values. Java converts these two values to an array of length 2. Line 22 passes 1 as start and an array of length 2 directly as nums.

You've seen that Java will create an empty array if no parameters are passed for a vararg. However, it is still possible to pass null explicitly:

```
walk(1, null);     // throws a NullPointerException
```

Since null isn't an int, Java treats it as an array reference that happens to be null. It just passes on the null array object to walk. Then the walk() method throws an exception because it tries to determine the length of null.

Accessing a vararg parameter is also just like accessing an array. It uses array indexing. For example:

```
16: public static void run(int... nums) {
17:    System.out.println(nums[1]);
18: }
19: public static void main(String[] args) {
20:    run(11, 22);     // 22
21: }
```

Line 20 calls a vararg method with two parameters. When the method gets called, it sees an array of size 2. Since indexes are 0 based, 22 is printed.

Applying Access Modifiers

You already saw that there are four access modifiers: public, private, protected, and default access. We are going to discuss them in order from most restrictive to least restrictive:

- private: Only accessible within the same class
- default (package private) access: private and other classes in the same package
- protected: default access and child classes
- public: protected and classes in the other packages

Private Access

Private access is easy. Only code in the same class can call private methods or access private fields.

Before we start, take a look at Figure 4.2. It shows the classes we'll use to explore private and default access. The big boxes are the names of the packages. The smaller boxes inside them are the classes in each package. You can refer back to this figure if you want to quickly see how the classes relate.

FIGURE 4.2 Classes used to show private and default access

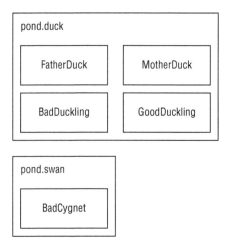

This is perfectly legal code because everything is one class:

```
1: package pond.duck;
2: public class FatherDuck {
3:   private String noise = "quack";
4:   private void quack() {
5:     System.out.println(noise);      // private access is ok
6:   }
7:   private void makeNoise() {
8:     quack();                        // private access is ok
9:   } }
```

So far, so good. FatherDuck makes a call to private method quack() on line 8 and uses private instance variable *noise* on line 5.

Now we add another class:

```
1: package pond.duck;
2: public class BadDuckling {
3:   public void makeNoise() {
4:     FatherDuck duck = new FatherDuck();
5:     duck.quack();                          // DOES NOT COMPILE
6:     System.out.println(duck.noise);        // DOES NOT COMPILE
7:   } }
```

BadDuckling is trying to access members it has no business touching. On line 5, it tries to access a private method in another class. On line 6, it tries to access a private instance variable in another class. Both generate compiler errors. Bad duckling!

Our bad duckling is only a few days old and doesn't know better yet. Luckily, you know that accessing private members of other classes is not allowed and you need to use a different type of access.

Default (Package Private) Access

Luckily, MotherDuck is more accommodating about what her ducklings can do. She allows classes in the same package to access her members. When there is no access modifier, Java uses the default, which is package private access. This means that the member is "private" to classes in the same package. In other words, only classes in the package may access it.

```
package pond.duck;

public class MotherDuck {
  String noise = "quack";
  void quack() {
    System.out.println(noise);      // default access is ok
  }
  private void makeNoise() {
    quack();                        // default access is ok
  } }
```

MotherDuck can call quack() and refer to *noise*. After all, members in the same class are certainly in the same package. The big difference is MotherDuck lets other classes in the same package access members (due to being package private) whereas FatherDuck doesn't (due to being private). GoodDuckling has a much better experience than BadDuckling:

```
package pond.duck;

public class GoodDuckling {
  public void makeNoise() {
    MotherDuck duck = new MotherDuck();
    duck.quack();                       // default access
    System.out.println(duck.noise);     // default access
  } }
```

GoodDuckling succeeds in learning to quack() and make *noise* by copying its mother. Notice that all the classes we've covered so far are in the same package pond.duck. This allows default (package private) access to work.

In this same pond, a swan just gave birth to a baby swan. A baby swan is called a cygnet. The cygnet sees the ducklings learning to quack and decides to learn from MotherDuck as well.

```
package pond.swan;
import pond.duck.MotherDuck;          // import another package
```

```
public class BadCygnet {
  public void makeNoise() {
    MotherDuck duck = new MotherDuck();
    duck.quack();                          // DOES NOT COMPILE
    System.out.println(duck.noise);        // DOES NOT COMPILE
  } }
```

Oh no! MotherDuck only allows lessons to other ducks by restricting access to the pond duck package. Poor little BadCygnet is in the pond.swan package and the code doesn't compile.

Remember that when there is no access modifier, only classes in the same package can access it.

Protected Access

Protected access allows everything that default (package private) access allows and more. The protected access modifier adds the ability to access members of a parent class. We'll cover creating subclasses in depth in Chapter 5. For now, we'll cover the simplest possible use of a child class.

Figure 4.3 shows the many classes we'll create in this section. There are a number of classes and packages, so don't worry about keeping them all in your head. Just check back with this figure as you go.

FIGURE 4.3   Classes used to show protected access

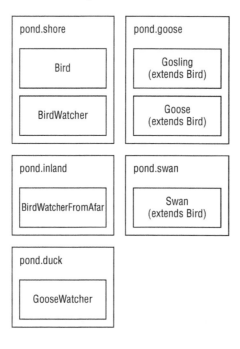

First, we create a `Bird` class and give protected access to its members:

```
package pond.shore;
public class Bird {
  protected String text = "floating";          // protected access
  protected void floatInWater() {               // protected access
    System.out.println(text);
} }
```

Next we create a subclass:

```
package pond.goose;
import pond.shore.Bird;                  // in a different package
public class Gosling extends Bird {      // extends means create subclass
  public void swim() {
    floatInWater();                      // calling protected member
    System.out.println(text);            // calling protected member
} }
```

This is a very simple subclass. It extends the `Bird` class. Extending means creating a subclass that has access to any protected or public members of the parent class. Running this code prints floating twice: once from calling `floatInWater()` and once from the print statement in `swim()`. Since `Gosling` is a subclass of `Bird`, it can access these members even though it is in a different package.

Remember that protected also gives us access to everything that default access does. This means that a class in the same package as `Bird` can access its protected members.

```
package pond.shore;                      // same package as Bird
public class BirdWatcher {
  public void watchBird() {
    Bird bird = new Bird();
    bird.floatInWater();                 // calling protected member
    System.out.println(bird.text);       // calling protected member
} }
```

Since `Bird` and `BirdWatcher` are in the same package, `BirdWatcher` can access members of the *bird* variable. The definition of protected allows access to subclasses and classes in the same package. This example uses the same package part of that definition.

Now let's try the same thing from a different package:

```
package pond.inland;
import pond.shore.Bird;                  // different package than Bird
public class BirdWatcherFromAfar {
  public void watchBird() {
    Bird bird = new Bird();
    bird.floatInWater();                 // DOES NOT COMPILE
```

```
    System.out.println(bird.text);      // DOES NOT COMPILE
  } }
```

BirdWatcherFromAfar is not in the same package as Bird and it doesn't inherit from Bird. This means that it is not allowed to access protected members of Bird.

Got that? Subclasses and classes in the same package are the only ones allowed to access protected members.

There is one gotcha for protected access. Consider this class:

```
1:  package pond.swan;
2:  import pond.shore.Bird;      // in different package than Bird
3:  public class Swan extends Bird {      // but subclass of bird
4:     public void swim() {
5:       floatInWater();                  // package access to superclass
6:       System.out.println(text);        // package access to superclass
7:     }
8:     public void helpOtherSwanSwim() {
9:       Swan other = new Swan();
10:      other.floatInWater();            // package access to superclass
11:      System.out.println(other.text);// package access to superclass
12:    }
13:    public void helpOtherBirdSwim() {
14:      Bird other = new Bird();
15:      other.floatInWater();                  // DOES NOT COMPILE
16:      System.out.println(other.text);        // DOES NOT COMPILE
17:    }
18: }
```

Take a deep breath. This is interesting. Swan is not in the same package as Bird, but does extend it—which implies it has access to the protected members of Bird since it is a subclass. And it does. Lines 5 and 6 refer to protected members via inheriting them.

Lines 10 and 11 also successfully use protected members of Bird. This is allowed because these lines refer to a Swan object. Swan inherits from Bird so this is okay. It is sort of a two-phase check. The Swan class is allowed to use protected members of Bird and we are referring to a Swan object. Granted, it is a Swan object created on line 9 rather than an inherited one, but it is still a Swan object.

Lines 15 and 16 do *not* compile. Wait a minute. They are almost exactly the same as lines 10 and 11! There's one key difference. This time a Bird reference is used. It is created on line 14. Bird is in a different package, and this code isn't inheriting from Bird, so it doesn't get to use protected members. Say what now? We just got through saying repeatedly that Swan inherits from Bird. And it does. However, the variable reference isn't a Swan. The code just happens to be in the Swan class.

It's okay to be confused. This is arguably one of the most confusing points on the exam. Looking at it a different way, the protected rules apply under two scenarios:

- A member is used without referring to a variable. This is the case on lines 5 and 6. In this case, we are taking advantage of inheritance and protected access is allowed.

- A member is used through a variable. This is the case on lines 10, 11, 15, and 16. In this case, the rules for the reference type of the variable are what matter. If it is a subclass, protected access is allowed. This works for references to the same class or a subclass.

We're going to try this again to make sure you understand what is going on. Can you figure out why these examples don't compile?

```
package pond.goose;
import pond.shore.Bird;
public class Goose extends Bird {
  public void helpGooseSwim() {
    Goose other = new Goose();
    other.floatInWater();
    System.out.println(other.text);
  }
  public void helpOtherGooseSwim() {
    Bird other = new Goose();
    other.floatInWater(); // DOES NOT COMPILE
    System.out.println(other.text); // DOES NOT COMPILE
  } }
```

The first method is fine. In fact, it is equivalent to the Swan example. Goose extends Bird. Since we are in the Goose subclass and referring to a Goose reference, it can access protected members. The second method is a problem. Although the object happens to be a Goose, it is stored in a Bird reference. We are not allowed to refer to members of the Bird class since we are not in the same package and Bird is not a subclass of Goose.

What about this one?

```
package pond.duck;
import pond.goose.Goose;
public class GooseWatcher {
  public void watch() {
    Goose goose = new Goose();
    goose.floatInWater();     // DOES NOT COMPILE
  } }
```

This code doesn't compile because we are not in the Goose class. The floatInWater() method is declared in Bird. GooseWatcher is not in the same package as Bird, nor does it extend Bird. Goose extends Bird. That only lets Goose refer to floatInWater() and not callers of Goose.

If this is still puzzling, try it out. Type in the code and try to make it compile. Then reread this section. Don't worry—it wasn't obvious to the authors the first time either!

Public Access

Protected access was a tough concept. Luckily, the last type of access modifier is easy: public means anyone can access the member from anywhere.

```
package pond.duck;
public class DuckTeacher {
  public String name = "helpful";       // public access
  public void swim() {                   // public access
    System.out.println("swim");
} }
```

DuckTeacher allows access to any class that wants it. Now we can try it out:

```
package pond.goose;
import pond.duck.DuckTeacher;
public class LostDuckling {
  public void swim() {
    DuckTeacher teacher = new DuckTeacher();
    teacher.swim();                                      // allowed
    System.out.println("Thanks" + teacher.name);         // allowed
} }
```

LostDuckling is able to refer to swim() and name on DuckTeacher because they are public. The story has a happy ending. LostDuckling has learned to swim and can find its parents—all because DuckTeacher made them public.

To review access modifiers, make sure you know why everything in Table 4.2 is true. Remember that a member is a method or field.

TABLE 4.2 Access modifiers

Can access	If that member is private?	If that member has default (package private) access?	If that member is protected?	If that member is public?
Member in the same class	Yes	Yes	Yes	Yes
Member in another class in same package	No	Yes	Yes	Yes

Can access	If that member is private?	If that member has default (package private) access?	If that member is protected?	If that member is public?
Member in a subclass in a different package	No	No	Yes	Yes
Method/field in a non-subclass class in a different package	No	No	No	Yes

Designing Static Methods and Fields

Except for the main() method, we've been looking at instance methods. Static methods don't require an instance of the class. They are shared among all users of the class. You can think of statics as being a member of the single class object that exist independently of any instances of that class.

Does Each Class Have Its Own Copy of the Code?

Each class has a copy of the instance variables. There is only one copy of the code for the instance methods. Each instance of the class can call it as many times as it would like. However, each call of an instance method (or any method) gets space on the stack for method parameters and local variables.

The same thing happens for static methods. There is one copy of the code. Parameters and local variables go on the stack.

Just remember that only data gets its "own copy." There is no need to duplicate copies of the code itself.

We have seen one static method since Chapter 1. The main() method is a static method. That means you can call it by the classname.

```
public class Koala {
  public static int count = 0;              // static variable
  public static void main(String[] args) {     // static method
    System.out.println(count);
  }
}
```

We said that the JVM basically calls Koala.main() to get the program started. You can do this too. We can have a KoalaTester that does nothing but call the main() method.

```
public class KoalaTester {
  public static void main(String[] args) {
    Koala.main(new String[0]);              // call static method
  }
}
```

Quite a complicated way to print 0, isn't it? When we run KoalaTester, it makes a call to the main() method of Koala, which prints the value of *count*. The purpose of all these examples is to show that main() can be called just like any other static method.

In addition to main() methods, static methods have two main purposes:

- For utility or helper methods that don't require any object state. Since there is no need to access instance variables, having static methods eliminates the need for the caller to instantiate the object just to call the method.

- For state that is shared by all instances of a class, like a counter. All instances must share the same state. Methods that merely use that state should be static as well.

Let's look at some examples covering other static concepts.

Calling a Static Variable or Method

Usually, accessing a static member is easy. You just put the classname before the method or variable and you are done. For example:

```
System.out.println(Koala.count);
Koala.main(new String[0]);
```

Both of these are nice and easy. There is one rule that is trickier. You can use an instance of the object to call a static method. The compiler checks for the type of the reference and uses that instead of the object—which is sneaky of Java. This code is perfectly legal:

```
5: Koala k = new Koala();
6: System.out.println(k.count);          // k is a Koala
7: k = null;
8: System.out.println(k.count);          // k is still a Koala
```

Believe it or not, this code outputs 0 twice. Line 6 sees that k is a Koala and count is a static variable, so it reads that static variable. Line 8 does the same thing. Java doesn't care that k happens to be null. Since we are looking for a static, it doesn't matter.

Remember to look at the reference type for a variable when you see a static method or variable. The exam creators will try to trick you into thinking a NullPointerException is thrown because the variable happens to be null. Don't be fooled!

One more time because this is really important: what does the following output?

```
Koala.count = 4;
Koala koala1 = new Koala();
Koala koala2 = new Koala();
koala1.count = 6;
koala2.count = 5;
System.out.println(Koala.count);
```

Hopefully, you answered 5. There is only one *count* variable since it is static. It is set to 4, then 6, and finally winds up as 5. All the Koala variables are just distractions.

Static vs. Instance

There's another way the exam creators will try to trick you regarding static and instance members. (Remember that "member" means field or method.) A static member cannot call an instance member. This shouldn't be a surprise since static doesn't require any instances of the class to be around.

The following is a common mistake for rookie programmers to make:

```
public class Static {
  private String name = "Static class";
  public static void first() {  }
  public static void second() {  }
  public void third() {  System.out.println(name); }
  public static void main(String args[]) {
    first();
    second();
    third();          // DOES NOT COMPILE
} }
```

The compiler will give you an error about making a static reference to a nonstatic method. If we fix this by adding static to third(), we create a new problem. Can you figure out what it is?

All this does is move the problem. Now, third() is referring to nonstatic name. Adding static to name as well would solve the problem. Another solution would have been to call third as an instance method—for example, new Static().third();.

The exam creators like this topic. A static method or instance method can call a static method because static methods don't require an object to use. Only an instance method can call another instance method on the same class without using a reference variable, because instance methods do require an object. Similar logic applies for the instance and static variables. Make sure you understand Table 4.3 before continuing.

TABLE 4.3   Static vs. instance calls

Type	Calling	Legal?	How?
Static method	Another static method or variable	Yes	Using the classname
Static method	An instance method or variable	No	Not without instantiating the object
Instance method	A static method or variable	Yes	Using the classname or a reference variable
Instance method	Another instance method or variable	Yes	Using a reference variable

Let's try one more example so you have more practice at recognizing this scenario. Do you understand why the following lines fail to compile?

```
1:  public class Gorilla {
2:     public static int count;
3:     public static void addGorilla() { count++; }
4:     public void babyGorilla() { count++; }
5:     public void announceBabies() {
6:        addGorilla();
7:        babyGorilla();
8:     }
9:     public static void announceBabiesToEveryone() {
10:       addGorilla();
11:       babyGorilla();      // DOES NOT COMPILE
12:    }
13:    public int total;
14:    public static double average = total / count;  // DOES NOT COMPILE
15: }
```

Lines 3 and 4 are fine because both static and instance methods can refer to a static variable. Lines 5–8 are fine because an instance method can call a static method. Line 11 doesn't compile because a static method cannot call an instance method. Similarly, line 14 doesn't compile because a static variable is trying to use an instance variable.

A common use for static variables is counting the number of instances:

```
public class Counter {
   private static int count;
   public Counter() { count++; }
```

```
  public static void main(String[] args) {
    Counter c1 = new Counter();
    Counter c2 = new Counter();
    Counter c3 = new Counter();
    System.out.println(count);            // 3
  }
}
```

Each time the constructor gets called, it increments *count* by 1. This example relies on the fact that static (and instance) variables are automatically initialized to the default value for that type, which is 0 for int. See Chapter 1 to review the default values.

Also notice that we didn't write Counter . count. We could have. It isn't necessary because we are already in that class so the compiler can infer it.

Static Variables

Some static variables are meant to change as the program runs. Counters are a common example of this. We want the count to increase over time. Just as with instance variables, you can initialize a static variable on the line it is declared:

```
public class Initializers {
  private static int counter = 0;          // initialization
}
```

Other static variables are meant to never change during the program. This type of variable is known as a *constant*. It uses the final modifier to ensure the variable never changes. static final constants use a different naming convention than other variables. They use all uppercase letters with underscores between "words." For example:

```
public class Initializers {
  private static final int NUM_BUCKETS = 45;
  public static void main(String[] args) {
    NUM_BUCKETS = 5;  // DOES NOT COMPILE
  } }
```

The compiler will make sure that you do not accidentally try to update a final variable. This can get interesting. Do you think the following compiles?

```
private static final ArrayList<String> values = new ArrayList<>();
public static void main(String[] args) {
  values.add("changed");
}
```

It actually does compile. *values* is a reference variable. We are allowed to call methods on reference variables. All the compiler can do is check that we don't try to reassign the final *values* to point to a different object.

Static Initialization

In Chapter 1, we covered instance initializers that looked like unnamed methods. Just code inside braces. Static initializers look similar. They add the static keyword to specify they should be run when the class is first used. For example:

```
private static final int NUM_SECONDS_PER_HOUR;
static {
  int numSecondsPerMinute = 60;
  int numMinutesPerHour = 60;
  NUM_SECONDS_PER_HOUR = numSecondsPerMinute * numMinutesPerHour;
}
```

The static initializer runs when the class is first used. The statements in it run and assign any static variables as needed. There is something interesting about this example. We just got through saying that final variables aren't allowed to be reassigned. The key here is that the static initializer is the first assignment. And since it occurs up front, it is okay.

Let's try another example to make sure you understand the distinction:

```
14: private static int one;
15: private static final int two;
16: private static final int three = 3;
17: private static final int four;     // DOES NOT COMPILE
18: static {
19:   one = 1;
20:   two = 2;
21:   three = 3;     // DOES NOT COMPILE
22:   two = 4;       // DOES NOT COMPILE
23: }
```

Line 14 declares a static variable that is not final. It can be assigned as many times as we like. Line 15 declares a final variable without initializing it. This means we can initialize it exactly once in a static block. Line 22 doesn't compile because this is the second attempt. Line 16 declares a final variable and initializes it at the same time. We are not allowed to assign it again, so line 21 doesn't compile. Line 17 declares a final variable that never gets initialized. The compiler gives a compiler error because it knows that the static blocks are the only place the variable could possibly get initialized. Since the programmer forgot, this is clearly an error.

Try to Avoid Static and Instance Initializers

Using static and instance initializers can make your code much harder to read. Everything that could be done in an instance initializer could be done in a constructor instead. The constructor approach is easier to read.

There is a common case to use a static initializer: when you need to initialize a static field and the code to do so requires more than one line. This often occurs when you want to initialize a collection like an `ArrayList`. When you do need to use a static initializer, put all the static initialization in the same block. That way, the order is obvious.

Static Imports

Back in Chapter 1, you saw that we could import a specific class or all the classes in a package:

```
import java.util.ArrayList;
import java.util.*;
```

We could use this technique to import:

```
import java.util.List;
import java.util.Arrays;
public class Imports {
  public static void main(String[] args) {
    List<String> list = Arrays.asList("one", "two");
  }
}
```

Imports are convenient because you don't need to specify where each class comes from each time you use it. There is another type of import called a static import. Regular imports are for importing classes. Static imports are for importing static members of classes. Just like regular imports, you can use a wildcard or import a specific member. The idea is that you shouldn't have to specify where each static method or variable comes from each time you use it. An example of when static interfaces shine are when you are referring to a lot of constants in another class.

In a large program, static imports can be overused. When importing from too many places, it can be hard to remember where each static member comes from.

The previous method has one static method call: `Arrays.asList`. Rewriting the code to use a static import yields the following:

```
import java.util.List;
import static java.util.Arrays.asList;          // static import
public class StaticImports {
  public static void main(String[] args) {
    List<String> list = asList("one", "two");    // no Arrays.
  } }
```

In this example, we are specifically importing the asList method. This means that any time we refer to asList in the class, it will call Arrays.asList().

An interesting case is what would happen if we created an asList method in our StaticImports class. Java would give it preference over the imported one and the method we coded would be used.

The exam will try to trick you with misusing static imports. This example shows almost everything you can do wrong. Can you figure out what is wrong with each one?

```
1: import static java.util.Arrays; // DOES NOT COMPILE
2: import static java.util.Arrays.asList;
3: static import java.util.Arrays.*;  // DOES NOT COMPILE
4: public class BadStaticImports {
5:    public static void main(String[] args) {
6:     Arrays.asList("one");  // DOES NOT COMPILE
7:  } }
```

Line 1 tries to use a static import to import a class. Remember that static imports are only for importing static members. Regular imports are for importing a class. Line 3 tries to see if you are paying attention to the order of keywords. The syntax is import static and not vice versa. Line 6 is sneaky. We imported the asList method on line 2. However, we did not import the Arrays class anywhere. This makes it okay to write asList("one"); but not Arrays.asList("one");.

There's only one more scenario with static imports. In Chapter 1, you learned that importing two classes with the same name gives a compiler error. This is true of static imports as well. The compiler will complain if you try to explicitly do a static import of two methods with the same name or two static variables with the same name. For example:

```
import static statics.A.TYPE;
import static statics.B.TYPE;     // DOES NOT COMPILE
```

Luckily when this happens, we can just refer to the static members via their classname in the code instead of trying to use a static import.

Passing Data Among Methods

Java is a "pass-by-value" language. This means that a copy of the variable is made and the method receives that copy. Assignments made in the method do not affect the caller. Let's look at an example:

```
2: public static void main(String[] args) {
3:    int num = 4;
4:    newNumber(num);
```

```
5:    System.out.println(num);      // 4
6: }
7: public static void newNumber(int num) {
8:    num = 8;
9: }
```

On line 3, num is assigned the value of 4. On line 4, we call a method. On line 8, the num parameter in the method gets set to 8. Although this parameter has the same name as the variable on line 3, this is a coincidence. The name could be anything. The exam will often use the same name to try to confuse you. The variable on line 3 never changes because no assignments are made to it.

Now that you've seen primitives, let's try an example with a reference type. What do you think is output by the following code?

```
public static void main(String[] args) {
  String name = "Webby";
  speak(name);
  System.out.println(name);
}
public static void speak(String name) {
  name = "Sparky";
}
```

The correct answer is Webby. Just as in the primitive example, the variable assignment is only to the method parameter and doesn't affect the caller.

Notice how we keep talking about variable assignments. This is because we can call methods on the parameters. As an example, we have code that calls a method on the StringBuilder passed into the method:

```
public static void main(String[] args) {
  StringBuilder name = new StringBuilder();
  speak(name);
  System.out.println(name); // Webby
}
public static void speak(StringBuilder s) {
  s.append("Webby");
}
```

In this case, the output is Webby because the method merely calls a method on the parameter. It doesn't reassign name to a different object. In Figure 4.4, you can see how pass-by-value is still used. s is a copy of the variable name. Both point to the same StringBuilder, which means that changes made to the StringBuilder are available to both references.

FIGURE 4.4   Copying a reference with pass-by-value

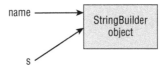

Real World Scenario

Pass-by-Value vs. Pass-by-Reference

Different languages handle parameters in different ways. Pass-by-value is used by many languages, including Java. In this example, the swap method does not change the original values. It only changes *a* and *b* within the method.

```
public static void main(String[] args) {
    int original1 = 1;
    int original2 = 2;
    swap(original1, original2);
    System.out.println(original1);      // 1
    System.out.println(original2);      // 2
}
public static void swap(int a, int b) {
    int temp = a;
    a = b;
    b = temp;
}
```

The other approach is pass-by-reference. It is used by default in a few languages, such as Perl. We aren't going to show you Perl code here because you are studying for the Java exam and we don't want to confuse you. The following example is in a made-up language that shows pass-by-reference:

```
original1 = 1;
original2 = 2;
swapByReference(original1, original2);
print(original1);       // 2 (not in Java)
print(original2);       // 1 (not in Java)

swapByReference(a, b) {
  temp = a;
  a = b;
  b = temp;
}
```

See the difference? In our made-up language, the caller is affected by variable assignments made in the method.

To review, Java uses pass-by-value to get data into a method. Assigning a new primitive or reference to a parameter doesn't change the caller. Calling methods on a reference to an object does affect the caller.

Getting data back from a method is easier. A copy is made of the primitive or reference and returned from the method. Most of the time, this returned value is used. For example, it might be stored in a variable. If the returned value is not used, the result is ignored. Watch for this on the exam. Ignored returned values are tricky.

Let's try an example. Pay attention to the return types.

```
1: public class ReturningValues {
2:   public static void main(String[] args) {
3:     int number = 1;                      // 1
4:     String letters = "abc";              // abc
5:     number(number);                      // 1
6:     letters = letters(letters);          // abcd
7:     System.out.println(number + letters); // 1abcd
8:   }
9:   public static int number(int number) {
10:     number++;
11:     return number;
12:   }
13:   public static String letters(String letters) {
14:     letters += "d";
15:     return letters;
16:   }
17: }
```

This is a tricky one because there is a lot to keep track of. When you see such questions on the exam, write down the values of each variable. Lines 3 and 4 are straightforward assignments. Line 5 calls a method. Line 10 increments the method parameter to 2 but leaves the *number* variable in the main() method as 1. While line 11 returns the value, the caller ignores it. The method call on line 6 doesn't ignore the result so *letters* becomes "abcd". Remember that this is happening because of the returned value and not the method parameter.

Overloading Methods

Now that you are familiar with the rules for declaring methods, it is time to look at creating methods with the same name in the same class. *Method overloading* occurs when there are different method signatures with the same name but different type parameters.

We've been calling overloaded methods for a while. System.out.println and StringBuilder's append methods provide many overloaded versions so you can pass just about anything to them without having to think about it. In both of these examples, the only change was the type of the parameter. Overloading also allows different numbers of parameters.

Everything other than the method name can vary for overloading methods. This means there can be different access modifiers, specifiers (like static), return types, and exception lists.

These are all valid overloaded methods:

```
public void fly(int numMiles) { }
public void fly(short numFeet) { }
public boolean fly() { return false; }
void fly(int numMiles, short numFeet) { }
public void fly(short numFeet, int numMiles) throws Exception { }
```

As you can see, we can overload by changing anything in the parameter list. We can have a different type, more types, or the same types in a different order. Also notice that the access modifier and exception list are irrelevant to overloading.

Now let's look at an example that is not valid overloading:

```
public void fly(int numMiles) { }
public int fly(int numMiles) { }      // DOES NOT COMPILE
```

This method doesn't compile because it only differs from the original by return type. The parameter lists are the same so they are duplicate methods as far as Java is concerned.

What about these two? Why does the second not compile?

```
public void fly(int numMiles) { }
public static void fly(int numMiles) { }      // DOES NOT COMPILE
```

Again, the parameter list is the same. The only difference is that one is an instance method and one is a static method.

Calling overloaded methods is easy. You just write code and Java calls the right one. For example, look at these two methods:

```
public void fly(int numMiles) {
  System.out.println("int");
}
public void fly(short numFeet) {
  System.out.println("short");
}
```

The call fly((short) 1); prints short. It looks for matching types and calls the appropriate method. Of course, it can be more complicated than this.

Now that you know the basics of overloading, let's look at some more complex scenarios that you may encounter on the exam.

Overloading and Varargs

Which method do you think is called if we pass an int[]?

```
public void fly(int[] lengths) { }
public void fly(int... lengths) { }      // DOES NOT COMPILE
```

Trick question! Remember that Java treats varargs as if they were an array. This means that the method signature is the same for both methods. Since we are not allowed to overload methods with the same parameter list, this code doesn't compile. Even though the code doesn't look the same, it compiles to the same parameter list.

Now that we've just gotten through explaining that they are the same, it is time to mention how they are not the same. It shouldn't be a surprise that you can call either method by passing an array:

```
fly(new int[] { 1, 2, 3 });
```

However, you can only call the varargs version with stand-alone parameters:

```
fly(1, 2, 3);
```

Obviously, this means they don't compile *exactly* the same. The parameter list is the same, though, and that is what you need to know with respect to overloading for the exam.

Autoboxing

In the previous chapter, you saw how Java will convert a primitive int to an object Integer to add it to an ArrayList through the wonders of autoboxing. This works for code you write too.

```
public void fly(Integer numMiles) { }
```

This means calling fly(3); will call the previous method as expected. However, what happens if we have both a primitive and an integer version?

```
public void fly(int numMiles) { }
public void fly(Integer numMiles) { }
```

Java will match the int numMiles version. Java tries to use the most specific parameter list it can find. When the primitive int version isn't present, it will autobox. However, when the primitive int version is provided, there is no reason for Java to do the extra work of autoboxing.

Reference Types

Given the rule about Java picking the most specific version of a method that it can, what do you think this code outputs?

```
public class ReferenceTypes {
  public void fly(String s) {
    System.out.print("string ");
  }

  public void fly(Object o) {
    System.out.print("object ");
  }
  public static void main(String[] args) {
    ReferenceTypes r = new ReferenceTypes();
```

```
    r.fly("test");
    r.fly(56);
} }
```

The answer is `"string object "`. The first call is a `String` and finds a direct match. There's no reason to use the `Object` version when there is a nice `String` parameter list just waiting to be called. The second call looks for an `int` parameter list. When it doesn't find one, it autoboxes to `Integer`. Since it still doesn't find a match, it goes to the `Object` one.

Primitives

Primitives work in a way similar to reference variables. Java tries to find the most specific matching overloaded method. What do you think happens here?

```
public class Plane {
  public void fly(int i) {
    System.out.print("int ");
  }
  public void fly(long l) {
    System.out.print("long ");
  }
  public static void main(String[] args) {
    Plane p = new Plane();
    p.fly(123);
    p.fly(123L);
} }
```

The answer is `"int long "`. The first call passes an `int` and sees an exact match. The second call passes a `long` and also sees an exact match. If we comment out the overloaded method with the `int` parameter list, the output becomes `"long long "`. Java has no problem calling a larger primitive. However, it will not do so unless a better match is not found.

Note that Java can only accept wider types. An `int` can be passed to a method taking a `long` parameter. Java will not automatically convert to a narrower type. If you want to pass a `long` to a method taking an `int` parameter, you have to add a cast to explicitly say narrowing is okay.

Putting It All Together

So far, all the rules for when an overloaded method is called should be logical. Java calls the most specific method it can. When some of the types interact, the Java rules focus on backward compatibility. In Java 1.4 and earlier, autoboxing and varargs didn't exist. Although that was a long time ago, old code still needs to work—which means autoboxing and varargs come last when Java looks at overloaded methods. Ready for the official order? Table 4.4 lays it out for you.

TABLE 4.4 Order Java uses to choose the right overloaded method

Rule	Example of what will be chosen for `glide(1,2)`
Exact match by type	`public String glide(int i, int j) {}`
Larger primitive type	`public String glide(long i, long j) {}`
Autoboxed type	`public String glide(Integer i, Integer j) {}`
Varargs	`public String glide(int... nums) {}`

Let's give this a practice run using the rules in Table 4.4. What do you think this outputs?

```java
public class Glider2 {
  public static String glide(String s) {
    return "1";
  }
  public static String glide(String... s) {
    return "2";
  }
  public static String glide(Object o) {
    return "3";
  }
  public static String glide(String s, String t) {
    return "4";
  }
  public static void main(String[] args) {
    System.out.print(glide("a"));
    System.out.print(glide("a", "b"));
    System.out.print(glide("a", "b", "c"));
} }
```

It prints out 142. The first call matches the signature taking a single `String` because that is the most specific match. The second call matches the signature, taking two `String` parameters since that is an exact match. It isn't until the third call that the varargs version is used since there are no better matches.

As accommodating as Java is with trying to find a match, it will only do one conversion:

```java
public class TooManyConversions {
  public static void play(Long l) { }
```

```
public static void play(Long... l) { }
public static void main(String[] args) {
  play(4);     // DOES NOT COMPILE
  play(4L);     // calls the Long version
} }
```

Here we have a problem. Java is happy to convert the int 4 to a long 4 or an Integer 4. It cannot handle converting in two steps to a long and then to a Long. If we had public static void play(Object o) { }, it would match because only one conversion would be necessary: from int to Integer. An Integer is an Object, as you'll see in Chapter 5.

Creating Constructors

As you learned in Chapter 1, a constructor is a special method that matches the name of the class and has no return type. Here's an example:

```
public class Bunny {
  public Bunny() {
    System.out.println("constructor");
  }
}
```

The name of the constructor, Bunny, matches the name of the class, Bunny, and there is no return type, not even void. That makes this a constructor. Can you tell why these two are not valid constructors for the Bunny class?

```
public bunny() { }     // DOES NOT COMPILE
public void Bunny() { }
```

The first one doesn't match the classname because Java is case sensitive. Since it doesn't match, Java knows it can't be a constructor and is supposed to be a regular method. However, it is missing the return type and doesn't compile. The second method is a perfectly good method, but is not a constructor because it has a return type.

Constructors are used when creating a new object. This process is called *instantiation* because it creates a new instance of the class. A constructor is called when we write new followed by the name of the class we want to instantiate. For example:

```
new Bunny()
```

When Java sees the new keyword, it allocates memory for the new object. Java also looks for a constructor and calls it.

A constructor is typically used to initialize instance variables. The this keyword tells Java you want to reference an instance variable. Most of the time, this is optional. The problem is that sometimes there are two variables with the same name. In a constructor, one is a parameter and one is an instance variable. If you don't say otherwise, Java gives you the one with the most granular scope, which is the parameter. Using `this.name` tells Java you want the instance variable.

Here's a common way of writing a constructor:

```
1: public class Bunny {
2:    private String color;
3:    public Bunny(String color) {
4:       this.color = color;
5: } }
```

On line 4, we assign the parameter color to the instance variable *color*. The right side of the assignment refers to the parameter because we don't specify anything special. The left side of the assignment uses `this` to tell Java we want it to use the instance variable.

Now let's look at some examples that aren't common but that you might see on the exam:

```
1: public class Bunny {
2:    private String color;
3:    private int height;
4:    private int length;
5:    public Bunny(int length, int theHeight) {
6:       length = this.length;     // backwards - no good!
7:       height = theHeight;         // fine because a different name
8:       this.color = "white";     // fine, but redundant
9:    }
10: public static void main(String[] args) {
11:    Bunny b = new Bunny(1, 2);
12:    System.out.println(b.length + " " + b.height + " " + b.color);
13: } }
```

Line 6 is incorrect and you should watch for it on the exam. The instance variable *length* starts out with a 0 value. That 0 is assigned to the method parameter *length*. The instance variable stays at 0. Line 7 is more straightforward. The parameter *theHeight* and instance variable *height* have different names. Since there is no naming collision, `this` is not required. Finally, line 8 shows that it is allowed to use `this` even when there is no duplication of variable names.

In this section, we'll look at default constructors, overloading constructors, final fields, and the order of initialization in a class.

Default Constructor

Every class in Java has a constructor whether you code one or not. If you don't include any constructors in the class, Java will create one for you without any parameters.

This Java-created constructor is called the *default constructor*. Sometimes we call it the default no-arguments constructor for clarity. Here's an example:

```
public class Rabbit {
  public static void main(String[] args) {
    Rabbit rabbit = new Rabbit();          // Calls default constructor
  }
}
```

In the Rabbit class, Java sees no constructor was coded and creates one. This default constructor is equivalent to typing this:

```
public Rabbit() {}
```

The default constructor has an empty parameter list and an empty body. It is fine for you to type this in yourself. However, since it doesn't do anything, Java is happy to supply it for you and save you some typing.

We keep saying *generated*. This happens during the compile step. If you look at the file with the .java extension, the constructor will still be missing. It is only in the compiled file with the .class extension that it makes an appearance.

Remember that a default constructor is only supplied if there are no constructors present. Which of these classes do you think has a default constructor?

```
class Rabbit1 {
}
class Rabbit2 {
  public Rabbit2() { }
}
class Rabbit3 {
  public Rabbit3(boolean b) { }
}
class Rabbit4 {
  private Rabbit4() { }
}
```

Only Rabbit1 gets a default no-argument constructor. It doesn't have a constructor coded so Java generates a default no-argument constructor. Rabbit2 and Rabbit3 both have public constructors already. Rabbit4 has a private constructor. Since these three classes have a constructor defined, the default no-argument constructor is not inserted for you.

Let's take a quick look at how to call these constructors:

```
1: public class RabbitsMultiply {
2:   public static void main(String[] args) {
```

```
3:    Rabbit1 r1 = new Rabbit1();
4:    Rabbit2 r2 = new Rabbit2();
5:    Rabbit3 r3 = new Rabbit3(true);
6:    Rabbit4 r4 = new Rabbit4(); // DOES NOT COMPILE
7:  } }
```

Line 3 calls the generated default no-argument constructor. Lines 4 and 5 call the user-provided constructors. Line 6 does not compile. Rabbit4 made the constructor private so that other classes could not call it.

Having a private constructor in a class tells the compiler not to provide a default no-argument constructor. It also prevents other classes from instantiating the class. This is useful when a class only has static methods or the class wants to control all calls to create new instances of itself.

Overloading Constructors

Up to now, you've only seen one constructor per class. You can have multiple constructors in the same class as long as they have different method signatures. When overloading methods, the method name needs to match. With constructors, the name is always the same since it has to be the same as the name of the class. This means constructors must have different parameters in order to be overloaded.

This example shows two constructors:

```
public class Hamster {
  private String color;
  private int weight;
  public Hamster(int weight) {                  // first constructor
    this.weight = weight;
    color = "brown";
  }
  public Hamster(int weight, String color) {    // second constructor
   this.weight = weight;
   this.color = color;
  }
}
```

One of the constructors takes a single int parameter. The other takes an int and a String. These parameter lists are different, so the constructors are successfully overloaded.

There is a problem here, though. There is a bit of duplication. In programming, even a bit of duplication tends to turn into a lot of duplication as we keep adding "just one more thing." What we really want is for the first constructor to call the second constructor with two parameters. You might be tempted to write this:

```
public Hamster(int weight) {
  Hamster(weight, "brown");     // DOES NOT COMPILE
}
```

This will not work. Constructors can be called only by writing new before the name of the constructor. They are not like normal methods that you can just call. What happens if we stick new before the constructor name?

```
public Hamster(int weight) {
  new Hamster(weight, "brown");     // Compiles but does not do what we want
}
```

This attempt does compile. It doesn't do what we want, though. When the constructor with one parameter is called, it creates an object with the default weight and color. It then constructs a different object with the desired weight and color and ignores the new object. That's not what we want. We want weight and color set on the object we are trying to instantiate in the first place.

Java provides a solution: this—yes, the same keyword we used to refer to instance variables. When this is used as if it were a method, Java calls another constructor on the same instance of the class.

```
public Hamster(int weight) {
  this(weight, "brown");
}
```

Success! Now Java calls the constructor that takes two parameters. weight and color get set on this instance.

this() has one special rule you need to know. If you choose to call it, the this() call must be the first noncommented statement in the constructor.

```
3: public Hamster(int weight) {
4:   System.out.println("in constructor");
5:   // ready to call this
6:   this(weight, "brown");     // DOES NOT COMPILE
7: }
```

Even though a print statement on line 4 doesn't change any variables, it is still a Java statement and is not allowed to be inserted before the call to this(). The comment on line 5 is just fine. Comments don't run Java statements and are allowed anywhere.

⊕ Real World Scenario

Constructor Chaining

Overloaded constructors often call each other. One common technique is to have each constructor add one parameter until getting to the constructor that does all the work. This approach is called *constructor chaining*. In this example, all three constructors are chained.

```java
public class Mouse {
   private int numTeeth;
   private int numWhiskers;
   private int weight;

   public Mouse(int weight) {
     this(weight, 16);  // calls constructor with 2 parameters
   }
   public Mouse(int weight, int numTeeth) {
    this(weight, numTeeth, 6);  // calls constructor with 3 parameters
   }
   public Mouse(int weight, int numTeeth, int numWhiskers) {
     this.weight = weight;
     this.numTeeth = numTeeth;
     this.numWhiskers = numWhiskers;
   }
   public void print() {
     System.out.println(weight + " " + numTeeth + " " + numWhiskers);
   }
   public static void main(String[] args) {
     Mouse mouse = new Mouse(15);
     mouse.print();
   }
}
```

This code prints 15 16 6. The main() method calls the constructor with one parameter. That constructor adds a second hard-coded value and calls the constructor with two parameters. That constructor adds one more hard-coded value and calls the constructor with three parameters. The three-parameter constructor assigns the instance variables.

Final Fields

As you saw earlier in the chapter, final instance variables must be assigned a value exactly once. We saw this happen in the line of the declaration and in an instance initializer. There is one more location this assignment can be done: in the constructor.

```
public class MouseHouse {
  private final int volume;
  private final String name = "The Mouse House";
  public MouseHouse(int length, int width, int height) {
   volume = length * width * height;
}}
```

The constructor is part of the initialization process, so it is allowed to assign final instance variables in it. By the time the constructor completes, all final instance variables must have been set.

Order of Initialization

Chapter 1 covered the order of initialization. Now that you've learned about static initializers, it is time to revisit that. Unfortunately, you do have to memorize this list. We'll give you lots of practice, but you do need to know this order by heart.

1. If there is a superclass, initialize it first (we'll cover this rule in the next chapter. For now, just say "no superclass" and go on to the next rule.)

2. Static variable declarations and static initializers in the order they appear in the file.

3. Instance variable declarations and instance initializers in the order they appear in the file.

4. The constructor.

   Let's try the first example:

```
1: public class InitializationOrderSimple {
2:    private String name = "Torchie";
3:    { System.out.println(name); }
4:    private static int COUNT = 0;
5:    static { System.out.println(COUNT); }
6:    static { COUNT += 10; System.out.println(COUNT); }
7:    public InitializationOrderSimple() {
8:     System.out.println("constructor");
9:    } }

1: public class CallInitializationOrderSimple {
2:    public static void main(String[] args) {
```

```
3:      InitializationOrderSimple init = new InitializationOrderSimple();
4:    } }
```

The output is:

```
0
10
Torchie
constructor
```

Let's look at why. Rule 1 doesn't apply because there is no superclass. Rule 2 says to run the `static` variable declarations and `static` initializers—in this case, lines 4, 5 and 6, which output 0 and 10. Rule 3 says to run the instance variable declarations and instance initializers—here, lines 2 and 3, which output Torchie. Finally, rule 4 says to run the constructor—here, lines 7–9, which output `constructor`.

The next example is a little harder. Keep in mind that the four rules apply only if an object is instantiated. If the class is referred to without a new call, only rules 1 and 2 apply. The other two rules relate to instances and constructors. They have to wait until there is code to instantiate the object.

What do you think happens here?

```
1: public class InitializationOrder {
2:    private String name = "Torchie";
3:    { System.out.println(name); }
4:    private static int COUNT = 0;
5:    static { System.out.println(COUNT); }
6:    { COUNT++;  System.out.println(COUNT); }
7:    public InitializationOrder() {
8:      System.out.println("constructor");
9:    }
10:  public static void main(String[] args) {
11:     System.out.println("read to construct");
12:     new InitializationOrder();
13:   }
14: }
```

The output looks like this:

```
0
read to construct
Torchie
1
constructor
```

Again, rule 1 doesn't apply because there is no superclass. Rule 2 tells us to look at the static variables and static initializers—lines 4 and 5, in that order. Line 5 outputs 0. Now that the statics are out of the way, the main() method can run. Next, we can use rule 3 to run the instance variables and instance initializers. Here that is lines 2 and 3, which output Torchie. Line 6 then outputs 1. Finally, rule 4 says to run the constructor—in this case, lines 7–9, which output constructor.

We are going to try one more example. This one is as hard as it gets. If you understand the output of this next one, congratulations on a job well done; if not, don't worry. Write some programs to play with this. Try typing in the examples in this section and making minor changes to see what happens. For example, you might try commenting out part of the code. This will give you a better feel for what is going on. Then come back and reread this section to try the examples.

Ready for the tough example? Here it is:

```
1: public class YetMoreInitializationOrder {
2:    static { add(2); }
3:    static void add(int num) { System.out.print(num + " "); }
4:    YetMoreInitializationOrder() { add(5); }
5:    static { add(4); }
6:    { add(6); }
7:    static { new YetMoreInitializationOrder(); }
8:    { add(8); }
9:    public static void main(String[] args) { } }
```

The correct answer is 2 4 6 8 5. Let's walk through why that is. There is no superclass, so we jump right to rule 2—the statics. There are three static blocks: on lines 2, 5, and 7. They run in that order. The static block on line 2 calls the add() method, which prints 2. The static block on line 5 calls the add() method, which prints 4. The last static block, on line 7, calls new to instantiate the object. This means we can go on to rule 3 to look at the instance variables and instance initializers. There are two of those: on lines 6 and 8. They both call the add() method and print 6 and 8, respectively. Finally, we go on to rule 4 and call the constructor, which calls the add() method one more time and prints 5.

This example is tricky for a few reasons. There's a lot to keep track of. Also, the question has a lot of one-line code blocks and methods, making it harder to visualize which is a block. Luckily, questions like this are rare on the exam. If you see one, just write down what is going on as you read the code.

Encapsulating Data

In Chapter 1, we had an example of a class with a field that wasn't private:

```
public class Swan {
  int numberEggs;      // instance variable
}
```

Why do we care? Since there is default (package private) access, that means any class in the package can set *numberEggs*. We no longer have control of what gets set in our own class. A caller could even write this:

```
    mother.numberEggs = -1;
```

This is clearly no good. We do not want the mother Swan to have a negative number of eggs!

Encapsulation to the rescue. Encapsulation means we set up the class so only methods in the class with the variables can refer to the instance variables. Callers are required to use these methods. Let's take a look at our newly encapsulated Swan class:

```
1: public class Swan {
2:   private int numberEggs;                      // private
3:   public int getNumberEggs() {                 // getter
4:     return numberEggs;
5:   }
6:   public void setNumberEggs(int numberEggs) {   // setter
7:     if (numberEggs >= 0)                         // guard condition
8:       this.numberEggs = numberEggs;
9:   } }
```

Note *numberEggs* is now private on line 2. This means only code within the class can read or write the value of *numberEggs*. Since we wrote the class, we know better than to set a negative number of eggs. We added a method on lines 3–5 to read the value, which is called an *accessor method* or a getter. We also added a method on lines 6–9 to update the value, which is called a *mutator method* or a setter. The setter has an if statement in this example to prevent setting the instance variable to an invalid value. This guard condition protects the instance variable.

On line 8, we used the this keyword that we saw in constructors to differentiate between the method parameter *numberEggs* and the instance variable *numberEggs*.

For encapsulation, remember that data (an instance variable) is private and getters/setters are public. Java defines a naming convention that is used in *JavaBeans*. JavaBeans are reusable software components. JavaBeans call an instance variable a *property*. The only thing you need to know about JavaBeans for the exam is the naming conventions listed in Table 4.5.

TABLE 4.5 Rules for JavaBeans naming conventions

Rule	Example
Properties are private.	`private int numEggs;`
Getter methods begin with is or get if the property is a boolean.	```java public boolean isHappy() { return happy; } ```
Getter methods begin with get if the property is not a boolean.	```java public int getNumEggs() { return numEggs; } ```
Setter methods begin with set.	```java public void setHappy(boolean happy) { this.happy = happy; } ```
The method name must have a prefix of set/get/is, followed by the first letter of the property in uppercase, followed by the rest of the property name.	```java public void setNumEggs(int num) { numEggs = num; } ```

From the last example in Table 4.5, you noticed that you can name the method parameter to set anything you want. Only the method name and property name have naming conventions here.

It's time for some practice. See if you can figure out which lines follow JavaBeans naming conventions:

```java
12: private boolean playing;
13: private String name;
14: public boolean getPlaying() { return playing; }
15: public boolean isPlaying() { return playing; }
16: public String name() { return name; }
17: public void updateName(String n) { name = n; }
18: public void setname(String n) { name = n; }
```

Lines 12 and 13 are good. They are private instance variables. Line 14 is correct. Since *playing* is a boolean, getter is allowed to begin with get or is. Line 15 is a correct getter for *playing*. Line 16 doesn't follow the JavaBeans naming conventions because it should be called getName. Lines 17 and 18 do not follow the JavaBeans naming conventions because they should be named setName. Remember that Java is case sensitive, so setname is not adequate to meet the naming convention.

Creating Immutable Classes

Encapsulating data is helpful because it prevents callers from making uncontrolled changes to your class. Another common technique is making classes immutable so they cannot be changed at all.

Immutable classes are helpful because you know they will always be the same. You can pass them around your application with a guarantee that the caller didn't change anything. This helps make programs easier to maintain. It also helps with performance by limiting the number of copies, as you saw with String in Chapter 3, "Core Java APIs."

One step in making a class immutable is to omit the setters. But wait: we still want the caller to be able to specify the initial value—we just don't want it to change after the object is created. Constructors to the rescue!

```java
public class ImmutableSwan {
  private int numberEggs;
  public ImmutableSwan(int numberEggs) {
    this.numberEggs = numberEggs;
  }
  public int getNumberEggs() {
    return numberEggs;
} }
```

In this example, we don't have a setter. We do have a constructor that allows a value to be set. Remember, immutable is only measured after the object is constructed. Immutable classes are allowed to have values. They just can't change after instantiation.

Real World Scenario

Return Types in Immutable Classes

When you are writing an immutable class, be careful about the return types. On the surface, this class appears to be immutable since there is no setter:

```java
public class NotImmutable {
  private StringBuilder builder;
  public NotImmutable(StringBuilder b) {
    builder = b;
  }
  public StringBuilder getBuilder() {
    return builder;
} }
```

The problem is that it isn't really. Consider this code snippet:

continues

continued

```
StringBuilder sb = new StringBuilder("initial");
NotImmutable problem = new NotImmutable(sb);
sb.append(" added");
StringBuilder gotBuilder = problem.getBuilder();
gotBuilder.append(" more");
System.out.println(problem.getBuilder());
```

This outputs "initial added more"—clearly not what we were intending. The problem is that we are just passing the same StringBuilder all over. The caller has a reference since it was passed to the constructor. Anyone who calls the getter gets a reference too.
A solution is to make a copy of the mutable object. This is called a defensive copy.

```
public Mutable(StringBuilder b) {
  builder = new StringBuilder(b);
}
public StringBuilder getBuilder() {
  return new StringBuilder(builder);
}
```

Now the caller can make changes to the initial sb object and it is fine. Mutable no longer cares about that object after the constructor gets run. The same goes for the getter: callers can change their StringBuilder without affecting Mutable.

Another approach for the getter is to return an immutable object:

```
public String getValue() {
  return builder.toString();
}
```

There's no rule that says we have to return the same type as we are storing. String is safe to return because it is immutable in the first place.

To review, encapsulation refers to preventing callers from changing the instance variables directly. Immutability refers to preventing callers from changing the instance variables at all.

Writing Simple Lambdas

Java is an object-oriented language at heart. You've seen plenty of objects by now. In Java 8, the language added the ability to write code using another style. *Functional programming* is a way of writing code more declaratively. You specify what you want to do rather than dealing with the state of objects. You focus more on expressions than loops.

Functional programming uses lambda expressions to write code. A *lambda expression* is a block of code that gets passed around. You can think of a lambda expression as an anonymous method. It has parameters and a body just like full-fledged methods do, but it doesn't have a name like a real method. Lambda expressions are often referred to as lambdas for short. You might also know them as closures if Java isn't your first language. If you had a bad experience with closures in the past, don't worry. They are far simpler in Java.

In other words, a lambda expression is like a method that you can pass as if it were a variable. For example, there are different ways to calculate age. One human year is equivalent to seven dog years. You want to write a method that takes an age() method as input. To do this in an object-oriented program, you'd need to define a Human subclass and a Dog subclass. With lambdas, you can just pass in the relevant expression to calculate age.

Lambdas allow you to write powerful code in Java. Only the simplest lambda expressions are on the OCA exam. The goal is to get you comfortable with the syntax and the concepts. This means you aren't truly doing functional programming yet. You'll see lambdas again on the OCP exam.

In this section, we'll cover an example of why lambdas are helpful, the syntax of lambdas, and how to use predicates.

Lambda Example

Our goal is to print out all the animals in a list according to some criteria. We'll show you how to do this without lambdas to illustrate how lambdas are useful. We start out with the Animal class:

```
public class Animal {
  private String species;
  private boolean canHop;
  private boolean canSwim;
  public Animal(String speciesName, boolean hopper, boolean swimmer) {
    species = speciesName;
    canHop = hopper;
    canSwim = swimmer;
  }
  public boolean canHop() { return canHop; }
  public boolean canSwim() { return canSwim; }
  public String toString() { return species; }
}
```

The Animal class has three instance variables, which are set in the constructor. It has two methods that get the state of whether the animal can hop or swim. It also has a toString() method so we can easily identify the Animal in programs.

We plan to write a lot of different checks, so we want an interface. You'll learn more about interfaces in the next chapter. For now, it is enough to remember that an interface specifies the methods that our class needs to implement:

```
public interface CheckTrait {
  boolean test(Animal a);
}
```

The first thing we want to check is whether the Animal can hop. We provide a class that can check this:

```
public class CheckIfHopper implements CheckTrait {
  public boolean test(Animal a) {
    return a.canHop();
  }
}
```

This class may seem simple—and it is. This is actually part of the problem that lambdas solve. Just bear with us for a bit. Now we have everything that we need to write our code to find the Animals that hop:

```
1: import java.util.*; public class TraditionalSearch {
2:   public static void main(String[] args) {
3:     List<Animal> animals = new ArrayList<Animal>();  // list of animals
4:     animals.add(new Animal("fish", false, true));
5:     animals.add(new Animal("kangaroo", true, false));
6:     animals.add(new Animal("rabbit", true, false));
7:     animals.add(new Animal("turtle", false, true));
8:
9:     print(animals, new CheckIfHopper());       // pass class that does check
10:   }
11:   private static void print(List<Animal> animals, CheckTrait checker) {
12:     for (Animal animal : animals) {
13:       if (checker.test(animal))                  // the general check
14:         System.out.print(animal + " ");
15:     }
16:     System.out.println();
17:   }
18: }
```

The print() method on line 11 method is very general—it can check for any trait. This is good design. It shouldn't need to know what specifically we are searching for in order to print a list of animals.

Now what happens if we want to print the Animals that swim? Sigh. We need to write another class CheckIfSwims. Granted, it is only a few lines. Then we need to add a new line under line 9 that instantiates that class. That's two things just to do another check.

Why can't we just specify the logic we care about right here? Turns out that we can with lambda expressions. We could repeat that whole class here and make you find the one line that changed. Instead, we'll just show you. We could replace line 9 with the following, which uses a lambda:

```
9:     print(animals, a -> a.canHop());
```

Don't worry that the syntax looks a little funky. You'll get used to it and we'll describe it in the next section. We'll also explain the bits that look like magic. For now, just focus on how easy it is to read. We are telling Java that we only care about Animals that can hop.

It doesn't take much imagination to figure how we would add logic to get the Animals that can swim. We only have to add one line of code—no need for an extra class to do something simple. Here's that other line:

```
print(animals, a -> a.canSwim());
```

How about Animals that cannot swim?

```
print(animals, a -> ! a.canSwim());
```

The point here is that it is really easy to write code that uses lambdas once you get the basics in place. This code uses a concept called deferred execution. *Deferred execution* means that code is specified now but will run later. In this case, later is when the print() method calls it.

Lambda Syntax

One of the simplest lambda expressions you can write is the one you just saw:

```
a -> a.canHop()
```

This means that Java should call a method with an Animal parameter that returns a boolean value that's the result of a.canHop(). We know all this because we wrote the code. But how does Java know?

Java relies on context when figuring out what lambda expressions mean. We are passing this lambda as the second parameter of the print() method. That method expects a CheckTrait as the second parameter. Since we are passing a lambda instead, Java tries to map our lambda to that interface:

```
boolean test(Animal a);
```

Since that interface's method takes an Animal, that means the lambda parameter has to be an Animal. And since that interface's method returns a boolean, we know the lambda returns a boolean.

The syntax of lambdas is tricky because many parts are optional. These two lines do the exact same thing:

```
a -> a.canHop()
```

```
(Animal a) -> { return a.canHop(); }
```

Let's look at what is going on here. The first example, shown in Figure 4.5, has three parts:

- Specify a single parameter with the name *a*
- The arrow operator to separate the parameter and body
- A body that calls a single method and returns the result of that method

FIGURE 4.5 Lambda syntax omitting optional parts

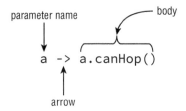

The second example also has three parts; it's just more verbose (see Figure 4.6):

- Specify a single parameter with the name a and stating the type is Animal
- The arrow operator to separate the parameter and body
- A body that has one or more lines of code, including a semicolon and a return statement

FIGURE 4.6 Lambda syntax, including optional parts

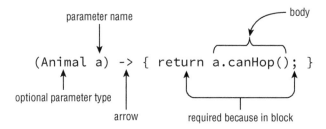

The parentheses can only be omitted if there is a single parameter and its type is not explicitly stated. Java does this because developers commonly use lambda expressions this way and they can do as little typing as possible.

It shouldn't be news to you that we can omit braces when we only have a single statement. We did this with if statements and loops already. What is different here is that the rules change when you omit the braces. Java doesn't require you to type return or use a semicolon when no braces are used. This special shortcut doesn't work when we have two or more statements. At least this is consistent with using {} to create blocks of code elsewhere.

Let's look at some examples of valid lambdas. Pretend that there are valid interfaces that can consume a lambda with zero, one, or two String parameters.

```
3: print(() -> true);                              // 0 parameters
4: print(a -> a.startsWith("test"));               // 1 parameter
5: print((String a) -> a.startsWith("test"));      // 1 parameter
6: print((a, b) -> a.startsWith("test"));          // 2 parameters
7: print((String a, String b) -> a.startsWith("test"));  // 2 parameters
```

Notice that all of these examples have parentheses around the parameter list except the one that takes only one parameter and doesn't specify the type. Line 3 takes 0 parameters and always returns the Boolean true. Line 4 takes one parameter and calls a method on it, returning the result. Line 5 does the same except that it explicitly defines the type of the variable. Lines 6 and 7 take two parameters and ignore one of them—there isn't a rule that says you must use all defined parameters.

Now let's make sure you can identify invalid syntax. Do you see what's wrong with each of these?

```
print(a, b -> a.startsWith("test"));            // DOES NOT COMPILE
print(a -> { a.startsWith("test"); });          // DOES NOT COMPILE
print(a -> { return a.startsWith("test") });    // DOES NOT COMPILE
```

The first line needs parentheses around the parameter list. Remember that the parentheses are *only* optional when there is one parameter and it doesn't have a type declared. The second line is missing the return keyword. The last line is missing the semicolon.

You might have noticed all of our lambdas return a boolean. That is because the scope for the OCA exam limits what you need to learn.

 Real World Scenario

What Variables Can My Lambda Access?

This topic isn't on the OCA exam, but you may come across it when practicing. Lambdas are allowed to access variables. Here's an example:

```
boolean wantWhetherCanHop = true;
print(animals, a -> a.canHop() == wantWhetherCanHop);
```

The trick is that they cannot access all variables. Instance and static variables are okay. Method parameters and local variables are fine if they are not assigned new values.

There is one more issue you might see with lambdas. We've been defining an argument list in our lambda expressions. Since Java doesn't allow us to redeclare a local variable, the following is an issue:

```
(a, b) -> { int a = 0; return 5;}     // DOES NOT COMPILE
```

We tried to redeclare a, which is not allowed. By contrast, the following line is okay because it uses a different variable name:

```
(a, b) -> { int c = 0; return 5;}
```

Predicates

In our earlier example, we created an interface with one method:

```
boolean test(Animal a);
```

Lambdas work with interfaces that have only one method. These are called functional interfaces—interfaces that can be used with functional programming. (It's actually more complicated than this, but for the OCA exam this definition is fine.)

You can imagine that we'd have to create lots of interfaces like this to use lambdas. We want to test Animals and Strings and Plants and anything else that we come across.

Luckily, Java recognizes that this is a common problem and provides such an interface for us. It's in the package java.util.function and the gist of it is as follows:

```
public interface Predicate<T> {
  boolean test(T t);
}
```

That looks a lot like our method. The only difference is that it uses this type T instead of Animal. That's the syntax for generics. It's like when we created an ArrayList and got to specify any type that goes in it.

This means we don't need our own interface anymore and can put everything related to our search in one class:

```
1: import java.util.*;
2: import java.util.function.*;
3: public class PredicateSearch {
4:   public static void main(String[] args) {
5:     List<Animal> animals = new ArrayList<Animal>();
6:     animals.add(new Animal("fish", false, true));
7:
8:     print(animals, a -> a.canHop());
9:   }
10:   private static void print(List<Animal> animals, Predicate<Animal>⏎
    checker) {
11:     for (Animal animal : animals) {
12:       if (checker.test(animal))
13:         System.out.print(animal + " ");
14:     }
15:     System.out.println();
16:   }
17: }
```

This time, line 10 is the only one that changed. We expect to have a Predicate passed in that uses type Animal. Pretty cool. We can just use it without having to write extra code.

Java 8 even integrated the `Predicate` interface into some existing classes. There is only one you need to know for the exam. `ArrayList` declares a `removeIf()` method that takes a `Predicate`. Imagine we have a list of names for pet bunnies. We decide we want to remove all of the bunny names that don't begin with the letter h because our little cousin really wants us to choose an H name. We could solve this problem by writing a loop. Or we could solve it in one line:

```
3: List<String> bunnies = new ArrayList<>();
4: bunnies.add("long ear");
5: bunnies.add("floppy");
6: bunnies.add("hoppy");
7: System.out.println(bunnies);      // [long ear, floppy, hoppy]
8: bunnies.removeIf(s -> s.charAt(0) != 'h');
9: System.out.println(bunnies);      // [hoppy]
```

Line 8 takes care of everything for us. It defines a predicate that takes a `String` and returns a `boolean`. The `removeIf()` method does the rest.

For the OCA exam, you only need to know how to implement lambda expressions that use the `Predicate` interface. Remember the one method in the interface called `test()`? It takes any one reference type parameter and returns a `boolean`. Functional programming is a large topic and just the basics are covered. On the OCP exam, you'll learn how to get rid of the loop entirely for more than just `removeIf()`. You'll also learn the rules for implementing your own functional interfaces as we did with `CheckTrait`.

Summary

As you learned in this chapter, Java methods start with an access modifier of `public`, `private`, `protected` or blank (default access). This is followed by an optional specifier such as `static`, `final`, or `abstract`. Next comes the return type, which is `void` or a Java type. The method name follows, using standard Java identifier rules. Zero or more parameters go in parentheses as the parameter list. Next come any optional exception types. Finally, zero or more statements go in braces to make up the method body.

Using the `private` keyword means the code is only available from within the same class. Default (package private) access means the code is only available from within the same package. Using the `protected` keyword means the code is available from the same package or subclasses. Using the `public` keyword means the code is available from anywhere. Static methods and static variables are shared by the class. When referenced from outside the class, they are called using the classname—for example, `StaticClass.method()`. Instance members are allowed to call static members, but static members are not allowed to call instance members. Static imports are used to import static members.

Java uses pass-by-value, which means that calls to methods create a copy of the parameters. Assigning new values to those parameters in the method doesn't affect the caller's variables.

Calling methods on objects that are method parameters changes the state of those objects and is reflected in the caller.

Overloaded methods are methods with the same name but a different parameter list. Java calls the most specific method it can find. Exact matches are preferred, followed by wider primitives. After that comes autoboxing and finally varargs.

Constructors are used to instantiate new objects. The default no-argument constructor is called when no constructor is coded. Multiple constructors are allowed and can call each other by writing this(). If this() is present, it must be the first statement in the constructor. Constructors can refer to instance variables by writing this before a variable name to indicate they want the instance variable and not the method parameter with that name. The order of initialization is the superclass (which we will cover in Chapter 5); static variables and static initializers in the order they appear; instance variables and instance initializers in the order they appear; and finally the constructor.

Encapsulation refers to preventing callers from changing the instance variables directly. This is done by making instance variables private and getters/setters public. Immutability refers to preventing callers from changing the instance variables at all. This uses several techniques, including removing setters. JavaBeans use methods beginning with is and get for boolean and non-boolean property types, respectively. Methods beginning with set are used for setters.

Lambda expressions, or lambdas, allow passing around blocks of code. The full syntax looks like (String a, String b) -> { return a.equals(b); }. The parameter types can be omitted. When only one parameter is specified without a type, the parentheses can also be omitted. The braces and return statement can be omitted for a single statement, making the short form a -> a.equals(b). Lambdas are passed to a method expecting an interface with one method. Predicate is a common interface. It has one method named test that returns a boolean and takes any type. The removeIf() method on ArrayList takes a Predicate.

Exam Essentials

Be able to identify correct and incorrect method declarations. A sample method signature is public static void method(String... args) throws Exception {}.

Identify when a method or field is accessible. Recognize when a method or field is accessed when the access modifier (private, protected, public, or default access) does not allow it.

Recognize valid and invalid uses of static imports. Static imports import static members. They are written as import static, not *static import*. Make sure they are importing static methods or variables rather than classnames.

State the output of code involving methods. Identify when to call static rather than instance methods based on whether the classname or object comes before the method.

Recognize the correct overloaded method. Exact matches are used first, followed by wider primitives, followed by autoboxing, followed by varargs. Assigning new values to method parameters does not change the caller, but calling methods on them does.

Evaluate code involving constructors.   Constructors can call other constructors by calling this() as the first line of the constructor. Recognize when the default constructor is provided. Remember the order of initialization is the superclass, static variables/initializers, instance variables/initializers, and the constructor.

Be able to recognize when a class is properly encapsulated.   Look for private instance variables and public getters and setters when identifying encapsulation.

Write simple lambda expressions.   Look for the presence or absence of optional elements in lambda code. Parameter types are optional. Braces and the return keyword are optional when the body is a single statement. Parentheses are optional when only one parameter is specified and the type is implicit. The Predicate interface is commonly used with lambdas because it declares a single method called test(), which takes one parameter.

Review Questions

1. Which of the following can fill in the blank in this code to make it compile? (Choose all that apply)

   ```
   public class Ant {
       _____ void method() { }
   }
   ```
   A. default
   B. final
   C. private
   D. Public
   E. String
   F. zzz:

2. Which of the following compile? (Choose all that apply)
   A. final static void method4() { }
   B. public final int void method() { }
   C. private void int method() { }
   D. static final void method3() { }
   E. void final method() {}
   F. void public method() { }

3. Which of the following methods compile? (Choose all that apply)
   A. public void methodA() { return;}
   B. public void methodB() { return null;}
   C. public void methodD() {}
   D. public int methodD() { return 9;}
   E. public int methodE() { return 9.0;}
   F. public int methodF() { return;}
   G. public int methodG() { return null;}

4. Which of the following compile? (Choose all that apply)
   A. public void moreA(int... nums) {}
   B. public void moreB(String values, int... nums) {}
   C. public void moreC(int... nums, String values) {}
   D. public void moreD(String... values, int... nums) {}
   E. public void moreE(String[] values, ...int nums) {}
   F. public void moreF(String... values, int[] nums) {}
   G. public void moreG(String[] values, int[] nums) {}

5. Given the following method, which of the method calls return 2? (Choose all that apply)

```
public int howMany(boolean b, boolean... b2) {
   return b2.length;
}
```

A. howMany();

B. howMany(true);

C. howMany(true, true);

D. howMany(true, true, true);

E. howMany(true, {true});

F. howMany(true, {true, true});

G. howMany(true, new boolean[2]);

6. Which of the following are true? (Choose all that apply)

A. Package private access is more lenient than protected access.

B. A public class that has private fields and package private methods is not visible to classes outside the package.

C. You can use access modifiers so only some of the classes in a package see a particular package private class.

D. You can use access modifiers to allow read access to all methods, but not any instance variables.

E. You can use access modifiers to restrict read access to all classes that begin with the word Test.

7. Given the following my.school.Classroom and my.city.School class definitions, which line numbers in main() generate a compiler error? (Choose all that apply)

```
1: package my.school;
2: public class Classroom {
3:    private int roomNumber;
4:    protected String teacherName;
5:    static int globalKey = 54321;
6:    public int floor = 3;
7:    Classroom(int r, String t) {
8:       roomNumber = r;
9:       teacherName = t; } }
```

```
1: package my.city;
2: import my.school.*;
3: public class School {
4:    public static void main(String[] args) {
5:       System.out.println(Classroom.globalKey);
6:       Classroom room = new Classroom(101, "Mrs. Anderson");
```

```
7:        System.out.println(room.roomNumber);
8:        System.out.println(room.floor);
9:        System.out.println(room.teacherName); } }
```

A. None, the code compiles fine.

B. Line 5

C. Line 6

D. Line 7

E. Line 8

F. Line 9

8. Which of the following are true? (Choose all that apply)

   A. Encapsulation uses package private instance variables.

   B. Encapsulation uses private instance variables.

   C. Encapsulation allows setters.

   D. Immutability uses package private instance variables.

   E. Immutability uses private instance variables.

   F. Immutability allows setters.

9. Which are methods using JavaBeans naming conventions for accessors and mutators? (Choose all that apply)

   A. `public boolean getCanSwim() {  return canSwim;}`

   B. `public boolean canSwim() {  return numberWings;}`

   C. `public int getNumWings() {  return numberWings;}`

   D. `public int numWings()    {  return numberWings;}`

   E. `public void setCanSwim(boolean b) {  canSwim = b;}`

10. What is the output of the following code?

```
1: package rope;
2: public class Rope {
3:   public static int LENGTH = 5;
4:   static {
5:     LENGTH = 10;
6:   }
```

```
7:  public static void swing() {
8:    System.out.print("swing ");
9:  }
10: }
```

```
1: import rope.*;
2: import static rope.Rope.*;
3: public class Chimp {
4:   public static void main(String[] args) {
5:     Rope.swing();
6:     new Rope().swing();
7:     System.out.println(LENGTH);
8:   }
9: }
```

A. swing swing 5

B. swing swing 10

C. Compiler error on line 2 of Chimp.

D. Compiler error on line 5 of Chimp.

E. Compiler error on line 6 of Chimp.

F. Compiler error on line 7 of Chimp.

11. Which are true of the following code? (Choose all that apply)

```
1:  public class Rope {
2:    public static void swing() {
3:      System.out.print("swing ");
4:    }
5:    public void climb() {
6:      System.out.println("climb ");
7:    }
8:    public static void play() {
9:      swing();
10:     climb();
11:   }
12:   public static void main(String[] args) {
13:     Rope rope = new Rope();
14:     rope.play();
15:     Rope rope2 = null;
16:     rope2.play();
17:   }
18: }
```

A. The code compiles as is.

B. There is exactly one compiler error in the code.

C. There are exactly two compiler errors in the code.

D. If the lines with compiler errors are removed, the output is climb climb .

E. If the lines with compiler errors are removed, the output is swing swing .

F. If the lines with compile errors are removed, the code throws a NullPointerException.

12. What is the output of the following code?

```
import rope.*;
import static rope.Rope.*;
public class RopeSwing {
  private static Rope rope1 = new Rope();
  private static Rope rope2 = new Rope();
  {
    System.out.println(rope1.length);
  }
  public static void main(String[] args) {
    rope1.length = 2;
    rope2.length = 8;
    System.out.println(rope1.length);
  }
}

package rope;
public class Rope {
  public static int length = 0;
}
```

A. 02

B. 08

C. 2

D. 8

E. The code does not compile.

F. An exception is thrown.

13. How many compiler errors are in the following code?

```
1: public class RopeSwing {
2:    private static final String leftRope;
3:    private static final String rightRope;
4:    private static final String bench;
5:    private static final String name = "name";
```

```
6:    static {
7:      leftRope = "left";
8:      rightRope = "right";
9:    }
10:    static {
11:      name = "name";
12:      rightRope = "right";
13:    }
14:    public static void main(String[] args) {
15:      bench = "bench";
16:    }
17: }
```

A. 0

B. 1

C. 2

D. 3

E. 4

F. 5

14. Which of the following can replace line 2 to make this code compile? (Choose all that apply)

```
1: import java.util.*;
2: // INSERT CODE HERE
3: public class Imports {
4:   public void method(ArrayList<String> list) {
5:     sort(list);
6:   }
7: }
```

A. import static java.util.Collections;

B. import static java.util.Collections.*;

C. import static java.util.Collections.sort(ArrayList<String>);

D. static import java.util.Collections;

E. static import java.util.Collections.*;

F. static import java.util.Collections.sort(ArrayList<String>);

15. What is the result of the following statements?

```
1:   public class Test {
2:     public void print(byte x) {
3:       System.out.print("byte");
4:     }
5:     public void print(int x) {
6:       System.out.print("int");
```

```
7:    }
8:    public void print(float x) {
9:       System.out.print("float");
10:   }
11:   public void print(Object x) {
12:      System.out.print("Object");
13:   }
14:   public static void main(String[] args) {
15:      Test t = new Test();
16:      short s = 123;
17:      t.print(s);
18:      t.print(true);
19:      t.print(6.789);
20:   }
21: }
```

A. bytefloatObject

B. intfloatObject

C. byteObjectfloat

D. intObjectfloat

E. intObjectObject

F. byteObjectObject

16. What is the result of the following program?

```
1: public class Squares {
2:   public static long square(int x) {
3:      long y = x * (long) x;
4:      x = -1;
5:      return y;
6:   }
7:   public static void main(String[] args) {
8:      int value = 9;
9:      long result = square(value);
10:     System.out.println(value);
11:   } }
```

A. -1

B. 9

C. 81

D. Compiler error on line 9.

E. Compiler error on a different line.

17. Which of the following are output by the following code? (Choose all that apply)

```java
public class StringBuilders {
   public static StringBuilder work(StringBuilder a,
StringBuilder b) {
     a = new StringBuilder("a");
     b.append("b");
     return a;
   }
   public static void main(String[] args) {
     StringBuilder s1 = new StringBuilder("s1");
     StringBuilder s2 = new StringBuilder("s2");
     StringBuilder s3 = work(s1, s2);
     System.out.println("s1 = " + s1);
     System.out.println("s2 = " + s2);
     System.out.println("s3 = " + s3);
   }
}
```

A. s1 = a

B. s1 = s1

C. s2 = s2

D. s2 = s2b

E. s3 = a

F. s3 = null

G. The code does not compile.

18. Which of the following are true? (Choose 2)

A. this() can be called from anywhere in a constructor.

B. this() can be called from any instance method in the class.

C. this.variableName can be called from any instance method in the class.

D. this.variableName can be called from any static method in the class.

E. You must include a default constructor in the code if the compiler does not include one.

F. You can call the default constructor written by the compiler using this().

G. You can access a private constructor with the main() method.

19. Which of these classes compile and use a default constructor? (Choose all that apply)

A. public class Bird { }

B. public class Bird { public bird() {} }

C. public class Bird { public bird(String name) {} }

D. public class Bird { public Bird() {} }

E. `public class Bird { Bird(String name) {} }`

F. `public class Bird { private Bird(int age) {} }`

G. `public class Bird { void Bird() { } }`

20. Which code can be inserted to have the code print 2?

```java
public class BirdSeed {
  private int numberBags;
  boolean call;

  public BirdSeed() {
    // LINE 1
    call = false;
    // LINE 2
  }
  public BirdSeed(int numberBags) {
    this.numberBags = numberBags;
  }
  public static void main(String[] args) {
    BirdSeed seed = new BirdSeed();
    System.out.println(seed.numberBags);
  } }
```

   A. Replace line 1 with `BirdSeed(2);`

   B. Replace line 2 with `BirdSeed(2);`

   C. Replace line 1 with `new BirdSeed(2);`

   D. Replace line 2 with `new BirdSeed(2);`

   E. Replace line 1 with `this(2);`

   F. Replace line 2 with `this(2);`

21. Which of the following complete the constructor so that this code prints out 50? (Choose all that apply)

```java
public class Cheetah {
  int numSpots;
  public Cheetah(int numSpots) {
    // INSERT CODE HERE
  }
  public static void main(String[] args) {
    System.out.println(new Cheetah(50).numSpots);
  }
}
```

   A. numSpots = numSpots;

   B. numSpots = this.numSpots;

   C. this.numSpots = numSpots;

   D. numSpots = super.numSpots;

   E. super.numSpots = numSpots;

   F. None of the above.

22. What is the result of the following?

```
1:  public class Order {
2:     static String result = "";
3:     { result += "c"; }
4:     static
5:     { result += "u"; }
6:     { result += "r"; }
7: }
```

```
1: public class OrderDriver {
2:   public static void main(String[] args) {
3:      System.out.print(Order.result + " ");
4:      System.out.print(Order.result + " ");
5:      new Order();
6:      new Order();
7:      System.out.print(Order.result + " ");
8:   }
9: }
```

   A. curur

   B. ucrcr

   C. u ucrcr

   D. u u curcur

   E. u u ucrcr

   F. ur ur urc

   G. The code does not compile.

23. What is the result of the following?

```
1: public class Order {
2:   String value = "t";
3:   { value += "a"; }
4:   { value += "c"; }
5:   public Order() {
```

```
6:    value += "b";
7:  }
8:  public Order(String s) {
9:    value += s;
10: }
11: public static void main(String[] args) {
12:   Order order = new Order("f");
13:   order = new Order();
14:   System.out.println(order.value);
15: } }
```

A. tacb

B. tacf

C. tacbf

D. tacfb

E. tacftacb

F. The code does not compile.

G. An exception is thrown.

24. Which of the following will compile when inserted in the following code? (Choose all that apply)

```
public class Order3 {
  final String value1 = "1";
  static String value2 = "2";
  String value3 = "3";
  {
    // CODE SNIPPET 1
  }
  static {
    // CODE SNIPPET 2
  }
}
```

A. value1 = "d"; instead of // CODE SNIPPET 1

B. value2 = "e"; instead of // CODE SNIPPET 1

C. value3 = "f"; instead of // CODE SNIPPET 1

D. value1 = "g"; instead of // CODE SNIPPET 2

E. value2 = "h"; instead of // CODE SNIPPET 2

F. value3 = "i"; instead of // CODE SNIPPET 2

25. Which of the following are true about the following code? (Choose all that apply)

```java
public class Create {
  Create() {
    System.out.print("1 ");
  }
  Create(int num) {
    System.out.print("2 ");
  }
  Create(Integer num) {
    System.out.print("3 ");
  }
  Create(Object num) {
    System.out.print("4 ");
  }
  Create(int... nums) {
    System.out.print("5 ");
  }
  public static void main(String[] args) {
    new Create(100);
    new Create(100L);
  }
}
```

A. The code prints out 2 4 .

B. The code prints out 3 4 .

C. The code prints out 4 2 .

D. The code prints out 4 4 .

E. The code prints 3 4 if you remove the constructor Create(int num).

F. The code prints 4 4 if you remove the constructor Create(int num).

G. The code prints 5 4 if you remove the constructor Create(int num).

26. What is the result of the following class?

```java
1: import java.util.function.*;
2:
3: public class Panda {
4:    int age;
5:    public static void main(String[] args) {
6:      Panda p1 = new Panda();
7:      p1.age = 1;
8:      check(p1, p -> p.age < 5);
```

```
9:    }
10:    private static void check(Panda panda, Predicate<Panda> pred) {
11:      String result = pred.test(panda) ? "match" : "not match";
12:      System.out.print(result);
13: } }
```

A. match

B. not match

C. Compiler error on line 8.

D. Compiler error on line 10.

E. Compiler error on line 11.

F. A runtime exception is thrown.

27. What is the result of the following code?

```
1: interface Climb {
2:    boolean isTooHigh(int height, int limit);
3: }
4:
5: public class Climber {
6:    public static void main(String[] args) {
7:    check((h, l) -> h.append(l).isEmpty(), 5);
8:    }
9:    private static void check(Climb climb, int height) {
10:      if (climb.isTooHigh(height, 10))
11:        System.out.println("too high");
12:      else
13:        System.out.println("ok");
14:  }
15: }
```

A. ok

B. too high

C. Compiler error on line 7.

D. Compiler error on line 10.

E. Compiler error on a different line.

F. A runtime exception is thrown.

28. Which of the following lambda expressions can fill in the blank? (Choose all that apply)

```
List<String> list = new ArrayList<>();
list.removeIf(_____);
```

A. `s -> s.isEmpty()`

B. `s -> {s.isEmpty()}`

C. `s -> {s.isEmpty();}`

D. `s -> {return s.isEmpty();}`

E. `String s -> s.isEmpty()`

F. `(String s) -> s.isEmpty()`

29. Which lambda can replace the `MySecret` class to return the same value? (Choose all that apply)

```
interface Secret {
  String magic(double d);
}

class MySecret implements Secret {
  public String magic(double d) {
    return "Poof";
  }
}
```

A. `caller((e) -> "Poof");`

B. `caller((e) -> {"Poof"});`

C. `caller((e) -> { String e = ""; "Poof" });`

D. `caller((e) -> { String e = ""; return "Poof"; });`

E. `caller((e) -> { String e = ""; return "Poof" });`

F. `caller((e) -> { String f = ""; return "Poof"; });`

Chapter

5

Class Design

OCA EXAM OBJECTIVES COVERED IN THIS CHAPTER:

✓ **Working with Inheritance**

- ▪ Describe inheritance and its benefits

- ▪ Develop code that demonstrates the use of polymorphism; including overriding and object type versus reference type

- ▪ Determine when casting is necessary

- ▪ Use super and this to access objects and constructors

- ▪ Use abstract classes and interfaces

In Chapter 1, "Java Building Blocks," we introduced the basic definition for a class in Java. In Chapter 4, "Methods and Encapsulation," we delved into constructors, methods, and modifiers, and showed how you can use them to build more structured classes. In this chapter, we'll take things one step further and show how class structure is one of the most powerful features in the Java language.

At its core, proper Java class design is about code reusability, increased functionality, and standardization. For example, by creating a new class that extends an existing class, you may gain access to a slew of inherited primitives, objects, and methods. Alternatively, by designing a standard interface for your application, you ensure that any class that implements the interface has certain required methods defined. Finally, by creating abstract class definitions, you're defining a platform that other developers can extend and build on top of.

Introducing Class Inheritance

When creating a new class in Java, you can define the class to inherit from an existing class. *Inheritance* is the process by which the new child subclass automatically includes any public or protected primitives, objects, or methods defined in the parent class.

For illustrative purposes, we refer to any class that inherits from another class as a *child class*, or a descendent of that class. Alternatively, we refer to the class that the child inherits from as the *parent class*, or an ancestor of the class. If child X inherits from class Y, which in turn inherits from class Z, then X would be considered an indirect child, or descendent, of class Z.

Java supports *single inheritance*, by which a class may inherit from only one direct parent class. Java also supports multiple levels of inheritance, by which one class may extend another class, which in turn extends another class. You can extend a class any number of times, allowing each descendent to gain access to its ancestor's members.

To truly understand single inheritance, it may helpful to contrast it with *multiple inheritance*, by which a class may have multiple direct parents. By design, Java doesn't support multiple inheritance in the language because studies have shown that multiple inheritance can lead to complex, often difficult-to-maintain code. Java does allow one exception to the single inheritance rule: classes may implement multiple interfaces, as you'll see later in this chapter.

Figure 5.1 illustrates the various types of inheritance models. The items on the left are considered single inheritance because each child has exactly one parent. You may notice that single inheritance doesn't preclude parents from having multiple children. The right side shows items that have multiple inheritance. For example, a dog object has multiple parent designations. Part of what makes multiple inheritance complicated is determining which parent to inherit values from in case of a conflict. For example, if you have an object or method defined in all of the parents, which one does the child inherit? There is no natural ordering for parents in this example, which is why Java avoids these issues by disallowing multiple inheritance altogether.

FIGURE 5.1 Types of inheritance

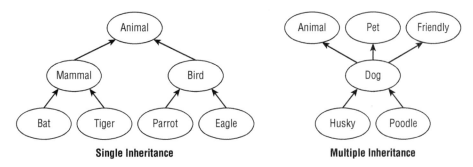

It is possible in Java to prevent a class from being extended by marking the class with the final modifier. If you try to define a class that inherits from a final class, the compiler will throw an error and not compile. Unless otherwise specified, throughout this chapter you can assume the classes we work with are not marked as final.

Extending a Class

In Java, you can extend a class by adding the parent class name in the definition using the extends keyword. The syntax of defining and extending a class is shown in Figure 5.2.

FIGURE 5.2 Defining and extending a class

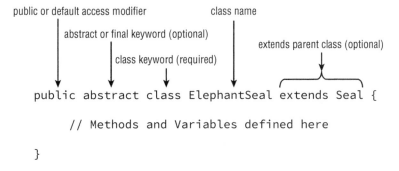

We'll discuss what it means for a class to be abstract and final, as well as the class access modifiers, later in this chapter.

Because Java allows only one public class per file, we can create two files, Animal.java and Lion.java, in which the Lion class extends the Animal class. Assuming they are in the same package, an import statement is not required in Lion.java to access the Animal class.

Here are the contents of Animal.java:

```
public class Animal {
  private int age;
  public int getAge() {
    return age;
  }
  public void setAge(int age) {
    this.age = age;
  }
}
```

And here are the contents of Lion.java:

```
public class Lion extends Animal {
  private void roar() {
    System.out.println("The "+getAge()+" year old lion says: Roar!");
  }
}
```

Notice the use of the extends keyword in Lion.java to indicate that the Lion class extends from the Animal class. In this example, we see that getAge() and setAge() are accessible by subclass Lion, because they are marked as public in the parent class. The primitive age is marked as private and therefore not accessible from the subclass Lion, as the following would not compile:

```
public class Lion extends Animal {
  private void roar() {
    System.out.println("The "+age+" year old lion says: Roar!");
    // DOES NOT COMPILE
  }
}
```

Despite the fact that age is inaccessible by the child class, if we have an instance of a Lion object, there is still an age value that exists within the instance. The age value just cannot be directly referenced by the child class nor any instance of the class. In this manner, the Lion object is actually "bigger" than the Animal object in the sense that it includes all the properties of the Animal object (although not all of those properties may be directly accessible) along with its own set of Lion attributes.

Applying Class Access Modifiers

As discussed in Chapter 4, you can apply access modifiers (public, private, protected, default) to both class methods and variables. It probably comes as no surprise that you can also apply access modifiers to class definitions, since we have been adding the public access modifier to nearly every class up to now.

> For the OCA exam, you should only be familiar with public and default package-level class access modifiers, because these are the only ones that can be applied to top-level classes within a Java file. The protected and private modifiers can only be applied to inner classes, which are classes that are defined within other classes, but this is well out of scope for the OCA exam.

The public access modifier applied to a class indicates that it can be referenced and used in any class. The default package private modifier, which is the lack of any access modifier, indicates the class can be accessed only by a class within the same package.

As you know, a Java file can have many classes but at most one public class. In fact, it may have no public class at all. One feature of using the default package private modifier is that you can define many classes within the same Java file. For example, the following definition could appear in a single Java file named Groundhog.java, since it contains only one public class:

```
class Rodent {}
```

```
public class Groundhog extends Rodent {}
```

If we were to update the Rodent class with the public access modifier, the Groundhog.java file would not compile unless the Rodent class was moved to its own Rodent.java file.

The rules for applying class access modifiers are identical for interfaces. There can be at most one public class or interface in a Java file. Like classes, top-level interfaces can also be declared with the public or default modifiers. We'll discuss interfaces in detail later in this chapter.

> For simplicity, any time you see multiple public classes or interfaces defined in the same code block in this chapter, assume each class is defined in its own Java file.

Creating Java Objects

Throughout our discussion of Java in this book, we have thrown around the word *object* numerous times—and with good reason. In Java, all classes inherit from a single class, java.lang.Object. Furthermore, java.lang.Object is the only class that doesn't have any parent classes.

You might be wondering, "None of the classes I've written so far extend java.lang .Object, so how do all classes inherit from it?" The answer is that the compiler has been automatically inserting code into any class you write that doesn't extend a specific class. For example, consider the following two equivalent class definitions:

```
public class Zoo {
}
```

```
public class Zoo extends java.lang.Object {
}
```

The key is that when Java sees you define a class that doesn't extend another class, it immediately adds the syntax extends java.lang.Object to the class definition.

If you define a new class that extends an existing class, Java doesn't add this syntax, although the new class still inherits from java.lang.Object. Since all classes inherit from java.lang.Object, extending an existing class means the child automatically inherits from java.lang.Object by construction. This means that if you look at the inheritance structure of any class, it will always end with java.lang.Object on the top of the tree, as shown in Figure 5.3.

FIGURE 5.3   Java object inheritance

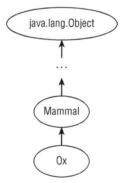

All objects inherit java.lang.Object

Defining Constructors

As you may recall from Chapter 4, every class has at least one constructor. In the case that no constructor is declared, the compiler will automatically insert a default no-argument constructor. In the case of extending a class, though, things are a bit more interesting.

In Java, the first statement of every constructor is either a call to another constructor within the class, using this(), or a call to a constructor in the direct parent class, using super(). If a parent constructor takes arguments, the super constructor would also take arguments. For simplicity in this section, we refer to the super() command as any parent constructor, even those that take an argument. Notice the use of both super() and super(age) in the following example:

```java
public class Animal {
  private int age;
  public Animal(int age) {
    super();
    this.age = age;
  }
}


public class Zebra extends Animal {
  public Zebra(int age) {
    super(age);
  }
  public Zebra() {
    this(4);
  }
}
```

In the first class, Animal, the first statement of the constructor is a call to the parent constructor defined in java.lang.Object, which takes no arguments. In the second class, Zebra, the first statement of the first constructor is a call to Animal's constructor, which takes a single argument. The class Zebra also includes a second no-argument constructor that doesn't call super() but instead calls the other constructor within the Zebra class using this(4).

Like the this() command that you saw in Chapter 4, the super() command may only be used as the first statement of the constructor. For example, the following two class definitions will not compile:

```java
public class Zoo {
  public Zoo() {
    System.out.println("Zoo created");
    super(); // DOES NOT COMPILE
  }
}


public class Zoo {
  public Zoo() {
    super();
    System.out.println("Zoo created");
```

```
    super();  // DOES NOT COMPILE
  }
}
```

The first class will not compile because the call to the parent constructor must be the first statement of the constructor, not the second statement. In the second code snippet, super() is the first statement of the constructor, but it also used as the third statement. Since super() can only be used as the first statement of the constructor, the code will likewise not compile.

If the parent class has more than one constructor, the child class may use any valid parent constructor in its definition, as shown in the following example:

```
public class Animal {
  private int age;
  private String name;
  public Animal(int age, String name) {
    super();
    this.age = age;
    this.name = name;
  }
  public Animal(int age) {
    super();
    this.age = age;
    this.name = null;
  }
}

public class Gorilla extends Animal {
  public Gorilla(int age) {
    super(age,"Gorilla");
  }
  public Gorilla() {
    super(5);
  }
}
```

In this example, the first child constructor takes one argument, age, and calls the parent constructor, which takes two arguments, age and name. The second child constructor takes no arguments, and it calls the parent constructor, which takes one argument, age. In this example, notice that the child constructors are not required to call matching parent constructors. Any valid parent constructor is acceptable as long as the appropriate input parameters to the parent constructor are provided.

Understanding Compiler Enhancements

Up to now, we defined numerous classes that did not explicitly call the parent constructor via the super() keyword, so why did the code compile? The answer is that the Java compiler automatically inserts a call to the no-argument constructor super() if the first statement is not a call to the parent constructor. For example, the following three class and constructor definitions are equivalent, because the compiler will automatically convert them all to the last example:

```
public class Donkey {
}

public class Donkey {
  public Donkey() {
  }
}

public class Donkey {
  public Donkey() {
    super();
    }
}
```

Make sure you understand the differences between these three Donkey class definitions and why Java will automatically convert them all to the last definition. Keep the process the Java compile performs in mind as we discuss the next few examples.

What happens if the parent class doesn't have a no-argument constructor? Recall that the no-argument constructor is not required and only inserted if there is no constructor defined in the class. In this case, the Java compiler will not help and you must create at least one constructor in your child class that explicitly calls a parent constructor via the super() command. For example, the following code will not compile:

```
public class Mammal {
  public Mammal(int age) {
  }
}

public class Elephant extends Mammal {  // DOES NOT COMPILE
}
```

In this example no constructor is defined within the Elephant class, so the compiler tries to insert a default no-argument constructor with a super() call, as it did in the Donkey example. The compiler stops, though, when it realizes there is no parent constructor that takes no arguments. In this example, we must explicitly define at least one constructor, as in the following code:

```
public class Mammal {
  public Mammal(int age) {
  }
}

public class Elephant extends Mammal {
  public Elephant() {  // DOES NOT COMPILE
  }
}
```

This code still doesn't compile, though, because the compiler tries to insert the no-argument super() as the first statement of the constructor in the Elephant class, and there is no such constructor in the parent class. We can fix this, though, by adding a call to a parent constructor that takes a fixed argument:

```
public class Mammal {
  public Mammal(int age) {
  }
}

public class Elephant extends Mammal {
  public Elephant() {
    super(10);
  }
}
```

This code will compile because we have added a constructor with an explicit call to a parent constructor. Note that the class Elephant now has a no-argument constructor even though its parent class Mammal doesn't. Subclasses may define no-argument constructors even if their parent classes do not, provided the constructor of the child maps to a parent constructor via an explicit call of the super() command.

You should be wary of any exam question in which the parent class defines a constructor that takes arguments and doesn't define a no-argument constructor. Be sure to check that the code compiles before answering a question about it.

Reviewing Constructor Rules

Let's review the rules we covered in this section.

Constructor Definition Rules:

1. The first statement of every constructor is a call to another constructor within the class using this(), or a call to a constructor in the direct parent class using super().

2. The super() call may not be used after the first statement of the constructor.

3. If no super() call is declared in a constructor, Java will insert a no-argument super() as the first statement of the constructor.

4. If the parent doesn't have a no-argument constructor and the child doesn't define any constructors, the compiler will throw an error and try to insert a default no-argument constructor into the child class.

5. If the parent doesn't have a no-argument constructor, the compiler requires an explicit call to a parent constructor in each child constructor.

Make sure you understand these rules; the exam will often provide code that breaks one or many of these rules and therefore doesn't compile.

Calling Constructors

Now that we have covered how to define a valid constructor, we'll show you how Java calls the constructors. In Java, the parent constructor is always executed before the child constructor. For example, try to determine what the following code outputs:

```
class Primate {
  public Primate() {
    System.out.println("Primate");
  }
}

class Ape extends Primate {
  public Ape() {
    System.out.println("Ape");
  }
}

public class Chimpanzee extends Ape {
  public static void main(String[] args) {
    new Chimpanzee();
  }
}
```

The compiler first inserts the super() command as the first statement of both the Primate and Ape constructors. Next, the compiler inserts a default no-argument constructor in the Chimpanzee class with super() as the first statement of the constructor. The code will execute with the parent constructors called first and yields the following output:

```
Primate
Ape
```

The exam creators are fond of questions similar to the previous one that try to get you to determine the output of statements involving constructors. Just remember to "think like the compiler" as much as possible and insert the missing constructors or statements as needed.

Calling Inherited Class Members

Java classes may use any `public` or `protected` member of the parent class, including methods, primitives, or object references. If the parent class and child class are part of the same package, the child class may also use any default members defined in the parent class. Finally, a child class may never access a `private` member of the parent class, at least not through any direct reference. As you saw in the first example in this chapter, a `private` member age may be accessed indirectly via a `public` or `protected` method.

To reference a member in a parent class, you can just call it directly, as in the following example with the output function `displaySharkDetails()`:

```
class Fish {
  protected int size;
  private int age;

  public Fish(int age) {
    this.age = age;
  }

  public int getAge() {
    return age;
  }
}

public class Shark extends Fish {

  private int numberOfFins = 8;

  public Shark(int age) {
    super(age);
    this.size = 4;
  }

  public void displaySharkDetails() {
    System.out.print("Shark with age: "+getAge());
```

```
        System.out.print(" and "+size+" meters long");
        System.out.print(" with "+numberOfFins+" fins");
    }
}
```

In the child class, we use the `public` method `getAge()` and `protected` member `size` to access values in the parent class.

As you may remember from Chapter 4, you can use the keyword `this` to access a member of the class. You may also use `this` to access members of the parent class that are accessible from the child class, since a child class inherits all of its parent members. Consider the following alternative definition to the `displaySharkDetails()` method in the previous example:

```
public void displaySharkDetails() {
    System.out.print("Shark with age: "+this.getAge());
    System.out.print(" and "+this.size+" meters long");
    System.out.print(" with "+this.numberOfFins+" fins");
}
```

In Java, you can explicitly reference a member of the parent class by using the `super` keyword, as in the following alternative definition of `displaySharkDetails()`:

```
public void displaySharkDetails() {
    System.out.print("Shark with age: "+super.getAge());
    System.out.print(" and "+super.size+" meters long");
    System.out.print(" with "+this.numberOfFins+" fins");
}
```

In the previous example, we could use `this` or `super` to access a member of the parent class, but is the same true for a member of the child class? Consider this example:

```
public void displaySharkDetails() {
    System.out.print("Shark with age: "+super.getAge());
    System.out.print(" and "+super.size+" meters long");
    System.out.print(" with "+super.numberOfFins+" fins"); // DOES NOT COMPILE
}
```

This code will not compile because `numberOfFins` is only a member of the current class, not the parent class. In other words, we see that `this` and `super` may both be used for methods or variables defined in the parent class, but only `this` may be used for members defined in the current class.

As you'll see in the next section, if the child class overrides a member of the parent class, `this` and `super` could have very different effects when applied to a class member.

---

super()* vs. *super

As discussed in Chapter 4, this() and this are unrelated in Java. Likewise, super() and super are quite different but may be used in the same methods on the exam. The first, super(), is a statement that explicitly calls a parent constructor and may only be used in the first line of a constructor of a child class. The second, super, is a keyword used to reference a member defined in a parent class and may be used throughout the child class.

The exam may try to trick you by using both super() and super in a constructor. For example, consider the following code:

```
public Rabbit(int age) {
  super();
  super.setAge(10);
}
```

The first statement of the constructor calls the parent's constructor, whereas the second statement calls a function defined in the parent class. Contrast this with the following code, which doesn't compile:

```
public Rabbit(int age) {
  super;  // DOES NOT COMPILE
  super().setAge(10);  // DOES NOT COMPILE
}
```

This code looks similar to the previous example, but neither line of the constructor will compile since they are using the keywords incorrectly. When you see super() or super on the exam, be sure to check that they are being used correctly.

Inheriting Methods

Inheriting a class grants us access to the public and protected members of the parent class, but also sets the stage for collisions between methods defined in both the parent class and the subclass. In this section, we'll review the rules for method inheritance and how Java handles such scenarios.

Overriding a Method

What if there is a method defined in both the parent and child class? For example, you may want to define a new version of an existing method in a child class that makes use of the definition in the parent class. In this case, you can *override* a method by declaring a new method with the signature and return type as the method in the parent class. As you may recall from Chapter 4, the method signature includes the name and list of input parameters.

When you override a method, you may reference the parent version of the method using the super keyword. In this manner, the keywords this and super allow you to select between the current and parent version of a method, respectively. We illustrate this with the following example:

```java
public class Canine {
  public double getAverageWeight() {
    return 50;
  }
}

public class Wolf extends Canine {
  public double getAverageWeight() {
    return super.getAverageWeight()+20;
  }
  public static void main(String[] args) {
    System.out.println(new Canine().getAverageWeight());
    System.out.println(new Wolf().getAverageWeight());
  }
}
```

In this example, in which the child class Wolf overrides the parent class Canine, the method getAverageWeight() runs without issue and outputs the following:

```
50.0
70.0
```

You might be wondering, was the use of super in the child's method required? For example, what would the following code output if we removed the super keyword in the getAverageWeight() method of the Wolf class?

```java
public double getAverageWeight() {
  return getAverageWeight()+20;  // INFINITE LOOP
}
```

In this example, the compiler would not call the parent Canine method; it would call the current Wolf method since it would think you were executing a recursive call. A recursive function is one that calls itself as part of execution, and it is common in programming. A recursive function must have a termination condition. In this example, there is no termination condition; therefore, the application will attempt to call itself infinitely and produce a stack overflow error at runtime.

Overriding a method is not without limitations, though. The compiler performs the following checks when you override a nonprivate method:

1. The method in the child class must have the same signature as the method in the parent class.

2. The method in the child class must be at least as accessible or more accessible than the method in the parent class.

3. The method in the child class may not throw a checked exception that is new or broader than the class of any exception thrown in the parent class method.

4. If the method returns a value, it must be the same or a subclass of the method in the parent class, known as *covariant return types*.

The first rule of overriding a method is somewhat self-explanatory. If two methods have the same name but different signatures, the methods are overloaded, not overridden. As you may recall from our discussion of overloaded methods in Chapter 4, the methods are unrelated to each other and do not share any properties.

Overloading vs. Overriding

Overloading a method and overriding a method are similar in that they both involve redefining a method using the same name. They differ in that an overloaded method will use a different signature than an overridden method. This distinction allows overloaded methods a great deal more freedom in syntax than an overridden method would have. For example, take a look at the following code sample:

```java
public class Bird {
  public void fly() {
    System.out.println("Bird is flying");
  }
  public void eat(int food) {
    System.out.println("Bird is eating "+food+" units of food");
  }
}

public class Eagle extends Bird {
  public int fly(int height) {
    System.out.println("Bird is flying at "+height+" meters");
    return height;
  }
  public int eat(int food) { // DOES NOT COMPILE
    System.out.println("Bird is eating "+food+" units of food");
    return food;
  }
}
```

The first method, fly(), is overloaded in the subclass Eagle, since the signature changes from a no-argument method to a method with one int argument. Because the method is being overloaded and not overridden, the return type can be changed from void to int without issue.

The second method, eat(), is overridden in the subclass Eagle, since the signature is the same as it is in the parent class Bird—they both take a single argument int. Because the method is being overridden, the return type of the method in Eagle must be a subclass of the return type of the method in Bird. In this example, the return type int is not a subclass of void; therefore, the compiler will throw an exception on this method definition.

Any time you see a method on the exam with the same name as a method in the parent class, determine whether the method is being overloaded or overridden first; doing so will help you with questions about whether the code will compile.

Let's review some examples of the last three rules of overriding methods so you can learn to spot the issues when they arise:

```java
public class Camel {
  protected String getNumberOfHumps() {
    return "Undefined";
  }
}

public class BactrianCamel extends Camel {
  private int getNumberOfHumps() {  // DOES NOT COMPILE
    return 2;
  }
}
```

In this example, the method in the child class doesn't compile for two reasons. First, it violates the second rule of overriding methods: the child method must be at least as accessible as the parent. In the example, the parent method uses the protected modifier, but the child method uses the private modifier, making it less accessible in the child method than in the parent method. It also violates the fourth rule of overriding methods: the return type of the parent method and child method must be covariant. In this example, the return type of the parent method is String, whereas the return type of the child method is int, neither of which is covariant with each other.

Any time you see a method that appears to be overridden on the exam, first check to make sure it is truly being overridden and not overloaded. Once you have confirmed it is being overridden, check that the access modifiers, return types, and any exceptions defined in the method are compatible with one another. Let's take a look at some example methods that use exceptions:

```java
public class InsufficientDataException extends Exception {}

public class Reptile {
  protected boolean hasLegs() throws InsufficientDataException {
    throw new InsufficientDataException();
  }
  protected double getWeight() throws Exception {
    return 2;
  }
}

public class Snake extends Reptile {
  protected boolean hasLegs() {
    return false;
  }
  protected double getWeight() throws InsufficientDataException{
    return 2;
  }
}
```

In this example, both parent and child classes define two methods, hasLegs() and getWeight(). The first method, hasLegs(), throws an exception InsufficientDataException in the parent class but doesn't throw an exception in the child class. This does not violate the third rule of overriding methods, though, as no new exception is defined. In other words, a child method may hide or eliminate a parent method's exception without issue.

The second method, getWeight(), throws Exception in the parent class and InsufficientDataException in the child class. This is also permitted, as InsufficientDataException is a subclass of Exception by construction.

Neither of the methods in the previous example violates the third rule of overriding methods, so the code compiles and runs without issue. Let's review some examples that do violate the third rule of overriding methods:

```java
public class InsufficientDataException extends Exception {}

public class Reptile {
  protected double getHeight() throws InsufficientDataException {
    return 2;
  }
  protected int getLength() {
    return 10;
  }
}
```

```
public class Snake extends Reptile {
  protected double getHeight() throws Exception {  // DOES NOT COMPILE
    return 2;
  }
  protected int getLength() throws InsufficientDataException { // DOES NOT COMPILE
    return 10;
  }
}
```

Unlike the earlier example, neither of the methods in the child class of this code will compile. The getHeight() method in the parent class throws an InsufficientDataException, whereas the method in the child class throws an Exception. Since Exception is not a subclass of InsufficientDataException, the third rule of overriding methods is violated and the code will not compile. Coincidentally, Exception is a superclass of InsufficientDataException.

Next, the getLength() method doesn't throw an exception in the parent class, but it does throw an exception, InsufficientDataException, in the child class. In this manner, the child class defines a new exception that the parent class did not, which is a violation of the third rule of overriding methods.

The last three rules of overriding a method may seem arbitrary or confusing at first, but as you'll see later in this chapter when we discuss polymorphism, they are needed for consistency of the language. Without these rules in place, it is possible to create contradictions within the Java language.

Redeclaring *private* Methods

The previous section defined the behavior if you override a public or protected method in the class. Now let's expand our discussion to private methods. In Java, it is not possible to override a private method in a parent class since the parent method is not accessible from the child class. Just because a child class doesn't have access to the parent method, doesn't mean the child class can't define its own version of the method. It just means, strictly speaking, that the new method is not an overridden version of the parent class's method.

Java permits you to redeclare a new method in the child class with the same or modified signature as the method in the parent class. This method in the child class is a separate and independent method, unrelated to the parent version's method, so none of the rules for overriding methods are invoked. For example, let's return to the Camel example we used in the previous section and show two related classes that define the same method:

```
public class Camel {
  private String getNumberOfHumps() {
    return "Undefined";
  }
}
```

```
public class BactrianCamel extends Camel {
  private int getNumberOfHumps() {
    return 2;
  }
}
```

This code compiles without issue. Notice that the return type differs in the child method from `String` to `int`. In this example, the method `getNumberOfHumps()` in the parent class is hidden, so the method in the child class is a new method and not an override of the method in the parent class. As you saw in the previous section, if the method in the parent class were `public` or `protected`, the method in the child class would not compile because it would violate two rules of overriding methods. The parent method in this example is `private`, so there are no such issues.

Hiding Static Methods

A *hidden method* occurs when a child class defines a static method with the same name and signature as a static method defined in a parent class. Method hiding is similar but not exactly the same as method overriding. First, the four previous rules for overriding a method must be followed when a method is hidden. In addition, a new rule is added for hiding a method, namely that the usage of the `static` keyword must be the same between parent and child classes. The following list summarizes the five rules for hiding a method:

1. The method in the child class must have the same signature as the method in the parent class.

2. The method in the child class must be at least as accessible or more accessible than the method in the parent class.

3. The method in the child class may not throw a checked exception that is new or broader than the class of any exception thrown in the parent class method.

4. If the method returns a value, it must be the same or a subclass of the method in the parent class, known as *covariant return types*.

5. The method defined in the child class must be marked as `static` if it is marked as `static` in the parent class (method hiding). Likewise, the method must not be marked as `static` in the child class if it is not marked as `static` in the parent class (method overriding).

Note that the first four are the same as the rules for overriding a method.
Let's review some examples of the new rule:

```
public class Bear {
  public static void eat() {
    System.out.println("Bear is eating");
  }
}
```

```java
public class Panda extends Bear {
  public static void eat() {
    System.out.println("Panda bear is chewing");
  }
  public static void main(String[] args) {
    Panda.eat();
  }
}
```

In this example, the code compiles and runs without issue. The eat() method in the child class hides the eat() method in the parent class. Because they are both marked as static, this is not considered an overridden method. Let's contrast this with examples that violate the fifth rule:

```java
public class Bear {
  public static void sneeze() {
    System.out.println("Bear is sneezing");
  }
  public void hibernate() {
    System.out.println("Bear is hibernating");
  }
}
```

```java
public class Panda extends Bear {
  public void sneeze() {  // DOES NOT COMPILE
    System.out.println("Panda bear sneezes quietly");
  }
  public static void hibernate() {  // DOES NOT COMPILE
    System.out.println("Panda bear is going to sleep");
  }
}
```

In this example, sneeze() is marked as static in the parent class but not in the child class. The compiler detects that you're trying to override a method that should be hidden and generates a compiler error. In the second method, hibernate() is an instance member in the parent class but a static method in the child class. In this scenario, the compiler thinks that you're trying to hide a method that should be overridden and also generates a compiler error.

As you saw in the previous example, hiding static methods is fraught with pitfalls and potential problems and as a practice should be avoided. Though you might see questions on the exam that contain hidden static methods that are syntactically correct, avoid hiding static methods in your own work, since it tends to lead to confusing and difficult-to-read code. You should not reuse the name of a static method in your class if it is already used in the parent class.

Overriding vs. Hiding Methods

In our description of hiding of static methods, we indicated there was a distinction between overriding and hiding methods. Unlike overriding a method, in which a child method replaces the parent method in calls defined in both the parent and child, hidden methods only replace parent methods in the calls defined in the child class.

At runtime the child version of an overridden method is always executed for an instance regardless of whether the method call is defined in a parent or child class method. In this manner, the parent method is never used unless an explicit call to the parent method is referenced, using the syntax *super.method()*. Alternatively, at runtime the parent version of a hidden method is always executed if the call to the method is defined in the parent class. Let's take a look at an example:

```java
public class Marsupial {
  public static boolean isBiped() {
    return false;
  }
  public void getMarsupialDescription() {
    System.out.println("Marsupial walks on two legs: "+isBiped());
  }
}
```

```java
public class Kangaroo extends Marsupial {
  public static boolean isBiped() {
    return true;
  }
  public void getKangarooDescription() {
    System.out.println("Kangaroo hops on two legs: "+isBiped());
  }
  public static void main(String[] args) {
    Kangaroo joey = new Kangaroo();
    joey.getMarsupialDescription();
    joey.getKangarooDescription();
  }
}
```

In this example, the code compiles and runs without issue, outputting the following:

```
Marsupial walks on two legs: false
Kangaroo hops on two legs: true
```

Notice that isBiped() returns false in the parent class and true in the child class. In the first method call, the parent method getMarsupialDescription() is used. The Marsupial class only knows about isBiped() from its own class definition, so it outputs false. In the second method call, the child executes a method of isBiped(), which hides the parent method's version and returns true.

Contrast this first example with the following example, which uses an overridden version of isBiped() instead of a hidden version:

```
class Marsupial {
  public boolean isBiped() {
    return false;
  }
  public void getMarsupialDescription() {
    System.out.println("Marsupial walks on two legs: "+isBiped());
  }
}

public class Kangaroo extends Marsupial {
  public boolean isBiped() {
    return true;
  }
  public void getKangarooDescription() {
    System.out.println("Kangaroo hops on two legs: "+isBiped());
  }
  public static void main(String[] args) {
    Kangaroo joey = new Kangaroo();
    joey.getMarsupialDescription();
    joey.getKangarooDescription();
  }
}
```

This code also compiles and runs without issue, but it outputs slightly different text:

```
Marsupial walks on two legs: true
Kangaroo hops on two legs: true
```

In this example, the isBiped() method is overridden, not hidden, in the child class. Therefore, it is replaced at runtime in the parent class with the call to the child class's method.

Make sure you understand these examples as they show how hidden and overridden methods are fundamentally different. This example makes uses of polymorphism, which we'll discuss later in this chapter.

Creating *final* methods

We conclude our discussion of method inheritance with a somewhat self-explanatory rule: final methods cannot be overridden. If you recall our discussion of modifiers from Chapter 4, you can create a method with the final keyword. By doing so, though, you forbid a child class from overriding this method. This rule is in place both when you override a method and when you hide a method. In other words, you cannot hide a static method in a parent class if it is marked as final.

Let's take a look at an example:

```
public class Bird {
  public final boolean hasFeathers() {
    return true;
  }
}


public class Penguin extends Bird {
  public final boolean hasFeathers() { // DOES NOT COMPILE
    return false;
  }
}
```

In this example, the method hasFeathers() is marked as final in the parent class Bird, so the child class Penguin cannot override the parent method, resulting in a compiler error. Note that whether or not the child method used the final keyword is irrelevant—the code will not compile either way.

Why Mark a Method as *final?*

Although marking methods as final prevents them from being overridden, it does have advantages in practice. For example, you'd mark a method as final when you're defining a parent class and want to guarantee certain behavior of a method in the parent class, regardless of which child is invoking the method.

For example, in the previous example with Birds, the author of the parent class may want to ensure the method hasFeathers() always returns true, regardless of the child class instance on which it is invoked. The author is confident that there is no example of a Bird in which feathers are not present.

The reason methods are not commonly marked as final in practice, though, is that it may be difficult for the author of a parent class method to consider all of the possible ways her child class may be used. For example, although all adult birds have feathers, a baby chick doesn't; therefore, if you have an instance of a Bird that is a chick, it would not have feathers. In short, the final modifier is only used on methods when the author of the parent method wants to guarantee very precise behavior.

Inheriting Variables

As you saw with method overriding, there were a lot of rules when two methods have the same signature and are defined in both the parent and child classes. Luckily, the rules for variables with the same name in the parent and child classes are a lot simpler, because Java doesn't allow variables to be overridden but instead hidden.

Hiding Variables

When you hide a variable, you define a variable with the same name as a variable in a parent class. This creates two copies of the variable within an instance of the child class: one instance defined for the parent reference and another defined for the child reference.

As when hiding a static method, you can't override a variable; you can only hide it. Also similar to hiding a static method, the rules for accessing the parent and child variables are quite similar. If you're referencing the variable from within the parent class, the variable defined in the parent class is used. Alternatively, if you're referencing the variable from within a child class, the variable defined in the child class is used. Likewise, you can reference the parent value of the variable with an explicit use of the super keyword. Consider the following example:

```java
public class Rodent {
  protected int tailLength = 4;
  public void getRodentDetails() {
    System.out.println("[parentTail="+tailLength+"]");
  }
}

public class Mouse extends Rodent {
  protected int tailLength = 8;
  public void getMouseDetails() {
    System.out.println("[tail="+tailLength +",parentTail="+super.tailLength+"]");
  }
  public static void main(String[] args) {
    Mouse mouse = new Mouse();
    mouse.getRodentDetails();
    mouse.getMouseDetails();
  }
}
```

This code compiles without issue and outputs the following when executed:

```
[parentTail=4]
[tail=8,parentTail=4]
```

Notice that the instance of Mouse contains two copies of the `tailLength` variables: one defined in the parent and one defined in the child. These instances are kept separate from each other, allowing our instance of Mouse to reference both `tailLength` values independently. In the first method call, `getRodentDetails()`, the parent method outputs the parent value of the `tailLength` variable. In the second method call, `getMouseDetails()`, the child method outputs both the child and parent version of the `tailLength` variables, using the super keyword to access the parent variable's value.

The important thing to remember is that there is no notion of overriding a member variable. For example, there is no code change that could be made to cause Java to override the value of `tailLength`, making it the same in both parent and child. These rules are the same regardless of whether the variable is an instance variable or a static variable.

 Real World Scenario

Don't Hide Variables in Practice

Although Java allows you to hide a variable defined in a parent class with one defined in a child class, it is considered an extremely poor coding practice. For example, take a look at the following code, which uses a hidden variable length, marked as public in both parent and child classes.

```java
public class Animal {
  public int length = 2;
}

public class Jellyfish extends Animal {
  public int length = 5;
  public static void main(String[] args) {
    Jellyfish jellyfish = new Jellyfish();
    Animal animal = new Jellyfish();
    System.out.println(jellyfish.length);
    System.out.println(animal.length);
  }
}
```

This code compiles without issue. Here's the output:

```
5
2
```

Notice the same type of object was created twice, but the reference to the object determines which value is seen as output. If the object Jellyfish was passed to a method by an Animal reference, as you'll see in the section "Understanding Polymorphism," later in this chapter, the wrong value might be used.

Hiding variables makes the code very confusing and difficult to read, especially if you start modifying the value of the variable in both the parent and child methods, since it may not be clear which variable you're updating.

When defining a new variable in a child class, it is considered good coding practice to select a name for the variable that is not already a public, protected, or default variable in use in a parent class. Hiding private variables is considered less problematic because the child class did not have access to the variable in the parent class to begin with.

Creating Abstract Classes

Let's say you want to define a parent class that other developers are going to subclass. Your goal is to provide some reusable variables and methods to developers in the parent class, whereas the developers provide specific implementations or overrides of other methods in the child classes. Furthermore, let's say you also don't want an instance of the parent class to be instantiated unless it is an instance of the child class.

For example, you might define an Animal parent class that a number of classes extend from and use but for which an instance of Animal itself cannot be instantiated. All subclasses of the Animal class, such as Swan, are required to implement a getName() method, but there is no implementation for the method in the parent Animal class. How do you ensure all classes that extend Animal provide an implementation for this method?

In Java, you can accomplish this task by using an abstract class and abstract method. An *abstract class* is a class that is marked with the abstract keyword and cannot be instantiated. An *abstract method* is a method marked with the abstract keyword defined in an abstract class, for which no implementation is provided in the class in which it is declared.

The following code is based on our Animal and Swan description:

```java
public abstract class Animal {
  protected int age;
  public void eat() {
    System.out.println("Animal is eating");
  }
  public abstract String getName();
}
```

```
public class Swan extends Animal {
  public String getName() {
    return "Swan";
  }
}
```

   The first thing to notice about this sample code is that the Animal class is declared abstract and Swan is not. Next, the member age and the method eat() are marked as protected and public, respectively; therefore, they are inherited in subclasses such as Swan. Finally, the abstract method getName() is terminated with a semicolon and doesn't provide a body in the parent class Animal. This method is implemented with the same name and signature as the parent method in the Swan class.

Defining an Abstract Class

The previous sample code illustrates a number of important rules about abstract classes. For example, an abstract class may include nonabstract methods and variables, as you saw with the variable age and the method eat(). In fact, an abstract class is not required to include any abstract methods. For example, the following code compiles without issue even though it doesn't define any abstract methods:

```
public abstract class Cow {
}
```

   Although an abstract class doesn't have to implement any abstract methods, an abstract method may only be defined in an abstract class. For example, the following code won't compile because an abstract method is not defined within an abstract class:

```
public class Chicken {
  public abstract void peck();  // DOES NOT COMPILE
}
```

   The exam creators are fond of questions like this one, which mixes nonabstract classes with abstract methods. They are also fond of questions with methods marked as abstract for which an implementation is also defined. For example, neither method in the following code will compile because the methods are marked as abstract:

```
public abstract class Turtle {
  public abstract void swim() {}  // DOES NOT COMPILE
  public abstract int getAge() {  // DOES NOT COMPILE
    return 10;
  }
}
```

The first method, swim(), doesn't compile because two braces are provided instead of a semicolon, and Java interprets this as providing a body to an abstract method. The second method, getAge(), doesn't compile because it also provides a body to an abstract method. Pay close attention to swim(), because you'll likely see a question like this on the exam.

Default Method Implementations in Abstract Classes

Although you can't provide a default implementation to an abstract method in an abstract class, you can still define a method with a body—you just can't mark it as abstract. As long as you do not mark it as final, the subclass still has the option to override it, as explained in the previous section.

Next, we note that an abstract class cannot be marked as final for a somewhat obvious reason. By definition, an abstract class is one that must be extended by another class to be instantiated, whereas a final class can't be extended by another class. By marking an abstract class as final, you're saying the class can never be instantiated, so the compiler refuses to process the code. For example, the following code snippet will not compile:

```
public final abstract class Tortoise {  // DOES NOT COMPILE
}
```

Likewise, an abstract method may not be marked as final for the same reason that an abstract method may not be marked as final. Once marked as final, the method can never be overridden in a subclass, making it impossible to create a concrete instance of the abstract class.

```
public abstract class Goat {
  public abstract final void chew();  // DOES NOT COMPILE
}
```

Finally, a method may not be marked as both abstract and private. This rule makes sense if you think about it. How would you define a subclass that implements a required method if the method is not accessible by the subclass itself? The answer is you can't, which is why the compiler will complain if you try to do the following:

```
public abstract class Whale {
  private abstract void sing();  // DOES NOT COMPILE
}

public class HumpbackWhale extends Whale {
  private void sing() {
    System.out.println("Humpback whale is singing");
  }
}
```

In this example, the abstract method `sing()` defined in the parent class `Whale` is not visible to the subclass `HumpbackWhale`. Even though `HumpbackWhale` does provide an implementation, it is not considered an override of the abstract method since the abstract method is unreachable. The compiler recognizes this in the parent class and throws an exception as soon as `private` and `abstract` are applied to the same method.

If we changed the access modified from `private` to `protected` in the parent class `Whale`, would the code compile? Let's take a look:

```
public abstract class Whale {
  protected abstract void sing();
}


public class HumpbackWhale extends Whale {
  private void sing() {  // DOES NOT COMPILE
    System.out.println("Humpback whale is singing");
  }
}
```

In this modified example, the code will still not compile but for a completely different reason. If you remember the rules earlier in this chapter for overriding a method, the subclass cannot reduce the visibility of the parent method, `sing()`. Because the method is declared `protected` in the parent class, it must be marked as `protected` or `public` in the child class. Even with abstract methods, the rules for overriding methods must be followed.

Creating a Concrete Class

When working with abstract classes, it is important to remember that by themselves, they cannot be instantiated and therefore do not do much other than define static variables and methods. For example, the following code will not compile as it is an attempt to instantiate an abstract class.

```
public abstract class Eel {
  public static void main(String[] args) {
    final Eel eel = new Eel();  // DOES NOT COMPILE
  }
}
```

An abstract class becomes useful when it is extended by a concrete subclass. A *concrete class* is the first nonabstract subclass that extends an abstract class and is required to implement all inherited abstract methods. When you see a concrete class extending an abstract class on the exam, check that it implements all of the required abstract methods. Let's review this with the following example.

```
public abstract class Animal {
  public abstract String getName();
}
```

```
public class Walrus extends Animal { // DOES NOT COMPILE
}
```

First, note that Animal is marked as abstract and Walrus is not. In this example, Walrus is considered the first concrete subclass of Animal. Second, since Walrus is the first concrete subclass, it must implement all inherited abstract methods, getName() in this example. Because it doesn't, the compiler rejects the code.

Notice that when we define a concrete class as the "first" nonabstract subclass, we include the possibility that another nonabstract class may extend an existing nonabstract class. The key point is that the first concrete class to extend the abstract class must implement all inherited abstract methods. For example, the following variation will also not compile:

```
public abstract class Animal {
  public abstract String getName();
}

public class Bird extends Animal { // DOES NOT COMPILE
}

public class Flamingo extends Bird {
  public String getName() {
    return "Flamingo";
  }
}
```

Even though a second subclass Flamingo implements the abstract method getName(), the first concrete subclass Bird doesn't; therefore, the Bird class will not compile.

Extending an Abstract Class

Let's expand our discussion of abstract classes by introducing the concept of extending an abstract class with another abstract. We'll repeat our previous Walrus example with one minor variation:

```
public abstract class Animal {
  public abstract String getName();
}

public class Walrus extends Animal { // DOES NOT COMPILE
}

public abstract class Eagle extends Animal {
}
```

In this example, we again have an abstract class Animal with a concrete subclass Walrus that doesn't compile since it doesn't implement a getName() method. We also have an abstract class Eagle, which like Walrus extends Animal and doesn't provide an implementation for getName(). In this situation, Eagle does compile because it is marked as abstract. Be sure you understand why Walrus doesn't compile and Eagle does in this example.

As you saw in this example, abstract classes can extend other abstract classes and are not required to provide implementations for any of the abstract methods. It follows, then, that a concrete class that extends an abstract class must implement all inherited abstract methods. For example, the following concrete class Lion must implement two methods, getName() and roar():

```
public abstract class Animal {
  public abstract String getName();
}

public abstract class BigCat extends Animal {
  public abstract void roar();
}

public class Lion extends BigCat {
  public String getName() {
    return "Lion";
  }
  public void roar() {
    System.out.println("The Lion lets out a loud ROAR!");
  }
}
```

In this sample code, BigCat extends Animal but is marked as abstract; therefore, it is not required to provide an implementation for the getName() method. The class Lion is not marked as abstract, and as the first concrete subclass, it must implement all inherited abstract methods not defined in a parent class.

There is one exception to the rule for abstract methods and concrete classes: a concrete subclass is not required to provide an implementation for an abstract method if an intermediate abstract class provides the implementation. For example, take a look at the following variation on our previous example:

```
public abstract class Animal {
  public abstract String getName();
}

public abstract class BigCat extends Animal {
  public String getName() {
```

```
      return "BigCat";
   }
   public abstract void roar();
}

public class Lion extends BigCat {
   public void roar() {
      System.out.println("The Lion lets out a loud ROAR!");
   }
}
```

In this example, `BigCat` provides an implementation for the abstract method `getName()` defined in the abstract `Animal` class. Therefore, `Lion` inherits only one abstract method, `roar()`, and is not required to provide an implementation for the method `getName()`.

Here's one way to think about this: if an intermediate class provides an implementation for an abstract method, that method is inherited by subclasses as a concrete method, not as an abstract one. In other words, the subclasses do not consider it an inherited abstract method because it is no longer abstract by the time it reaches the subclasses.

The following are lists of rules for abstract classes and abstract methods that we have covered in this section. Review and understand these rules before taking the exam.

Abstract Class Definition Rules:

1. Abstract classes cannot be instantiated directly.

2. Abstract classes may be defined with any number, including zero, of abstract and non-abstract methods.

3. Abstract classes may not be marked as `private`, `protected`, or `final`.

4. An abstract class that extends another abstract class inherits all of its abstract methods as its own abstract methods.

5. The first concrete class that extends an abstract class must provide an implementation for all of the inherited abstract methods.

Abstract Method Definition Rules:

1. Abstract methods may only be defined in abstract classes.

2. Abstract methods may not be declared `private` or `final`.

3. Abstract methods must not provide a method body/implementation in the abstract class for which is it declared.

4. Implementing an abstract method in a subclass follows the same rules for overriding a method. For example, the name and signature must be the same, and the visibility of the method in the subclass must be at least as accessible as the method in the parent class.

Implementing Interfaces

Although Java doesn't allow multiple inheritance, it does allow classes to implement any number of interfaces. An *interface* is an abstract data type that defines a list of abstract public methods that any class implementing the interface must provide. An interface can also include a list of constant variables and default methods, which we'll cover in this section. In Java, an interface is defined with the `interface` keyword, analogous to the `class` keyword used when defining a class. A class invokes the interface by using the `implements` keyword in its class definition. Refer to Figures 5.4 and 5.5 for proper syntax usage.

FIGURE 5.4 Defining an interface

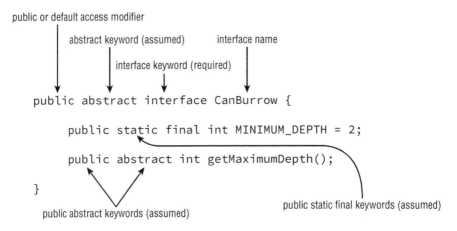

FIGURE 5.5 Implementing an interface

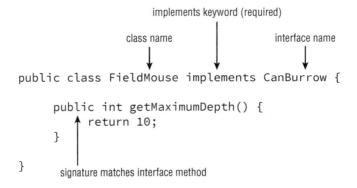

As you see in this example, an interface is not declared an abstract class, although it has many of the same properties of abstract class. Notice that the method modifiers in this example, abstract and public, are assumed. In other words, whether or not you provide them, the compiler will automatically insert them as part of the method definition.

A class may implement multiple interfaces, each separated by a comma, such as in the following example:

```
public class Elephant implements WalksOnFourLegs, HasTrunk, Herbivore {
}
```

In the example, if any of the interfaces defined abstract methods, the concrete class Elephant would be required to implement those methods.

New to Java 8 is the notion of default and static interface methods, which we'll cover at the end of this section.

Defining an Interface

It may be helpful to think of an interface as a specialized kind of abstract class, since it shares many of the same properties and rules as an abstract class. The following is a list of rules for creating an interface, many of which you should recognize as adaptions of the rules for defining abstract classes.

1. Interfaces cannot be instantiated directly.

2. An interface is not required to have any methods.

3. An interface may not be marked as final.

4. All top-level interfaces are assumed to have public or default access. They are assumed to be abstract whether this keyword is used or not. Therefore, making a method private, protected or final will trigger a compiler error as it is incompatible with these assumptions.

5. All nondefault methods in an interface are assumed to have the modifiers abstract and public in their definition. Therefore, marking a method as private, protected, or final will trigger compiler errors as these are incompatible with the abstract and public keywords.

The fourth rule doesn't apply to inner interfaces, although inner classes and interfaces are not in scope for the OCA exam. The first three rules are identical to the first three rules for creating an abstract class. Imagine we have an interface WalksOnTwoLegs, defined as follows:

```
public interface WalksOnTwoLegs {}
```

It compiles without issue, since interfaces are not required to define any methods. Now consider the following two examples, which do not compile:

```
public class TestClass {
  public static void main(String[] args) {
    WalksOnTwoLegs example = new WalksOnTwoLegs();  // DOES NOT COMPILE
```

```
  }
}
```

```
public final interface WalksOnEightLegs {  // DOES NOT COMPILE
}
```

The first example doesn't compile, as WalksOnTwoLegs is an interface and cannot be instantiated directly. The second example, WalksOnEightLegs, doesn't compile since interfaces may not be marked as final for the same reason that abstract classes cannot be marked as final.

The fourth and fifth rule about "assumed keywords" might be new to you, but you should think of these in the same light as the compiler inserting a default no-argument constructor or super() statement into your constructor. You may provide these modifiers yourself, although the compiler will insert them automatically if you do not. For example, the following two interface definitions are equivalent, as the compiler will convert them both to the second example:

```
public interface CanFly {
  void fly(int speed);
  abstract void takeoff();
  public abstract double dive();
}
```

```
public abstract interface CanFly {
  public abstract void fly(int speed);
  public abstract void takeoff();
  public abstract double dive();
}
```

In this example, the abstract keyword is first automatically added to the interface definition. Then, each method is prepended with abstract and public keywords. If the method already has either of these keywords, then no change is required. Let's take a look at an example that violates the assumed keywords:

```
private final interface CanCrawl {  // DOES NOT COMPILE
  private void dig(int depth);  // DOES NOT COMPILE
  protected abstract double depth();  // DOES NOT COMPILE
  public final void surface();  // DOES NOT COMPILE
}
```

Every single line of this example doesn't compile. The first line doesn't compile for two reasons. First, it is marked as final, which cannot be applied to an interface since it conflicts with the assumed abstract keyword. Next, it is marked as private, which conflicts with the public or default required access for interfaces. The second and third line do not compile because all interface methods are assumed to be public and marking them as private or protected throws a compiler error. Finally, the last line doesn't compile because the method is marked as final and since interface methods are assumed to be abstract, the compiler throws an exception for using both abstract and final keywords on a method.

 Adding the assumed keywords to an interface is a matter of personal preference, although it is considered good coding practice to do so. Code with the assumed keywords written out tends to be easier and clearer to read, and leads to fewer potential conflicts, as you saw in the previous examples.

Be sure to review the previous example and understand why each of the lines doesn't compile. There will likely be at least one question on the exam in which an interface or interface method uses an invalid modifier.

Inheriting an Interface

There are two inheritance rules you should keep in mind when extending an interface:

1. An interface that extends another interface, as well as an abstract class that implements an interface, inherits all of the abstract methods as its own abstract methods.

2. The first concrete class that implements an interface, or extends an abstract class that implements an interface, must provide an implementation for all of the inherited abstract methods.

Like an abstract class, an interface may be extended using the extends keyword. In this manner, the new child interface inherits all the abstract methods of the parent interface. Unlike an abstract class, though, an interface may extend multiple interfaces. Consider the following example:

```
public interface HasTail {
   public int getTailLength();
}

public interface HasWhiskers {
   public int getNumberOfWhiskers();
}

public interface Seal extends HasTail, HasWhiskers {
}
```

Any class that implements the Seal interface must provide an implementation for all methods in the parent interfaces—in this case, getTailLength() and getNumberOfWhiskers().

What about an abstract class that implements an interface? In this scenario, the abstract class is treated in the same way as an interface extending another interface. In other words, the abstract class inherits the abstract methods of the interface but is not required to implement them. That said, like an abstract class, the first concrete class to extend the abstract class must implement all the inherited abstract methods of the interface. We illustrate this in the following example:

```java
public interface HasTail {
  public int getTailLength();
}

public interface HasWhiskers {
  public int getNumberOfWhiskers();
}

public abstract class HarborSeal implements HasTail, HasWhiskers {
}

public class LeopardSeal implements HasTail, HasWhiskers {  // DOES NOT COMPILE
}
```

In this example, we see that HarborSeal is an abstract class and compiles without issue. Any class that extends HarborSeal will be required to implement all of the methods in the HasTail and HasWhiskers interface. Alternatively, LeopardSeal is not an abstract class, so it must implement all the interface methods within its definition. In this example, LeopardSeal doesn't provide an implementation for the interface methods, so the code doesn't compile.

Classes, Interfaces, and Keywords

The exam creators are fond of questions that mix class and interface terminology. Although a class can implement an interface, a class cannot extend an interface. Likewise, whereas an interface can extend another interface, an interface cannot implement another interface. The following examples illustrate these principles:

```java
public interface CanRun {}

public class Cheetah extends CanRun {}  // DOES NOT COMPILE

public class Hyena {}

public interface HasFur extends Hyena {} // DOES NOT COMPILE
```

The first example shows a class trying to extend an interface that doesn't compile. The second example shows an interface trying to extend a class, which also doesn't compile.

Be wary of examples on the exam that mix class and interface definitions. Make sure the only connection between a class and an interface is with the *class implements interface* syntax.

Abstract Methods and Multiple Inheritance

Since Java allows for multiple inheritance via interfaces, you might be wondering what will happen if you define a class that inherits from two interfaces that contain the same abstract method:

```
public interface Herbivore {
  public void eatPlants();
}

public interface Omnivore {
  public void eatPlants();
  public void eatMeat();
}
```

In this scenario, the signatures for the two interface methods eatPlants() are compatible, so you can define a class that fulfills both interfaces simultaneously:

```
public class Bear implements Herbivore, Omnivore {
  public void eatMeat() {
    System.out.println("Eating meat");
  }
  public void eatPlants() {
    System.out.println("Eating plants");
  }
}
```

Why does this work? Remember that interface methods in this example are abstract and define the "behavior" that the class implementing the interface must have. If two abstract interface methods have identical behaviors—or in this case the same method signature— creating a class that implements one of the two methods automatically implements the second method. In this manner, the interface methods are considered duplicates since they have the same signature.

What happens if the two methods have different signatures? If the method name is the same but the input parameters are different, there is no conflict because this is considered a method overload. We demonstrate this principle in the following example:

```
public interface Herbivore {
  public int eatPlants(int quantity);
}
```

```
public interface Omnivore {
  public void eatPlants();
}

public class Bear implements Herbivore, Omnivore {
  public int eatPlants(int quantity) {
    System.out.println("Eating plants: "+quantity);
    return quantity;
  }
  public void eatPlants() {
    System.out.println("Eating plants");
  }
}
```

In this example, we see that the class that implements both interfaces must provide implements of both versions of eatPlants(), since they are considered separate methods. Notice that it doesn't matter if the return type of the two methods is the same or different, because the compiler treats these methods as independent.

Unfortunately, if the method name and input parameters are the same but the return types are different between the two methods, the class or interface attempting to inherit both interfaces will not compile. The reason the code doesn't compile has less to do with interfaces and more to do with class design, as discussed in Chapter 4. It is not possible in Java to define two methods in a class with the same name and input parameters but different return types. Given the following two interface definitions for Herbivore and Omnivore, the following code will not compile:

```
public interface Herbivore {
  public int eatPlants();
}

public interface Omnivore {
  public void eatPlants();
}

public class Bear implements Herbivore, Omnivore { // DOES NOT COMPILE
  public int eatPlants() {  // DOES NOT COMPILE
    System.out.println("Eating plants: 10");
    return 10;
  }
  public void eatPlants() {  // DOES NOT COMPILE
    System.out.println("Eating plants");
  }
}
```

The code doesn't compile, as the class defines two methods with the same name and input parameters but different return types. If we were to remove either definition of eatPlants(), the compiler would stop because the definition of Bear would be missing one of the required methods. In other words, there is no implementation of the Bear class that inherits from Herbivore and Omnivore that the compiler would accept.

The compiler would also throw an exception if you define an interface or abstract class that inherits from two conflicting interfaces, as shown here:

```
public interface Herbivore {
  public int eatPlants();
}

public interface Omnivore {
  public void eatPlants();
}

public interface Supervore extends Herbivore, Omnivore {} // DOES NOT COMPILE

public abstract class AbstractBear implements Herbivore, Omnivore {}

                                              // DOES NOT COMPILE
```

Even without implementation details, the compiler detects the problem with the abstract definition and prevents compilation.

This concludes our discussion of abstract interface methods and multiple inheritance. We'll return to this discussion shortly after we introduce default interface methods. You'll see that things work a bit differently with default interface methods.

Interface Variables

Let's expand our discussion of interfaces to include interface variables, which can be defined within an interface. Like interface methods, interface variables are assumed to be public. Unlike interface methods, though, interface variables are also assumed to be static and final.

Here are two interface variables rules:

1. Interface variables are assumed to be public, static, and final. Therefore, marking a variable as private or protected will trigger a compiler error, as will marking any variable as abstract.

2. The value of an interface variable must be set when it is declared since it is marked as final.

In this manner, interface variables are essentially constant variables defined on the interface level. Because they are assumed to be static, they are accessible even without an instance of the interface. Like our earlier `CanFly` example, the following two interface definitions are equivalent, because the compiler will automatically convert them both to the second example:

```
public interface CanSwim {
  int MAXIMUM_DEPTH = 100;
  final static boolean UNDERWATER = true;
  public static final String TYPE = "Submersible";
}
```

```
public interface CanSwim {
  public static final int MAXIMUM_DEPTH = 100;
  public static final boolean UNDERWATER = true;
  public static final String TYPE = "Submersible";
}
```

As we see in this example, the compiler will automatically insert `public static final` to any constant interface variables it finds missing those modifiers. Also note that it is a common coding practice to use uppercase letters to denote constant values within a class.

Based on these rules, it should come as no surprise that the following entries will not compile:

```
public interface CanDig {
  private int MAXIMUM_DEPTH = 100;  // DOES NOT COMPILE
  protected abstract boolean UNDERWATER = false;  // DOES NOT COMPILE
  public static String TYPE;  // DOES NOT COMPILE
}
```

The first example, `MAXIMUM_DEPTH`, doesn't compile because the `private` modifier is used, and all interface variables are assumed to be `public`. The second line, `UNDERWATER`, doesn't compile for two reasons. It is marked as `protected`, which conflicts with the assumed modifier public, and it is marked as `abstract`, which conflicts with the assumed modifier `final`. Finally, the last example, `TYPE`, doesn't compile because it is missing a value. Unlike the other examples, the modifiers are correct, but as you may remember from Chapter 4, you must provide a value to a `static final` member of the class when it is defined.

Default Interface Methods

With the release of Java 8, the authors of Java have introduced a new type of method to an interface, referred to as a default method. A *default method* is a method defined within an interface with the `default` keyword in which a method body is provided. Contrast default methods with "regular" methods in an interface, which are assumed to be abstract and may not have a method body.

A default method within an interface defines an abstract method with a default implementation. In this manner, classes have the option to override the default method if they need to, but they are not required to do so. If the class doesn't override the method, the default implementation will be used. In this manner, the method definition is concrete, not abstract.

The purpose of adding default methods to the Java language was in part to help with code development and backward compatibility. Imagine you have an interface that is shared among dozens or even hundreds of users that you would like to add a new method to. If you just update the interface with the new method, the implementation would break among all of your subscribers, who would then be forced to update their code. In practice, this might even discourage you from making the change altogether. By providing a default implementation of the method, though, the interface becomes backward compatible with the existing codebase, while still providing those individuals who do want to use the new method with the option to override it.

The following is an example of a default method defined in an interface:

```
public interface IsWarmBlooded {
  boolean hasScales();
  public default double getTemperature() {
    return 10.0;
  }
}
```

This example defines two interface methods, one is a normal abstract method and the other a default method. Note that both methods are assumed to be `public`, as all methods of an interface are all `public`. The first method is terminated with a semicolon and doesn't provide a body, whereas the second default method provides a body. Any class that implements `IsWarmBlooded` may rely on the default implementation of `getTemperature()` or override the method and create its own version.

Note that the default access modifier as defined in Chapter 4 is completely different from the default method defined in this chapter. We defined a default access modifier in Chapter 4 as lack of an access modifier, which indicated a class may access a class, method, or value within another class if both classes are within the same package. In this chapter, we are specifically talking about the keyword `default` as applied to a method within an interface. Because all methods within an interface are assumed to be `public`, the access modifier for a default method is therefore `public`.

The following are the default interface method rules you need to be familiar with:

1. A default method may only be declared within an interface and not within a class or abstract class.

2. A default method must be marked with the `default` keyword. If a method is marked as `default`, it must provide a method body.

3. A default method is not assumed to be `static`, `final`, or `abstract`, as it may be used or overridden by a class that implements the interface.

4. Like all methods in an interface, a default method is assumed to be public and will not compile if marked as private or protected.

The first rule should give you some comfort in that you'll only see default methods in interfaces. If you see them in a class on the exam, assume the code will not compile. The second rule just denotes syntax, as default methods must use the default keyword. For example, the following code snippets will not compile:

```java
public interface Carnivore {
  public default void eatMeat();  // DOES NOT COMPILE
  public int getRequiredFoodAmount() {  // DOES NOT COMPILE
    return 13;
  }
}
```

In this example, the first method, eatMeat(), doesn't compile because it is marked as default but doesn't provide a method body. The second method, getRequiredFood Amount(), also doesn't compile because it provides a method body but is not marked with the default keyword.

Unlike interface variables, which are assumed static class members, default methods cannot be marked as static and require an instance of the class implementing the interface to be invoked. They can also not be marked as final or abstract, because they are allowed to be overridden in subclasses but are not required to be overridden.

When an interface extends another interface that contains a default method, it may choose to ignore the default method, in which case the default implementation for the method will be used. Alternatively, the interface may override the definition of the default method using the standard rules for method overriding, such as not limiting the accessibility of the method and using covariant returns. Finally, the interface may redeclare the method as abstract, requiring classes that implement the new interface to explicitly provide a method body. Analogous options apply for an abstract class that implements an interface.

For example, the following interface overrides one default interface method and redeclares a second interface method as abstract:

```java
public interface HasFins {
  public default int getNumberOfFins() {
    return 4;
  }
  public default double getLongestFinLength() {
    return 20.0;
  }
  public default boolean doFinsHaveScales() {
    return true;
  }
}
```

```
public interface SharkFamily extends HasFins {
  public default int getNumberOfFins() {
    return 8;
  }
  public double getLongestFinLength();
  public boolean doFinsHaveScales() {  // DOES NOT COMPILE
    return false;
  }
}
```

In this example, the first interface, HasFins, defines three default methods: getNumberOfFins(), getLongestFinLength(), and doFinsHaveScales(). The second interface, SharkFamily, extends HasFins and overrides the default method getNumberOfFins() with a new method that returns a different value. Next, the SharkFamily interface replaces the default method getLongestFinLength() with a new abstract method, forcing any class that implements the SharkFamily interface to provide an implementation of the method. Finally, the SharkFamily interface overrides the doFinsHaveScales() method but doesn't mark the method as default. Since interfaces may only contain methods with a body that are marked as default, the code will not compile.

Because default methods are new to Java 8, there will probably be a few questions on the exam about them, although they likely will not be any more difficult than the previous example.

Default Methods and Multiple Inheritance

You may have realized that by allowing default methods in interfaces, coupled with the fact a class may implement multiple interfaces, Java has essentially opened the door to multiple inheritance problems. For example, what value would the following code output?

```
public interface Walk {
  public default int getSpeed() {
    return 5;
  }
}

public interface Run {
  public default int getSpeed() {
    return 10;
  }
}

public class Cat implements Walk, Run {  // DOES NOT COMPILE
  public static void main(String[] args) {
    System.out.println(new Cat().getSpeed());
  }
}
```

In this example, `Cat` inherits the two default methods for `getSpeed()`, so which does it use? Since `Walk` and `Run` are considered siblings in terms of how they are used in the `Cat` class, it is not clear whether the code should output 5 or 10. The answer is that the code outputs neither value—it fails to compile.

If a class implements two interfaces that have default methods with the same name and signature, the compiler will throw an error. There is an exception to this rule, though: if the subclass overrides the duplicate default methods, the code will compile without issue—the ambiguity about which version of the method to call has been removed. For example, the following modified implementation of `Cat` will compile and output 1:

```java
public class Cat implements Walk, Run {
  public int getSpeed() {
    return 1;
  }

  public static void main(String[] args) {
    System.out.println(new Cat().getSpeed());
  }
}
```

You can see that having a class that implements or inherits two duplicate default methods forces the class to implement a new version of the method, or the code will not compile. This rule holds true even for abstract classes that implement multiple interfaces, because the default method could be called in a concrete method within the abstract class.

Static Interface Methods

Java 8 also now includes support for static methods within interfaces. These methods are defined explicitly with the `static` keyword and function nearly identically to static methods defined in classes, as discussed in Chapter 4. In fact, there is really only one distinction between a static method in a class and an interface. A static method defined in an interface is not inherited in any classes that implement the interface.

Here are the static interface method rules you need to be familiar with:

1. Like all methods in an interface, a static method is assumed to be `public` and will not compile if marked as `private` or `protected`.

2. To reference the static method, a reference to the name of the interface must be used.

The following is an example of a static method defined in an interface:

```java
public interface Hop {
  static int getJumpHeight() {
    return 8;
  }
}
```

The method getJumpHeight() works just like a static method as defined in a class. In other words, it can be accessed without an instance of the class using the Hop.getJumpHeight() syntax. Also, note that the compiler will automatically insert the access modifier public since all methods in interfaces are assumed to be public.

The following is an example of a class Bunny that implements Hop:

```java
public class Bunny implements Hop {
  public void printDetails() {
    System.out.println(getJumpHeight()); // DOES NOT COMPILE
  }
}
```

As you can see, without an explicit reference to the name of the interface the code will not compile, even though Bunny implements Hop. In this manner, the static interface methods are not inherited by a class implementing the interface. The following modified version of the code resolves the issue with a reference to the interface name Hop:

```java
public class Bunny implements Hop {
  public void printDetails() {
    System.out.println(Hop.getJumpHeight());
  }
}
```

It follows, then, that a class that implements two interfaces containing static methods with the same signature will still compile at runtime, because the static methods are not inherited by the subclass and must be accessed with a reference to the interface name. Contrast this with the behavior you saw for default interface methods in the previous section: the code would compile if the subclass overrode the default methods and would fail to compile otherwise. You can see that static interface methods have none of the same multiple inheritance issues and rules as default interface methods do.

Understanding Polymorphism

Java supports *polymorphism*, the property of an object to take on many different forms. To put this more precisely, a Java object may be accessed using a reference with the same type as the object, a reference that is a superclass of the object, or a reference that defines an interface the object implements, either directly or through a superclass. Furthermore, a cast is not required if the object is being reassigned to a super type or interface of the object.

Let's illustrate this polymorphism property with the following example:

```java
public class Primate {
  public boolean hasHair() {
    return true;
```

```
    }
}

public interface HasTail {
  public boolean isTailStriped();
}

public class Lemur extends Primate implements HasTail {
  public boolean isTailStriped() {
    return false;
  }
  public int age = 10;
  public static void main(String[] args) {
    Lemur lemur = new Lemur();
    System.out.println(lemur.age);

    HasTail hasTail = lemur;
    System.out.println(hasTail.isTailStriped());

    Primate primate = lemur;
    System.out.println(primate.hasHair());
    }
}
```

This code compiles and executes without issue and yields the following output:

```
10
false
true
```

The most important thing to note about this example is that only one object, Lemur, is created and referenced. The ability of an instance of Lemur to be passed as an instance of an interface it implements, HasTail, as well as an instance of one of its superclasses, Primate, is the nature of polymorphism.

Once the object has been assigned a new reference type, only the methods and variables available to that reference type are callable on the object without an explicit cast. For example, the following snippets of code will not compile:

```
    HasTail hasTail = lemur;
    System.out.println(hasTail.age);  // DOES NOT COMPILE
```

```
Primate primate = lemur;
System.out.println(primate.isTailStriped());  // DOES NOT COMPILE
```

In this example, the reference `hasTail` has direct access only to methods defined with the `HasTail` interface; therefore, it doesn't know the variable age is part of the object. Likewise, the reference `primate` has access only to methods defined in the `Primate` class, and it doesn't have direct access to the `isTailStriped()` method.

Object vs. Reference

In Java, all objects are accessed by reference, so as a developer you never have direct access to the object itself. Conceptually, though, you should consider the object as the entity that exists in memory, allocated by the Java runtime environment. Regardless of the type of the reference you have for the object in memory, the object itself doesn't change. For example, since all objects inherit `java.lang.Object`, they can all be reassigned to `java.lang.Object`, as shown in the following example:

```
Lemur lemur = new Lemur();
```

```
Object lemurAsObject = lemur;
```

Even though the Lemur object has been assigned a reference with a different type, the object itself has not changed and still exists as a Lemur object in memory. What has changed, then, is our ability to access methods within the Lemur class with the `lemurAsObject` reference. Without an explicit cast back to Lemur, as you'll see in the next section, we no longer have access to the Lemur properties of the object.

We can summarize this principle with the following two rules:

1. The type of the object determines which properties exist within the object in memory.

2. The type of the reference to the object determines which methods and variables are accessible to the Java program.

It therefore follows that successfully changing a reference of an object to a new reference type may give you access to new properties of the object, but those properties existed before the reference change occurred.

Let's illustrate this property using the previous example in Figure 5.6. As you can see in the figure, the same object exists in memory regardless of which reference is pointing to it. Depending on the type of the reference, we may only have access to certain methods. For example, the `hasTail` reference has access to the method `isTailStriped()` but doesn't have access to the variable age defined in the Lemur class. As you'll learn in the next section, it is possible to reclaim access to the variable age by explicitly casting the hasTail reference to a reference of type Lemur.

FIGURE 5.6 Object vs. reference

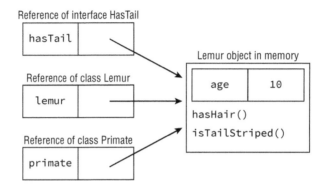

Casting Objects

In the previous example, we created a single instance of a Lemur object and accessed it via superclass and interface references. Once we changed the reference type, though, we lost access to more specific methods defined in the subclass that still exist within the object. We can reclaim those references by casting the object back to the specific sub-class it came from:

```
Primate primate = lemur;
Lemur lemur2 = primate; // DOES NOT COMPILE

Lemur lemur3 = (Lemur)primate;
System.out.println(lemur3.age);
```

In this example, we first try to convert the primate reference back to a lemur reference, lemur2, without an explicit cast. The result is that the code will not compile. In the second example, though, we explicitly cast the object to a subclass of the object Primate and we gain access to all the methods available to the Lemur class.

Here are some basic rules to keep in mind when casting variables:

1. Casting an object from a subclass to a superclass doesn't require an explicit cast.
2. Casting an object from a superclass to a subclass requires an explicit cast.
3. The compiler will not allow casts to unrelated types.
4. Even when the code compiles without issue, an exception may be thrown at runtime if the object being cast is not actually an instance of that class.

The third rule is important; the exam may try to trick you with a cast that the compiler doesn't allow. For example, we were able to cast a `Primate` reference to a `Lemur` reference, because `Lemur` is a subclass of `Primate` and therefore related.

Consider this example:

```
public class Bird {}

public class Fish {
  public static void main(String[] args) {
    Fish fish = new Fish();
    Bird bird = (Bird)fish;   // DOES NOT COMPILE
  }
}
```

In this example, the classes `Fish` and `Bird` are not related through any class hierarchy that the compiler is aware of; therefore, the code will not compile.

Casting is not without its limitations. Even though two classes share a related hierarchy, that doesn't mean an instance of one can automatically be cast to another. Here's an example:

```
public class Rodent {
}

public class Capybara extends Rodent {
  public static void main(String[] args) {
    Rodent rodent = new Rodent();
    Capybara capybara = (Capybara)rodent; // Throws ClassCastException at runtime
  }
}
```

This code creates an instance of `Rodent` and then tries to cast it to a subclass of `Rodent`, `Capybara`. Although this code will compile without issue, it will throw a `ClassCastException` at runtime since the object being referenced is not an instance of the `Capybara` class. The thing to keep in mind in this example is the object that was created is not related to the `Capybara` class in any way.

 Although this topic is out of scope for the OCA exam, keep in mind that the `instanceof` operator can be used to check whether an object belongs to a particular class and to prevent `ClassCastExceptions` at runtime. Unlike the previous example, the following code snippet doesn't throw an exception at runtime and performs the cast only if the `instanceof` operator returns true.

```
if(rodent instanceof Capybara) {
  Capybara capybara = (Capybara)rodent;
}
```

When reviewing a question on the exam that involves casting and polymorphism, be sure to remember what the instance of the object actually is. Then, focus on whether the compiler will allow the object to be referenced with or without explicit casts.

Virtual Methods

The most important feature of polymorphism—and one of the primary reasons we have class structure at all—is to support virtual methods. A *virtual method* is a method in which the specific implementation is not determined until runtime. In fact, all non-final, non-static, and non-private Java methods are considered virtual methods, since any of them can be overridden at runtime. What makes a virtual method special in Java is that if you call a method on an object that overrides a method, you get the overridden method, even if the call to the method is on a parent reference or within the parent class.

We'll illustrate this principle with the following example:

```java
public class Bird {
  public String getName() {
    return "Unknown";
  }
  public void displayInformation() {
    System.out.println("The bird name is: "+getName());
  }
}

public class Peacock extends Bird {
  public String getName() {
    return "Peacock";
  }
  public static void main(String[] args) {
    Bird bird = new Peacock();
    bird.displayInformation();
  }
}
```

This code compiles and executes without issue and outputs the following:

```
The bird name is: Peacock
```

As you saw in similar examples in the section "Overriding a Method," the method getName() is overridden in the child class Peacock. More importantly, though, the value of the getName() method at runtime in the displayInformation() method is replaced with the value of the implementation in the subclass Peacock.

In other words, even though the parent class `Bird` defines its own version of `getName()` and doesn't know anything about the `Peacock` class during compile-time, at runtime the instance uses the overridden version of the method, as defined on the instance of the object. We emphasize this point by using a reference to the `Bird` class in the `main()` method, although the result would have been the same if a reference to `Peacock` was used.

You now know the true purpose of overriding a method and how it relates to polymorphism. The nature of the polymorphism is that an object can take on many different forms. By combining your understanding of polymorphism with method overriding, you see that objects may be interpreted in vastly different ways at runtime, especially in methods defined in the superclasses of the objects.

Polymorphic Parameters

One of the most useful applications of polymorphism is the ability to pass instances of a subclass or interface to a method. For example, you can define a method that takes an instance of an interface as a parameter. In this manner, any class that implements the interface can be passed to the method. Since you're casting from a subtype to a supertype, an explicit cast is not required. This property is referred to as *polymorphic parameters* of a method, and we demonstrate it in the following example:

```java
public class Reptile {
  public String getName() {
    return "Reptile";
  }
}

public class Alligator extends Reptile {
  public String getName() {
    return "Alligator";
  }
}

public class Crocodile extends Reptile {
  public String getName() {
    return "Crocodile";
  }
}

public class ZooWorker {
  public static void feed(Reptile reptile) {
    System.out.println("Feeding: "+reptile.getName());
  }
```

```
  public static void main(String[] args) {
    feed(new Alligator());
    feed(new Crocodile());
    feed(new Reptile());
  }
}
```

This code compiles and executes without issue, yielding the following output:

```
Feeding: Alligator
Feeding: Crocodile
Feeding: Reptile
```

Let's focus on the feed(Reptile reptile) method in this example. As you can see, that method was able to handle instances of Alligator and Crocodile without issue, because both are subclasses of the Reptile class. It was also able to accept a matching type Reptile class. If we had tried to pass an unrelated class, such as the previously defined Rodent or Capybara classes, or a superclass such as java.lang.Object, to the feed() method, the code would not have compiled.

Polymorphic Parameters and Code Reusability

If you're defining a method that will be accessible outside the current class, either to subclasses of the current class or publicly to objects outside the current class, it is considered good coding practice to use the superclass or interface type of input parameters whenever possible.

As you may remember from Chapter 3, "Core Java APIs," the type java.util.List is an interface, not a class. Although there are many classes that implement java.util.List, such as java.util.ArrayList and java.util.Vector, when you're passing an existing List you're not usually interested in the particular subclass of the List. In this manner, a method that passes a List should use the interface type java.util.List as the polymorphic parameter type, rather than a specific class that implements List, as the code will be more reusable for other types of lists.

For example, it is common to see code such as the following that uses the interface reference type over the class type for greater reusability:

```
java.util.List list = new java.util.ArrayList();
```

Polymorphism and Method Overriding

Let's conclude this chapter by returning to the last three rules for method overriding to demonstrate how polymorphism requires them to be included as part of the Java specification. You'll see that without such rules in place, it is easy to construct an example with polymorphism in Java.

The first rule is that an overridden method must be at least as accessible as the method it is overriding. Let's assume this rule is not necessary and consider the following example:

```java
public class Animal {
  public String getName() {
    return "Animal";
  }
}
```

```java
public class Gorilla extends Animal {
  protected String getName() {  // DOES NOT COMPILE
    return "Gorilla";
  }
}
```

```java
public class ZooKeeper {
  public static void main(String[] args) {
    Animal animal = new Gorilla();
    System.out.println(animal.getName());
  }
}
```

For the purpose of this discussion, we'll ignore the fact that the implementation of getName() in the Gorilla class doesn't compile because it is less accessible than the version it is overriding in the Animal class.

As you can see, this example creates an ambiguity problem in the ZooKeeper class. The reference animal.getName() is allowed because the method is public in the Animal class, but due to polymorphism, the Gorilla object itself has been overridden with a less accessible version, not available to the ZooKeeper class. This creates a contradiction in that the compiler should not allow access to this method, but because it is being referenced as an instance of Animal, it is allowed. Therefore, Java eliminates this contradiction, thus disallowing a method from being overridden by a less accessible version of the method.

Likewise, a subclass cannot declare an overridden method with a new or broader exception than in the superclass, since the method may be accessed using a reference to the superclass. For example, if an instance of the subclass is passed to a method using a superclass reference, then the enclosing method would not know about any new checked exceptions that exist on methods for this object, potentially leading to compiled code with "unchecked" checked exceptions. Therefore, the Java compiler disallows overriding methods with new or broader exceptions.

Finally, overridden methods must use covariant return types for the same kinds of reasons as just discussed. If an object is cast to a superclass reference and the overridden method is called, the return type must be compatible with the return type of the parent method. If the return type in the child is too broad, it will result an inherent cast exception when accessed through the superclass reference.

For example, if the return type of a method is Double in the parent class and is overridden in a subclass with a method that returns Number, a superclass of Double, then the subclass method would be allowed to return any valid Number, including Integer, another subclass of Number. If we are using the object with a reference to the superclass, that means an Integer could be returned when a Double was expected. Since Integer is not a subclass of Double, this would lead to an implicit cast exception as soon as the value was referenced. Java solves this problem by only allowing covariant return types for overridden methods.

Summary

This chapter took the basic class structure we presented in Chapter 4 and expanded it by introducing the notion of inheritance. Java classes follow a multilevel single-inheritance pattern in which every class has exactly one direct parent class, with all classes eventually inheriting from java.lang.Object. Java interfaces simulate a limited form of multiple inheritance, since Java classes may implement multiple interfaces.

Inheriting a class gives you access to all of the public and protected methods of the class, but special rules for constructors and overriding methods must be followed or the code will not compile. For example, if the parent class doesn't include a no-argument constructor, an explicit call to a parent constructor must be provided in the child's constructors. Pay close attention on the exam to any class that defines a constructor with arguments and doesn't define a no-argument constructor.

We reviewed overloaded, overridden, and hidden methods and showed how they differ, especially in terms of polymorphism. We also introduced the notion of hiding variables, although we strongly discourage this in practice as it often leads to confusing, difficult-to-maintain code.

We introduced abstract classes and interfaces and showed how you can use them to define a platform for other developers to interact with. By definition, an abstract type cannot be instantiated directly and requires a concrete subclass for the code to be used. Since default and static interface methods are new to Java 8, expect to see at least one question on them on the exam.

Finally, this chapter introduced the concept of polymorphism, central to the Java language, and showed how objects can be accessed in a variety of forms. Make sure you understand when casts are needed for accessing objects, and be able to spot the difference between compile-time and runtime cast problems.

Exam Essentials

Be able to write code that extends other classes. A Java class that extends another class inherits all of its public and protected methods and variables. The first line of every constructor is a call to another constructor within the class using this() or a call to a constructor of the parent class using the super() call. If the parent class doesn't contain a no-argument constructor, an explicit call to the parent constructor must be provided. Parent methods and objects can be accessed explicitly using the super keyword. Finally, all classes in Java extend java.lang.Object either directly or from a superclass.

Understand the rules for method overriding. The Java compiler allows methods to be overridden in subclasses if certain rules are followed: a method must have the same signature, be at least as accessible as the parent method, must not declare any new or broader exceptions, and must use covariant return types.

Understand the rules for hiding methods and variables. When a static method is re-created in a subclass, it is referred to as method hiding. Likewise, variable hiding is when a variable name is reused in a subclass. In both situations, the original method or variable still exists and is used in methods that reference the object in the parent class. For method hiding, the use of static in the method declaration must be the same between the parent and child class. Finally, variable and method hiding should generally be avoided since it leads to confusing and difficult-to-follow code.

Recognize the difference between method overriding and method overloading. Both method overloading and overriding involve creating a new method with the same name as an existing method. When the method signature is the same, it is referred to as method overriding and must follow a specific set of override rules to compile. When the method signature is different, with the method taking different inputs, it is referred to as method overloading and none of the override rules are required.

Be able to write code that creates and extends abstract classes. In Java, classes and methods can be declared as abstract. Abstract classes cannot be instantiated and require a concrete subclass to be accessed. Abstract classes can include any number, including zero, of abstract and nonabstract methods. Abstract methods follow all the method override rules and may only be defined within abstract classes. The first concrete subclass of an abstract class must implement all the inherited methods. Abstract classes and methods may not be marked as final or private.

Be able to write code that creates, extends, and implements interfaces.   Interfaces are similar to a specialized abstract class in which only abstract methods and constant static final variables are allowed. New to Java 8, an interface can also define default and static methods with method bodies. All members of an interface are assumed to be public. Methods are assumed to be abstract if not explicitly marked as default or static. An interface that extends another interface inherits all its abstract methods. An interface cannot extend a class, nor can a class extend an interface. Finally, classes may implement any number of interfaces.

Be able to write code that uses default and static interface methods.   A default method allows a developer to add a new method to an interface used in existing implementations, without forcing other developers using the interface to recompile their code. A developer using the interface may override the default method or use the provided one. A static method in an interface follows the same rules for a static method in a class.

Understand polymorphism.   An object in Java may take on a variety of forms, in part depending on the reference used to access the object. Methods that are overridden will be replaced everywhere they are used, whereas methods and variables that are hidden will only be replaced in the classes and subclasses that they are defined. It is common to rely on polymorphic parameters—the ability of methods to be automatically passed as a superclass or interface reference—when creating method definitions.

Recognize valid reference casting.   An instance can be automatically cast to a superclass or interface reference without an explicit cast. Alternatively, an explicit cast is required if the reference is being narrowed to a subclass of the object. The Java compiler doesn't permit casting to unrelated types. You should be able to discern between compiler-time casting errors and those that will not occur until runtime and that throw a CastClassException.

Review Questions

1. What modifiers are implicitly applied to all interface methods? (Choose all that apply)
   - **A.** protected
   - **B.** public
   - **C.** static
   - **D.** void
   - **E.** abstract
   - **F.** default

2. What is the output of the following code?
```
1: class Mammal {
2:    public Mammal(int age) {
3:       System.out.print("Mammal");
4:    }
5: }
6: public class Platypus extends Mammal {
7:    public Platypus() {
8:       System.out.print("Platypus");
9:    }
10:   public static void main(String[] args) {
11:      new Mammal(5);
12:   }
13: }
```
   - **A.** Platypus
   - **B.** Mammal
   - **C.** PlatypusMammal
   - **D.** MammalPlatypus
   - **E.** The code will not compile because of line 7.
   - **F.** The code will not compile because of line 11.

3. Which of the following statements can be inserted in the blank line so that the code will compile successfully? (Choose all that apply)
```
public interface CanHop {}
public class Frog implements CanHop {
   public static void main(String[] args) {
      _____ frog = new TurtleFrog();
   }
}
```

```
public class BrazilianHornedFrog extends Frog {}
public class TurtleFrog extends Frog {}
```

A. Frog

B. TurtleFrog

C. BrazilianHornedFrog

D. CanHop

E. Object

F. Long

4. Which statement(s) are correct about the following code? (Choose all that apply)

```
public class Rodent {
    protected static Integer chew() throws Exception {
      System.out.println("Rodent is chewing");
      return 1;
    }
}
public class Beaver extends Rodent {
    public Number chew() throws RuntimeException {
      System.out.println("Beaver is chewing on wood");
      return 2;
    }
}
```

A. It will compile without issue.

B. It fails to compile because the type of the exception the method throws is a subclass of the type of exception the parent method throws.

C. It fails to compile because the return types are not covariant.

D. It fails to compile because the method is protected in the parent class and public in the subclass.

E. It fails to compile because of a static modifier mismatch between the two methods.

5. Which of the following may only be hidden and not overridden? (Choose all that apply)

A. private instance methods

B. protected instance methods

C. public instance methods

D. static methods

E. public variables

F. private variables

6. Choose the correct statement about the following code:

```
1: interface HasExoskeleton {
2:    abstract int getNumberOfSections();
3: }
4: abstract class Insect implements HasExoskeleton {
5:    abstract int getNumberOfLegs();
6: }
7: public class Beetle extends Insect {
8:    int getNumberOfLegs() { return 6; }
9: }
```

    A. It compiles and runs without issue.

    B. The code will not compile because of line 2.

    C. The code will not compile because of line 4.

    D. The code will not compile because of line 7.

    E. It compiles but throws an exception at runtime.

7. Which of the following statements about polymorphism are true? (Choose all that apply)

    A. A reference to an object may be cast to a subclass of the object without an explicit cast.

    B. If a method takes a superclass of three objects, then any of those classes may be passed as a parameter to the method.

    C. A method that takes a parameter with type `java.lang.Object` will take any reference.

    D. All cast exceptions can be detected at compile-time.

    E. By defining a public instance method in the superclass, you guarantee that the specific method will be called in the parent class at runtime.

8. Choose the correct statement about the following code:

```
1: public interface Herbivore {
2:    int amount = 10;
3:    public static void eatGrass();
4:    public int chew() {
5:       return 13;
6:    }
7: }
```

    A. It compiles and runs without issue.

    B. The code will not compile because of line 2.

    C. The code will not compile because of line 3.

    D. The code will not compile because of line 4.

    E. The code will not compile because of lines 2 and 3.

    F. The code will not compile because of lines 3 and 4.

9. Choose the correct statement about the following code:

```
1: public interface CanFly {
2:    void fly();
3: }
4: interface HasWings {
5:    public abstract Object getWindSpan();
6: }
7: abstract class Falcon implements CanFly, HasWings {
8: }
```

  A. It compiles without issue.

  B. The code will not compile because of line 2.

  C. The code will not compile because of line 4.

  D. The code will not compile because of line 5.

  E. The code will not compile because of lines 2 and 5.

  F. The code will not compile because the class `Falcon` doesn't implement the interface methods.

10. Which statements are true for both abstract classes and interfaces? (Choose all that apply)

  A. All methods within them are assumed to be abstract.

  B. Both can contain `public static final` variables.

  C. Both can be extended using the `extends` keyword.

  D. Both can contain default methods.

  E. Both can contain static methods.

  F. Neither can be instantiated directly.

  G. Both inherit `java.lang.Object`.

11. What modifiers are assumed for all interface variables? (Choose all that apply)

  A. `public`

  B. `protected`

  C. `private`

  D. `static`

  E. `final`

  F. `abstract`

12. What is the output of the following code?

```
1: interface Nocturnal {
2:    default boolean isBlind() { return true; }
3: }
4: public class Owl implements Nocturnal {
```

```
5:    public boolean isBlind() { return false; }
6:      public static void main(String[] args) {
7:      Nocturnal nocturnal = (Nocturnal)new Owl();
8:      System.out.println(nocturnal.isBlind());
9:      }
10: }
```

A. true

B. false

C. The code will not compile because of line 2.

D. The code will not compile because of line 5.

E. The code will not compile because of line 7.

F. The code will not compile because of line 8.

13. What is the output of the following code?

```
1: class Arthropod {
2:    public void printName(double input) { System.out
   .print("Arthropod"); }
3: }
4: public class Spider extends Arthropod {
5:    public void printName(int input) { System.out.print("Spider"); }
6:    public static void main(String[] args) {
7:      Spider spider = new Spider();
8:      spider.printName(4);
9:      spider.printName(9.0);
10:   }
11: }
```

A. SpiderArthropod

B. ArthropodSpider

C. SpiderSpider

D. ArthropodArthropod

E. The code will not compile because of line 5.

F. The code will not compile because of line 9.

14. Which statements are true about the following code? (Choose all that apply)

```
1: interface HasVocalCords {
2:    public abstract void makeSound();
3: }
4: public interface CanBark extends HasVocalCords {
5:    public void bark();
6: }
```

A. The CanBark interface doesn't compile.

B. A class that implements HasVocalCords must override the makeSound() method.

C. A class that implements CanBark inherits both the makeSound() and bark() methods.

D. A class that implements CanBark only inherits the bark() method.

E. An interface cannot extend another interface.

15. Which of the following is true about a concrete subclass? (Choose all that apply)

   A. A concrete subclass can be declared as abstract.

   B. A concrete subclass must implement all inherited abstract methods.

   C. A concrete subclass must implement all methods defined in an inherited interface.

   D. A concrete subclass cannot be marked as final.

   E. Abstract methods cannot be overridden by a concrete subclass.

16. What is the output of the following code?

```
1: abstract class Reptile {
2:   public final void layEggs() { System.out.println("Reptile laying eggs");
   }
3:     public static void main(String[] args) {
4:       Reptile reptile = new Lizard();
5:       reptile.layEggs();
6:     }
7: }
8: public class Lizard extends Reptile {
9:   public void layEggs() { System.out.println("Lizard laying eggs"); }
10: }
```

   A. Reptile laying eggs

   B. Lizard laying eggs

   C. The code will not compile because of line 4.

   D. The code will not compile because of line 5.

   E. The code will not compile because of line 9.

17. What is the output of the following code?

```
1: public abstract class Whale {
2:   public abstract void dive() {};
3:   public static void main(String[] args) {
4:     Whale whale = new Orca();
5:     whale.dive();
6:   }
7: }
```

```
8: class Orca extends Whale {
9:    public void dive(int depth) { System.out.println("Orca diving"); }
10: }
```

A. Orca diving

B. The code will not compile because of line 2.

C. The code will not compile because of line 8.

D. The code will not compile because of line 9.

E. The output cannot be determined from the code provided.

18. What is the output of the following code? (Choose all that apply)

```
1: interface Aquatic {
2:    public default int getNumberOfGills(int input) { return 2; }
3: }
4: public class ClownFish implements Aquatic {
5:    public String getNumberOfGills() { return "4"; }
6:    public String getNumberOfGills(int input) { return "6"; }
7:    public static void main(String[] args) {
8:      System.out.println(new ClownFish().getNumberOfGills(-1));
9:    }
10: }
```

A. 2

B. 4

C. 6

D. The code will not compile because of line 5.

E. The code will not compile because of line 6.

F. The code will not compile because of line 8.

19. Which of the following statements can be inserted in the blank so that the code will compile successfully? (Choose all that apply)

```
public class Snake {}
public class Cobra extends Snake {}
public class GardenSnake {}
public class SnakeHandler {
   private Snake snake;
   public void setSnake(Snake snake) { this.snake = snake; }
   public static void main(String[] args) {
     new SnakeHandler().setSnake(_____);
   }
}
```

A. new Cobra()

B. new GardenSnake()

C. new Snake()

D. new Object()

E. new String("Snake")

F. null

20. What is the result of the following code?

```
1: public abstract class Bird {
2:    private void fly() { System.out.println("Bird is flying"); }
3:    public static void main(String[] args) {
4:      Bird bird = new Pelican();
5:      bird.fly();
6:    }
7: }
8: class Pelican extends Bird {
9:    protected void fly() { System.out.println("Pelican is flying"); }
10: }
```

A. Bird is flying

B. Pelican is flying

C. The code will not compile because of line 4.

D. The code will not compile because of line 5.

E. The code will not compile because of line 9.

Chapter

6

Exceptions

Many things can go wrong in a program. Java uses exceptions to deal with some of these scenarios. The OCA exam covers only the basics of working with exceptions. The rest are on the OCP exam.

Understanding Exceptions

A program can fail for just about any reason. Here are just a few possibilities:

- The code tries to connect to a website, but the Internet connection is down.
- You made a coding mistake and tried to access an invalid index in an array.
- One method calls another with a value that the method doesn't support.

As you can see, some of these are coding mistakes. Others are completely beyond your control. Your program can't help it if the Internet connection goes down. What it *can* do is deal with the situation.

First, we'll look at the role of exceptions. Then we'll cover the various types of exceptions, followed by an explanation of how to throw an exception in Java.

The Role of Exceptions

An *exception* is Java's way of saying, "I give up. I don't know what to do right now. You deal with it." When you write a method, you can either deal with the exception or make it the calling code's problem.

As an example, think of Java as a child who visits the zoo. The *happy path* is when nothing goes wrong. The child continues to look at the animals until the program nicely ends. Nothing went wrong and there were no exceptions to deal with.

This child's younger sister doesn't experience the happy path. In all the excitement she trips and falls. Luckily, it isn't a bad fall. The little girl gets up and proceeds to look at more animals. She has handled the issue all by herself. Unfortunately, she falls again later in the day and starts crying. This time, she has declared she needs help by crying. The story ends well. Her daddy rubs her knee and gives her a hug. Then they go back to seeing more animals and enjoy the rest of the day.

These are the two approaches Java uses when dealing with exceptions. A method can handle the exception case itself or make it the caller's responsibility. You saw both in the trip to the zoo.

You saw an exception in Chapter 1, "Java Building Blocks," with a very simple Zoo example. You wrote a class that printed out the name of the zoo:

```
1: public class Zoo {
2:    public static void main(String[] args) {
3:       System.out.println(args[0]);
4:       System.out.println(args[1]);
5: } }
```

Then you tried to call it without enough arguments:

```
$ javac Zoo.java
$ java Zoo Zoo
```

On line 4, Java realized there's only one element in the array and index 1 is not allowed. Java threw up its hands in defeat and threw an exception. It didn't try to handle the exception. It just said, "I can't deal with it" and the exception was displayed:

```
ZooException in thread "main"
java.lang.ArrayIndexOutOfBoundsException: 1
at Zoo.main(Zoo.java:4)
```

Exceptions can and do occur all the time, even in solid program code. In our example, toddlers falling is a fact of life. When you write more advanced programs, you'll need to deal with failures in accessing files, networks, and outside services. On the OCA exam, exceptions deal largely with mistakes in programs. For example, a program might try to access an invalid position in an array. The key point to remember is that exceptions alter the program flow.

🌐 Real World Scenario

Return Codes vs. Exceptions

Exceptions are used when "something goes wrong." However, the word "wrong" is subjective. The following code returns –1 instead of throwing an exception if no match is found:

```
public int indexOf(String[] names, String name) {
  for (int i = 0; i < names.length; i++) {
    if (names[i].equals(name)) { return i; }
  }
  return -1;
}
```

continues

continued

This approach is common when writing a method that does a search. For example, imagine being asked to find the name Joe in the array. It is perfectly reasonable that Joe might not appear in the array. When this happens, a special value is returned. An exception should be reserved for exceptional conditions like *names* being null.

In general, try to avoid return codes. Return codes are commonly used in searches, so programmers are expecting them. In other methods, you will take your callers by surprise by returning a special value. An exception forces the program to deal with them or end with the exception if left unhandled, whereas a return code could be accidentally ignored and cause problems later in the program. An exception is like shouting, "Deal with me!"

Understanding Exception Types

As we've explained, an exception is an event that alters program flow. Java has a `Throwable` superclass for all objects that represent these events. Not all of them have the word exception in their classname, which can be confusing. Figure 6.1 shows the key subclasses of `Throwable`.

FIGURE 6.1   Categories of exception

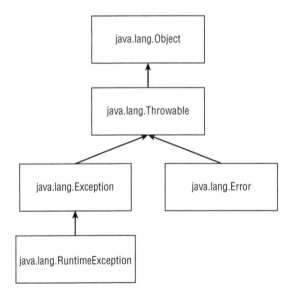

Error means something went so horribly wrong that your program should not attempt to recover from it. For example, the disk drive "disappeared." These are abnormal conditions that you aren't likely to encounter.

A *runtime exception* is defined as the `RuntimeException` class and its subclasses. Runtime exceptions tend to be unexpected but not necessarily fatal. For example, accessing an invalid array index is unexpected. Runtime exceptions are also known as *unchecked exceptions*.

Runtime vs. at the Time the Program is Run

A runtime (unchecked) exception is a specific type of exception. All exceptions occur at the time that the program is run. (The alternative is compile time, which would be a compiler error.) People don't refer to them as run time exceptions because that would be too easy to confuse with runtime! When you see runtime, it means unchecked.

A *checked exception* includes Exception and all subclasses that do not extend RuntimeException. Checked exceptions tend to be more anticipated—for example, trying to read a file that doesn't exist.

Checked exceptions? What are we checking? Java has a rule called the *handle or declare rule*. For checked exceptions, Java requires the code to either handle them or declare them in the method signature.

For example, this method declares that it might throw an exception:

```java
void fall() throws Exception {
  throw new Exception();
}
```

Notice that you're using two different keywords here. throw tells Java that you want to throw an Exception. throws simply declares that the method might throw an Exception. It also might not. You will see the throws keyword more later in the chapter.

Because checked exceptions tend to be anticipated, Java enforces that the programmer do something to show the exception was thought about. Maybe it was handled in the method. Or maybe the method declares that it can't handle the exception and someone else should.

An example of a runtime exception is a NullPointerException, which happens when you try to call a member on a null reference. This can occur in any method. If you had to declare runtime exceptions everywhere, every single method would have that clutter!

Checked vs. Unchecked (Runtime) Exceptions

In the past, developers used checked exceptions more often than they do now. According to Oracle, they are intended for issues a programmer "might reasonably be expected to recover from." Then developers started writing code where a chain of methods kept declaring the same exception and nobody actually handled it. Some libraries started using runtime exceptions for issues a programmer might reasonably be expected to recover from. Many programmers can hold a debate with you on which approach is better. For the OCA exam, you need to know the rules for how checked versus unchecked exceptions function. You don't have to decide philosophically whether an exception should be checked or unchecked.

Throwing an Exception

Any Java code can throw an exception; this includes code you write. For the OCP exam, you'll learn how to create your own exception classes. The OCA exam is limited to exceptions that someone else has created. Most likely, they will be exceptions that are provided with Java. You might encounter an exception that was made up for the exam. This is fine. The question will make it obvious that these are exceptions by having the classname end with exception. For example, "MyMadeUpException" is clearly an exception.

On the exam, you will see two types of code that result in an exception. The first is code that's wrong. For example:

```
String[] animals = new String[0];
System.out.println(animals[0]);
```

This code throws an `ArrayIndexOutOfBoundsException`. That means questions about exceptions can be hidden in questions that appear to be about something else.

On the OCA exam, the vast majority of questions have a choice about not compiling and about throwing an exception. Pay special attention to code that calls a method on a null or that references an invalid array or `ArrayList` index. If you spot this, you know the correct answer is that the code throws an exception.

The second way for code to result in an exception is to explicitly request Java to throw one. Java lets you write statements like these:

```
throw new Exception();
throw new Exception("Ow! I fell.");
throw new RuntimeException();
throw new RuntimeException("Ow! I fell.");
```

The `throw` keyword tells Java you want some other part of the code to deal with the exception. This is the same as the young girl crying for her daddy. Someone else needs to figure out what to do about the exception.

When creating an exception, you can usually pass a `String` parameter with a message or you can pass no parameters and use the defaults. We say *usually* because this is a convention. Someone could create an exception class that does not have a constructor that takes a message. The first two examples create a new object of type `Exception` and throw it. The last two show that the code looks the same regardless of which type of exception you throw.

These rules are very important. Be sure to closely study everything in Table 6.1.

TABLE 6.1   Types of exceptions

Type	How to recognize	Okay for program to catch?	Is program required to handle or declare?
Runtime exception	Subclass of RuntimeException	Yes	No
Checked exception	Subclass of Exception but not subclass of RuntimeException	Yes	Yes
Error	Subclass of Error	No	No

Using a *try* Statement

Now that you know what exceptions are, let's explore how to handle them. Java uses a *try statement* to separate the logic that might throw an exception from the logic to handle that exception. Figure 6.2 shows the syntax of a try statement.

FIGURE 6.2   The syntax of a *try* statement

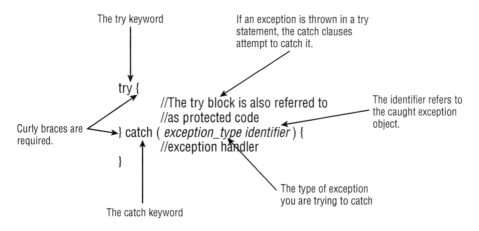

The code in the try block is run normally. If any of the statements throw an exception that can be caught by the exception type listed in the catch block, the try block stops running and execution goes to the catch statement. If none of the statements in the try block throw an exception that can be caught, the *catch clause* is not run.

You probably noticed the words "block" and "clause" used interchangeably. The exam does this as well, so we are getting you used to it. Both are correct. "Block" is correct because there are braces present. "Clause" is correct because they are part of a try statement.

There aren't a ton of syntax rules here. The curly braces are required for the try and catch blocks.

In our example, the little girl gets up by herself the first time she falls. Here's what this looks like:

```
3: void explore() {
4:    try {
5:      fall();
6:      System.out.println("never get here");
7:    } catch (RuntimeException e) {
8:       getUp();
9:    }
10:   seeAnimals();
11: }
12: void fall() {  throw new RuntimeException(); }
```

First, line 5 calls the fall() method. Line 12 throws an exception. This means Java jumps straight to the catch block, skipping line 6. The girl gets up on line 8. Now the try statement is over and execution proceeds normally with line 10.

Now let's look at some invalid try statements that the exam might try to trick you with. Do you see what's wrong with this one?

```
try  // DOES NOT COMPILE
  fall();
catch (Exception e)
  System.out.println("get up");
```

The problem is that the braces are missing. It needs to look like this:

```
try {
  fall();
} catch (Exception e) {
  System.out.println("get up");
}
```

try statements are like methods in that the curly braces are required even if there is only one statement inside the code blocks. if statements and loops are special in this respect as they allow you to omit the curly braces.

What about this one?

```
try {// DOES NOT COMPILE
  fall();
}
```

This code doesn't compile because the try block doesn't have anything after it. Remember, the point of a try statement is for something to happen if an exception is thrown. Without another clause, the try statement is lonely.

Now that you know the basics, let's start adding more features to exceptions. The following sections show you how to add a finally clause to a try statement and catch different types of exceptions and describe what happens if an exception is thrown in catch or finally.

Adding a *finally* Block

The try statement also lets you run code at the end with a *finally clause* regardless of whether an exception is thrown. Figure 6.3 shows the syntax of a try statement with this extra functionality.

FIGURE 6.3   The syntax of a *try* statement with *finally*

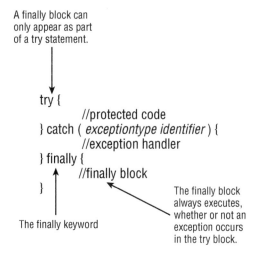

There are two paths through code with both a catch and a finally. If an exception is thrown, the finally block is run after the catch block. If no exception is thrown, the finally block is run after the try block completes.

Let's go back to our young girl example, this time with `finally`:

```
12: void explore() {
13:    try {
14:       seeAnimals();
15:       fall();
16:    } catch (Exception e) {
17:       getHugFromDaddy();
18:    } finally {
19:       seeMoreAnimals();
20:    }
21:    goHome();
22: }
```

The girl falls on line 15. If she gets up by herself, the code goes on to the `finally` block and runs line 19. Then the `try` statement is over and the code proceeds on line 21. If the girl doesn't get up by herself, she throws an exception. The `catch` block runs and she gets a hug on line 17. Then the `try` statement is over and the code proceeds on line 21. Either way, the ending is the same. The `finally` block is executed and the `try` statement ends.

> On the OCA exam, a try statement must have catch and/or finally. Having both is fine. Having neither is a problem. On the OCP exam, you'll learn about a special syntax for a try statement called try-with-resources that allows neither a catch nor a finally block. On the OCA exam, you get to assume a try statement is just a regular try statement and not a try-with-resources statement.

The exam will try to trick you with missing clauses or clauses in the wrong order. Do you see why the following do or do not compile?

```
25: try { // DOES NOT COMPILE
26:    fall();
27: } finally {
28:    System.out.println("all better");
29: } catch (Exception e) {
30:    System.out.println("get up");
31: }
32:
33: try { // DOES NOT COMPILE
34:    fall();
35: }
36:
37: try {
```

```
38:    fall();
39: } finally {
40:    System.out.println("all better");
41: }
```

The first example (lines 25–31) does not compile because the catch and finally blocks are in the wrong order. The second example (lines 33–35) does not compile because there must be a catch or finally block. The third example (lines 37–41) is just fine. catch is not required if finally is present.

One problem with finally is that any realistic uses for it are out of the scope of the OCA exam. finally is typically used to close resources such as files or databases—both of which are topics on the OCP exam. This means most of the examples you encounter on the OCA exam with finally are going to look contrived. For example, you'll get asked questions such as what this code outputs:

```
String s = "";
try {
  s += "t";
} catch(Exception e) {
  s += "c";
} finally {
  s += "f";
}
s += "a";
System.out.print(s);
```

The answer is tfa. The try block is executed. Since no exception is thrown, Java goes straight to the finally block. Then the code after the try statement is run. We know; this is a silly example. Expect to see examples like this on the OCA exam.

System.exit

There is one exception to "the finally block always runs after the catch block" rule: Java defines a method that you call as System.exit(0);. The integer parameter is the error code that gets returned. System.exit tells Java, "Stop. End the program right now. Do not pass go. Do not collect $200." When System.exit is called in the try or catch block, finally does not run.

Catching Various Types of Exceptions

So far, you have been catching only one type of exception. Now let's see what happens when different types of exceptions can be thrown from the same method.

Creating your own exceptions is not on the OCA exam, but it is on the OCP exam. However, the OCA exam can define basic exceptions to show you the hierarchy. You only need to do two things with this information. First, you must be able to recognize if the exception is a checked or an unchecked exception. Second, you need to determine if any of the exceptions are subclasses of the others.

```
class AnimalsOutForAWalk extends RuntimeException { }
class ExhibitClosed extends RuntimeException { }
class ExhibitClosedForLunch extends ExhibitClosed { }
```

In this example, there are three custom exceptions. All are unchecked exceptions because they directly or indirectly extend RuntimeException. Now we catch both types of exceptions and handle them by printing out the appropriate message:

```
public void visitPorcupine() {
  try {
    seeAnimal();
  } catch (AnimalsOutForAWalk e) {// first catch block
    System.out.print("try back later");
  } catch (ExhibitClosed e) {// second catch block
    System.out.print("not today");
  }
}
```

There are three possibilities for when this code is run. If seeAnimal() doesn't throw an exception, nothing is printed out. If the animal is out for a walk, only the first catch block runs. If the exhibit is closed, only the second catch block runs.

A rule exists for the order of the catch blocks. Java looks at them in the order they appear. If it is impossible for one of the catch blocks to be executed, a compiler error about unreachable code occurs. This happens when a superclass is caught before a subclass. Remember, we warned you to pay attention to any subclass exceptions.

In the porcupine example, the order of the catch blocks could be reversed because the exceptions don't inherit from each other. And yes, we have seen a porcupine be taken for a walk on a leash.

The following example shows exception types that do inherit from each other:

```
public void visitMonkeys() {
  try {
    seeAnimal();
  } catch (ExhibitClosedForLunch e) {// subclass exception
    System.out.print("try back later");
  } catch (ExhibitClosed e) {// superclass exception
    System.out.print("not today");
  }
}
```

If the more specific ExhibitClosedForLunch exception is thrown, the first catch block runs. If not, Java checks if the superclass ExhibitClosed exception is thrown and catches it. This time, the order of the catch blocks does matter. The reverse does not work.

```
public void visitMonkeys() {
  try {
    seeAnimal();
  } catch (ExhibitClosed e) {
    System.out.print("not today");
  } catch (ExhibitClosedForLunch e) {// DOES NOT COMPILE
    System.out.print("try back later");
  }
}
```

This time, if the more specific ExhibitClosedForLunch exception is thrown, the catch block for ExhibitClosed runs—which means there is no way for the second catch block to ever run. Java correctly tells us there is an unreachable catch block.

Let's try this one more time. Do you see why this code doesn't compile?

```
public void visitSnakes() {
  try {
    seeAnimal();
  } catch (RuntimeException e) {
    System.out.print("runtime exception");
  } catch (ExhibitClosed e) {// DOES NOT COMPILE
    System.out.print("not today");
  } catch (Exception e) {
    System.out.print("exception");
  }
}
```

It's the same problem. ExhibitClosed is a RuntimeException. If it is thrown, the first catch block takes care of it, making sure there no way to get to the second catch block.

To review catching multiple exceptions, remember that at most one catch block will run and it will be the first catch block that can handle it.

Throwing a Second Exception

So far, we've limited ourselves to one try statement in each example. However, a catch or finally block can have any valid Java code in it—including another try statement.

Even though the topic of reading files is on the OCP exam, the OCA exam may ask you about exception handling with those classes. This is actually a gift. When you see such a question, you know the problem has to be about basic Java syntax or exception handling!

The following code tries to read a file:

```
16: public static void main(String[] args) {
17:    FileReader reader = null;
18:    try {
19:       reader = read();
20:    } catch (IOException e) {
21:       try {
22:        if (reader != null)  reader.close();
23:       } catch (IOException inner) {
24:       }
25:    }
26: }
27: private static FileReader read() throws IOException {
28:    // CODE GOES HERE
29: }
```

The easiest case is if line 28 doesn't throw an exception. Then the entire catch block on lines 20–25 is skipped. Next, consider if line 28 throws a NullPointerException. That isn't an IOException, so the catch block on lines 20–25 will still be skipped.

If line 28 does throw an IOException, the catch block on lines 20–25 does get run. Line 22 tries to close the reader. If that goes well, the code completes and the main() method ends normally. If the close() method does throw an exception, Java looks for more catch blocks. This exception is caught on line 23. Regardless, the exception on line 28 is handled. A different exception might be thrown, but the one from line 28 is done.

Most of the examples you see with exception handling on the exam are abstract. They use letters or numbers to make sure you understand the flow. This one shows that only the last exception to be thrown matters. (This is true for the OCA exam. It will change a bit on the OCP exam.)

```
26: try {
27:    throw new RuntimeException();
28: } catch (RuntimeException e) {
29:    throw new RuntimeException();
30: } finally {
31:    throw new Exception();
32: }
```

Line 27 throws an exception, which is caught on line 28. The catch block then throws an exception on line 29. If there were no finally block, the exception from line 29 would be thrown. However, the finally block runs after the catch block. Since the finally block throws an exception of its own on line 31, this one gets thrown. The exception from the catch block gets forgotten about. This is why you often see another try/catch inside a finally block—to make sure it doesn't mask the exception from the catch block.

Next we are going to show you the hardest example you can be asked related to exceptions. What do you think this method returns? Go slowly. It's tricky.

```
30: public String exceptions() {
31:    String result = "";
32:    String v = null;
33:    try {
34:       try {
35:          result += "before ";
36:          v.length();
37:          result += "after ";
38:       } catch (NullPointerException e) {
39:          result += "catch";
40:          throw new RuntimeException();
41:       } finally {
42:          result += "finally ";
43:          throw new Exception();
44:       }
45:    } catch (Exception e) {
46:       result += "done";
47:    }
48:    return result;
49: }
```

The correct answer is before catch finally done. Everything is normal up until line 35, when "before" is added. Line 36 throws a NullPointerException. Line 37 is skipped as Java goes straight to the catch block. Line 38 does catch the exception, and "catch" is added on line 39. Then line 40 throws a RuntimeException. The finally block runs after the catch regardless of whether an exception is thrown; it adds "finally" to result. At this point, we have completed the inner try statement that ran on lines 34–44. The outer catch block then sees an exception was thrown and catches it on line 45; it adds "done" to result.

Recognizing Common Exception Types

You need to recognize three types of exceptions for the OCA exam: runtime exceptions, checked exceptions, and errors. We'll look at common examples of each type. For the exam, you'll need to recognize which type of an exception it is and whether it's thrown by the JVM or a programmer. So you can recognize them, we'll show you some code examples for those exceptions.

Runtime Exceptions

Runtime exceptions extend `RuntimeException`. They don't have to be handled or declared. They can be thrown by the programmer or by the JVM. Common runtime exceptions include the following:

ArithmeticException   Thrown by the JVM when code attempts to divide by zero

ArrayIndexOutOfBoundsException   Thrown by the JVM when code uses an illegal index to access an array

ClassCastException   Thrown by the JVM when an attempt is made to cast an object to a subclass of which it is not an instance

IllegalArgumentException   Thrown by the programmer to indicate that a method has been passed an illegal or inappropriate argument

NullPointerException   Thrown by the JVM when there is a `null` reference where an object is required

NumberFormatException   Thrown by the programmer when an attempt is made to convert a string to a numeric type but the string doesn't have an appropriate format

ArithmeticException

Trying to divide an `int` by zero gives an undefined result. When this occurs, the JVM will throw an `ArithmeticException`:

```
int answer = 11 / 0;
```

Running this code results in the following output:

```
Exception in thread "main" java.lang.ArithmeticException: / by zero
```

Java doesn't spell out the word "divide." That's okay, though, because we know that / is the division operator and that Java is trying to tell us division by zero occurred.

The thread "main" is telling us the code was called directly or indirectly from a program with a `main` method. On the OCA exam, this is all the output we will see. Next comes the name of the exception, followed by extra information (if any) that goes with the exception.

ArrayIndexOutOfBoundsException

You know by now that array indexes start with 0 and go up to 1 less than the length of the array—which means this code will throw an `ArrayIndexOutOfBoundsException`:

```
int[] countsOfMoose = new int[3];
System.out.println(countsOfMoose[-1]);
```

This is a problem because there's no such thing as a negative array index. Running this code yields the following output:

```
Exception in thread "main" java.lang.ArrayIndexOutOfBoundsException: -1
```

At least Java tells us what index was invalid. Can you see what's wrong with this one?

```
int total = 0;
int[] countsOfMoose = new int[3];
for (int i = 0; i <= countsOfMoose.length; i++)
  total += countsOfMoose[i];
```

The problem is that the for loop should have < instead of <=. On the final iteration of the loop, Java tries to call countsOfMoose[3], which is invalid. The array includes only three elements, making 2 the largest possible index. The output looks like this:

```
Exception in thread "main" java.lang.ArrayIndexOutOfBoundsException: 3
```

ClassCastException

Java tries to protect you from impossible casts. This code doesn't compile because Integer is not a subclass of String:

```
String type = "moose";
Integer number = (Integer) type;  // DOES NOT COMPILE
```

More complicated code thwarts Java's attempts to protect you. When the cast fails at runtime, Java will throw a ClassCastException:

```
String type = "moose";
Object obj = type;
Integer number = (Integer) obj;
```

The compiler sees a cast from Object to Integer. This could be okay. The compiler doesn't realize there's a String in that Object. When the code runs, it yields the following output:

```
Exception in thread "main" java.lang.ClassCastException: java.lang.String
cannot be cast to java.lang.Integer
```

Java tells us both types that were involved in the problem, making it apparent what's wrong.

IllegalArgumentException

IllegalArgumentException is a way for your program to protect itself. We first saw the following setter method in the Swan class in Chapter 4, "Methods and Encapsulation."

```
6:  public void setNumberEggs(int numberEggs) {// setter
7:    if (numberEggs >= 0) // guard condition
8:      this.numberEggs = numberEggs;
9:  }
```

This code works, but we don't really want to ignore the caller's request when they tell us a Swan has –2 eggs. We want to tell the caller that something is wrong—preferably in a very obvious way that the caller can't ignore so that the programmer will fix the problem. Exceptions are an efficient way to do this. Seeing the code end with an exception is a great reminder that something is wrong:

```
public void setNumberEggs(int numberEggs) {
  if (numberEggs < 0)
    throw new IllegalArgumentException(
        "# eggs must not be negative");
  this.numberEggs = numberEggs;
}
```

The program throws an exception when it's not happy with the parameter values. The output looks like this:

```
Exception in thread "main" java.lang.IllegalArgumentException: # eggs must not
be negative
```

Clearly this is a problem that must be fixed if the programmer wants the program to do anything useful.

NullPointerException

Instance variables and methods must be called on a non-null reference. If the reference is null, the JVM will throw a NullPointerException. It's usually subtle, such as this example, which checks whether you remember instance variable references default to null.

```
String name;

public void printLength() throws NullPointerException {
  System.out.println(name.length());
}
```

Running this code results in this output:

```
Exception in thread "main" java.lang.NullPointerException
```

NumberFormatException

Java provides methods to convert strings to numbers. When these are passed an invalid value, they throw a NumberFormatException. The idea is similar to IllegalArgumentException. Since this is a common problem, Java gives it a separate class. In fact, NumberFormatException is a subclass of IllegalArgumentException. Here's an example of trying to convert something non-numeric into an int:

```
Integer.parseInt("abc");
```

The output looks like this:

```
Exception in thread "main" java.lang.NumberFormatException: For input string:
"abc"
```

Checked Exceptions

Checked exceptions have Exception in their hierarchy but not RuntimeException. They must be handled or declared. They can be thrown by the programmer or by the JVM. Common checked exceptions include the following:

FileNotFoundException Thrown programmatically when code tries to reference a file that does not exist

IOException Thrown programmatically when there's a problem reading or writing a file

For the OCA exam, you only need to know that these are checked exceptions. Also keep in mind that FileNotFoundException is a subclass of IOException, although the exam will remind you of that fact if it comes up. You'll see these two exceptions in more detail on the OCP exam.

Errors

Errors extend the Error class. They are thrown by the JVM and should not be handled or declared. Errors are rare, but you might see these:

ExceptionInInitializerError Thrown by the JVM when a static initializer throws an exception and doesn't handle it

StackOverflowError Thrown by the JVM when a method calls itself too many times (this is called *infinite recursion* because the method typically calls itself without end)

NoClassDefFoundError Thrown by the JVM when a class that the code uses is available at compile time but not runtime

ExceptionInInitializerError

Java runs static initializers the first time a class is used. If one of the static initializers throws an exception, Java can't start using the class. It declares defeat by throwing an ExceptionInInitializerError. This code shows an ArrayIndexOutOfBounds in a static initializer:

```
static {
  int[] countsOfMoose = new int[3];
  int num = countsOfMoose[-1];
}
public static void main(String[] args) { }
```

This code yields information about two exceptions:

```
Exception in thread "main" java.lang.ExceptionInInitializerError
Caused by: java.lang.ArrayIndexOutOfBoundsException: -1
```

We get the `ExceptionInInitializerError` because the error happened in a static initializer. That information alone wouldn't be particularly useful in fixing the problem. Therefore, Java also tells us the original cause of the problem: the `ArrayIndexOutOfBoundsException` that we need to fix.

The `ExceptionInInitializerError` is an error because Java failed to load the whole class. This failure prevents Java from continuing.

StackOverflowError

When Java calls methods, it puts parameters and local variables on the stack. After doing this a very large number of times, the stack runs out of room and overflows. This is called a `StackOverflowError`. Most of the time, this error occurs when a method calls itself.

```
public static void doNotCodeThis(int num) {
  doNotCodeThis(1);
}
```

The output contains this line:

```
Exception in thread "main" java.lang.StackOverflowError
```

Since the method calls itself, it will never end. Eventually, Java runs out of room on the stack and throws the error. This is called infinite recursion. It is better than an infinite loop because at least Java will catch it and throw the error. With an infinite loop, Java just uses all your CPU until you can kill it.

NoClassDefFoundError

This error won't show up in code on the exam—you just need to know that it is an error. `NoClassDefFoundError` occurs when Java can't find the class at runtime.

Calling Methods That Throw Exceptions

When you're calling a method that throws an exception, the rules are the same as within a method. Do you see why the following doesn't compile?

```
class NoMoreCarrotsException extends Exception {}
public class Bunny {
  public static void main(String[] args) {
    eatCarrot();// DOES NOT COMPILE
  }
  private static void eatCarrot() throws NoMoreCarrotsException {
  }
}
```

The problem is that NoMoreCarrotsException is a checked exception. Checked exceptions must be handled or declared. The code would compile if we changed the main() method to either of these:

```
public static void main(String[] args)
  throws NoMoreCarrotsException {// declare exception
  eatCarrot();
}
public static void main(String[] args) {
  try {
    eatCarrot();
  } catch (NoMoreCarrotsException e ) {// handle exception
    System.out.print("sad rabbit");
  }
}
```

You might have noticed that eatCarrot() didn't actually throw an exception; it just declared that it could. This is enough for the compiler to require the caller to handle or declare the exception.

The compiler is still on the lookout for unreachable code. Declaring an unused exception isn't considered unreachable code. It gives the method the option to change the implementation to throw that exception in the future. Do you see the issue here?

```
public void bad() {
  try {
    eatCarrot();
  } catch (NoMoreCarrotsException e ) {// DOES NOT COMPILE
    System.out.print("sad rabbit");
  }
}
public void good() throws NoMoreCarrotsException {
  eatCarrot();
}
private static void eatCarrot() { }
```

Java knows that eatCarrot() can't throw a checked exception—which means there's no way for the catch block in bad() to be reached. In comparison, good() is free to declare other exceptions.

Subclasses

Now that you have a deeper understanding of exceptions, let's look at overriding methods with exceptions in the method declaration. When a class overrides a method from a superclass or implements a method from an interface, it's not allowed to add new checked exceptions to the method signature. For example, this code isn't allowed:

```
class CanNotHopException extends Exception { }
class Hopper {
  public void hop() { }
}
class Bunny extends Hopper {
  public void hop() throws CanNotHopException { } // DOES NOT COMPILE
}
```

Java knows hop() isn't allowed to throw any checked exceptions because the superclass Hopper doesn't declare any. Imagine what would happen if subclasses could add checked exceptions—you could write code that calls Hopper's hop() method and not handle any exceptions. Then if Bunny was used in its place, the code wouldn't know to handle or declare CanNotHopException.

A subclass is allowed to declare fewer exceptions than the superclass or interface. This is legal because callers are already handling them.

```
class Hopper {
  public void hop() throws CanNotHopException { }
}
class Bunny extends Hopper {
  public void hop()   { }
}
```

A subclass not declaring an exception is similar to a method declaring it throws an exception that it never actually throws. This is perfectly legal.

Similarly, a class is allowed to declare a subclass of an exception type. The idea is the same. The superclass or interface has already taken care of a broader type. Here's an example:

```
class Hopper {
  public void hop() throws Exception { }
}
class Bunny extends Hopper {
  public void hop() throws CanNotHopException { }
}
```

Bunny could declare that it throws Exception directly, or it could declare that it throws a more specific type of Exception. It could even declare that it throws nothing at all.

This rule applies only to checked exceptions. The following code is legal because it has a runtime exception in the subclass's version:

```
class Hopper {
  public void hop() { }
}
```

```
class Bunny extends Hopper {
  public void hop() throws IllegalStateException { }
}
```

The reason that it's okay to declare new runtime exceptions in a subclass method is that the declaration is redundant. Methods are free to throw any runtime exceptions they want without mentioning them in the method declaration.

Printing an Exception

There are three ways to print an exception. You can let Java print it out, print just the message, or print where the stack trace comes from. This example shows all three approaches:

```
5: public static void main(String[] args) {
6:     try {
7:       hop();
8:     } catch (Exception e) {
9:       System.out.println(e);
10:      System.out.println(e.getMessage());
11:      e.printStackTrace();
12:    }
13: }
14: private static void hop() {
15:     throw new RuntimeException("cannot hop");
16: }
```

This code results in the following output:

```
java.lang.RuntimeException: cannot hop
cannot hop
java.lang.RuntimeException: cannot hop
at trycatch.Handling.hop(Handling.java:15)
at trycatch.Handling.main(Handling.java:7)
```

The first line shows what Java prints out by default: the exception type and message. The second line shows just the message. The rest shows a stack trace.

The stack trace is usually the most helpful one because it shows where the exception occurred in each method that it passed through. On the OCA exam, you will mostly see the first approach. This is because the exam often shows code snippets.

The stack trace shows all the methods on the stack. Figure 6.4 shows what the stack looks like for this code. Every time you call a method, Java adds it to the stack until it completes. When an exception is thrown, it goes through the stack until it finds a method that can handle it or it runs out of stack.

FIGURE 6.4 A method stack

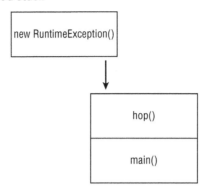

 Real World Scenario

Why Swallowing Exception Is Bad

Because checked exceptions require you to handle or declare them, there is a temptation to catch them so they "go away." But doing so can cause problems. In the following code, there's a problem reading in the file:

```java
public static void main(String[] args) {
  String textInFile = null;
  try {
    readInFile();
  } catch (IOException e) {
    // ignore exception
  }
  // imagine many lines of code here
  System.out.println(textInFile.replace(" ", ""));
}
private static void readInFile() throws IOException {
  throw new IOException();
}
```

The code results in a NullPointerException. Java doesn't tell you anything about the original IOException because it was handled. Granted, it was handled poorly, but it *was* handled.

When writing your own code, print out a stack trace or at least a message when catching an exception. Also, consider whether continuing is the best course of action. In our example, the program can't do anything after it fails to read in the file. It might as well have just thrown the IOException.

Summary

An exception indicates something unexpected happened. A method can handle an exception by catching it or declaring it for the caller to deal with. Many exceptions are thrown by Java libraries. You can throw your own exception with code such as throw new Exception().

Subclasses of java.lang.Error are exceptions that a programmer should not attempt to handle. Subclasses of java.lang.RuntimeException are runtime (unchecked) exceptions. Subclasses of java.lang.Exception, but not java.lang.RuntimeException are checked exceptions. Java requires checked exceptions to be handled or declared.

If a try statement has multiple catch blocks, at most one catch block can run. Java looks for an exception that can be caught by each catch block in the order they appear, and the first match is run. Then execution continues after the try statement. If both catch and finally throw an exception, the one from finally gets thrown.

Common runtime exceptions include:

- ArithmeticException
- ArrayIndexOutOfBoundsException
- ClassCastException
- IllegalArgumentException
- NullPointerException
- NumberFormatException

IllegalArgumentException and NumberFormatException are typically thrown by the programmer, whereas the others are typically thrown by the JVM.

Common checked exceptions include:

- IOException
- FileNotFoundException

Common errors include:

- ExceptionInInitializerError
- StackOverflowError
- NoClassDefFoundError

When a method overrides a method in a superclass or interface, it is not allowed to add checked exceptions. It is allowed to declare fewer exceptions or declare a subclass of a declared exception. Methods declare exceptions with the keyword throws.

Exam Essentials

Differentiate between checked and unchecked exceptions.   Unchecked exceptions are also known as runtime exceptions and are subclasses of java.lang.RuntimeException. All other subclasses of java.lang.Exception are checked exceptions.

Understand the flow of a try statement.   A try statement must have a catch or a finally block. Multiple catch blocks are also allowed, provided no superclass exception type appears in an earlier catch block than its subclass. The finally block runs last regardless of whether an exception is thrown.

Identify whether an exception is thrown by the programmer or the JVM.   Illegal ArgumentException and NumberFormatException are commonly thrown by the programmer. Most of the other runtime exceptions are typically thrown by the JVM.

Declare methods that declare exceptions.   The throws keyword is used in a method declaration to indicate an exception might be thrown. When overriding a method, the method is allowed to throw fewer exceptions than the original version.

Recognize when to use throw versus throws.   The throw keyword is used when you actually want to throw an exception—for example, throw new RuntimeException(). The throws keyword is used in a method declaration.

Review Questions

1. Which of the following statements are true? (Choose all that apply)

   A. Runtime exceptions are the same thing as checked exceptions.

   B. Runtime exceptions are the same thing as unchecked exceptions.

   C. You can declare only checked exceptions.

   D. You can declare only unchecked exceptions.

   E. You can handle only `Exception` subclasses.

2. Which of the following pairs fill in the blanks to make this code compile? (Choose all that apply)

   ```
   7: public void ohNo() _____ Exception {
   8:     _____ Exception();
   9: }
   ```

   A. On line 7, fill in `throw`

   B. On line 7, fill in `throws`

   C. On line 8, fill in `throw`

   D. On line 8, fill in `throw new`

   E. On line 8, fill in `throws`

   F. On line 8, fill in `throws new`

3. When are you required to use a `finally` block in a regular `try` statement (not a try-with-resources)?

   A. Never.

   B. When the program code doesn't terminate on its own.

   C. When there are no `catch` blocks in a `try` statement.

   D. When there is exactly one `catch` block in a `try` statement.

   E. When there are two or more `catch` blocks in a `try` statement.

4. Which exception will the following throw?

   ```
   Object obj = new Integer(3);
   String str = (String) obj;
   System.out.println(str);
   ```

   A. `ArrayIndexOutOfBoundsException`

   B. `ClassCastException`

   C. `IllegalArgumentException`

   D. `NumberFormatException`

   E. None of the above.

5. Which of the following exceptions are thrown by the JVM? (Choose all that apply)

A. `ArrayIndexOutOfBoundsException`

B. `ExceptionInInitializerError`

C. `java.io.IOException`

D. `NullPointerException`

E. `NumberFormatException`

6. What will happen if you add the statement `System.out.println(5 / 0);` to a working `main()` method?

A. It will not compile.

B. It will not run.

C. It will run and throw an `ArithmeticException`.

D. It will run and throw an `IllegalArgumentException`.

E. None of the above.

7. What is printed besides the stack trace caused by the `NullPointerException` from line 16?

```
1: public class DoSomething {
2:   public void go() {
3:     System.out.print("A");
4:     try {
5:         stop();
6:     } catch (ArithmeticException e) {
7:         System.out.print("B");
8:     } finally {
9:         System.out.print("C");
10:    }
11:    System.out.print("D");
12:  }
13:  public void stop() {
14:    System.out.print("E");
15:    Object x = null;
16:    x.toString();
17:    System.out.print("F");
18:  }
19:  public static void main(String[] args) {
20:    new DoSomething().go();
21:  }
22: }
```

A. AE

B. AEBCD

C. AEC

D. AECD

E. No output appears other than the stack trace.

8. What is the output of the following snippet, assuming a and b are both 0?

```
3:      try {
4:          return a / b;
5:      } catch (RuntimeException e) {
6:          return -1;
7:      } catch (ArithmeticException e) {
8:          return 0;
9:      } finally {
10:         System.out.print("done");
11:     }
```

A. -1

B. 0

C. done-1

D. done0

E. The code does not compile.

F. An uncaught exception is thrown.

9. What is the output of the following program?

```
1: public class Laptop {
2:   public void start() {
3:     try {
4:       System.out.print("Starting up ");
5:       throw new Exception();
6:     } catch (Exception e) {
7:       System.out.print("Problem ");
8:       System.exit(0);
9:     } finally {
10:        System.out.print("Shutting down ");
11:    }
12:  }
13:  public static void main(String[] args) {
14:    new Laptop().start();
15:  } }
```

A. Starting up

B. Starting up Problem

C. Starting up Problem Shutting down

D. `Starting up Shutting down`

E. The code does not compile.

F. An uncaught exception is thrown.

10. What is the output of the following program?

```
1:   public class Dog {
2:     public String name;
3:     public void parseName() {
4:       System.out.print("1");
5:       try {
6:         System.out.print("2");
7:         int x = Integer.parseInt(name);
8:         System.out.print("3");
9:       } catch (NumberFormatException e) {
10:        System.out.print("4");
11:      }
12:    }
13:    public static void main(String[] args) {
14:      Dog leroy = new Dog();
15:      leroy.name = "Leroy";
16:      leroy.parseName();
17:      System.out.print("5");
18:   } }
```

A. 12

B. 1234

C. 1235

D. 124

E. 1245

F. The code does not compile.

G. An uncaught exception is thrown.

11. What is the output of the following program?

```
1:   public class Cat {
2:     public String name;
3:     public void parseName() {
4:       System.out.print("1");
5:       try {
6:         System.out.print("2");
7:         int x = Integer.parseInt(name);
8:         System.out.print("3");
```

```
9:      } catch (NullPointerException e) {
10:        System.out.print("4");
11:      }
12:      System.out.print("5");
13:    }
14:    public static void main(String[] args) {
15:      Cat leo = new Cat();
16:      leo.name = "Leo";
17:      leo.parseName();
18:      System.out.print("6");
19:    }
20: }
```

A. 12, followed by a stack trace for a NumberFormatException

B. 124, followed by a stack trace for a NumberFormatException

C. 12456

D. 12456

E. 1256, followed by a stack trace for a NumberFormatException

F. The code does not compile.

G. An uncaught exception is thrown.

12. What is printed by the following? (Choose all that apply)

```
1:  public class Mouse {
2:    public String name;
3:    public void run() {
4:      System.out.print("1");
5:      try {
6:        System.out.print("2");
7:        name.toString();
8:        System.out.print("3");
9:      } catch (NullPointerException e) {
10:        System.out.print("4");
11:        throw e;
12:      }
13:      System.out.print("5");
14:    }
15:    public static void main(String[] args) {
16:      Mouse jerry = new Mouse();
17:      jerry.run();
18:      System.out.print("6");
19:    } }
```

A. 1

B. 2

C. 3

D. 4

E. 5

F. 6

G. The stack trace for a `NullPointerException`

13. Which of the following statements are true? (Choose all that apply)

   A. You can declare a method with `Exception` as the return type.

   B. You can declare any subclass of `Error` in the `throws` part of a method declaration.

   C. You can declare any subclass of `Exception` in the `throws` part of a method declaration.

   D. You can declare any subclass of `Object` in the `throws` part of a method declaration.

   E. You can declare any subclass of `RuntimeException` in the `throws` part of a method declaration.

14. Which of the following can be inserted on line 8 to make this code compile? (Choose all that apply)

   ```
   7: public void ohNo() throws IOException {
   8:    // INSERT CODE HERE
   9: }
   ```

   A. `System.out.println("it's ok");`

   B. `throw new Exception();`

   C. `throw new IllegalArgumentException();`

   D. `throw new java.io.IOException();`

   E. `throw new RuntimeException();`

15. Which of the following are unchecked exceptions? (Choose all that apply)

   A. `ArrayIndexOutOfBoundsException`

   B. `IllegalArgumentException`

   C. `IOException`

   D. `NumberFormatException`

   E. Any exception that extends `RuntimeException`

   F. Any exception that extends `Exception`

16. Which scenario is the best use of an exception?

   A. An element is not found when searching a list.

   B. An unexpected parameter is passed into a method.

   C. The computer caught fire.

   D. You want to loop through a list.

   E. You don't know how to code a method.

17. Which of the following can be inserted into `Lion` to make this code compile? (Choose all that apply)

```
class HasSoreThroatException extends Exception {}
class TiredException extends RuntimeException {}
interface Roar {
  void roar() throws HasSoreThroatException;
}
class Lion implements Roar {// INSERT CODE HERE
}
```

   A. `public void roar(){}`

   B. `public void roar() throws Exception{}`

   C. `public void roar() throws HasSoreThroatException{}`

   D. `public void roar() throws IllegalArgumentException{}`

   E. `public void roar() throws TiredException{}`

18. Which of the following are true? (Choose all that apply)

   A. Checked exceptions are allowed to be handled or declared.

   B. Checked exceptions are required to be handled or declared.

   C. Errors are allowed to be handled or declared.

   D. Errors are required to be handled or declared.

   E. Runtime exceptions are allowed to be handled or declared.

   F. Runtime exceptions are required to be handled or declared.

19. Which of the following can be inserted in the blank to make the code compile? (Choose all that apply)

```
public static void main(String[] args) {
  try {
    System.out.println("work real hard");
  } catch (_____ e) {
  } catch (RuntimeException e) {
  }
}
```

   A. `Exception`

   B. `IOException`

   C. `IllegalArgumentException`

   D. `RuntimeException`

    E. StackOverflowError

    F. None of the above.

20. What does the output of the following contain? (Choose all that apply)

```
12: public static void main(String[] args) {
13:    System.out.print("a");
14:    try {
15:      System.out.print("b");
16:      throw new IllegalArgumentException();
17:    } catch (IllegalArgumentException e) {
18:      System.out.print("c");
19:      throw new RuntimeException("1");
20:    } catch (RuntimeException e) {
21:      System.out.print("d");
22:      throw new RuntimeException("2");
23:    } finally {
24:      System.out.print("e");
25:      throw new RuntimeException("3");
26:    }
27: }
```

    A. abce

    B. abde

    C. An exception with the message set to "1"

    D. An exception with the message set to "2"

    E. An exception with the message set to "3"

    F. Nothing; the code does not compile.

Appendix A

Answers to Review Questions

Chapter 1: Java Building Blocks

1. A, B, E. Option A is valid because you can use the dollar sign in identifiers. Option B is valid because you can use an underscore in identifiers. Option C is not a valid identifier because true is a Java reserved word. Option D is not valid because the dot (.) is not allowed in identifiers. Option E is valid because Java is case sensitive, so Public is not a reserved word and therefore a valid identifier. Option F is not valid because the first character is not a letter, $, or _.

2. D. Boolean fields initialize to false and references initialize to null, so empty is false and brand is null. Brand = null is output.

3. B, D, E. Option A (line 4) compiles because short is an integral type. Option B (line 5) generates a compiler error because int is an integral type, but 5.6 is a floating-point type. Option C (line 6) compiles because it is assigned a String. Options D and E (lines 7 and 8) do not compile because short and int are primitives. Primitives do not allow methods to be called on them. Option F (line 9) compiles because length() is defined on String.

4. A, B. Adding the variable at line 2 makes result an instance variable. Since instance variables are in scope for the entire life of the object, option A is correct. Option B is correct because adding the variable at line 4 makes result a local variable with a scope of the whole method. Adding the variable at line 6 makes result a local variable with a scope of lines 6–7. Since it is out of scope on line 8, the println does not compile and option C is incorrect. Adding the variable at line 9 makes result a local variable with a scope of lines 9 and 10. Since line 8 is before the declaration, it does not compile and option D is incorrect. Finally, option E is incorrect because the code can be made to compile.

5. C, D. Option C is correct because it imports Jelly by classname. Option D is correct because it imports all the classes in the jellies package, which includes Jelly. Option A is incorrect because it only imports classes in the aquarium package—Tank in this case—and not those in lower-level packages. Option B is incorrect because you cannot use wildcards anyplace other than the end of an import statement. Option E is incorrect because you cannot import parts of a class with a regular import statement. Option F is incorrect because options C and D do make the code compile.

6. E. The first two imports can be removed because java.lang is automatically imported. The second two imports can be removed because Tank and Water are in the same package, making the correct answer E. If Tank and Water were in different packages, one of these two imports could be removed. In that case, the answer would be option D.

7. A, B, C. Option A is correct because it imports all the classes in the aquarium package including aquarium.Water. Options B and C are correct because they import Water by classname. Since importing by classname takes precedence over wildcards, these compile. Option D is incorrect because Java doesn't know which of the two wildcard Water classes to use. Option E is incorrect because you cannot specify the same classname in two imports.

8. B. Option B is correct because arrays start counting from zero and strings with spaces must be in quotes. Option A is incorrect because it outputs Blue. C is incorrect because it outputs Jay. Option D is incorrect because it outputs Sparrow. Options E and F are incorrect because they output Error: Could not find or load main class Bird-Display.class.

9. A, C, D, E. Option A is correct because it is the traditional main() method signature and variables may begin with underscores. Options C and D are correct because the array operator may appear after the variable name. Option E is correct because varargs are allowed in place of an array. Option B is incorrect because variables are not allowed to begin with a digit. Option F is incorrect because the argument must be an array or varargs. Option F is a perfectly good method. However, it is not one that can be run from the command line because it has the wrong parameter type.

10. E. Option E is the canonical main() method signature. You need to memorize it. Option A is incorrect because the main() method must be public. Options B and F are incorrect because the main() method must have a void return type. Option C is incorrect because the main() method must be static. Option D is incorrect because the main() method must be named main.

11. C, D. Option C is correct because all non-primitive values default to null. Option D is correct because float and double primitives default to 0.0. Options B and E are incorrect because int primitives default to 0.

12. G. Option G is correct because local variables do not get assigned default values. The code fails to compile if a local variable is not explicitly initialized. If this question were about instance variables, options D and F would be correct. A boolean primitive defaults to false and a float primitive defaults to 0.0.

13. A, D. Options A and D are correct because boolean primitives default to false and int primitives default to 0.

14. D. The package name represents any folders underneath the current path, which is named.A in this case. Option C is incorrect because package names are case sensitive, just like variable names and other identifiers.

15. A, E. Underscores are allowed as long as they are directly between two other digits. This means options A and E are correct. Options B and C are incorrect because the underscore is adjacent to the decimal point. Option D is incorrect because the underscore is the last character.

16. B, C, D. 0b is the prefix for a binary value and is correct. 0x is the prefix for a hexadecimal value. This value can be assigned to many primitive types, including int and double, making options C and D correct. Option A is incorrect because 9L is a long value. long amount = 9L would be allowed. Option E is incorrect because the underscore is immediately before the decimal. Option F is incorrect because the underscore is the very last character.

17. A, E. Bunny is a class, which can be seen from the declaration: public class Bunny. bun is a reference to an object. main() is a method.

18. C, D, E. package and import are both optional. If both are present, the order must be package, then import, then class. Option A is incorrect because class is before package and import. Option B is incorrect because import is before package. Option F is incorrect because class is before package. Option G is incorrect because class is before import.

19. B, D. The Rabbit object from line 3 has two references to it: one and three. The references are nulled out on lines 6 and 8, respectively. Option B is correct because this makes the object eligible for garbage collection after line 8. Line 7 sets the reference four to the now null one, which means it has no effect on garbage collection. The Rabbit object from line 4 only has a single reference to it: two. Option D is correct because this single reference becomes null on line 9. The Rabbit object declared on line 10 becomes eligible for garbage collection at the end of the method on line 12. Calling System.gc() has no effect on eligibility for garbage collection.

20. B, E. Calling System.gc() suggests that Java might wish to run the garbage collector. Java is free to ignore the request, making option E correct. finalize() runs if an object attempts to be garbage collected, making option B correct.

21. A. While the code on line 3 does compile, it is not a constructor because it has a return type. It is a method that happens to have the same name as the class. When the code runs, the default constructor is called and count has the default value (0) for an int.

22. B, E. C++ has operator overloading and pointers. Java made a point of not having either. Java does have references to objects, but these are pointing to an object that can move around in memory. Option B is correct because Java is platform independent. Option E is correct because Java is object oriented. While it does support some parts of functional programming, these occur within a class.

23. C, D. Java puts source code in .java files and bytecode in .class files. It does not use a .bytecode file. When running a Java program, you pass just the name of the class without the .class extension.

Chapter 2: Operators and Statements

1. A, D. Option A is the equality operator and can be used on numeric primitives, boolean values, and object references. Options B and C are both arithmetic operators and cannot be applied to a boolean value. Option D is the logical complement operator and is used exclusively with boolean values. Option E is the modulus operator, which can only be used with numeric primitives. Finally, option F is a relational operator that compares the values of two numbers.

2. A, B, D. The value x + y is automatically promoted to int, so int and data types that can be promoted automatically from int will work. Options A, B, D are such data types. Option C will not work because boolean is not a numeric data type. Options E and F will not work without an explicit cast to a smaller data type.

3. F. In this example, the ternary operator has two expressions, one of them a String and the other a boolean value. The ternary operator is permitted to have expressions that don't have matching types, but the key here is the assignment to the String reference. The compiler knows how to assign the first expression value as a String, but the second boolean expression cannot be set as a String; therefore, this line will not compile.

4. B, C, D, F. The code will not compile as is, so option A is not correct. The value 2 * x is automatically promoted to long and cannot be automatically stored in y, which is in an int value. Options B, C, and D solve this problem by reducing the long value to int. Option E does not solve the problem and actually makes it worse by attempting to place the value in a smaller data type. Option F solves the problem by increasing the data type of the assignment so that long is allowed.

5. C. This code does not contain any compilation errors or an infinite loop, so options D, E, and F are incorrect. The break statement on line 8 causes the loop to execute once and finish, so option C is the correct answer.

6. F. The code does not compile because two else statements cannot be chained together without additional if-then statements, so the correct answer is option F. Option E is incorrect as Line 6 by itself does not cause a problem, only when it is paired with Line 7. One way to fix this code so it compiles would be to add an if-then statement on line 6. The other solution would be to remove line 7.

7. D. As you learned in the section "Ternary Operator," although parentheses are not required, they do greatly increase code readability, such as the following equivalent statement:

System.out.println((x > 2) ? ((x < 4) ? 10 : 8) : 7)

We apply the outside ternary operator first, as it is possible the inner ternary expression may never be evaluated. Since (x>2) is true, this reduces the problem to:

System.out.println((x < 4) ? 10 : 8)

Since x is greater than 2, the answer is 8, or option D in this case.

8. B. This example is tricky because of the second assignment operator embedded in line 5. The expression (z=false) assigns the value false to z and returns false for the entire expression. Since y does not equal 10, the left-hand side returns true; therefore, the exclusive or (^) of the entire expression assigned to x is true. The output reflects these assignments, with no change to y, so option B is the only correct answer. The code compiles and runs without issue, so option F is not correct.

9. F. In this example, the update statement of the for loop is missing, which is fine as the statement is optional, so option D is incorrect. The expression inside the loop increments i but then assigns i the old value. Therefore, i ends the loop with the same value that it starts with: 0. The loop will repeat infinitely, outputting the same statement over and over again because i remains 0 after every iteration of the loop.

10. D. Line 4 generates a possible loss of precision compiler error. The cast operator has the highest precedence, so it is evaluated first, casting a to a byte. Then, the addition is evaluated, causing both a and b to be promoted to int values. The value 90 is an int and cannot be assigned to the byte sum without an explicit cast, so the code does not compile. The code could be corrected with parentheses around (a + b), in which case option C would be the correct answer.

11. A. The * and % have the same operator precedence, so the expression is evaluated from left-to-right. The result of 5 * 4 is 20, and 20 % 3 is 2 (20 divided by 3 is 18, the remainder is 2). The output is 2 and option A is the correct answer.

12. D. The variable x is an int and s is a reference to a String object. The two data types are incomparable because neither variable can be converted to the other variable's type. The compiler error occurs on line 5 when the comparison is attempted, so the answer is option D.

13. A. The code compiles successfully, so options C and D are incorrect. The value of b after line 4 is false. However, the if-then statement on line 5 contains an assignment, not a comparison. The variable b is assigned true on line 3, and the assignment operator returns true, so line 5 executes and displays Success, so the answer is option A.

14. C. The code compiles successfully, so option F is incorrect. On line 5, the pre-increment operator is used, so c is incremented to 4 and the new value is returned to the expression. The value of result is computed by adding 8 to the original value of 4, resulting in a new value of 12, which is output on line 6. Therefore, option C is the correct answer.

15. E. This is actually a much simpler problem than it appears to be. The while statement on line 4 is missing parentheses, so the code will not compile, and option E is the correct answer. If the parentheses were added, though, option F would be the correct answer since the loop does not use curly braces to include x++ and the boolean expression never changes. Finally, if curly braces were added around both expressions, the output would be 10, 6 and option B would be correct.

16. D. The variable y is declared within the body of the do-while statement, so it is out of scope on line 6. Line 6 generates a compiler error, so option D is the correct answer.

17. D. The code compiles without issue, so option F is incorrect. After the first execution of the loop, i is decremented to 9 and result to 13. Since i is not 8, keep going remains true, and the loop continues. On the next iteration, i is decremented to 8 and result to 11. On the second execution, i does equal 8, so keepGoing is set to false. At the conclusion of the loop, the loop terminates since keepGoing is no longer true. The value of result is 11, and the correct answer is option D.

18. B. The expression on line 5 is true when row * col is an even number. On the first iteration, row = 1 and col = 1, so the expression on line 6 is false, the continue is skipped, and count is incremented to 1. On the second iteration, row = 1 and col = 2, so the expression on line 6 is true and the continue ends the outer loop with count still at 1. On the third iteration, row = 2 and col = 1, so the expression on line 6 is true and the continue ends the outer loop with count still at 1. On the fourth iteration, row = 3 and col = 1, so the expression on line 6 is false, the continue is skipped, and count is incremented to 2. Finally, on the fifth and final iteration, row = 3 and col = 2, so the expression on line 6 is true and the continue ends the outer loop with count still at 2. The result of 2 is displayed, so the answer is option B.

19. D. Prior to the first iteration, m = 9, n = 1, and x = 0. After the iteration of the first loop, m is updated to 8, n to 3, and x to the sum of the new values for m + n, 0 + 11 = 11. After the iteration of the second loop, m is updated to 7, n to 5, and x to the sum of the new values for m + n, 11 + 12 = 23. After the iteration of the third loop, m is updated to 6, n to 7, and x to the sum of the new values for m + n, 23 + 13 = 36. On the fourth iteration of the loop, m > n evaluates to false, as 6 < 7 is not true. The loop ends and the most recent value of x, 36, is output, so the correct answer is option D.

20. B. The code compiles and runs without issue, so options C, D, and E are not correct. The value of grade is 'B' and there is a matching case statement that will cause "great" to be printed. There is no break statement after the case, though, so the next case statement will be reached, and "good" will be printed. There is a break after this case statement, though, so the switch statement will end. The correct answer is thus option B.

Chapter 3: Core Java APIs

1. G. Line 5 does not compile. This question is checking to see if you are paying attention to the types. numFish is an int and 1 is an int. Therefore, we use numeric addition and get 5. The problem is that we can't store an int in a String variable. Supposing line 5 said String anotherFish = numFish + 1 + "";. In that case, the answer would be options A and D. The variable defined on line 5 would be the string "5", and both output statements would use concatenation.

2. A, C, D. The code compiles fine. Line 3 points to the String in the string pool. Line 4 calls the String constructor explicitly and is therefore a different object than s. Lines 5 and 7 check for object equality, which is true, and so print one and three. Line 6 uses object reference equality, which is not true since we have different objects. Line 7 also compares references but is true since both references point to the object from the string pool. Line 8 also compares references but is true since both references point to the object from the string pool. Finally, line 9 compares one object from the string pool with one that was explicitly constructed and returns false.

3. B, C, E. Immutable means the state of an object cannot change once it is created. Immutable objects can be garbage collected just like mutable objects. String is immutable. StringBuilder can be mutated with methods like append(). Although

StringBuffer isn't on the exam, you should know about it anyway in case older questions haven't been removed.

4.   B. This example uses method chaining. After the call to append(), sb contains "aaa". That result is passed to the first insert() call, which inserts at index 1. At this point sb contains abbaa. That result is passed to the final insert(), which inserts at index 4, resulting in abbaccca.

5.   F. The question is trying to distract you into paying attention to logical equality versus object reference equality. It is hoping you will miss the fact that line 4 does not compile. Java does not allow you to compare String and StringBuilder using ==.

6.   B. A String is immutable. Calling concat() returns a new String but does not change the original. A StringBuilder is mutable. Calling append() adds characters to the existing character sequence along with returning a reference to the same object.

7.   B, D, E. length() is simply a count of the number of characters in a String. In this case, there are six characters. charAt() returns the character at that index. Remember that indexes are zero based, which means that index 3 corresponds to d and index 6 corresponds to 1 past the end of the array. A StringIndexOutOfBoundsException is thrown for the last line.

8.   A, D, E. substring() has two forms. The first takes the index to start with and the index to stop immediately before. The second takes just the index to start with and goes to the end of the String. Remember that indexes are zero based. The first call starts at index 1 and ends with index 2 since it needs to stop before index 3. The second call starts at index 7 and ends in the same place, resulting in an empty String. This prints out a blank line. The final call starts at index 7 and goes to the end of the String.

9.   C. This question is trying to see if you know that String objects are immutable. Line 4 returns "PURR" but the result is ignored and not stored in s. Line 5 returns "purr" since there is no whitespace present but the result is again ignored. Line 6 returns "ur" because it starts with index 1 and ends before index 3 using zero-based indexes. The result is ignored again. Finally, on line 6 something happens. We concatenate four new characters to s and now have a String of length 8.

10.   F. a += 2 expands to a = a + 2. A String concatenated with any other type gives a String. Lines 14, 15, and 16 all append to a, giving a result of "2cfalse". The if statement on line 18 returns true because the values of the two String objects are the same using object equality. The if statement on line 17 returns false because the two String objects are not the same in memory. One comes directly from the string pool and the other comes from building using String operations.

11.   E. Line 6 adds 1 to total because substring() includes the starting index but not the ending index. Line 7 adds 0 to total. Line 8 is a problem: Java does not allow the indexes to be specified in reverse order and the code throws a StringIndexOutOf-BoundsException.

12. A. First, we delete the characters at index 2 until the character one before index 8. At this point, 0189 is in `numbers`. The following line uses method chaining. It appends a dash to the end of the characters sequence, resulting in `0189-`, and then inserts a plus sign at index 2, resulting in `01+89-`.

13. F. This is a trick question. The first line does not compile because you cannot assign a `String` to a `StringBuilder`. If that line were `StringBuilder b = new StringBuilder("rumble")`, the code would compile and print rum4. Watch out for this sort of trick on the exam. You could easily spend a minute working out the character positions for no reason at all.

14. A, C. The `reverse()` method is the easiest way of reversing the characters in a `StringBuilder`; therefore, option A is correct. Option B does not reverse the string. However, `substring()` returns a `String`, which is not stored anywhere. Option C uses method chaining. First it creates the value `"JavavaJ$"`. Then it removes the first three characters, resulting in `"avaJ$"`. Finally, it removes the last character, resulting in `"avaJ"`. Option D throws an exception because you cannot delete the character after the last index. Remember that `deleteCharAt()` uses indexes that are zero based and `length()` counts starting with 0.

15. C, E, F. Option C uses the variable name as if it were a type, which is clearly illegal. Options E and F don't specify any size. Although it is legal to leave out the size for later dimensions of a multidimensional array, the first one is required. Option A declares a legal 2D array. Option B declares a legal 3D array. Option D declares a legal 2D array. Remember that it is normal to see on the exam types you might not have learned. You aren't expected to know anything about them.

16. C. Arrays define a property called `length`. It is not a method, so parentheses are not allowed.

17. F. The `ArrayList` class defines a method called `size()`.

18. A, C, D, E. An array is not able to change size and can have multiple dimensions. Both an array and `ArrayList` are ordered and have indexes. Neither is immutable. The elements can change in value.

19. B, C. An array does not override `equals()` and so uses object equality. `ArrayList` does override `equals()` and defines it as the same elements in the same order. The compiler does not know when an index is out of bounds and thus can't give you a compiler error. The code will throw an exception at runtime, though.

20. D. The code does not compile because `list` is instantiated using generics. Only `String` objects can be added to `list` and 7 is an `int`.

21. C. After line 4, values has one element (4). After line 5, values has two elements (4, 5). After line 6, values has two elements (4, 6) because `set()` does a replace. After line 7, values has only one element (6).

22. D. The code compiles and runs fine. However, an array must be sorted for `binarySearch()` to return a meaningful result.

23. A. Line 4 creates a fixed size array of size 4. Line 5 sorts it. Line 6 converts it back to an array. The brackets aren't in the traditional place, but they are still legal. Line 7 prints the first element, which is now –1.

24. C. Converting from an array to an `ArrayList` uses `Arrays.asList(names)`. There is no `asList()` method on an array instance. If this code were corrected to compile, the answer would be option A.

25. D. After sorting, hex contains `[30, 3A, 8, FF]`. Remember that numbers sort before letters and strings sort alphabetically. This makes 30 come before 8. A binary search correctly finds 8 at index 2 and 3A at index 1. It cannot find 4F but notices it should be at index 2. The rule when an item isn't found is to negate that index and subtract 1. Therefore, we get –2–1, which is –3.

26. A, B, D. Lines 5 and 7 use autoboxing to convert an `int` to an `Integer`. Line 6 does not because `valueOf()` returns an `Integer`. Line 8 does not because `null` is not an `int`. The code does compile. However, when the `for` loop tries to unbox `null` into an `int`, it fails and throws a `NullPointerException`.

27. B. The first `if` statement is false because the variables do not point to the same object. The second `if` statement is true because `ArrayList` implements equality to mean the same elements in the same order.

28. D, F. Options A and B are incorrect because `LocalDate` does not have a public constructor. Option C is incorrect because months start counting with 1 rather than 0. Option E is incorrect because it uses the old pre–Java 8 way of counting months, again beginning with 0. Options D and F are both correct ways of specifying the desired date.

29. D. A `LocalDate` does not have a time element. Therefore, it has no method to add hours and the code does not compile.

30. F. Java throws an exception if invalid date values are passed. There is no 40th day in April—or any other month for that matter.

31. B. The date starts out as April 30, 2018. Since dates are immutable and the plus methods have their return values ignored, the result is unchanged. Therefore, option B is correct.

32. E. Even though d has both date and time, the formatter only outputs time.

33. B. `Period` does not allow chaining. Only the last `Period` method called counts, so only the two years are subtracted.

Chapter 4: Methods and Encapsulation

1. B, C. `void` is a return type. Only the access modifier or optional specifiers are allowed before the return type. Option C is correct, creating a method with private access. Option B is correct, creating a method with default access and the optional specifier `final`. Since default access does not require a modifier, we get to jump right to `final`.

Option A is incorrect because default access omits the access modifier rather than specifying default. Option D is incorrect because Java is case sensitive. It would have been correct if public were the choice. Option E is incorrect because the method already has a void return type. Option F is incorrect because labels are not allowed for methods.

2. A, D. Options A and D are correct because the optional specifiers are allowed in any order. Options B and C are incorrect because they each have two return types. Options E and F are incorrect because the return type is before the optional specifier and access modifier, respectively.

3. A, C, D. Options A and C are correct because a void method is allowed to have a return statement as long as it doesn't try to return a value. Options B and G do not compile because null requires a reference object as the return type. void is not a reference object since it is a marker for no return type. int is not a reference object since it is a primitive. Option D is correct because it returns an int value. Option E does not compile because it tries to return a double when the return type is int. Since a double cannot be assigned to an int, it cannot be returned as one either. Option F does not compile because no value is actually returned.

4. A, B, G. Options A and B are correct because the single vararg parameter is the last parameter declared. Option G is correct because it doesn't use any vararg parameters at all. Options C and F are incorrect because the vararg parameter is not last. Option D is incorrect because two vararg parameters are not allowed in the same method. Option E is incorrect because the . . . for a vararg must be after the type, not before it.

5. D, G. Option D passes the initial parameter plus two more to turn into a vararg array of size 2. Option G passes the initial parameter plus an array of size 2. Option A does not compile because it does not pass the initial parameter. Options E and F do not compile because they do not declare an array properly. It should be new boolean[] {true}. Option B creates a vararg array of size 0 and option C creates a vararg array of size 1.

6. D. Option D is correct. This is the common implementation for encapsulation by setting all fields to be private and all methods to be public. Option A is incorrect because protected access allows everything that package private access allows and additionally allows subclasses access. Option B is incorrect because the class is public. This means that other classes can see the class. However, they cannot call any of the methods or read any of the fields. It is essentially a useless class. Option C is incorrect because package private access applies to the whole package. Option E is incorrect because Java has no such capability.

7. B, C, D, F. The two classes are in different packages, which means private access and default (package private) access will not compile. Additionally, protected access will not compile since School does not inherit from Classroom. Therefore, only line 8 will compile because it uses public access.

8. B, C, E. Encapsulation requires using methods to get and set instance variables so other classes are not directly using them. Instance variables must be private for this to work. Immutability takes this a step further, allowing only getters, so the instance variables do not change state.

9. A, C, E. Options B and D are incorrect because they don't follow the naming convention of beginning with get/is/set. Options C and E follow normal getter and setter conventions. Option A is correct, but the book doesn't explain this and is out of scope for the exam so give yourself credit if you answered C and E.

10. B. Rope runs line 3, setting LENGTH to 5, then immediately after runs the static initializer, which sets it to 10. Line 5 calls the static method normally and prints swing . Line 6 also calls the static method. Java allows calling a static method through an instance variable. Line 7 uses the static import on line 2 to reference LENGTH.

11. B, E. Line 10 does not compile because static methods are not allowed to call instance methods. Even though we are calling play() as if it were an instance method and an instance exists, Java knows play() is really a static method and treats it as such. If line 10 is removed, the code works. It does not throw a NullPointerException on line 16 because play() is a static method. Java looks at the type of the reference for rope2 and translates the call to Rope.play().

12. D. There are two details to notice in this code. First, note that RopeSwing has an instance initializer and not a static initializer. Since RopeSwing is never constructed, the instance initializer does not run. The other detail is that *length* is static. Changes from one object update this common static variable.

13. E. static final variables must be set exactly once, and it must be in the declaration line or in a static initialization block. Line 4 doesn't compile because *bench* is not set in either of these locations. Line 15 doesn't compile because final variables are not allowed to be set after that point. Line 11 doesn't compile because *name* is set twice: once in the declaration and again in the static block. Line 12 doesn't compile because *rightRope* is set twice as well. Both are in static initialization blocks.

14. B. The two valid ways to do this are import static java.util.Collections.*; and import static java.util.Collections.sort;. Option A is incorrect because you can only do a static import on static members. Classes such as Collections require a regular import. Option C is nonsense as method parameters have no business in an import. Options D, E, and F try to trick you into reversing the syntax of import static.

15. E. The argument on line 17 is a short. It can be promoted to an int, so print() on line 5 is invoked. The argument on line 18 is a boolean. It can be autoboxed to a Boolean, so print() on line 11 is invoked. The argument on line 19 is a double. It can be autoboxed to a Double, so print() on line 11 is invoked. Therefore, the output is intObjectObject and the correct answer is option E.

16. B. Since Java is pass-by-value and the variable on line 8 never gets reassigned, it stays as 9. In the method square, *x* starts as 9. *y* becomes 81 and then *x* gets set to –1. Line 9 does set *result* to 81. However, we are printing out *value* and that is still 9.

17. B, D, E. Since Java is pass-by-value, assigning a new object to *a* does not change the caller. Calling append() does affect the caller because both the method parameter and

caller have a reference to the same object. Finally, returning a value does pass the reference to the caller for assignment to *s3*.

18. C, G. Since the `main()` method is in the same class, it can call `private` methods in the class. `this()` may only be called as the first line of a constructor. `this.variableName` can be called from any instance method to refer to an instance variable. It cannot be called from a static method because there is no instance of the class to refer to. Option F is tricky. The default constructor is only written by the compiler if no user-defined constructors were provided. `this()` can only be called from a constructor in the same class. Since there can be no user-defined constructors in the class if a default constructor was created, it is impossible for option F to be true.

19. A, G. Options B and C don't compile because the constructor name must match the classname. Since Java is case sensitive, these don't match. Options D, E, and F all compile and provide one user-defined constructor. Since a constructor is coded, a default constructor isn't supplied. Option G defines a method, but not a constructor. Option A does not define a constructor, either. Since no constructor is coded, a default constructor is provided for options A and G.

20. E. Options A and B will not compile because constructors cannot be called without `new`. Options C and D will compile but will create a new object rather than setting the fields in this one. Option F will not compile because `this()` must be the first line of a constructor. Option E is correct.

21. C. Within the constructor *numSpots* refers to the constructor parameter. The instance variable is hidden because they have the same name. *this.numSpots* tells Java to use the instance variable. In the `main()` method, *numSpots* refers to the instance variable. Option A sets the constructor parameter to itself, leaving the instance variable as 0. Option B sets the constructor parameter to the value of the instance variable, making them both 0. Option C is correct, setting the instance variable to the value of the constructor parameter. Options D and E do not compile.

22. E. On line 3 of `OrderDriver`, we refer to `Order` for the first time. At this point the statics in `Order` get initialized. In this case, the statics are the `static` declaration of *result* and the `static` initializer. *result* is u at this point. On line 4, *result* is the same because the `static` initialization is only run once. On line 5, we create a new `Order`, which triggers the instance initializers in the order they appear in the file. Now *result* is ucr. Line 6 creates another `Order`, triggering another set of initializers. Now *result* is ucrcr. Notice how the `static` is on a different line than the initialization code in lines 4–5 of `Order`. The exam may try to trick you by formatting the code like this to confuse you.

23. A. Line 12 instantiates an `Order`. Java runs the declarations and instance initializers first in the order they appear. This sets *value* to tacf. Line 13 creates another `Order` and initializes *value* to tacb. The object on line 13 is stored in the same variable line 12 used. This makes the object created on line 12 unreachable. When *value* is printed, it is the instance variable in the object created on line 13.

24. B, C, E. *value1* is a final instance variable. It can only be set once: in the variable declaration, an instance initializer, or a constructor. Option A does not compile because the final variable was already set in the declaration. *value2* is a static variable. Both instance and static initializers are able to access static variables, making options B and E correct. *value3* is an instance variable. Options D and F do not compile because a static initializer does not have access to instance variables.

25. A, E. The 100 parameter is an int and so calls the matching int constructor. When this constructor is removed, Java looks for the next most specific constructor. Java prefers autoboxing to varargs, and so chooses the Integer constructor. The 100L parameter is a long. Since it can't be converted into a smaller type, it is autoboxed into a Long and then the constructor for Object is called.

26. A. This code is correct. Line 8 creates a lambda expression that checks if the age is less than 5. Since there is only one parameter and it does not specify a type, the parentheses around the type parameter are optional. Line 10 uses the Predicate interface, which declares a test() method.

27. C. The interface takes two int parameters. The code on line 7 attempts to use them as if one is a StringBuilder. It is tricky to use types in a lambda when they are implicitly specified. Remember to check the interface for the real type.

28. A, D, F. removeIf() expects a Predicate, which takes a parameter list of one parameter using the specified type. Options B and C are incorrect because they do not use the return keyword. It is required inside braces for lambda bodies. Option E is incorrect because it is missing the parentheses around the parameter list. This is only optional for a single parameter with an inferred type.

29. A, F. Option B is incorrect because it does not use the return keyword. Options C, D, and E are incorrect because the variable e is already in use from the lambda and cannot be redefined. Additionally, option C is missing the return keyword and option E is missing the semicolon.

Chapter 5: Class Design

1. B. All interface methods are implicitly public, so option B is correct and option A is not. Interface methods may be declared as static or default but are never implicitly added, so options C and F are incorrect. Option D is incorrect—void is not a modifier; it is a return type. Option E is a tricky one, because prior to Java 8 all interface methods would be assumed to be abstract. Since Java 8 now includes default and static methods and they are never abstract, you cannot assume the abstract modifier will be implicitly applied to all methods by the compiler.

2. E. The code will not compile because the parent class Mammal doesn't define a no-argument constructor, so the first line of a Platypus constructor should be an explicit call to super(int age).

3. A, B, D, E. The blank can be filled with any class or interface that is a supertype of TurtleFrog. Option A is a superclass of TurtleFrog, and option B is the same class, so both are correct. BrazilianHornedFrog is not a superclass of TurtleFrog, so option C is incorrect. TurtleFrog inherits the CanHop interface, so option D is correct. All classes inherit Object, so option E is correct. Finally, Long is an unrelated class that is not a superclass of TurtleFrog, and is therefore incorrect.

4. C, E. The code doesn't compile, so option A is incorrect. Option B is also not correct because the rules for overriding a method allow a subclass to define a method with an exception that is a subclass of the exception in the parent method. Option C is correct because the return types are not covariant; in particular, Number is not a subclass of Integer. Option D is incorrect because the subclass defines a method that is more accessible than the method in the parent class, which is allowed. Finally, option E is correct because the method is declared as static in the parent class and not so in the child class. For nonprivate methods in the parent class, both methods must use static (hide) or neither should use static (override).

5. A, D, E, F. First off, options B and C are incorrect because protected and public methods may be overridden, not hidden. Option A is correct because private methods are always hidden in a subclass. Option D is also correct because static methods cannot be overridden, only hidden. Options E and F are correct because variables may only be hidden, regardless of the access modifier.

6. D. The code fails to compile because Beetle, the first concrete subclass, doesn't implement getNumberOfSections(), which is inherited as an abstract method; therefore, option D is correct. Option B is incorrect because there is nothing wrong with this interface method definition. Option C is incorrect because an abstract class is not required to implement any abstract methods, including those inherited from an interface. Option E is incorrect because the code fails at compilation-time.

7. B, C. A reference to an object requires an explicit cast if referenced with a subclass, so option A is incorrect. If the cast is to a superclass reference, then an explicit cast is not required. Because of polymorphic parameters, if a method takes the superclass of an object as a parameter, then any subclass references may be used without a cast, so option B is correct. All objects extend java.lang.Object, so if a method takes that type, any valid object, including null, may be passed; therefore, option C is correct. Some cast exceptions can be detected as errors at compile-time, but others can only be detected at runtime, so D is incorrect. Due to the nature of polymorphism, a public instance method can be overridden in a subclass and calls to it will be replaced even in the superclass it was defined, so E is incorrect.

8. F. The interface variable amount is correctly declared, with public, static and final being assumed and automatically inserted by the compiler, so option B is incorrect. The method declaration for eatGrass() on line 3 is incorrect because the method has been marked as static but no method body has been provided. The method declaration for chew() on line 4 is also incorrect, since an interface method that provides a body must be marked as default or static explicitly. Therefore, option F is the correct answer since this code contains two compile-time errors.

9. A. Although the definition of methods on lines 2 and 5 vary, both will be converted to public abstract by the compiler. Line 4 is fine, because an interface can have public or default access. Finally, the class Falcon doesn't need to implement the interface methods because it is marked as abstract. Therefore, the code will compile without issue.

10. B, C, E, F. Option A is wrong, because an abstract class may contain concrete methods. Since Java 8, interfaces may also contain concrete methods in form of static or default methods. Although all variables in interfaces are assumed to be public static final, abstract classes may contain them as well, so option B is correct. Both abstract classes and interfaces can be extended with the extends keyword, so option C is correct. Only interfaces can contain default methods, so option D is incorrect. Both abstract classes and interfaces can contain static methods, so option E is correct. Both structures require a concrete subclass to be instantiated, so option F is correct. Finally, though an instance of an object that implements an interface inherits java.lang. Object, the interface itself doesn't; otherwise, Java would support multiple inheritance for objects, which it doesn't. Therefore, option G is incorrect.

11. A, D, E. Interface variables are assumed to be public static final; therefore, options A, D, and E are correct. Options B and C are incorrect because interface variables must be public—interfaces are implemented by classes, not inherited by interfaces. Option F is incorrect because variables can never be abstract.

12. B. This code compiles and runs without issue, outputting false, so option B is the correct answer. The first declaration of isBlind() is as a default interface method, assumed public. The second declaration of isBlind() correctly overrides the default interface method. Finally, the newly created Owl instance may be automatically cast to a Nocturnal reference without an explicit cast, although adding it doesn't break the code.

13. A. The code compiles and runs without issue, so options E and F are incorrect. The printName() method is an overload in Spider, not an override, so both methods may be called. The call on line 8 references the version that takes an int as input defined in the Spider class, and the call on line 9 references the version in the Arthropod class that takes a double. Therefore, SpiderArthropod is output and option A is the correct answer.

14. C. The code compiles without issue, so option A is wrong. Option B is incorrect, since an abstract class could implement HasVocalCords without the need to override the makeSound() method. Option C is correct; any class that implements CanBark automatically inherits its methods, as well as any inherited methods defined in the parent interface. Because option C is correct, it follows that option D is incorrect. Finally, an interface can extend multiple interfaces, so option E is incorrect.

15. B. Concrete classes are, by definition, not abstract, so option A is incorrect. A concrete class must implement all inherited abstract methods, so option B is correct. Option C is incorrect; a superclass may have already implemented an inherited interface, so the concrete subclass would not need to implement the method. Concrete classes can be both final and not final, so option D is incorrect. Finally, abstract methods must be overridden by a concrete subclass, so option E is incorrect.

16. E. The code doesn't compile, so options A and B are incorrect. The issue with line 9 is that `layEggs()` is marked as `final` in the superclass `Reptile`, which means it cannot be overridden. There are no errors on any other lines, so options C and D are incorrect.

17. B. This may look like a complex question, but it is actually quite easy. Line 2 contains an invalid definition of an abstract method. Abstract methods cannot contain a body, so the code will not compile and option B is the correct answer. If the body {} was removed from line 2, the code would still not compile, although it would be line 8 that would throw the compilation error. Since `dive()` in `Whale` is abstract and `Orca` extends `Whale`, then it must implement an overridden version of `dive()`. The method on line 9 is an overloaded version of `dive()`, not an overridden version, so `Orca` is an invalid subclass and will not compile.

18. E. The code doesn't compile because line 6 contains an incompatible override of the `getNumberOfGills(int input)` method defined in the `Aquatic` interface. In particular, `int` and `String` are not covariant returns types, since `String` is not a subclass of `int`. Note that line 5 compiles without issue; `getNumberOfGills()` is an overloaded method that is not related to the parent interface method that takes an `int` value.

19. A, C, F. First off, `Cobra` is a subclass of `Snake`, so option A can be used. `GardenSnake` is not defined as a subclass of `Snake`, so it cannot be used and option B is incorrect. The class `Snake` is not marked as `abstract`, so it can be instantiated and passed, so option C is correct. Next, `Object` is a superclass of `Snake`, not a subclass, so it also cannot be used and option D is incorrect. The class `String` is unrelated in this example, so option E is incorrect. Finally, a `null` value can always be passed as an object value, regardless of type, so option F is correct.

20. A. The code compiles and runs without issue, so options C, D, and E are incorrect. The trick here is that the method `fly()` is marked as `private` in the parent class `Bird`, which means it may only be hidden, not overridden. With hidden methods, the specific method used depends on where it is referenced. Since it is referenced within the `Bird` class, the method declared on line 2 was used, and option A is correct. Alternatively, if the method was referenced within the `Pelican` class, or if the method in the parent class was marked as `protected` and overridden in the subclass, then the method on line 9 would have been used.

Chapter 6: Exceptions

1. B. Runtime exceptions are also known as unchecked exceptions. They are allowed to be declared, but they don't have to be. Checked exceptions must be handled or declared. Legally, you can handle `java.lang.Error` subclasses, but it's not a good idea.

2. B, D. In a method declaration, the keyword `throws` is used. To actually throw an exception, the keyword `throw` is used and a new exception is created.

3. C. A `try` statement is required to have a `catch` clause and/or `finally` clause. If it goes the `catch` route, it is allowed to have multiple `catch` clauses.

4. B. The second line tries to cast an `Integer` to a `String`. Since `String` does not extend `Integer`, this is not allowed and a `ClassCastException` is thrown.

5. A, B, D. `java.io.IOException` is thrown by many methods in the `java.io` package, but it is always thrown programmatically. The same is true for `NumberFormatException`; it is thrown programmatically by the wrapper classes of `java.lang`. The other three exceptions are all thrown by the JVM when the corresponding problem arises.

6. C. The compiler tests the operation for a valid type but not a valid result, so the code will still compile and run. At runtime, evaluation of the parameter takes place before passing it to the `print()` method, so an `ArithmeticException` object is raised.

7. C. The `main()` method invokes go and A is printed on line 3. The `stop` method is invoked and E is printed on line 14. Line 16 throws a `NullPointerException`, so `stop` immediately ends and line 17 doesn't execute. The exception isn't caught in go, so the go method ends as well, but not before its `finally` block executes and C is printed on line 9. Because `main()` doesn't catch the exception, the stack trace displays and no further output occurs, so AEC was the output printed before the stack trace.

8. E. The order of `catch` blocks is important because they're checked in the order they appear after the `try` block. Because `ArithmeticException` is a child class of `Runtime-Exception`, the catch block on line 7 is unreachable. (If an `ArithmeticException` is thrown in `try` block, it will be caught on line 5.) Line 7 generates a compiler error because it is unreachable code.

9. B. The `main()` method invokes `start` on a new `Laptop` object. Line 4 prints `Starting up`; then line 5 throws an `Exception`. Line 6 catches the exception, line 7 prints `Problem`, and then line 8 calls `System.exit`, which terminates the JVM. The `finally` block does not execute because the JVM is no longer running.

10. E. The `parseName` method is invoked within `main()` on a new `Dog` object. Line 4 prints 1. The `try` block executes and 2 is printed. Line 7 throws a `NumberFormatException`, so line 8 doesn't execute. The exception is caught on line 9, and line 10 prints 4. Because the exception is handled, execution resumes normally. `parseName` runs to completion, and line 17 executes, printing 5. That's the end of the program, so the output is 1245.

11. A. The `parseName` method is invoked on a new `Cat` object. Line 4 prints 1. The `try` block is entered, and line 6 prints 2. Line 7 throws a `NumberFormatException`. It isn't caught, so `parseName` ends. `main()` doesn't catch the exception either, so the program terminates and the stack trace for the `NumberFormatException` is printed.

12. A, B, D, G. The `main()` method invokes run on a new `Mouse` object. Line 4 prints 1 and line 6 prints 2, so options A and B are correct. Line 7 throws a `NullPointerException`, which causes line 8 to be skipped, so C is incorrect. The exception is caught on line 9 and line 10 prints 4, so option D is correct. Line 11 throws the exception again, which causes `run()` to immediately end, so line 13 doesn't execute and option E is incorrect. The `main()` method doesn't catch the exception either, so line 18 doesn't execute and option F is incorrect. The uncaught `NullPointerException` causes the stack trace to be printed, so option G is correct.

13. A, B, C, E. Classes listed in the throws part of a method declaration must extend java.lang.Throwable. This includes Error, Exception, and RuntimeException. Arbitrary classes such as String can't go there. Any Java type, including Exception, can be declared as the return type. However, this will simply return the object rather than throw an exception.

14. A, C, D, E. A method that declares an exception isn't required to throw one, making option A correct. Runtime exceptions can be thrown in any method, making options C and E correct. Option D matches the exception type declared and so is also correct. Option B is incorrect because a broader exception is not allowed.

15. A, B, D, E. ArrayIndexOutOfBoundsException, IllegalArgumentException, and NumberFormatException are runtime exceptions. Sorry, you have to memorize them. Any class that extends RuntimeException is a runtime (unchecked) exception. Classes that extend Exception but not RuntimeException are checked exceptions.

16. B. IllegalArgumentException is used when an unexpected parameter is passed into a method. Option A is incorrect because returning null or -1 is a common return value for this scenario. Option D is incorrect because a for loop is typically used for this scenario. Option E is incorrect because you should find out how to code the method and not leave it for the unsuspecting programmer who calls your method. Option C is incorrect because you should run!

17. A, C, D, E. The method is allowed to throw no exceptions at all, making option A correct. It is also allowed to throw runtime exceptions, making options D and E correct. Option C is also correct since it matches the signature in the interface.

18. A, B, C, E. Checked exceptions are required to be handled or declared. Runtime exceptions are allowed to be handled or declared. Errors are allowed to be handled or declared, but this is bad practice.

19. C, E. Option C is allowed because it is a more specific type than RuntimeException. Option E is allowed because it isn't in the same inheritance tree as RuntimeException. It's not a good idea to catch either of these. Option B is not allowed because the method called inside the try block doesn't declare an IOException to be thrown. The compiler realizes that IOException would be an unreachable catch block. Option D is not allowed because the same exception can't be specified in two different catch blocks. Finally, option A is not allowed because it's more general than RuntimeException and would make that block unreachable.

20. A, E. The code begins normally and prints a on line 13, followed by b on line 15. On line 16, it throws an exception that's caught on line 17. Remember, only the most specific matching catch is run. Line 18 prints c, and then line 19 throws another exception. Regardless, the finally block runs, printing e. Since the finally block also throws an exception, that's the one printed.

Appendix B

Study Tips

This appendix covers suggestions and recommendations for how you should prepare for the certification exam. If you're an experienced test taker, or you've taken a certification test before, most of this should be common knowledge. For those who are taking the exam for the first time, don't panic! We'll present a number of tips and strategies in this appendix to help you prepare for the exam.

Studying for the Test

Before you even sign up and take the test, you need to study the material. Studying includes the following tasks:

- Create a study plan.
- Read the Study Guide material.
- Create and run sample applications.
- Solve the Review Questions at the end of each chapter.
- Create flashcards and/or use the ones we've provided.
- Take the three practice exams.

The book is divided into chapters with corresponding exam objectives, to make it easier to assimilate. The earlier chapters on syntax and operators are especially important since they are used throughout the code samples on the exam. Unless we explicitly stated something was out of scope for the exam, you will be required to have a strong understanding of all the information in this book.

Creating a Study Plan

Rome wasn't built in a day, so you shouldn't attempt to study for only one day. Even if you have been certified with a previous version of Java, the new test includes features and components unique to Java 8 that are covered in this text.

Once you have decided to take the test, which we assume you have already since you're reading this book, you should construct a study plan that fits with your schedule. We recommend you set aside some amount of time each day, even if it's just a few minutes during lunch, to read or practice for the exam. The idea is to keep your momentum going throughout the exam preparation process. The more consistent you are in how you study, the better prepared you will be for the exam. Try to avoid taking a few days or weeks off from studying, or you're likely to spend a lot of time relearning existing material instead of moving on to new material.

Let's say you begin studying on January 1. Assuming you allot two weeks per chapter, we constructed a study plan in Table B.1 that you can use as a schedule throughout the study process. Of course, if you're new to Java, two weeks per chapter may not be enough; if you're an experienced Java developer, you may only need a few days per chapter.

TABLE B.1   Sample study plan

Date	Task
January 1–January 11	Read Introduction, Appendix B, and Chapter 1
January 12–January 14	Answer Chapter 1 Review Questions
January 15–January 25	Read Chapter 2
January 26–January 28	Answer Chapter 2 Review Questions
January 29–February 8	Read Chapter 3
February 9–February 11	Answer Chapter 3 Review Questions
February 12–February 22	Read Chapter 4
February 23–February 25	Answer Chapter 4 Review Questions
February 26–March 8	Read Chapter 5
March 9–March 11	Answer Chapter 5 Review Questions
March 12–March 22	Read Chapter 6
March 23–March 25	Answer Chapter 6 Review Questions
March 26–April 2	Take practice exams and practice with flashcards
April 3	Take exam

Your own study plan will vary based on your familiarity with Java, your personal and work schedule, and your learning abilities. The idea is to create a plan early on that has self-imposed deadlines that you can follow throughout the studying process. When someone asks how you're doing preparing for the exam, you should have a strong sense of what you've learned so far, what you're currently studying, and how many weeks you need to be prepared to the take the exam.

Creating and Running Sample Applications

Although some people can learn Java just by reading a textbook, that's not how we recommend you study for a certification exam. We want you to be writing your own Java sample applications throughout this book so that you don't just learn the material but you also understand the material. For example, it may not be obvious why the following line of code does not compile, but if you try to compile it yourself, the Java compiler will tell you the problem.

```
float value = 102.0;   // DOES NOT COMPILE
```

In this section, we will discuss how to test Java code and the tools available to assist you in this process.

 A lot of people post on the CodeRanch.com forum asking, "Why does this code not compile?" and we encourage you to post the compiler error message anytime you need help. We recommend you also read the compiler message when posting, since it may provide meaningful information about why the code failed to compile.

In the previous example, the compiler failed to compile with the message `Type mismatch: cannot convert from double to float`. This message indicates that we are trying to convert a double value, `102.0`, to a float variable reference using an implicit cast. If we add an explicit cast to `(float)` or change the value to `102.0f`, the code will compile without issue.

Sample Test Class

Throughout this book, we present numerous code snippets and ask you whether they'll compile and what their output will be. These snippets are designed to be placed inside a simple Java application that starts, executes the code, and terminates. As described in Chapter 1, "Java Building Blocks," you can accomplish this by compiling and running a public class containing a `public static void main(String[] args)` method, such as the following:

```java
public class TestClass {
  public static void main(String[] args) {
    // Add test code here

    // Add any print statements here
    System.out.println("Hello World!");
  }
}
```

This application isn't particularly interesting—it just outputs "Hello World" and exits. That said, we can insert many of the code snippets present in this book in the `main()` method to determine if the code compiles, as well as what the code outputs when it does compile. We strongly recommend you become familiar with this sample application, so much so that you could write it from memory, without the comments.

We recommend that while reading this book you make note of any sections that you do not fully understand and revisit them when in front of a computer screen with a Java compiler and Java runtime. You should start by copying the code snippet into your test class, and then try experimenting with the code as much as possible. For example, we indicated the previous sample line of code would not compile, but would any of the following compile?

```java
float value1 = 102;
float value2 = (int)102.0;
float value3 = 1f * 0.0;
float value4 = 1f * (short)0.0;
float value5 = 1f * (boolean)0;
```

Try out these samples on your computer and see if the result matches your expectation. Here's a hint: Two of these fives lines will not compile.

 Real World Scenario

IDE Software

While studying for the exam, you should develop code using a text editor and command-line Java compiler. Some of you may have existing experience with Integrated Development Environments (IDEs) such as Eclipse or IntelliJ. An IDE is a software application that facilitates software development for computer programmers.

Although such tools are extremely valuable in developing software, they can interfere with your ability to readily spot problems on the exam. For example, when a line code does not compile, the IDE will often underline it in red, whereas on the exam, you'll have to find the line that does not compile, if there is one, on your own.

If you do choose to study with an IDE, make sure you understand everything it is doing in the background for you. For the exam, you'll need to know how to manually compile code from the command line, and this experience is rarely learned using an IDE. You'll also need to understand why the code does not compile without relying on the tips and suggestions provided by the IDE.

Identifying Your Weakest Link

The best advice we can give you to do well on the exam is to practice writing sample applications that push the limits of what you already know, as much and as often as possible. For example, if the previous samples with float values were too difficult for you, then you should spend even more time studying numeric promotion and casting expressions.

Prior to taking the OCA exam, you may already be an experienced Java developer, but there is a difference between being able to write Java code and being a certified Java developer. For example, you might go years without writing a ternary expression or using an abstract class, but that does not mean they are not important features of the Java language. You may also be unaware of some of the more complex features that exist within the Java language. On top of that, there are new features to Java 8, such as lambda expressions and default interface methods, which as of this writing very few professional software developers are using.

The Review Questions in each chapter are designed to help you hone in on those features of the Java language that you may be weak in and that are required knowledge for the exam. For each chapter, you should note which questions you got wrong, understand why you got them wrong, and study those areas even more.

Often, the reason you got a question wrong on the exam is that you did not fully understand the concept. Many topics in Java have subtle rules that you often need to see for yourself to truly understand. For example, you cannot write a class that implements two interfaces that define the same default method unless you override the default method in the class. Writing and attempting to compile your own sample interfaces and classes that reference the default method may illuminate this concept far better than we could ever explain it.

Finally, we find developers who practice writing code while studying for the Java certification tend to write better Java code in their professional career. Anyone can write a Java class that can compile, but just because a class compiles does not mean it is well designed. For example, imagine a class where all class methods and variables were declared public, simply because the developer did not understand the other access modifiers, such as protected and private. Studying for the certification helps you to learn those features that may be applicable in your daily coding experience but that you never knew existed within the Java language.

"Overstudying" Practice Exams

Although we recommend reading this book and writing your own sample applications multiple times, redoing practice exams over and over can have a negative impact in the long run. For example, some individuals study the practice exam questions so much that they end up memorizing them. In this scenario, they can easily become overconfident—they can achieve perfect scores on the practice exams but may fail on the actual exam.

If you get a practice exam question correct, you should move on, and if you get it incorrect you should review the part of the chapter that covers it until you can answer it correctly. Remember that for legal reasons the practice exam questions are not real exam questions, so it is important you learn the material the questions are based on.

On the other hand, we recommend you repeat Review Questions as often as you like to master a chapter. Review Questions are designed to teach you important concepts in the chapter, and you should understand them completely before leaving a section. Furthermore, they help improve your ability to recognize certain types of problems present in many code snippets.

Taking the Test

Studying how to take a test can be just as important as the studying the material itself. For example, you could answer every question correctly, but only make it halfway through the exam, resulting in a failing score! If you're not historically a good test taker, or you've never taken a certification exam before, we recommend you read this section because it contains notes that are relevant to many software certification exams.

Understanding the Question

The majority of questions on the exam will contain code snippets and ask you to answer questions about them. For those containing code snippets, the number one question we recommend you answer before attempting to solve the question is:

Does the code compile?

It sounds simple but many people dive into answering the question without checking whether or not the code actually compiles. If you can determine whether or not a particular set of code compiles, and what line or lines cause it to not compile, answering the question often becomes easy.

Checking the Answers

To determine whether the code will compile, you should briefly review the answer choices to see what options are available. If there are no choices of the form "Code does not compile," then you can be reasonably assured all the lines of the code will compile and you do not need to spend time checking syntax. These questions are often, but not always, among the easiest questions because you can skip determining whether the code compiles and instead focus on what it does.

If the answer choices do include some answers of the form "Does not compile due to line 5," you should immediately focus on those lines and determine whether they compile. For example, take a look at the answer choices for the following question:

18. What is the output of the following code?

- Code Omitted -

    A. Monday

    B. Tuesday

    C. Friday

    D. The code does not compile due to line 4.

    E. The code does not compile due to line 6.

The answer choices act as a guide instructing you to focus on line 4 or 6 for compilation errors. If the question indicates only one answer choice is allowed, it also tells you at most only one line of code contains a compilation problem and the other line is correct. Although the reason line 4 or 6 may not compile could be related to other lines of code, the key is that those other lines do not throw compiler errors themselves. By quickly browsing the list of answers, you can save time by focusing only on those lines of code that are possible candidates for not compiling.

If you are able to identify a line of code that does not compile, you will be able to finish the question a lot quicker. Often, the most difficult questions are the ones where the code does in fact compile, but one of the answer choices is "Does not compile" without indicating any line numbers. In these situations, you will have to spend extra time verifying that each and every line compiles. If they are taking too much time, we recommend marking these for "Review" and coming back to them later.

Determining What the Question Is Asking

A lot of times, a question may appear to be asking one thing but will actually be asking another. For example, the following question may appear to be asking about method overloading and abstract classes:

12. What is the output of the following code?

```
1: abstract class Mammal {
2:    protected boolean hasFur() { return false; }
3: }
4: class Capybara implements Mammal {
5:    public boolean hasFur() { return true; }
6:    public static void main(String[] args) {
7:       System.out.println(new Capybara().hasFur());
8:    }
9: }
```

It turns out this question is a lot simpler than it looks. A class cannot implement another class—it can only extend another class—so line 4 will cause the code to fail to compile. If you notice this compiler problem early on, you'll likely be able to answer this question quickly and easily.

Taking Advantage of Context Clues

Let's face it—there will be things you're likely to forget on the day of the exam. Between being nervous about taking the test and being a bit overtired when you read a particular chapter, you're likely to encounter at least one question where you do not have a high degree of confidence. Luckily, you do not need to score a perfect 100% to pass.

One advanced test-taking skill that can come in handy is to use information from one question to help answer another. For example, we mentioned in an earlier section that you can assume a question's code block will compile and run if "Does not compile" and "Throw an exception at runtime" are not available in the list of answers. If you have a piece of code that you know compiles and a related piece of code that you're not so sure about, you can use information from the former question to help solve the latter question.

Use a similar strategy when a question asks which single line will not compile. If you're able to determine the line that does not compile with some degree of confidence, you can use the remaining code that you know does compile as a guide to help answer other questions.

By using context clues of other questions on the exam, you may be able to more easily solve questions that you are unsure about.

Reviewing Common Compiler Issues

The following is a brief list of common things to look for when trying to determine whether code compiles. Bear in mind that this is only a partial list. We recommend you review each chapter for a comprehensive list of reasons that code will not compile. Also, if you have not finished reading the book, you should set aside this list and return to it when you are preparing to take the exam.

Common Tips to Determine if Code Compiles:

- Keep an eye out for all reserved words. [Chapter 1]

- Verify brackets—{}—and parentheses—()—are being used correctly. [Chapter 1]

- Verify new is used appropriately for creating objects. [Chapter 1]

- Ignore all line indentation especially with if-then statements that do not use brackets {}. [Chapter 2]

- Make sure operators use compatible data types, such as the logical complement operator (!) only applied to boolean values, and arithmetic operators (+, -, ++, --) only applied to numeric values. [Chapter 2]

- For any numeric operators, check for automatic numeric promotion and order or operation when evaluating an expression. [Chapter 2]

- Verify switch statements use acceptable data types. [Chapter 2]

- Remember == is not the same as equals(). [Chapter 3]

- String values are immutable. [Chapter 3]

- Non-void methods must return a value that matches or is a subclass of the return type of the method. [Chapter 4]

- If two classes are involved, make sure access modifiers allow proper access of variables and methods. [Chapter 4]

- Nonstatic methods and variables require an object instance to access. [Chapter 4]

- If a class is missing a default no-argument constructor or the provided constructors do not explicitly call super(), assume the compiler will automatically insert them. [Chapter 5]

- Make sure abstract methods do not define an implementation, and likewise concrete methods always define an implementation. [Chapter 5]

- You implement an interface and extend a class. [Chapter 5]
- A class can be cast to a reference of any superclass it inherits from or interface it implements. [Chapter 5]
- Checked exceptions must be caught; unchecked exceptions may be caught but do not need to be. [Chapter 6]
- try blocks require a catch and/or finally block for the OCA exam. [Chapter 6]

We have listed the chapter each tip is found in so that you can go back and review any that you do not fully understand. Once you've determined that the code does in fact compile, proceed with tracing the application logic and trying to determine what the code actually does.

Applying Process of Elimination

Although you might not immediately know the correct answer to a question, if you can reduce the question from five answers down to three, your odds of guessing the correct answer will be markedly improved. For example, if you can reduce a question from four answers to two answers, you double your chances of guessing the correct answer. In this section, we will discuss how to apply the process of elimination to help improve your score.

Using the Provided Writing Material

Depending on your particular testing center, you may be provided with a stack of blank paper or a whiteboard to use to help you answer questions. If you sit down and are not provided with anything, please make sure to ask for such materials.

After determining whether a question compiles and what it is asking for, you should then jot down a list of all the answers. You should then proceed to cross out the ones you know are not correct. We provided a sample of what this might look like in Figure B.1.

FIGURE B.1 Eliminating answer choices

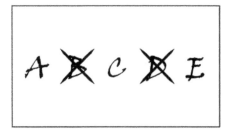

If you're using paper and you decide to come back to this question, be sure to write down the question number and save it for later. If you're using a whiteboard and decide to come back to a question later, you may have to redo some of the work, given the limited space on a whiteboard. For those questions you want to come back to later, we suggest jotting down the remaining answer choices on the side of the whiteboard. Some test-taking software allows you to mark and save which answer choices you've eliminated, although in our experience this does not always work reliably in practice.

> Although you aren't allowed to bring any written notes with you into the exam, you're allowed to write things down you remember at the start of the exam on the provided writing material. If there's a particular facet of the Java language that you have difficulty remembering, try memorizing it before the exam and write it down as soon as the exam starts. You can then use it as a guide for the rest of the exam. Of course, this strategy only works for a handful of topics, since there's a limit to what you're likely to remember in a short time.
>
> For example, you may have trouble remembering the list of acceptable data types in switch statements. If so, we recommend you memorize that information before the exam and write it down as soon as the exam starts for use in various questions.

Understanding Relationships Between Answers

The exam writers, as well as the writers of this book, are fond of answers that are related to each other. We can apply the process of elimination to remove entire sets of answers from selection, not just a single answer. For example, take a look at the following question:

22. What is the output of the following application?

```
3: int x = 0;
4: while(++x < 5) { x+=1; }
5: String message = x > 5 ? "Greater than" : "Less Than";
6: System.out.println(message+","+x);
```

A. Greater than,5
B. Greater than,6
C. Greater than,7
D. Less than,5
E. Less than,6
F. Less than,7

In this question, notice that half of the answers output Greater than, whereas the other half output Less than. Based on the code, as well as the answers available, the question cannot output both values. That means if you can determine what the ternary expression on line 5 evaluates to, you can eliminate half the answers!

You might also notice that this particular question does not include any "Does not compile" or "Code throws an exception at runtime" answers, meaning you can be assured this snippet of code does compile and run without issue. If you have a question similar to this, you can compare the syntax and use this as a guide for solving other related questions.

Guessing the Correct Answer

Unlike with some other standardized tests, there's no penalty for answering a question incorrectly versus leaving it blank. If you're nearly out of time, or you just can't decide on an answer, select a random answer and move on. If you've been able to eliminate even one answer, then your guess will be better than blind luck.

Answer All Questions!

You should set a hard stop of 5 minutes of time remaining on the exam to ensure that you've answered each and every question. Remember, if you fail to answer a question you'll definitely get it wrong and lose points, but if you guess, there's at least a chance you'll be correct. There's no harm in guessing!

When in doubt, we generally recommend picking a random answer that includes "Does not compile" if available, although which choice you select is not nearly as important as making sure to not leave any unanswered questions on the exam!

Optimizing Your Time

One of the most difficult test-taking skills to master is balancing your time on the exam. Although Oracle often varies the precise number of questions on the exam and the amount of time you have to answer them, the general rule of thumb is that you have about one and half minutes per question.

Of course, it can be stressful to frequently look at the time remaining while taking the exam, so the key is pacing yourself. Some questions will take you longer than two minutes to solve, but hopefully others will only take less than a minute. The more time you save on the easier questions, the more time you'll have for the harder questions.

Checking the Time Remaining

The exam software includes a clock that tells you the amount of time you have left on the exam. We don't recommend checking the clock after each and every question to determine your pace. After all, doing such a calculation will waste time and probably make you nervous and stressed out. We do recommend you check the time remaining at certain points while taking the exam to determine whether you should try to increase your pace.

For example, if the exam lasts two hours and is 90 questions long, the following would be a good pace to try to keep.

- 120 Minutes Remaining: Start exam.
- 90 Minutes Remaining: One third of the exam finished.

- 60 Minutes Remaining: Two thirds of the exam finished.

- 30 Minutes Remaining: First pass of all questions complete.

- 5 Minutes Remaining: Finished reviewing all questions marked for "Review." Select answers to all questions left blank.

As you're taking the exam you may realize you're falling behind. In this scenario, you need to start allotting less time per question, which may involve more guessing, or you'll end up with some questions that you never even answered. As discussed in the previous section, guessing an answer to a question is better than not answering the question at all.

Skipping Hard Questions

If you do find you are having difficulty with a particular set of questions, just skip them. The exam provides a feature to mark questions for "Review" that you can later come back to. Remember that all questions on the exam, easy or difficult, are weighted the same. It is a far better use of your time to spend five minutes answering ten easy questions than the same amount of time answering one difficult question.

You might come to a question that looks difficult and immediately realize it is going to take a lot of time. In this case, skip it before even starting on it. You can save the most difficult problems for the end so that you can get all the easy ones solved early on. Of course, you shouldn't mark every question for "Review," so use that sparingly. For example, if you only need 30 more seconds to solve a specific question, it is better to finish it so you do not have to come back to it later. The trick is to not get stuck on a difficult question for a long period of time.

Improving Your Test-Taking Speed

Answering certification exam questions quickly does not come naturally to most people. It takes a bit of practice and skill to look at a question, a code sample, and 4–6 answers, and be able to answer it within a minute or two. The best way to practice is to keep solving the review questions at the end of each chapter until you can read, understand, and answer them in under a minute.

Once you've completed all of the material and practiced with the review questions enough that you can answer them quickly and correctly, you should try one of the three 60-question practice exams that come with this Study Guide. You should treat it like the real exam, setting aside two hours and finishing it in one sitting.

Although we recommend you try to avoid taking the practice exams so much that you memorize the questions and answers, we do recommend you keep taking them until you can finish each practice exam in under two hours. Remember not to move on to the next one until you can pass the previous exam in the allotted time. If not, study more and go back to drilling on the Review Questions. The idea is that you want to be good at quickly reading through the question, honing in on the key concept the question is asking, and being able to select the answer that best represents it.

Getting a Good Night's Rest

Although a lot of people are inclined to cram as much material as they can in the hours leading up to the exam, most studies have shown that this is a poor test-taking strategy. The best thing we can recommend you do before the exam is to get a good night's rest!

Given the length of the exam and number of questions, the exam can be quite draining, especially if this is your first time taking a certification exam. You might come in expecting to be done 30 minutes early, only to discover you are only a quarter of the way through the exam with half the time remaining. At some point, you may begin to panic, and it is in these moments that these test-taking skills are most important. Just remember to take a deep breath, stay calm, eliminate as many wrong answers as you can, and make sure to answer each and every question. It is for stressful moments like these that being well rested with a good night's sleep will be most beneficial!

Index

Note to the Reader: Throughout this index **boldfaced** page numbers indicate primary discussions of a topic. *Italicized* page numbers indicate illustrations.

N

O